UNEMPLOYMENT AND THE FUTURE OF WORK

An Enquiry for the Churches

CCBI
Inter-Church House
35-41 Lower Marsh
London SE1 7RL

ISBN 0 85169 238 9

© 1997 Council of Churches for Britain and Ireland

CCBI
Inter-Church House
35-41 Lower Marsh
London SE1 7RL

Typeset and printed by Delta Press, Hove, East Sussex

Cover design by Mark Whitchurch Art & Design

CONTENTS

Page

Foreword by Rt Revd David Sheppard   v

Introduction   1

Part One: The Need for Decision   13

1. The Changing Nature of Work   13
2. Unemployment and Poverty   31
3. National and Regional Variations   54
4. Work and Income   69

Part Two: The Choices we can Make   82

5. Expanding Employment   82
6. Fair Pay and Conditions of Work   102
7. Work for the Unemployed   122
8. Work and the Benefit System   133
9. Education and Training   144
10. The Work Ethic and Full Employment   158

Part Three: What the Churches can do   175

11. Christian Mission and the World of Work   175

A Concluding Reflection: Working Still   195

Appendix A: The Conduct of the Enquiry   199

Appendix B: Bibliography   205

Annex A: *Christian Teaching on Work and the Economy*
            by Revd Dr Peter Sedgwick   219

Annex B: *Low Pay* by Gabrielle Cox   229

Annex C: *The Idea of an Employment Guarantee* by David Price 241

Annex D: *The Future of Work:* Evidence submitted by
            Church Action on Poverty   251

Annex E: *Social Security and Unemployment* by David Price   263

Annex F: *The Concept of the Work Ethic* by
            Rt Revd Michael Bourke   281

Annex G: *Simone Weil on 'The Spirituality of Work'* by
            Revd Dr Andrew Shanks   285

Annex H: *Unemployment and the Future of Work:*
            Introduction by Revd Simon Jones to papers
            submitted by the Baptist Union.   289

Annex I: *Some Thoughts on Theological Method* by
            Revd Malcolm Brown   293

FOREWORD

Will there ever be enough jobs to go round? That was the question which prompted this enquiry. New technology brings prosperity for many people, but for many others it means redundancy and unemployment. As the world economy becomes more and more competitive some people are giving up hope that they will ever work again. Is mass unemployment here to stay?

That is one question that needs to be asked about work, but it is not the only one. Some new questions need to be asked as well. Are all of the new jobs worth doing? It is not only the level of pay which can be scandalous; the conditions of work can also be oppressive and unfair. The challenge is not just to create more jobs, but to create better jobs as well. 'Any old job' will not do.

Some questions like these have been around for many years now, but they are becoming more urgent all the time. Children are now growing up in homes and in communities where regular work has been unknown for a generation or more. They are learning to accept unemployment as a way of life. At the same time there is increasing reluctance among some taxpayers to pay for the welfare benefits on which unemployed people depend. They compete for a limited public budget, which some people believe already absorbs too much of the national income. The system is being made tougher, and people are being forced into increasing hardship as a result. We seem, in some parts of our islands, to be heading for a social crisis, as mutual resentment between the haves and the have-nots builds up. The situation has been neglected, and allowed to deteriorate, for far too long already.

This report includes a cry of pain heard by the Working Party in many parts of our countries: they describe a deep wound in the body, dividing those who are left out of decent opportunities from the favoured majority. They call for costly, long term measures. None of us should expect that such a deep wound could be healed without sacrifice. The Church has a freedom to look at these matters, with our presence in every neighbourhood and the skills which we can draw on from within our membership.

Underlying social justice matters are spiritual issues. Underneath these subjects of Unemployment and the Future of Work lie despair, waste of God-given talents, contempt, hiding the eyes from the pain of brothers and sisters. The Report quotes the organiser of Tear Fund UK Action as saying, 'When people at the bottom of society's heap are treated with dignity and respect, their spiritual needs start to be addressed.' The first words of the Second Vatican Council's statement *Gaudium et Spes* puts it like this, 'The joy and hope, the grief and anguish of the men of our time, especially of those who are poor or afflicted in any way, are the joy and hope, the grief and anguish of the followers of Christ as well.'

The subject has frequently been near the top of the agenda for the Social

Responsibility network of the Council of Churches for Britain and Ireland. The instruments of Ecumenical partnership (CCBI and the four national bodies) are charged with co-ordinating church initiatives, rather than initiating them. The initiative for an independent Churches' Enquiry sprang out of discussions in the Social Responsibility network of the CCBI. Churches in the four nations appointed members of a Sponsoring Group. With the blessing of the Church Representatives Meeting of the CCBI we raised the money for the Enquiry, and appointed a Working Party.

We are deeply thankful for the commitment of members of the working party over eighteen months in visiting widely, listening to many who are most closely involved and wrestling with these great issues. They come from a great variety of backgrounds, from many different places, many different churches. They brought a wide range of experience to draw on. In the course of the enquiry they have visited many places in England, Scotland, Wales and Ireland, some regarded as prosperous, some as deprived. They have met people in positions of power and influence, people with technical expertise in economics and social policy, people who are tackling the problem of unemployment in various practical ways; they have talked at length to people with personal experience of what long-term unemployment and poverty are actually like. Especially our thanks go to Andrew Britton, who has brought his economic wisdom and his Christian faith to bear as Executive Secretary of the Working Party. In turn we are grateful for the skills and commitment brought by Ruth Badger, seconded by the Church of England Board for Social Responsibility to serve as secretary to the Sponsoring Body. We also express our gratitude to Katie Lane and Deborah Cunningham for patient and accurate secretarial work.

We have been glad to receive the Report from the Working Party. We believe it has a very solid base. It reflects also the passion with which members of the Working Party expressed to us what they had seen and heard. **We offer it to the Churches and our nations as a prophetic word and, we believe, a highly significant contribution to this debate. We warmly commend it for study and in many instances for action.**

We hope that it will alert public opinion to the seriousness of the challenge that we face. We hope that it will increase the priority given over the long term to employment issues in policy making. We hope that it will convince those with the responsibility of power that something can and must be done.

Rt Revd David Sheppard,
Bishop of Liverpool
Chairman, Sponsoring Group for the Churches'
Enquiry into Unemployment and the Future of Work
Liverpool, February 1997

INTRODUCTION

A Divided Society

From our year of visiting all the countries and regions of Britain and Ireland, north and south, we have returned shocked and saddened by the sharpness of contrast we have found everywhere between a favoured majority on the one hand and those on the other who are left out. Such contrasts should not be tolerated. They imply a complacency among the contented that has to be challenged.

Even in the relatively prosperous South-West of England we were told of places where nearly all the young men were without work. In the North-East we learnt about big spending in the new supermarkets, but hopeless poverty on housing estates where almost no-one is in work. In the North-West we visited world-class manufacturing firms, but also heard of the anger and frustration of those who could find nothing but dead-end, low-paid and seemingly pointless work to do. Wherever we went we saw increasing riches and increasing poverty side by side.

A high level of unemployment has come to be taken for granted in the national consciousness, although it is recognised that it causes social breakdown and personal tragedy. It is an evil which has put down deep roots. People who are unemployed feel that they have become invisible, that society is indifferent to them, if not actively hostile. Not so long ago a figure of one million unemployed was recognised in Britain as a national disgrace. Now a figure of 'only' two million (and that on a revised definition) is pointed to as a great achievement. The recent monthly falls in the totals of the registered unemployed are greatly welcome, of course. But they are liable to aggravate our blindness, if they direct attention from the need for a radical shift in national thinking. For those who actually suffer unemployment the pain is as acute as ever.

It is wrong in such prosperous times as ours for men and women to be deprived for long periods of the chance to earn their living. In the UK in October 1996, nearly three-quarters of a million people had been unemployed for more than a year. For people over the age of 55 the *average* duration for a spell of unemployment in Britain was more than 60 weeks. In the North-East we were told that many of those over 45 who lose their jobs expect never to work again.

It is wrong to allow children to grow up where the right and duty to work are forgotten after generations of unemployment. Yet lack of work in many families is now an inheritance. On Merseyside we were told that children as young as twelve look forward to a life on Income Support.

It is often suggested that wages must fall to 'price the less skilled back into work'. But when technological advances have raised prosperity for most of

1

us beyond the dreams of our grandparents, it is wrong that people in work should still lack the means to pay for a decent standard of living. Yet wages as low as £2 an hour are commonplace in many areas. The average (median) wages of people leaving unemployment to take a job are only £4 an hour.

At the other end of the scale competition and insecurity often lead to overwork and anxiety which are dangerous to health as well as damaging to economic efficiency. This is compounded by the increasingly long hours of work which are often demanded and which workers are naturally reluctant to refuse if their jobs may be at risk. This contributes to increasing strain on marriages and can lead to neglect of proper attention to children. One witness said tellingly: 'Two parents working flat-out is a pretty poor model for the future'. The Institute of Management reports that almost 90 per cent of their members believe that stress is now having an adverse effect on their morale, health, work effectiveness and relationships.

The divisions and contrasts we have seen show how the accepted mix of market economy and democratic process fails many of our fellow-citizens. Yet in the British election campaign the political parties are competing for votes by promising low taxation. When so many are living in poverty and unemployment, it is wrong to give priority to the claims of those who are already well off. None of the political parties has put forward a programme which offers much real hope of improvement to those in the greatest need.

The Christian Vision

We address this report, not only to the churches who set up the enquiry, but to our fellow citizens in Britain and Ireland, whether or not they are church members, whether or not they share our Christian faith. This means that we must make clear where our own starting point is to be found in that faith, and how it affects the way we address the subjects of unemployment and the future of work. Everything we have to say is grounded in our experience of the life of the Church and in our understanding of the Bible. From this we draw our vision of what it would mean for human potential to be ultimately fulfilled in a society that was ordered and governed by God.

A member of an earlier working party, Peter Baelz, wrote in proposing some Christian perspectives on economics:

> 'The vision of the Kingdom prescribes certain fundamental criteria for evaluating the goals and objectives of a fully human society. In God's Kingdom there is universal peace and harmony, combining justice and prosperity in a truly personal and fulfilling community. Its universality (it is for <u>everyone</u>, we emphasise) puts in question any social or economic system which allows the world to be divided into the powerful and the powerless, the rich and the poor, or allows one group of people,

whether a class, a nation or a group of nations to pursue its own welfare at the expense of the welfare of others.

Its harmony and justice stem from the recognition that persons have a fundamental dignity of their own since they are made in God's image, independently of what they achieve or fail to achieve (and independently, of course, of their productivity!). *Thus, the whole community shares the responsibility for meeting the basic needs of each of its members, while each of its members accepts his or her own responsibility for contributing to the common good of all.*

Such a community is incompatible with an unbridled individualism, which in the name of freedom allows inequitable access to material and human resources. It is also incompatible with an unchecked collectivism, which in the name of equality and the good of the majority exercises an ever more rigid control over the thoughts and actions of its members. Neither freedom nor equality represents an absolute value. Both need to be set within the context of fraternity, which stresses the givenness of mutual belonging as prior to any relationship based solely on shared interests.

The dynamic in the Kingdom of God is shared care and concern, reflecting the indiscriminate love of God Himself. This love is directed towards the meeting of human needs, material needs such as food and shelter but also spiritual needs, such as freedom, responsibility and creativity.'
(Perspectives on Economics, Church of England BSR, 1984)

That vision of a good, and particularly a fraternal, society inspires every section of our report. It provides us with a compass-bearing for change and an ultimate standard of comparison for our survey of the current working-world and its failure.

More specifically, in describing and interpreting what we have learnt and in proposing a way forward we draw on particular narratives and images of scripture. These uniquely illuminate human tendencies and human possibilities, offering warnings and suggesting fruitful avenues of change:

* Christians go back to the biblical description of men and women as 'made in God's image'. This points to humanity's being endowed with a sacred and indestructible dignity and with stewardship of a world that God himself saw 'was good'. All humans have the potential for creativity, responsibility and love; none may ever be treated as disposable, menial or unwanted. That is to say, among other things, that the economy is there to serve human beings, not human beings to serve the economy.

* We see Jesus, the man who was God, described as the Lord's servant, insisting in his life and words that human dignity be expressed in the love of others. He himself gave living expression to that love as dutiful son fulfilling his family responsibilities to his mother, in services to family and community before his more public service as teacher and healer. Therefore we cannot do other than think of the economy as one way in which society provides us with opportunities to serve one another and meet each other's needs. To work may sometimes be tedious, oppressive and exhausting but it is the way we are enabled to contribute to sustaining and transforming the world.

* We do not have to do anything to earn the love of God; it is a free gift. Neither do we have to earn the love and fellowship of one another. Our daily work is one way of expressing our gratitude for these gifts. Yet in our society most people's wage or salary both rewards their creative effort and marks their standing as a contributing member. No-one therefore should be excluded from paid work.

* In the Biblical account of creation God rested when his work was complete. Like him, we men and women need the opportunity to step back from time to time, lean on our spade, relax and even admire our handiwork a little. That rhythm - work and relaxation- is fundamental. To encourage overwork, whether from anxiety, ambition or greed, is to misunderstand our own essential fragility and so threaten our capacity to create and to engage with our families, friends and society.

* We are commanded never to allow the full range of our attention and energy to be harnessed to a single man-made object or idea. That is to create, as it were, a false substitute for God. The virtues of the 'free market', for example, can tempt people to an excessive veneration, recognised in our religious tradition as the sin of idolatry. Such seductive economic and political ideas, equally available at both ends of the party-political spectrum, are dangerous. They impoverish our God-given critical faculties; they limit (by simple-mindedness) our imaginative response to the huge raw aspects of the world of actual, particular humans.

* Jesus taught within a tradition which set store by the idea of 'jubilee'. The energies that powered an economy and its markets, indeed enterprise itself, were recognised to have dangerous self-reinforcing tendencies. Unchecked, the economically strong grew stronger at the expense of the weakening weak. Justice and overall prosperity there-fore demanded countervailing arrangements: the agreed periodical

4

restoration of a just balance by the cancellation every 50 years of debt and obligations.

* The same God-given tradition looked not only for a justly ordered society but for its citizens to go about their affairs with a generous spirit, and not pursue economic advantage to the limit; to leave the windfalls on the ground, not to reap to the field's very edges, not to return to collect a forgotten sheaf, so as to leave proper scope for poor people to go gleaning.

* It may be the conventional wisdom in the world of affairs that economic growth is the precondition of helping the poor and those at disadvantage. The Bible proposes a radical alternative, which threatens our 'commonsense' assumptions for policy: namely that only a just and caring society can achieve real and lasting prosperity.

* Above all we are urged to see a good society as one of mutuality and inter-dependence. Its life is best seen as organic and its citizens as living members of a living body. We are 'members one of another'. We are commanded to resist the temptation to turn a blind eye to others' sufferings. We must learn to feel their fortunes as in part our own.

As the English and Welsh Catholic Bishops recently found in writing their statement on *The Common Good*, we too are 'not without resources' in debating these issues. 'There is an abundance of wisdom in scripture, in the teachings of the early fathers of the Church and the writings of numerous Christian thinkers down the ages.' (There is such abundance indeed that we have invited Peter Sedgwick to make a survey of it, which appears at Annex A to this report.)

St. Augustine, we learn, led the way in relating economic behaviour to the Christian faith, pointing out to a group of idle monks that labour was a means of self-expression, and the Garden of Eden a place both of work and of delight. Work predated man's sinfulness and was not to be seen as punishment for it. Culture, he said, sprang from the elemental experience of fashioning the world by manual labour and the use of reason.

John Wesley argued for great diligence in work, urging that 'everyone ought, in his lawful vocation and calling, to give himself to labour'. He stressed the importance of 'honest and godly exercise and labour, and everyone follow[ing] his own business'.

Among pioneers in the economic territory we have been exploring, William Temple most helpfully warns us not to try to *deduce* specific policies from the faith: 'Christian faith does not by itself enable its adherents to foresee how a vast multitude of people, each partly selfish and partly generous, and an intricate economic mechanism will in fact be affected by a particular economic or political innovation'.

We have been inspired by the Roman Catholics' careful crystallisation from time to time of their own social teaching. From the Second Vatican Council in 1965 came this insight:

'When a man by his handiwork and technical skill cultivates the earth to make it yield fruit and become a fit place for living in and when he consciously takes part in the various forms of social life, he carries out the design of God, manifested from the beginning, that he should subdue the earth and perfect the work of creation as he perfects himself; at the same time he observes the great commandments of Christ that he should spend himself in the service of his fellows.'

(*Gaudium et Spes*, para 67)

Our faith also tells us something about the way in which an enquiry like this should be conducted. We should look at unemployment and the future of work particularly from the viewpoint of the poor and the powerless themselves. They have little vested interest in the labour market as it is now, so they are more likely to consider radical changes. They know some of the realities of life in our divided society, of which many find it more comfortable to stay ignorant. As Christians we are called to listen to what they are saying and to pass the message on.

Many people might applaud us if we did no more than state a faith, derive some principles from our tradition and then leave it to others (politicians, civil servants, economists, scientists and 'experts' in general) to work out the practicalities. 'The Church should not be getting into politics', they would repeat. They would be wrong; we see our job quite otherwise. Our faith is precisely in a God who is not above the battle and who is visible for us in the mundane detail of the life of a working man, Jesus the Palestinian carpenter's son. We are therefore bound, as we think our readers inside and outside the Church will see, to grapple with the detail of policy options. We have to move beyond the idealised call for justice and the Christian promise of future deliverance, into grappling alongside others with the detail of how justice is to be made a practical reality or society brought to embody a new compassion.

Our faith compels us, as we think it compels the Church, to engage in argument about ways and means, sustainable, non-inflationary growth rates, industrial competitiveness, the usefulness or not of minimum wage legislation, the practicalities of large-scale job creation, an affordable system of Social Security benefits which can encourage as well as support. That engagement makes up the meat of this report.

Even in our debates on practical detail, however, we have found ourselves bringing the churches' particular insights to bear in deciding what weight to give to the pros and cons which surround almost all the different courses of action. So, in our discussion of the merits of a national minimum wage, it is in the end as some protection against individuals' loss of dignity and to raise a sign for justice that we support it, though aware that it could never on its own be an effective remedy for poverty. We have also recommended that higher taxation can no longer be ruled out of consideration by competent politicians. To achieve that would mean a change of heart among the electorate towards a 'higher doctrine' of taxation - as it were a vital spiritual transformation towards seeing tax as a willing contribution to the common good.

What Needs to be Done

The most fundamental question we have had to address is this: should we still, as church leaders have in the past, argue the case that enough paid work should be created for everyone, or should we adopt a new set of values in the belief that full employment is essentially a thing of the past?

We have concluded that the value of work is central to Christian understanding of the human condition, not an optional extra. Society should not give up on paid work, not even for the relatively low-skilled, not even on the estates we have visited where at present there is almost no paid work being done. The alternative, which would mean making long-term unemployment an accepted and acceptable way of life, is not realistic, and would not be compatible with human dignity if it were ever achieved.

During the period of our enquiry the monthly figures of claimant unemployed have been falling consistently. The most gloomy predictions of the past have been proved wrong. The British economy, when judged conventionally by growth rates, inflation trend, and the balance of our overseas transactions, is not in terminal decline; far from it. It is currently showing signs of remarkable resilience. At a time of relative optimism, it should be possible to get a hearing for proposals which might seem too ambitious if the economy were depressed.

But we must not be lulled into thinking all is well. Our criteria for 'economic success' are far too narrow for today's conditions. They can even blind us to our weaknesses. We need instead to learn to assess society's 'wealth' as its well-being as a whole, and not merely some average well-being but that (so far as we can) of each individual. We need moreover to judge how far our economic arrangements are serving to help bind people together or how far (by contrast) to set them apart or even against each other. Competition has strong economic virtues but on its own it is not a recipe for national happiness or cohesion.

The fall in unemployment shows that there is nothing inevitable about the loss of jobs. But closer inspection shows that the improvement we are seeing in the labour market does not go nearly far enough. Already there are warnings that the recovery of output cannot be sustained for much longer and that unemployment must level off around its present rate, which is still very high by historical standards. Moreover the recovery is passing by some regions and many of the individuals who have been worst hit by previous recessions. Some of the fall in unemployment is simply the result of people who have failed to find work over a long period giving up looking for it. And the jobs which are being created are often temporary, part-time and very low paid.

Our report is addressed to the longer-term problems of the economy rather than the ups and downs which happen from year to year. In that perspective the situation deteriorated sharply in the 1970s and 1980s, with rising unemployment and inequality, and no great improvement is evident in the 1990s. If these trends are actually to be reversed, on a lasting basis, there needs to be a change in the character of economic expansion not just for a year or two, but probably for several decades.

To achieve that implies a re-ordering of quite fundamental policy priorities. 'Enough good work for every one' has to become an explicit national aim in its own right - that is to say an objective central enough for other, otherwise worthwhile, projects to be sacrificed from time to time in pursuit of it. The aim of enough good work cannot be allowed to remain a hoped-for, but ultimately optional, by-product to economic growth.

Those priorities, however, cannot in practice be followed except in a climate where the public at large is steadily being led to share them. Politicians need to lead with conviction, not merely to respond to present majority appetite. We hope a voice from the churches can help to change public perceptions of what can and should be done.

The economy needs to expand in directions which will create more and better jobs. In particular this means expanding the service sector, both private and public. Some, at least, of this expansion will have to be financed by taxation. Society as a whole will benefit, not only the poor and powerless but the rich and powerful as well. With a better and fuller sense of common life, our countries could be better places for all to live in.

For example, jobs could be created in health and education, in childcare and help for the elderly, or in tourism, entertainment and maintenance of the environment. There is plenty of work to be done, work for people who would otherwise be unemployed. This is work which would meet real needs and at the same time enable more people to make a real contribution to the community. In doing that they would be able to support themselves, instead of depending on the grudging support of the benefit system. We make some more specific suggestions as to how this could be done in Part Two of our report.

We also make suggestions as to how conditions of employment could be improved. The problem of low pay certainly needs to be tackled and we support the proposal for a statutory minimum wage in Britain. Conditions of work should be made fairer and more reliable. Obviously we are seeing a change in the relations of employer and employee, but that does not mean that people at work need less protection. On the contrary we hope that the rights of workers will be taken as seriously in the future as the rights of consumers are taken now. Perhaps trade union ambitions have become too modest. One way to improve the conditions of the least well-treated would be for the union movement to organise them and negotiate on their behalf.

Recent changes in employment policy and the benefit system often give the impression that the unemployed are to blame for their situation. The new Jobseeker's Allowance has been seen as a way of identifying the workshy and the cheats, so that they can be excluded from the receipt of welfare benefits. That approach is unjust; it is also fundamentally mistaken. Something quite different is required. In our report we describe a fresh start for the long-term unemployed under which society would share with them the responsibility for finding good jobs for them to do. We also suggest some changes to the benefit system itself which would make the transition to work rather easier and more attractive. As it is, it can encourage some to distance themselves from working society.

Our concern is especially directed to the plight of those who have few readily-marketable skills. They are the ones most likely to experience unemployment or low pay. Clearly the best long-term solution is to improve both schooling and vocational training so that no-one lacks the ability to earn a good living in the economy of the future. We have some suggestions to make about how that might be achieved, but we also warn against regarding education and training as the solution to all our problems. There will always be some people more skilled and productive than others. It matters a lot how willing the successful and lucky ones are to share their good fortune with the rest.

One of the principal means by which the strong help the weak in our society is by paying their taxes, part of which the state uses to combat poverty. As the political debate is being conducted in Britain the case for redistributive taxation seems to be going by default. We see paying taxes as a contribution to the common good, which people should make without resentment. The increase in employment which we need for the good of society will, in our view, be much easier to secure if the existing self-imposed constraint on taxation and total public spending is removed.

We have conducted our enquiry in the run-up to a general election in

Britain. Some of the policy measures we discuss in our report have been issues in that campaign - the statutory minimum wage is an obvious example. But none of the political parties has put forward a programme which seriously tackles the central questions we raise about unemployment and the future of work. Some politicians have said to us that these are not matters on which they would want to express an opinion. We hope that the churches do not feel so constrained!

Our own aim is not partisan. It is to help set the agenda, to prick the national conscience, by raising the saliency of unemployment as an issue, and to ask the public as a whole to accept the responsibility for effective practical remedies which will be costly to themselves.

What the Churches Can Do

This enquiry is itself a sign that the churches take seriously their duty to say what the Christian faith implies for social conditions as well as individual behaviour. We hope that they will see this as a continuing process, of debate amongst Christians about the meaning of the Gospel and also debate with others in society about the application of the values we hold in common. It is all too easy for the church to retreat into a private sphere, to become an escape route from the world and not a means of redeeming it.

In Part Three of our report we describe what we have seen of the mission of the churches and Christian organisations to the world of work and unemployment. A great deal is being done, some of it not very well known either to the public or within the churches themselves. Churches are deeply involved in supporting and counselling people who are unemployed, in helping people to find work, in training and community regeneration projects. The churches are providing action as well as words.

We are impressed by the contribution of both industrial missioners and social responsibility officers, who are employed by the churches to engage full-time or part-time in mission and witness outside the parish or congregational structures. These are front-line troops for the church. They need more support and recognition than they have been getting recently in some parts of the country.

The life of the churches will always be centred primarily on local worshipping communities. These are the grass roots of church politics and the foundations on which national and regional structures are built. If the churches are to contribute more, by action or by words, to the great issues which we have addressed in this enquiry, then there has to be a real involvement at this local level. This must also mean drawing in the unemployed and low-paid as full members of the community. Church activities are for all, and not merely the comfortably off, the well-dressed and the respectable.

We think that every parish church or congregation should be expressing concern about unemployment and the future of work, in their prayers and in giving their support to employment and community projects. This concern should be expressed not just by a few enthusiasts, not just at the occasional weekday evening meeting. It should be expressed regularly to us all and by us all at the main Sunday services when we meet together to offer ourselves and our own work to God in thanksgiving and praise.

Notes

Our **main findings** *are summarised on page 174 of this report. The combination of policies which we believe to be most likely to provide good work for everyone would include:*

- tax reform to create many more jobs in the private sector (see chapter 5)
- much more employment in the public sector, financed by higher taxation (see chapter 5)
- a fresh start for the long-term unemployed (see chapter 7)
- a national minimum wage (see chapter 6)
- better conditions of work and fairer pay bargaining (see chapter 6)
- reform of the benefit system (see chapter 8)
- priority for basic skills (see chapter 9)
- a national employment forum (see chapter 10)

The conduct of the enquiry, *its methods of work and its proceedings are described in Appendix A. The enquiry was launched in September 1995 and this report was completed in February 1997. Meetings were held in London, in most regions of England, in Wales, in Scotland and Northern Ireland and in the Irish Republic. Informal evidence was received from a wide range of organisations and individuals including political leaders, employers, trade unionists, economists, theologians, community workers, and people with experience of unemployment and poverty. We are most grateful to all those who have shared with us their expertise, their experience and their convictions. We also wish to express our gratitude to the organisations and individuals, listed in that Appendix, who have provided financial support for the enquiry.*

We have included as Annexes, nine papers prepared for the enquiry on which we have drawn in writing our report. We are particularly grateful to the authors and we commend their papers to readers of this report.

We hope that the enquiry will encourage continuing debate and proposals for action within the churches and in society at large. A number of conferences and meetings are already planned. To receive further information, or to make suggestions for follow-up activities, contact:

The Co-ordinating Secretary for Public Affairs, CCBI, Inter-Church House, 35-41 Lower Marsh, London SE1 7RL

<u>or</u>   The Senior Chaplain, Mission in the Economy, Church House, 1 Hanover
Street, Liverpool L1 3DW (on behalf of the Industrial Mission Association)

<u>or</u>   The Executive Secretary, Churches' Enquiry into Unemployment and the
Future of Work, Christchurch, 27 Blackfriars Road, London SE1 8NY.

The enquiry has been conducted under the auspices of the Council of Churches
for Britain and Ireland, the ecumenical body to which almost all the main churches
of both islands belong. The **inclusion of Ireland, both north and south,** within
the scope of the enquiry has been an important aspect of our work. It has given us
fresh insights and suggested conclusions which we would not otherwise have reached.
The Irish economy is, in many important respects, quite different from that of
Britain and the contrasts help illuminate the strengths and weaknesses of the policy
regimes in both.

We have not been able, given the resources at our disposal and the experience of
most of our members, to devote as much attention to the situation in Ireland as to
that in Britain. Our visits to Dublin and Belfast are described in chapter 3 and
there is also a section in chapter 5 in which we offer some comments specifically on
the high level of unemployment in the Republic, despite all that is being done to
reduce it. Moreover the main message of our report, which is developed in all the
chapters of it, applies just as much to Ireland as to Britain, and indeed to all of the
more advanced economies of the world.

PART ONE: THE NEED FOR DECISION

Chapter One

The Changing Nature of Work

Historians looking back to the closing decades of the twentieth century may well identify our own times as the crucial period of a new industrial revolution. Certainly they will identify some profound changes in the nature of work. It is too soon to make such historical judgments, as these changes are still taking place around us now and their full implications are far from clear. But already we can see that there are pervasive effects on economic organisation and living standards, on family and household structure, and on community and social cohesion.

Our way of thinking about work in our society is so conditioned by the modern world as it developed out of the industrial revolution of the late eighteenth century that it is not easy for us to stand back and view it as if from the outside. Yet this is necessary if we are to address the issues, and make the choices, on which depend the character of our society in the future. Our Christian inheritance can be invaluable, stretching back as it does over two thousand years and not a mere two hundred. It is not dependent on the experience of just one form of economic organisation. It gives us a framework of values, or a decisive point of reference, as we try our best to address some important and complex questions about the future of work and of employment.

The issues addressed in this report are of great concern to all sections of society, and they are being actively studied from many different points of view. We have been conscious throughout our work that other enquiries are in progress covering some of the same ground. This has been a source of encouragement to us, and we have kept closely in touch with what they are doing. The Royal Society of Arts has a programme called 'Redefining Work'; the Joseph Rowntree Trust is supporting a research programme on 'Work and Opportunity'; the Leverhulme Foundation is supporting a programme of research on employment creation; the Carnegie Trust is undertaking a new initiative on the plight of young people with special emphasis on the transition into paid work; the Employment Policy Institute has a central role in stimulating debate and disseminating information. These are just some British examples of what is, quite rightly, a wide and diverse range of activity, directed towards some of the most crucial issues of our times. We believe that, as an expert working party set up by the churches, we have an important and distinctive contribution to make to the debate.

We have found it helpful to distinguish three different strands in the web of social change, although they are all closely related and mutually

13

interactive. The **first** is the introduction of new technology, especially in communications and information processing. The **second** is the changing composition of the labour force, with male participation rates falling and female participation growing. This has profound implications for the workplace as well as the home. The **third** is the liberalisation or deregulation of markets resulting in greater intensity of competition both within our countries and internationally. Much else is happening in our society at the same time which could be thought relevant to our enquiry, not least the changes in religious belief and the role of our own churches, but it is on these three trends we will concentrate our attention. We will describe them in a preliminary way in this chapter of our report. Their consequences are the challenge that we see to society today. We have no choice but to enter a new age, with new technology, global markets and increasingly equal opportunities for men and women in employment, but we **do** have a choice about the future of work and of unemployment in that new society.

New Technology

We are told that before long the storage and transformation of information in any form will become almost costless, and so will be its communication to anywhere in the world. Once an information system is set up and running there will be almost no need for human beings to be involved in any of these operations anymore. In the past machines have replaced physical effort and stamina, now they are replacing patience and manual dexterity, knowledge and skill as well. To give just one example we met out of the thousands we might have observed and quoted, computers have now taken over from scientists with PhDs the task of carrying out routine tests on the chemical properties of newly-developed medicines. This illustrates the point that it is not only what are conventionally thought of as 'unskilled' jobs which can be made redundant by technical change. Currently, we are advised, it is particularly the skilled or semi-skilled jobs in data processing that are most at risk, not least the new jobs created by earlier generations of computer technology.

On our industrial visits we have been impressed, like any group of relative innocents, by the precision of computer driven manufacturing machinery, for example in a modern shipbuilding yard. A vast and complex structure can be assembled according to a pre-set design and time schedule with relatively little human effort, because the process is guided by the information which is stored and transmitted very cheaply and accurately in a multitude of computer installations. We may see such processes as humbling or threatening, but we should also celebrate them as magnificent achievements of human ingenuity.

Another, not altogether trivial, example is worth recording. One member of our working party, Kumar Jacob, is a manager in a software company which designs and makes computer games. Some of us visited the firm and were duly impressed by the technology on display. Computer games, of this very sophisticated kind, may suggest lessons to be learnt about the use of computers at work as well as at play. They depend for their fascination on the interaction of human and mechanical abilities. The role of the human mind is active, not passive, requiring imagination and strategic vision very different to that possessed by the machine. We must bear this in mind when futurologists tell us that computers will make all human labour obsolete.

A recent American book, *The End of Work* by Jeremy Rifkin, begins with a disturbing vision:

> 'From the beginning, civilisation has been structured, in large part, around the concept of work. From the Palaeolithic hunter/gatherer and Neolithic farmer to the medieval craftsman and assembly line worker of the current century, work has been an integral part of daily existence. Now, for the first time, human labour is being systematically eliminated from the production process.'

In another passage he considers the long-term implications of artificial intelligence. 'Nicholas Negroponte of the MIT Media Lab', he tells us

> 'envisions a new generation of computers so human in their behaviour and intelligence that they are thought of more as companions and colleagues than mechanical aids'.

We need to reflect critically on this 'envisioning'. It raises some deep questions, including some religious questions, about what it means to be human and about how human work differs from the work we can get out of a machine, however intelligent. When we say that human beings are made 'in the image of God' we mean, amongst other things, that they are creative. Much of the work which human beings actually do is not like the work of God at all, because it is repetitive, boring and essentially mechanical. That kind of work could well be mechanised. But the element which we describe as creative is different in kind as well as degree. No machine now in existence is creative in that sense; it is a matter of dispute amongst scientists and philosophers whether a truly creative machine is possible as a matter of principle.

There is, in any case, a great range of tasks which of their very nature only a human being can perform. They involve human relationships. The more obvious examples may come from the caring professions, but a similar point could be made about jobs which involve persuasion, selling something or public relations, and about jobs which involve aesthetic or moral judgement.

It is no accident that careers guidance nowadays puts so much stress on the need for 'interpersonal skills'. A well-drilled computer programme may be able to mimic some such skills, but only as a form of deception. A vast number of jobs require the real thing.

Even if, as we believe, new technology does not exactly spell the end of work, it does nevertheless imply some fundamental changes in its nature. On the whole these changes should be beneficial, as were most of the long-term effects of earlier industrial revolutions. If machines can take over what is mechanical in human work, what is left should be better suited for humans to do. E F Schumacher in *Good Work* described most forms of work, whether manual or white-collared, as 'utterly uninteresting and meaningless'. 'Mechanical, artificial, divorced from nature, utilizing only the smallest part of man's potential capabilities' he described work in an industrial society as 'sentencing the great majority of workers to spending their working lives in a way which contains no worthy challenge, no stimulus to self-perfection, no chance of development, no element of Beauty, Truth, or Goodness.' His son, Christian Schumacher, has developed the concept of 'Whole Work', based on analogies between the structure of human work and Christian theology. He says that every job should involve planning, doing and evaluating; every job should perform some complete transformation, whether of material or of information, for which the workers can take responsibility; workers should be organised into teams whose members are responsible for one another. These ideas also relate well to new styles of management made possible by new technology. People work better when they are treated more as human beings, less as machines. It becomes increasingly possible to do this, as information processing takes over the mechanical parts of human work.

Simone Weil, who described the actual experience of work in very negative terms, wrote in *The Need for Roots* (written in 1943) that liberation would come from new technology. 'A considerable development of the adjustable automatic machine, serving a variety of purposes', she wrote 'would go far to satisfy these needs' - that is the need for variety and creativity as well as relative safety and comfort. 'What is essential is the idea itself of posing in technical terms problems concerning the effect of machines upon the moral well-being of the workmen.' Half a century later the need to pose such problems is even more evident, and the potential to solve them greatly enhanced. Technical advance can and should be a liberating and humanising influence on the future of work. Whether it is in fact so depends on the economic system and the choices people make within it.

A textbook on the subject, *The Economic Analysis of Technological Change* by Paul Stoneman, concludes as follows:

'The nature of the development of the economy that is likely to result from this complicated and involved process of technological change is not necessarily going to be ideal. Reductions in price and increases in consumer welfare may result, but these may only be generated at a cost... Nobody pretends that, in a world where decisions are made on the basis of private costs and benefits, the world will normally behave in a socially optimal way.'

When a new product or process is introduced there will always, in a market system, be winners and losers. Some of the winners will be easy to identify because they will be the owners of the innovating firms and those workers who have a stake in them. The other winners will be more difficult to point out because they will be members of the general public who enjoy a better product at a lower price. The losers will of course be the owners of the firms that compete with the innovation and especially the workers who lose their jobs. Typically they will move to much lower paid employment, if indeed they do not remain unemployed. Much of this report will be about how society treats, or should treat, those who find themselves in that position.

Even at this stage, however, we can make one thing clear. We have not seen or heard anything which convinces us that work has no future. Certainly there are needs to be met and many of those needs can be met only by human effort. It is not only the very clever, well educated or uniquely qualified people whose work is needed. Even a four-year-old child can do some things much more efficiently than the best computers in the world. The problem is one of social organisation. How can we match the potential of the people who want to work with the needs that exist, given the stock of equipment and the resources, and given the state of technical know-how? There is no reason why we should assume that this problem has no feasible solution.

The Supply of Labour

As our society gets richer one might suppose that people would choose to work less hard. With a larger stock of capital invested in machinery and infrastructure, with increased knowledge and technical efficiency, the same standard of living could be achieved with less human effort. It would be reasonable to expect - indeed it would be a prediction of standard economic theory - that most people would choose to take some of the benefit of higher productivity as increased leisure, or perhaps in undertaking some kind of unpaid work which they enjoyed doing, rather than taking the whole of the benefit as higher income and more consumption of goods and services. Yet looking back over the past generation there has been little change overall to the supply of labour to the market economy. One indicator of this is the proportion of the population aged 15 to 64 who are recorded as being in the labour force, that is to say either in work or actively seeking work. For the advanced industrial countries in aggregate (the OECD area) that proportion was 69.6 per cent in 1960 and 70.8 per cent in 1990. The fall in the male participation rate was almost exactly offset by the increase in the female participation rate. Similarly in Britain between 1985 and 1996 the activity rate overall was unchanged at 62.8 per cent: the rate for men fell from 76.4 to 72.3 per cent whilst the rate for women rose from 50.3 to 53.8 per cent. Chart 1 shows the numbers of men and women employed in Britain since the late 1960s.

CHART 1: EMPLOYMENT OF MALES AND FEMALES (INCLUDING SELF EMPLOYMENT)

Thousands

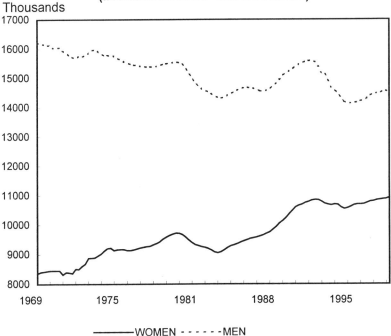

————WOMEN - - - - - -MEN

The fact that women as well as men now expect to take part in paid work is itself a change in the nature of work and of society of immense significance. It is at least as important and as challenging as the development of new technology. We need again to take a long historical perspective and note how the industrial revolution brought about a very sharp distinction between the work that men and women do. In a pre-industrial society men and women were more often working together and organising their work in similar ways. In a post-industrial society, if that is the right term to describe the pattern of life and work now emerging, men and women may again see their tasks as, in many if not all respects, the same.

The sociologist Anthony Giddens has described how heavy industry required a division of labour in which men's physical strength and endurance was stretched to the limit. This was possible only if women were able to give them both practical and emotional support:

'Women became 'specialists in love' as men lost touch with the emotional origins of a society in which work was the icon. Seemingly of little importance, because relegated to the private sphere, women's 'labour of love' became as important to productivism as the autonomy of work itself.' (*Beyond Left and Right*, 1994, pages 196-7)

In pre-industrial society the family was often the unit of production. Husband and wives, parents and children, worked together at common tasks, typically farming a small plot of land, doing some small-scale manufacturing, or running a small shop. Following the industrial revolution all this changed. By the early twentieth century work had come to mean quite different things to different members of the family. The husband was the breadwinner, working full-time, if he could, from when he left school to when he retired. Typically he worked as part of a large team in a hierarchical organisation with its own sense of community and strong bonds of mutual loyalty. His responsibility was limited to just one function within a larger whole that he did not need to understand. Work was like being in the army. It required discipline, loyalty, stamina and courage. It was a duty you owed to your wife and children. It was your fate, not something to be chosen or changed.

All this is now passing into history. Many of the traditionally male jobs, in mining and manufacturing for example, have disappeared. At the same time traditionally female jobs, in services for example, have increased. These changes in the composition of output are one part of the revolution which is going on, but not the whole of it. Thanks to changing attitudes and legislation women have access to jobs previously closed to them. At the same time some women are obliged to take low paid jobs to supplement the family income. It is a complex picture. The changing composition of the labour force has effects which interact with the changes that are due to new technology and new approaches to personnel management. The structure of work in most industries is becoming less hierarchical, with more scope for initiative at all levels. Work is still as a rule separated physically from the home, but they are no longer two different worlds. Employers sometimes try to be more 'family-friendly'. Work and family are both having to make compromises. We are in a period of transition, a period of particular stress, as the old patterns conflict with the new. Women are often trying to fulfil the roles of housewife and worker simultaneously, which is a very demanding combination indeed. There will be pressure for further changes both at work and at home.

During our visits we have heard concern expressed that there are now no longer enough jobs for men. Employment is declining in manufacturing, transport, mining and other industries which have in the past been largely male territory, while at the same time employment is expanding in service industries which have been mainly reserved for women. Moreover full-time employment is declining, while part-time employment grows, a trend which obviously suits many women with responsibility for young children.

The participation rate for men is falling - that is to say the proportion of the male population either in work or actively seeking work. It is very difficult to say to what extent this fall is voluntary and how far it is a recognition that good jobs are hard to find. More young men are prolonging their education, in the hope of improving their chances in the labour market. Others seem to have dropped out of the labour force altogether, and may well be involved in unrecorded casual work or in criminal activities. At the other end of the age range early retirement is becoming very common indeed. The typical situation is that men in their fifties or even forties lose one job as a result of closure or redundancy and then cannot find another. There may be work of a kind to be had, but it is low-paid, perhaps also seen as low-status, may involve long hours and high levels of stress, may involve living away from home or moving to a new part of the country. If many men decide not to take up such work opportunities, it does not necessarily mean that early retirement is really the option that they wanted to take.

The Carnegie Inquiry into the Third Age has investigated in some depth the employment situation for men and women over the age of fifty. They propose a phased transition from work to retirement. The general picture is one of frustration rather than relief at shedding the burdens of work. The section of their report on future prospects concludes: 'In general the position is bleak... Labour market pressures in the 1990s are unlikely to be sufficient to force change'. At the conference in 1996, when the third stage of the programme was presented, there was a call from angry members of the audience for legislation that explicitly outlawed employment discrimination by age. Despite all the talk there has been in the past about the coming of the leisure society, what many people still want, it seems, is to continue in paid work for as long as they physically can.

Such, indeed, is the apparent enthusiasm for paid work in our society even today that we shall need in this report to consider what remedies there are to the problems that result from overwork. Many individuals, of course, have no option but to overwork given the job that they are doing and given the attitudes of their employers and colleagues. When trade unions were more powerful they were more effective in limiting hours of work. But looking at society as a whole it is extraordinary how we have come to expect and accept hours of work, and a pace of work, which would have been called intolerable by many of our predecessors say twenty years ago. Perhaps a generation ago some people were inclined to take things too easy, but now the opposite danger is much more in evidence.

In reflecting on these changes in the supply of labour we miss a sense of the proper balance between work and the rest of life. We admire the enterprise, the enthusiasm, the persistence and sheer hard grind on which our collective prosperity is built. Yet we know that human fulfilment also requires periods of rest and recreation, time for family life, for cultural involvement, for prayer and worship. These are social as well as individual needs. In the Old Testament Law the observance of the Sabbath day was both a duty and a right. We need something analogous to that in our own society. If we can no longer observe Sunday as a work-free day for everyone, we can nevertheless reflect in other ways the attitudes that it fostered. Even if, in a post-industrial age, work becomes more creative and more humane, everybody will still need to get away from it from time to time to enjoy or endure all the rest that life has to offer.

Competition and World Markets

The third strand we have sought to unravel in the web of social change is the liberalisation of markets and the increased competition that goes with it. The old regulations that kept national markets apart have largely been abolished and within each country many of the rules which limited what firms could do have gone as well. In our own deliberations this is the strand which has caused the most profound concern and aroused the strongest feelings. We have been led into wider issues of the relationship between social justice and the market system, economics and the Christian gospel. What we have to say about unemployment and the future of work necessarily reflects what we believe about these even broader questions.

There is no doubt that economic life everywhere has become more competitive, both within countries and in the world as a whole. International competition owes something to the development of better communications, easing the transfer of information anywhere in the world. Cheaper transport may also be important. But in recent years the most significant change results from the elimination of political barriers to trade and the reduction of regulations limiting access to world markets. This has direct consequences for markets in tradeable goods and services as well as markets for capital. It has important indirect consequences for labour markets as well. Many international firms are in a position to locate their production where labour costs are lowest, pressing wages downwards and worsening conditions of work in relatively rich countries like our own. On the other hand the expansion of world markets benefits consumers in our countries who get more variety to choose from as well as lower prices for the goods and services they buy. Many firms in Britain and Ireland also benefit from wider markets for their products, as we have observed at first hand on our visits. Some people gain and others lose.

Globalisation and new technology interact powerfully with one another. New technology both destroys and creates jobs, but not necessarily in the same parts of the world. New jobs in data-processing can be created anywhere in the world, provided it is within reach of a telephone. Airline booking, insurance underwriting, software writing, copy editing - the list is endless of the jobs which are now being done wherever it is most convenient and cheap. These are some of the occupations for which demand will be growing fastest, and the rich advanced countries like our own will be too expensive to capture them.

One prominent British politician suggested to us that we should take up the unfashionable cause of protectionism as a means of safeguarding jobs at home. The argument is that Britain could opt out of international competition, so as to preserve our older industries without necessarily losing the opportunities to expand production in some new industries as well. We decline the invitation to support that cause. It does not seem to us plausible that Britain could stand aside from the globalisation of markets, without becoming increasingly isolated and impoverished. It would, of course, be incompatible with many treaty commitments, not least those with the European Union. In fact we see the opening of our markets to international trade as being in the interests of the country as a whole, as well as a means of helping development in some poorer countries. Christians must be concerned for the whole world and its poor. It is important to add, however, that the burden of adjustment to global markets is something which should be shared by society as a whole, not just carried by the communities which depend on industries where Britain no longer has a comparative advantage in world trade.

There are further qualifications which must be made to the generally beneficial effects of trade. One is the environmental damage which too often results from the development of products for export in relatively poor countries, the destruction of the tropical rain forests being just one of many such ecological disasters. Another is the over-use of energy resources in transportation. Moreover, countries which consume the products of cheap labour abroad cannot avoid all moral responsibility for the conditions in which those products are made. Increasingly charities are offering the alternative to individual consumers of purchasing goods which are traded on conditions which can be described as fair. This means cutting out unnecessary profit by traders and ensuring that most of the purchase price goes to the people who do most of the work. This is admirable, but our national governments could have far more direct influence on conditions in poor countries if they were prepared to use it. We do not see this as a reason for holding back the development of international trade. On the contrary we see the expansion of trade as the most promising route to the reduction of poverty. However, we deplore some of the effects of unregulated production and employment. In societies which are themselves unjust and uncaring, the opening up of markets for trade can make the working conditions of some very poor people even more intolerable and unfair.

In the sections of an advanced economy like ours which engage in international trade there is no real alternative to pursuing competitiveness and higher productivity. Firms which do not keep their costs under control and keep abreast of new technology will not survive long, as much of British industry has learnt in the past to its cost. The incomes earned from trade by world-class firms and industries can be used in part to generate employment elsewhere in the economy, especially in the service sectors, both public and private.

Typically the future of industry in countries like Britain and Ireland will be in relatively high technology activities, involving research and development rather than cheap mass production. This puts us in competition with other advanced industrial countries, most of them enjoying living standards as high as our own. We would not want, for several reasons, to see the future as being in competition with industry in the low-wage economies of the so-called Third World. As a strategy for Britain it does not appear likely to succeed, or only at the cost of a sharp fall in the living standards of much of the population. It would also mean trying to prosper at the expense of people in poorer countries whose need is in fact much greater than our own.

Competition Within the Home Economy

Competition within domestic markets has been increased by the deliberate policy of deregulation as well as the backwash of developments in the world at large. In the public sector conditions like those in a market have been created wherever possible, so as to encourage the same motivation and exert the same discipline. The intention has been to promote innovation and efficiency in public services, but on our travels we have met many people who regard these developments with anger or dismay.

The arguments in favour of a market system are well-known. It can allocate economic resources to the use where there is most demand for them, without the need for central planning. It leaves people free to make their own choices, within the limits of the economic resources they control. It rewards self-reliance, prudence, thrift, enterprise, diligence and other qualities which promote social as well as individual prosperity. The issue is not whether there should be a market system, but how it should be regulated and what activities should be within its domain. Some economic activities certainly do need regulation and planning, for example traffic in town or fishing in the sea. No-one should be seriously advocating a market system with no role for government at all.

Whilst accepting the need for a market system we must also draw attention to the moral dangers inherent in it. In the last twenty years or so there has grown up a tendency to treat the market as if it were an arbiter of social value. It is as if some people thought that the outcome of market forces, the equilibrium between supply and demand, was necessarily right and fair. This is nonsense - no system of exchange will put right an injustice in the initial distribution of the resources which each person brings to the market. We must never venerate the market as if it were some kind of god - or idol. The fact that we have adopted a market system, and not a command economy, does not relieve us, individually and collectively, of all responsibility for the outcome in social as well as economic terms.

Christianity and the market system have never been altogether at ease with one another, and probably never will be. To put it no stronger, the market does not actively encourage the Christian virtues of compassion and generosity; neither does it promote social justice or moderation in the enjoyment of material things. On the contrary it sometimes excuses or even encourages a kind of selfishness and a kind of callousness which would be totally unacceptable if they were shown in relationships face-to-face. It may also be a vehicle for ambition and greed, or an obsessive need to accumulate wealth. Some of these unattractive features of the market system have been very much in evidence, alongside much that is good, in our society over the last twenty years or so.

Economists draw a distinction between markets in which competition is 'perfect' or 'imperfect'. Under perfect competition individual producers and consumers have no effect on prices, because there are so many other producers and consumers in the market. An individual farmer for example has no effect on the market price of potatoes. Under perfect competition 'the market' is an altogether impersonal force, and business is transacted, as it were, at arm's length. Imperfect competition, which in fact characterises many of the most important markets in modern economies, is another matter altogether. Individual producers or purchasers, who are often giant companies, exercise considerable market power. They are very conscious how their behaviour will influence the price of the things that they buy and sell. They have also to calculate how their behaviour will alter the behaviour of their main competitors. Relationships of co-operation, rivalry or outright warfare develop between firms. The smaller players in such a market, the consumers of the final product or the producers of raw material for example, find themselves at a strategic disadvantage. The benefits of the market system in allocating economic resources efficiently can be claimed for perfect competition, but not with such confidence for imperfect. Elements of monopoly power will disturb the action of Adam Smith's 'invisible hand'.

The difference has a moral as well as an economic significance. The successful use of market power often requires a firm to drive others into extinction or to exploit those that are weaker than itself. Such behaviour would be unacceptable in a personal relationship and it cannot be exempt from moral judgement simply because it takes place in a business context.

Our main concern in this enquiry is with the market for labour. As economists and other social scientists recognise, the hiring of labour is seldom a purely market transaction like the idealised process of exchange described in the elementary textbooks. Relationships at work involve commitment and trust, co-operation and a sense of fellowship as well as contracts of employment and competition for the best jobs. Wages reflect conventions, norms and hierarchies as well as supply and demand. They reflect the bargaining strength of employees and the role played by trade unions. But in recent years reality is coming a little closer to the textbooks and labour is being treated more and more like a commodity. This may or may not increase economic efficiency, but in any case it impoverishes human relations. These are issues to which we will return again and again later in this report.

We are not suggesting that the labour market should be abolished. That might be desirable in a small community, in which everyone knows and cares for one another, but not on a national or a global scale. It might be necessary in wartime, but at the cost of restrictions on individual liberty which would be intolerable under any other circumstances. What we are suggesting is that the labour market should be fair, and also that it should be used as a means to achieve social objectives, including the expansion of employment and improved conditions of work. The best guarantee of fairness is likely to be a bargain struck between market participants who are reasonably evenly matched: employees, usually speaking collectively through their representatives, on one side, employers on the other. We cannot separate the growth of unfair employment practice from the decline over the past fifteen years in the membership and power of the trade unions.

This weakening of worker representation results partly from the changing composition of the labour force (more part-timers, more small firms, a smaller public sector) but also from deliberate government policy expressed in new legislation. It is very likely that the decline of unionisation, of itself, has contributed significantly to the growing inequality of pay, especially the increase in the proportion of very low paid jobs. The effect on unemployment is less easy to assess. Certainly unions have resisted redundancies, and stronger unions could have done so more successfully. It is less clear how they would have affected the expansion of employment in other areas. Some of the countries with a good record of job creation have strong unions, others do not. The relationship is a complex one, not fully understood by economists.

In the 1950s and 1960s trade unions in Britain were generally agreed to have a very important and constructive role to play in both the public and the private sector, at local and national level. In the 1970s however relations became antagonistic and the behaviour of some unions was perceived as irresponsible. The public sector strikes of the 1978-9 'winter of discontent' remain a particular vivid memory in the minds of politicians of all parties, as well as the general public. George Woodcock, at one time General Secretary of the TUC, uttered the following prophetic warning in 1975:

'The most likely alternative to co-operation is that governments will have to modify or abandon their commitment to maintain a high level of employment, and their consequential responsibilities for economic growth, stable prices and good industrial relations. If this country were to return to the industrial instability and the heavy unemployment of pre-war days, that would certainly not improve the ability of the trade unions collectively to secure greater social justice and fairness for their members.'

Trade union influence has been weakened since the 1980s as Woodcock foresaw. These developments are important to our enquiry. The balance of industrial power, which in the 1970s was tipped in favour of the unions, is now too heavily weighted in the opposite direction. As a result many workers are now employed on a 'take-it-or-leave-it' basis. Too often that is the reality behind the comfortable-sounding phrases about 'individual negotiations' and 'individual contracts'.

The powers of the state to regulate, to tax and to spend, should be deployed so that behaviour which supports social objectives, creating new jobs, for example, is encouraged, whilst behaviour which is socially damaging, paying excessively low wages, for example, is discouraged or even prevented.

This puts considerable responsibility and power into the hands of politicians and officials, who will have to decide what the regulations should be, what taxes should go up and how (and where) the money should be spent. We are, of course, aware that such powers can be misused. Individuals pursue their self interest and exploit others within bureaucracies or voluntary bodies as well as within commercial enterprises. There is no getting away from the sinful nature of human beings; our Christian belief encourages us to be realistic at the same time as we are idealistic. We would nevertheless put forward the following simple proposition: when the economy is not producing what justice demands, in particular not producing enough good jobs to go round, then it is right for the government to take action which will make the market work better. These are some very broad generalisations, our reflections on a debate which has been going on since the eighteenth century, if not before. Against that background we can look at the more immediate historical context of the enquiry.

Varieties of the Market System

Recent decades have seen the collapse of communism in eastern Europe and the old Soviet Union and the attempt, by no means successful so far, to replace it with a market economy. The command economies proved unsuccessful, especially at adopting new technologies and responding to consumer demand. They also depended on the suppression of democracy and human rights. It was good to see them go. The attempt, however, to move from one extreme to another is now shown to have been misguided. The chaos now emerging in some parts of eastern Europe demonstrates only too clearly how a market system can operate well only in the context of well-designed and enforced regulation. Nearer home we have seen the failure of mixed economies to cope with the various crises that hit them in the 1970s. The trend towards deregulation and greater reliance on market forces results in large part from the recognition of that failure and reaction against the style of economic policy associated with it. We now have a variety of market systems in different parts of the world in which the role of government policies differs quite a lot.

Economic policy and its institutional setting are very different in the United States and in the countries of Continental Europe, although both are examples of the market system. To oversimplify the contrast, the American system makes a virtue of keeping the role of government to a minimum, whilst the European system sees government, industry and workforce representatives as partners in achieving economic and social goals.

In America social security provision for the unemployed is limited to a short period with no equivalent of means-tested Income Support or Jobseeker's Allowance except for families with young children. Provision on the Continent varies considerably but in some countries, as also in Ireland, social security benefits are much more generous than in Britain and available for an unlimited period. In America there is a minimum wage, although it is very low; in some European countries there is a national minimum wage which seems very high in comparison with levels of pay now common in Britain. In Ireland there is no national minimum wage, but there is a system similar to the wage council rates which used to operate in Britain. America relies on individual employment rights enforceable in the courts; Europe relies more on collective bargaining and on regulation of employment by law. Most European countries have relatively large public sectors and relative high rates of taxation. In Ireland also personal taxation is higher than it is in Britain, although company taxation is relatively low. The dispersion of wages in America is wide, and getting wider, whilst in Europe it remains relatively narrow. To oversimplify again, the main labour market problems in America are low pay and non-participation, whilst in Continental Europe the main problem is unemployment and especially long-term unemployment.

Much of the political debate in Britain is about the choice between these two models. Under Conservative governments since 1979 the movement has been generally in the American direction, partly as a result of spontaneous changes in the culture of business and society but also very much as a result of legislation and changes in economic policy. The parties in opposition, both Labour and the Liberal Democrats, as well as the trade union movement, have been much more in sympathy with most aspects of the European model, supporting for example the social chapter of the Maastricht Treaty. Nevertheless it would be a mistake to associate any of the political parties in Britain with just one model of the market economy, since opinion in all of them is divided.

Much Christian opinion in America strongly supports the market economy as it is in that country, with particular emphasis on freedom and the rights of the individual. In 1986 however, the National Conference of US Catholic Bishops in Washington issued a statement called *Economic Justice for All* which was very critical of some trends in that country, especially the neglect of the poor and the lack of social protection. A vigorous debate followed within the American churches, in which some prominent Catholics came out strongly against the views expressed by the Bishops. As the substance of this report will imply, we feel that the American Catholic Bishops made a lot of valid and very telling points.

This does not mean however that all is well with the European model. The situation in both France and Germany at the time of writing this report is a cause for grave and increasing concern. Jacques Delors has written:

'Today the problems of unemployment and social exclusion constitute the main challenge to European society as a whole. They are neither marginal nor accidental but threaten the very foundations of the European social model by casting doubt upon it and leading to unbearable personal situations.'
(Preface to Uniapac Report: *Committed Entrepreneurial Action Against Unemployment*)

How could we possibly support a model which produces unemployment rates of 12½ per cent in France, 9 per cent in Germany, 10 per cent in Sweden and 22 per cent in Spain? There must be something profoundly wrong with the Irish economy as well since the rate of unemployment is 12½ per cent in that country, substantially higher than it is in Britain. The condition of the unemployed in Continental Europe cries out for justice just as much as the condition of the working poor in America. To put that right will require major reforms to the European model, not just a few 'schemes' which tinker at the edges.

The Benefits and the Costs of Change

We have identified three strands in the fabric of change: the rapid introduction of new technology, the changing role of women in the labour force, and an intensification of competitive pressure throughout the world. Bringing these three together creates a need for flexibility and a general sense of insecurity. Flexibility is not just a word which employers use when they have to cut wages or make staff redundant. It is a quality which our society must have if we are to benefit from change and the opportunities it can bring.

The White Paper of the European Commission, *Growth, Competitiveness and Employment,* published in 1994 distinguishes two different needs for flexibility in the labour market, flexibility which is external to the firm and flexibility which is internal. External flexibility includes movement of labour between geographical regions and between industries or occupations, with the provision for retraining which that implies. It means less emphasis on preserving old jobs and more emphasis on creating new ones. It means better arrangements for matching those who are seeking work with the work that they could do. Internal flexibility concerns the reorganisation of the existing workforce whilst maintaining continuity of employment. 'The aim' according to the White Paper, 'is to adjust the workforce without making people redundant wherever this can be avoided'. These are fine words, but behind them lie some very difficult choices as to who bears most of the cost of adjustment. How much falls on the firm as employers, and hence indirectly on its shareholders and customers? How much falls on individual employees? How much should society as a whole pick up through the mechanism of taxation and public spending? We will return to these issues later in the report.

There can be no doubting the increased sense of economic insecurity which is felt by people in all walks of life. It is not in fact easy to find statistics to back up the common perception that job changes are much more frequent now than they were ten or twenty years ago. The data show a mixed picture, in part because people are reluctant to quit a job if they feel that a new job would be even less secure. Undoubtedly many of the new jobs now being created are temporary, and many of the small firms creating them are themselves in a precarious position. Some uncertainty is inseparable from economic enterprise and some people thrive on it. There are others, however, who are especially vulnerable and who have been made to feel increasingly so in recent years.

In times of rapid social change and insecurity, churches and other religious institutions are often seen as places of refuge in which people can shelter and find comfort. This may rest on the belief that God does not change, and neither do the truths on which our faith is built. It is dangerous however if it means that religion is backward-looking, a nostalgia for the way of life that was appropriate to a previous generation. To avoid any possible misunderstanding of this kind we want to assert vigorously that the future, especially the future of work, belongs to God, just as much as the past. The changes we have described in the nature of work could all be used to bring society a little closer to the vision which the Christian gospel reveals. Faith and hope in the future are cardinal virtues. But what we observe is a great deal of cost, avoidable cost unequally borne, as well as the benefit from change. This avoidable cost is what our report must be mainly about.

Our enquiry was set up to consider the two issues of the future of work and of unemployment. They are, of course, related in ways which we shall explore in the next chapter of our report. They have become so closely identified, however, in the popular mind that some people think the future of work is unemployment. This is a fatalistic attitude, based on mistaken views we shall challenge. But first we must address the phenomenon of mass unemployment, a social evil of the greatest magnitude.

Chapter Two

Unemployment and Poverty

According to the national charity Church Action on Poverty, unemployment and low pay are 'two sides of the same coin'. In this chapter of our report we shall be looking at how they relate to one another and asking why both unemployment and low pay have been becoming so much more prevalent at a time when our society as a whole has been becoming so much richer. First we need to set out some facts and figures, taken from standard statistical sources.

Facts and Figures

In December 1996 the claimant count in the United Kingdom stood at 6.7 per cent. This is somewhat below the rate used for international comparisons. In the summer months of 1996 the standardised percentage rate of unemployment was 8.2 per cent in the United Kingdom and 12.5 per cent in the Irish Republic; it averaged 10.8 per cent in the European Union and 5.3 per cent in the United States. The rate varies considerably across countries. (Despite the efforts made to make the figures comparable they must inevitably reflect the different classifications and terminology in use.) In 1995 for example unemployment was exceptionally low in Japan at 3.1 per cent and in Switzerland at about 3.2 per cent, but exceptionally high in Spain at 22.9 per cent and in Finland at 16.6 per cent. Clearly unemployment is not a universal consequence of modern technology or a market economy. The situation is much more complicated than that.

It is important to look at the figures in a historical perspective. In Britain in the mid 1920s unemployment was recorded at around 8 per cent, no different from the level recorded last year. During the depression of the early 1930s it rose to over 15 per cent and then fell back to about 8 or 9 per cent again towards the end of the decade. The second world war quickly secured full employment, with recorded unemployment rates below 1 per cent from 1942 to 1945. The remarkable fact, looking back from the present day, is that full employment was then maintained in Britain right up to the end of the 1960s. For twenty-five years after the end of the war unemployment varied between 1.2 and 2.6 per cent, rising and falling a little with the rhythm of the economic cycle. At that time it was thought that the problem of unemployment had been solved.

In the 1970s the unemployment percentage (on a slightly different definition now) began to show an upward trend (see Chart 2 overleaf). It passed 5 per cent in 1976 and 10 per cent in 1982. Since then it has not shown any clear trend: some economists believe that the underlying rate, abstracting from the cycle of boom and recession, has fallen back somewhat in the 1990s.

The peak year of 1993 seems a little below the peak year of 1983, but adjustments for changes in the definitions used cannot be made with certainty. In the Irish Republic there was also a steep rise in unemployment between the late 1970s and the mid 1980s with the rate having levelled off and even eased back a little since then. If we look at the industrialised world as a whole (the OECD area) the pattern is much the same. What needs to be explained, therefore, is both the steep rise in unemployment which took place between 25 and 10 years ago and its persistence at high levels ever since.

CHART 2: CLAIMANT UNEMPLOYMENT

Thousands

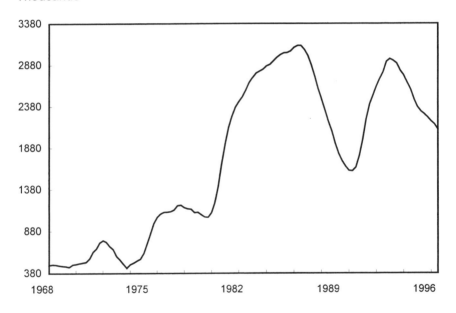

The area statistics for unemployment vary greatly from one part of the country to another. Claimant unemployment as a proportion of the workforce in December 1996 was 13 per cent in South Tyneside, 15 per cent in Cumnock in Scotland, 15½ per cent in Strabane in Northern Ireland. At the other extreme it was under 3 per cent in Andover, Clitheroe and Windermere. These figures are based on what are called 'travel-to-work' areas; figures for smaller areas are higher - for example over 20 per cent in some wards in Manchester.

In December 1996 the claimant unemployment rate in the United Kingdom for men was 9.1 per cent as against 3.7 per cent for women. The much lower rate for women reflects the fact that many women are not eligible to claim benefits when they are unemployed. Young people below the age of 18 are not in the claimant count because they are not eligible for benefit when unemployed. For young men aged 18 or 19 the rate was 18 per cent in October 1996, compared with 11½ per cent for young women in the same age group. The rate is lower in successive age cohorts up to age 50, when it rises again. These figures highlight the particular problem of unemployment amongst young men which was drawn to our attention again and again as we travelled round the country.

An article in the June 1996 edition of *Labour Market Trends*, based on the Spring 1995 Labour Force Survey, shows unemployment analysed by ethnic origin. For 'whites' the percentage was 8.2 per cent, compared with 18.7 per cent for all ethnic minorities. The main reason for this large difference is almost certainly racial discrimination in employment.

We will be devoting particular attention in this report to the issue of long-term unemployment. In October 1996 2.0 million people were recorded as claimant unemployed in the UK; of these 0.7 million had been unemployed for over a year and 0.4 million for over two years. In proportional terms, long-term unemployment is predominately male rather than female. The figures for long-term unemployment in Ireland are substantially higher (see chapter 3 below).

These duration statistics do not show the whole of the problém, however, since many people experience repeated spells of unemployment rather than one continuous long period. Some indication of this is given by the figures for intervals between claims. Of those people in the UK who became unemployed claimants in July 1996, only 26 per cent had never claimed before; as many as 49 per cent had claimed within the last year and 36 per cent within the last six months. It is too easily assumed that short-term unemployment is not a serious social problem. This might be true if it affected us all equally. In fact for many people unemployment is never far away, even if they do obtain employment from time to time, breaking up the really long spells out of work.

As normally measured the statistics for unemployment only include those who are actively seeking work. The Labour Force Survey also identifies those who have given up looking for work because they do not expect to find it, those who would like to work but are not available to start work straight away and others who simply say that they would like a job and who might well therefore be drawn into the labour force if demand were more buoyant. On this basis total unemployment in the summer of 1996 was not 2.3 million as in the Labour Force Survey figures usually quoted, but 4.5 million. (For a fuller description of this measure see *Employment Audit* published by the Employment Policy Institute.)

The fall in male unemployment during the current recovery phase of the cycle in the United Kingdom is matched in roughly equal measure by an increase in male employment and a fall in male participation rates. In other words, even in a cyclical upturn, men are still leaving the active labour force in large numbers. This is an unusual state of affairs and should be a cause for serious concern. One reason is the increasing number of men whose benefit payments are being stopped for one reason or another (see Chapter 8 below). Another explanation is that men are not often looking for part-time or temporary work. Since unemployment began to fall two-thirds of the extra people at work are working part-time and three-quarters of the new full-time jobs are temporary. Another explanation may be the rates of pay on offer. 'Entry' jobs taken by people moving from unemployment to work, on average, pay only half as much per week as the wage of all jobs in the economy. These figures are taken from the *Employment Audit*. The authors comment:

'It is clear that a period of unemployment could hold out the prospect of a return to work at a much lower rate of pay. Perhaps it is fear of paying this penalty associated with unemployment, and the possibility of 'trading down' in the labour market, that lies at the heart of people's apparent insecurity and anxiety about keeping their jobs in the 1990s.'

The situation in Britain today has some of the characteristics of a 'dual' labour market. On the one hand there are the people in steady jobs, who may not feel themselves to be very well paid or secure, but who do have some power simply by virtue of being 'insiders'. They have developed some kind of relationship of trust and mutual support with their colleagues and their employers. All this may be at risk, but whilst it lasts it gives protection from the cold winds of increasing competition. On the other hand we have those who are unemployed or in temporary and insecure work - the 'outsiders' in the labour market. They have no power at all and must sell their labour for whatever price it can reach in what is now quite clearly a buyer's market. This duality helps to explain why we are such a divided society.

Before leaving the facts and figures on unemployment some comment is needed on the problems of measurement. The most commonly quoted figure for unemployment is the claimant count in Britain (or the Live Register in Ireland). The number of people claiming benefit as unemployed depends not only on the numbers seeking work but also on the rules for benefit entitlement. For example the recent fall in the claimant count results in part from the tightening of eligibility tests both before and after the changeover to the Jobseeker's Allowance. So many changes have been made to the criteria for benefit in recent years that the claimant count can not be regarded as a satisfactory measure either of the pressure of demand for labour or of the social problems which arise from the shortage of jobs. The Labour Force Survey provides a better guide, but it is not necessarily an undistorted measure. When changes are made in conditions for benefit they are likely to have some effect on the way in which people describe their own situation in response to a questionnaire. It is increasingly coming to be recognised in the UK that the unemployment figures refer to just one category of those without paid work. They do not include the involuntary retired, the single parents who would like to work, the sick or disabled who are by no means totally incapable, and other identifiable groups which are increasing in importance.

The *Employment Audit* also provides information on the distribution of pay derived from the New Earnings Survey. In 1985 the lowest decile of full-time male earnings (that is the man who was ten per cent up from the bottom of the pile) earned 63 per cent of the median (the man in the middle of the distribution). By 1995 the ratio had fallen to 57 per cent. Just recently the pay of those near the bottom of the scale has not even kept pace with inflation. Near the top of the pile, the highest decile has risen from 184 per cent of the median to 205 per cent over the same ten years. Broadly speaking the rich are getting richer and the poor are getting poorer. In historical terms this widening of the wage distribution is very unusual indeed. It shows up both within occupations and also between occupations. In the early 1980s it was widely interpreted as a reversal of the compression of differentials by the incomes policies of the 1970s, but it has now gone much further than that. Part of the explanation must be the decline in the influence of trade unions and the decentralisation of pay bargaining, but deregulation and privatisation are important too.

These figures tell the same story as those given in the official publication, *Social Trends 1996* (page 108)

> 'Between 1971 and 1993 average (median) real disposable income rose by 45 per cent. However the incomes at the decile points have diverged from the median over time, increasing the gap between those with high and low incomes. Income in the ninth decile in 1971 was just over three times that for the first decile; in 1993 it had increased to over four times that for the first decile.'

The same publication shows that between 1981 and 1992/3, the real income of the bottom fifth of the population was almost unchanged, while the income at the top fifth rose by 45 per cent.

On another definition, using data from 'Households Below Average Income', for the population as a whole real average net income rose by 40 per cent between 1979 and 1993/94, but for the bottom decile it fell by 13 per cent over the same period.

The Current Economic Upturn in the UK

During the period of our enquiry the British economy has been going through a favourable phase with steady growth and low inflation. The claimant count of the unemployed fell from 8.2 per cent in September 1995 to 6.7 per cent in December 1996. The recovery began four years ago following the deep recession at the beginning of the decade. It is essential therefore to see the economic situation in its cyclical context: economies go through phases of optimism and pessimism and it is all too early for commentators to get carried along with the current mood. We have been here before. In the mid 1980s for example a long cyclical recovery was very widely misinterpreted as a permanent change of trend. It took the experience of another recession to correct that illusion. Similarly in the depth of a recession commentators too easily become apocalyptic. Only a few years ago it was widely believed that the UK economy was in an irreversible decline. That mistake can also be corrected now. At the present time the economy is showing remarkable resilience, unemployment is falling and as yet inflation has not accelerated much in consequence. Similar periods have occurred in previous cycles. The question which needs to be asked is whether anything fundamental has changed when this cyclical upturn is compared with its predecessors.

We are helped to make this comparison by an article in the December 1996 issue of *Labour Market Trends* written by Julian Morgan of the National Institute of Economic and Social Research. As well as comparing the British upturns of the 1990s and 1980s with one another, he also compares both with corresponding cyclical movements in six other countries. The fall in unemployment in the UK in this upturn has come earlier than it did in the 1980s. The contrast between behaviour in the two decades is much greater in the UK than in the other countries examined. That is the story of unemployment, but the story about employment is different. In the first three years of the 1990s upturn employment continued to fall, even though unemployment was also falling - there was an unusually sharp fall in participation rates. A significant part of the explanation is the increasing numbers being classified as disabled or sick. Moreover, as the author comments:

'These data may underestimate the true numbers of discouraged workers as changes in the administration of unemployment benefits, with increasingly strict eligibility requirements, may have led to a change in registration behaviour. This has been an ongoing process with, for example, the introduction of 'Restart' interviewing in 1986 and the more recent 'Jobseekers Allowance'. Also some people who have a health problem which affects their ability to find work and who were previously classified as unemployed, may have shifted to claim Sickness Benefit which does not carry onerous conditions to look for work.'

One lesson to draw from this is that a fall in unemployment cannot always be taken at face value. Moreover the behaviour of unemployment in a cyclical recovery may not be typical. Suppose, for example, that deregulation of the labour market and other structural changes in the 1980s have made it easier both to hire and to fire labour. Then we would expect to see exceptional losses of employment in the recession years followed by exceptional, but perhaps temporary, gains in the recovery. What we have seen so far in the UK is consistent with that view. It does not bode well for the future, when we come to the next period of slowdown or recession - as, sooner or later, no doubt we will.

It remains true that unemployment in the UK has fallen further without damage to inflation than seemed likely a few years ago. One reason may be that, compared with the 1980s cycle, the recovery has been more widely dispersed geographically so that there is less risk of inflationary pressure caused by regional bottlenecks. Another, less welcome, explanation may be connected with the dispersion of earnings. The new jobs being created are typically paid a small fraction of the average wage. This enables firms to keep their costs low and competition obliges them to keep their prices low as well.

It is difficult (especially in an election year) for anyone to make a sober and dispassionate assessment of the performance of the economy. It would be curmudgeonly not to welcome the cyclical upturn in output, from which many people, including many poor people, are benefitting at the present time. On a purely statistical measure of performance, combining unemployment and inflation, the economy is clearly doing very well. But looking behind the statistics, there are reasons to question whether that is the right judgement. Are we really better off as a society when it becomes more difficult to establish eligibility for unemployment benefits? Are we really better off as a society if we keep costs under control by paying poverty wages? We see it as part of our task in this enquiry to point out the limitations of the criteria by which our society judges economic failure and success.

Youth Unemployment

In October 1996 the rate of UK claimant unemployed was 7.1 per cent overall, but as high as 14.9 per cent for those aged 18 or 19, and 12.1 per cent for those aged 20 to 24. (There are no comparable figures for the unemployed under 18 as they are not entitled to claim benefits.)

In the 1980s youth unemployment was identified as a specially worrying aspect of the general problem of rising unemployment, but it was associated with the post-war bulge in the population. A recent OECD study describes the changes over a period of fourteen years. In 1980 the population aged 15 to 24 was about 41 per cent of the population aged 25-54. In 1994 the ratio had fallen to about 32 percent. One might have thought therefore that the particular problem of youth employment would be getting less serious. Moreover more young people are staying in education: between 1984 and 1994 the proportion of 18 to 22 year olds in education in the UK rose from 27 to 35 per cent. That should have further reduced excess supply in the labour market. Nevertheless the fall in youth unemployment rates (from 23½ per cent to 17½ per cent for 18 to 22 year olds between 1984 and 1994) was disappointingly small.

Rates of youth unemployment vary considerably between countries, not always in line with rates of unemployment for the population as a whole. For example the rate for young men in 1994 was only 7.2 per cent in Germany, but 33.9 per cent in France. The transition from school to employment is relatively well planned in Germany with its tradition of vocational guidance and apprenticeship (see chapter 9 below). In other countries, notably the United States, it is recognised that young people, especially the minority who do not stay on at college, are very likely to switch from one job to another before settling down, and to have more or less frequent spells of unemployment in between.

The reason for special concern about youth unemployment is not just that it is relatively high, but also that it comes at a crucial stage in a lifetime. The anxiety must be that young people who fail to obtain work experience at this stage will miss out an essential induction into adult responsibility and independence. For this reason various government schemes have been designed for this age group in particular. It is also the main focus for the initiatives proposed by the Labour Party in their 'new deal'.

However the main explanation for youth unemployment is the deficiency of demand for labour overall. A study of youth unemployment in 15 countries was carried out for the OECD by David Blanchflower and Richard Freeman in 1996. They concluded that

'the most likely cause for the adverse labour market experiences of youths is the high overall rate of unemployment. Neither changes in demography nor expansion of low-wage industries nor reductions in the wages of youth were able to counteract the effects of the macro-economy on the prospects of young workers'.

At the same time as we have been conducting our enquiry, the Employment Policy Institute has been working with the Prince's Trust to prepare a consultation document called *What Works? Jobs for Young People*. They have visited Glasgow, Cardiff, Manchester and Birmingham and discussed the problems of the youth labour market with a range of experts and with young unemployed people themselves. We would emphasise two points from this interesting and wide-ranging report.

The first concerns what they call 'status zero'. This is the classification of school leavers who are neither in employment nor in receipt of education or training.

> 'A relatively small but not insignificant minority of youths -
> between 5 and 10 per cent of the school-leaving cohort depending
> on the general state of the economy - still end up jobless and enter
> [this] depressingly labelled category...People who slip through the
> education, training and employment nets at this very young age
> are clearly those most at risk of remaining unemployed into young
> adulthood and ending up on the margins of society.'

The second point concerns racial discrimination. In some parts of London for example, we know that a majority of young black men are unemployed. At the consultations conducted by the Employment Policy Institute the point was made that 'tougher anti-race-discrimination legislation targeted at private and public sector employers would have to be an element of any major onslaught on youth and adult long-term unemployment'. What we have heard in the course of our own enquiry confirms that view (see Chapter 6 below for further discussion of unfair discrimination in the labour market).

The Experience of Unemployment and Poverty

It is dangerous to generalise about the experience of unemployment and poverty since it is different for each individual. Meeting people who are unemployed and poor, there is no way of observing why these people rather than some others, including oneself, should not be experiencing this misfortune. Misfortune is all that they have in common. Clearly unemployment interacts with other kinds of trouble, including ill-health, depression, homelessness, family break-up and divorce. These seem as likely to be consequences of unemployment as to be its cause. Some of the unemployed people we have met clearly do lack motivation or have health problems which would make it difficult for them to work, but these appear to be a minority even amongst the long-term unemployed. The only handicap that many face is the absence of recent work experience on their CVs.

We were told by the chief executive of the Wise Group, a Glasgow business which provides work for the long-term unemployed, that about three-quarters of the people they take on turn out to be perfectly capable of doing the jobs they are given - see Chapter 7 below. Two church-based employment projects we visited in London both told us that their hardest task was to overcome the despair felt by the long-term unemployed and convincing them that they could work again. Our evidence suggests that most of the unemployed want, often want desperately, to work again. We met, or heard about, a few exceptions. Some people do adapt to the fact of unemployment and find ways of coping with it. One person described his experience of unemployment in the past as the life of a 'government-sponsored philosopher'. Others find things to do which are useful to themselves and their communities, and which help to fill the gap left by lack of paid work. Obviously there is an 'informal economy' in which some of the unemployed may supplement their benefit income illegally, but we remain as uncertain as everyone else about its size.

Life on social security is dreary in the extreme. Those who have not experienced it seldom realise quite how dreary it is. It really is difficult to meet what everyone in our society regards as essential needs, like an adequate diet for the whole family, warmth, shelter and a decent appearance. Unforeseen expenditure results in debt which cannot be paid back. It takes real ingenuity to survive on social security. There are many heroes and heroines who do just that for years on end and get little thanks or recognition from the rest of us for doing so.

We have been impressed by the detailed knowledge of the benefit system shown by some unemployed people and their families. They can often put the experts on the subject to shame. They have been quick to point out to us the inequities and absurdities built into the system and we thank them for their help with our enquiry. But what has sickened us most of all is the grudging way in which the system operates. It must be deeply humiliating for a mother to have to ask a public official for special help to buy clothes for her children, and doubly so to have her request turned down. Yet this is part of life, year after year, for many mothers and their children growing up in our society now.

The unemployed find themselves blamed for what society has done to them. Sometimes they may feel themselves that their situation is their own fault, even if they have tried very hard indeed to put it right. So they come to be cut off from their friends and relations, getting much less support and sympathy than they would for example if they were sick, disabled or merely old. One of the difficulties we have had in our enquiry is that people who are unemployed do not necessarily want to talk to us about their situations. All this is well-known and well-documented by social scientists. But it needs to be repeated, because nothing is being done to change it. The main motive for reform seems to be the reduction of public spending. This confirms the feelings of most unemployed people that the government is not on their side.

Studies using OPCS longitudinal data have compared mortality rates for unemployed men with those for all men in the same age range, from 1971 to 1989. They consistently show significantly raised mortality amongst unemployed men in all social classes (*Social Trends*, 1996, pages 21-22). Such statistical evidence, although long-established and well-known, fails to catch popular attention. The public needs to be told what being unemployed is really like.

The people best qualified to describe the effects of unemployment are those who experience it themselves. The passages below are taken from the presentation made to the working party by an unemployed man in South Wales.

'I was very pleased to be asked to take part in this forum. The reality is that the unemployed are almost never asked to comment on anything, let alone something that is as central to their lives as unemployment'.

'Unemployment affects directly my life, my universe and every-thing I do, and indeed everything I am as an individual today. I say today, because I realise I am nothing like the person I once was when I worked. Unemployment changes people. In fact I'd go so far as to say unemployment is a soul changing experience.'

'The most obvious benefit that work brings us is of course a regular wage or salary. This enables us to not only live largely as we choose in society, but also to operate as makers of our own destiny, in that we have some financial control over our own lives. Money also enables us to play a full and active role in the normal societal, and cultural life prevalent in our society.'

'Financial reward, important as it is, and particularly so in our society, is not the only reason we work, and perhaps not even the primary reason. Work not only puts food in our mouths, but it feeds our psyche and our egos. Work gives us roles to play in society, not just the role of teacher, doctor, labourer or painter, but also those of contributor, responsible person and breadwinner.'

'If working brings us some measure of economic, social, psycho-logical and spiritual security, as I've indicated, then to find oneself unemployed means being faced with a whole range of problems which combined affect us economically, socially, psychologically and spiritually at one and the same time. Being long-term unemployed is to be bereft of some of the cornerstones that work provides to the stability of the individual, and without that stability the individual is obliged to reassess how he sees himself and his role in society.'

'I fear the brown envelope that drops on my mat and know before I open it there's no way I can pay the demand. I fear the knock on the door that might be the bailiff or debt collector who is bent upon relieving me of the few possessions I have left... Fear of the collection plate is a principal reason I no longer attend church as often as I would like.'

'Confidence is one of the first things to go. Self-esteem and self-respect soon follow. The effects of one rejection after another, for work you believed you were well able to do, bring about a change in the way you see yourself. The question 'what's wrong with me?' occurs early. Eventually you accept there must be something not quite right about you. All those prospective employers surely can't be wrong. One result of all this is a changed view of yourself, and sadly it is all too likely that any new image will be built around the negative connotations society applies to the unemployed: idle scrounger, cheat, parasite. We provide nothing good with which the unemployed can evolve new positive self-images.'

"What are you doing for Christmas' is a question I'm often asked and sometimes ask in turn of my friends. Too often I receive the reply 'Nothing, Christmas is just another day'. It isn't necessary for me to enquire what is meant by this. I already know - while I believe most of my friends to be Christians, although they would never admit it.'

'In my experience as people slide further into poverty there appears to be an equivalent growth in their generosity of spirit. Maybe this isn't really the case. Perhaps it only appears that way when those who have little are prepared to share what they have in support of another's greater misfortune. It may be that such generosity is only more noticeable when it comes from a group where we would not expect to find it so readily. Nevertheless it is there. And I believe it stems in part from the empathy of the unemployed with the misfortunes of others - and the knowledge that it could be their turn to suffer similar misfortune.'

On our visit to Merseyside we were told of a local enquiry which was collecting typical true-life stories about unemployment and at the same time asking how helpful they had found the churches to be in this situation. For example:

A man trained as a civil servant in the field of computer technology. He was made redundant after twenty-two years in what he had confidently expected would be a job for life. For two weeks he felt 'kicked in the stomach', let down, with his skills devalued. After nine months unemployment he found contract work using his skills.

A woman, trained initially as a teacher, and after a long period of continuous employment was made redundant. She felt angry and shocked, as it was totally unexpected. She felt it was the end of her useful life. She has applied for other jobs without success. She felt the church gave her great support, and that worship and preaching spoke to her needs. The experience has helped her to 'empathise' with other people - to understand what they are going through.

A married man with a young family working in a managerial position for a foreign company was made redundant two weeks before Christmas. Anger followed and a deep sense of powerlessness. Looking for a job was a full-time job, and depressing. He was unemployed for six months and eventually accepted a job at a much lower level of ability and pay. The people in the church were a great strength, but he found the constant praying for the 'unemployed' as a category was less than helpful.

A married couple both became unemployed almost simultaneously. They felt shocked, angry and depressed. Later they came to terms with their situation. 'Not having dependent children makes a difference...and being made redundant in your 50s is not as bad as being made redundant in your 40s.' The wife said she felt she received considerable support and inspiration from the church.

There are so many people unemployed, and so many different experiences of that condition. It hits some people harder than others, just like bereavement or serious illness. All we can say, at the end of our enquiry, is that we feel that the experience of unemployment, as it is in our society today, is an experience which no-one should be expected to endure. Something has to be done.

'Idleness and Want'

William Beveridge, writing in 1944, said:

'Idleness is not the same as want, but a separate evil, which men do not escape by having an income. They must also have the chance of rendering useful service and of feeling that they are doing so'.

By 'idleness' he meant lack of work - there is no hint of 'laziness' in his use of the word. Archbishop William Temple made the same point in his book *Christianity and the Social Order* published in 1942.

> 'The worst evil... is creating in the unemployed a sense that they have fallen out of the common life. However much their physical needs may be supplied... the gravest part of their trouble remains; they are not wanted! This is the thing that has the power to corrupt the soul of any man who is not already well advanced in saintliness... Nothing will touch the real need except to enable the man to do something which is needed by the community. For it is part of the principle of personality that we should live for one another.'

Although these quotations reflect the experience of a previous generation, they still ring true today. It is still true that the unemployed suffer from social exclusion as well as poverty. It is still true that they need to be given back their proper place in society. But the issue which now arises, which may not have arisen in the same way in the 1930s, is what kind of work, on what conditions, would achieve the aims we share with Beveridge and with Temple. In other words what kind of job actually gives 'the chance of rendering useful service'? In previous generations it was assumed that a job meant full-time work at a wage that would support a family. The conditions might well be tough, but the product probably was 'something which is needed by the community'. How do we now relate this to, let us say, a temporary part-time job at £2 an hour or less selling useless products over the telephone?

The question has to be asked whether the experience of insecure, part-time work at low pay is so much better than the experience of unemployment with much the same income from social security. Some would say it all depends how worthwhile the work actually is to the community as well as the individual. When we speak of the dignity of work in contrast to the indignity of unemployment, we must remember that many of the jobs open to the unemployed may not give them much sense of real achievement or usefulness.

Others would say that the value of a job depends on the experience it gives and the opportunities it may open up in the future. When people who have been out of work accept a job offer it often involves them in a kind of gamble. They have to give up a source of income from the state, which may be less than they really need, but which is at least reliable and familiar. Instead they have a job which involves them in some extra expenditure, which requires them to reorganise life for themselves and their families, which may fold up at short notice, with sometimes no real certainty that the wages that are promised will actually be paid. Once you are known to have a job anyone you owe money to will press hard to be paid. Stress levels will probably rise and the risk of ill health may get worse. The incentive is that one job may lead to another which is better paid and more worthwhile. Employers value evidence that an applicant can hold down a job of any kind. New contacts will be made. Confidence will be restored. An interesting research study called *Into Work?* published by the Joseph Rowntree Foundation, found that many of those leaving unemployment were taking jobs which left them no better off, or even worse off, financially. They apparently felt a powerful need to work and believed that their decision to take even an unsatisfactory job would pay off in the long run.

This is the reality of the labour market in the 1990s. It means that we have to rethink the aims which lay behind the objective of full employment and the words of Beveridge and Temple. They assumed that solving the problem of 'idleness' as they called it, would also solve the problem of 'want'. That cannot now be taken for granted. They clearly thought in terms of jobs for 'men', without necessarily intending that there should be jobs for women as well. Now we need to think in terms of households and families in which several people work, or want to work, either full-time or part-time. Not everyone in the labour market is seeking a wage that would support a whole family. And that has obvious implications for the wages that some employers pay. We conclude that our task as a working party is not just to reflect on the level of unemployment, but also to see that in the wider context of poverty as it affects people of working age and their families. This means looking at levels of pay and at the benefit system as well as at the availability of work.

Poverty can be either an absolute or a relative concept. Absolute poverty means the inability to meet needs which are regarded as essential. By those standards the poor of today are far richer than those who were in 'want' in the 1930s. Poor people in our society are also, of course, much better off than poor people in Africa or Latin America. But these comparisons are not those which poor people actually make. They compare their poverty here and now with the living standards of other people here and now, their neighbours, the parents of children who go to the same school, the people they see on television or read about in the newspapers.

Since the late 1970s most benefit levels in Britain have generally moved in line with the retail price index, so that their real value in these terms has been maintained. (Nevertheless today's benefit claimants are in many respects worse off than their predecessors twenty years ago, for example because of the replacement of grants to meet special needs by loans which are repayable and may be refused.) Meanwhile the real value of personal incomes has risen by more than 40 per cent. In relative terms therefore the

45

poverty of those on benefits has increased markedly. Undoubtedly this means that people living on benefit feel much poorer. Undoubtedly their feeling of exclusion - indeed the reality of their exclusion - has got much worse. That is one issue which we have to address.

Many religions, not least Christianity, make a virtue of poverty, entered into voluntarily. There is indeed a sense in which the good life does not depend on income or expenditure, beyond the minimum which depends on physical needs. But that is to abstract poverty from its social context. The poverty we are concerned with in this enquiry is not voluntary nor inspired by any religious teaching. It is a sign of exclusion from society and a sign that something is morally wrong in the society which does the excluding. It is the powerful and the wealthy who must take most responsibility for such exclusion. In such a society it is morally and spiritually dangerous to be rich.

If we are to evaluate the options open to society faced with the challenge of unemployment and poverty we need to form a view as to how the situation has come about. It can be seen as a failure of the market system, as a failure of government policy or a failure of society itself. We shall try out each of these perspectives in turn.

The Failures of the Market

In a properly functioning market, relative prices should adjust so as to get rid of excess supply or excess demand. In other words the market should 'clear'. So the persistence of unemployment, or excess supply of labour, would seem to point to some kind of market failure. One way of explaining what has gone wrong in the labour market is to find out what it is that prevents it from clearing. Economists in recent years have devoted a great deal of attention to this question.

One answer is that there is a deficiency of aggregate demand, or total spending, as Keynes claimed was the case in the 1930s. In other words the problem lies not so much in the labour market itself as in the markets for the goods and services which labour could produce. The market solution to an excess supply of goods and services is for the price level to fall. If the quantity of money is fixed, then as prices fall the real purchasing power of the money people hold will rise and the level of demand will be restored. This process of adjustment, however, may be very slow. To speed things up the monetary authorities can actually increase the supply of money, cut interest rates or induce a fall in the exchange rate. This is what happened in Britain in 1992. Cuts in the exchange rate and interest rates stimulated an economic recovery, and unemployment fell.

The course of events in the British economy in the early 1990s actually gives a vivid demonstration of the effectiveness of monetary policy changes to stimulate demand. The fall in the exchange rate, when sterling was driven out of the European exchange rate mechanism, made British goods less expensive compared with goods produced elsewhere. The cut in interest rates at the same time made it cheaper to borrow to finance either consumer spending or house purchase. Once the recovery got under way confidence was rebuilt and no further stimulus was required. At the time of writing this report the question being asked was how much and how soon interest rates would have to be raised to prevent inflation accelerating. So far such fears have been shown to lack foundation and the Chancellor has been proved right in holding out against the inflation pessimists for so long.

The limits to what can be achieved in this way are illustrated by the events in Britain in the late 1980s. At that time output grew rapidly, helped by relaxation of credit control as well as cuts in taxes and interest rates. As unemployment fell sharply, inflation began to accelerate and the balance of payments went into deficit. The productive capacity of the economy was overstretched, even with more than one and a half million people unemployed. The lesson most economists draw from this, and similar episodes in other countries, is that the unemployment problem is not just one of deficient demand for goods and services. Even with the British economy operating at full capacity somewhere between one and two million people would still be out of work. Recent events in the Republic of Ireland are consistent into this view of unemployment. The Irish economy has grown very rapidly, so fast that it has been compared with the 'tiger economies' of the Pacific rim. There seems to be no shortage of demand around the world for goods and services produced in Ireland. Nevertheless the level of unemployment there remains very high indeed, higher than in any region of Great Britain. No-one is suggesting that the problem of the Irish labour market could be solved by an indiscriminate expansion of aggregate demand.

Two kinds of theory, not mutually exclusive, have been suggested to explain the unemployment that remains even when there is no shortage of aggregate demand. One says that the labour market is not sufficiently competitive, even now. Employees still press for wages which are too high to bring supply and demand into line, and employers still pay them to retain loyalty and motivation. The other kind of theory says that labour markets are sufficiently competitive, but that the existence of social security benefits means that wages cannot fall to the point where the market would clear. If this latter theory is correct then the best solution is not to reduce benefits, but to raise the equilibrium wage. The real problem is that the unemployed lack the skills or other qualities which would enable them to do a worthwhile job at a decent wage.

This takes us back to the changes which are taking place in the nature of work, which were the subject of the previous chapter. New technology, changes in the composition of the workforce, enhanced competition at home and abroad - all these are major changes to which economies have to adjust. It takes time to adjust to these changes, just as it took time to adjust to the world oil price increases in the 1970s. It certainly takes time to create new jobs to replace those lost when many firms simultaneously adopt policies of 'downsizing'.

But it is not just a matter of slow adjustment. It is no good just waiting for the market to sort things out. More fundamentally the problem is that the changes which are taking place in the nature of work all tend to reduce the demand for unskilled labour, or labour equipped with out-dated skills. If there were no unemployment insurance or social security, no minimum wage legislation and weak trade unions, the market might drive wages down to the subsistence level, or below. In America, where the welfare system is less comprehensive and less generous than in Europe, wages have indeed fallen and unemployment has not been nearly so high. The problem becomes one of poverty in work, social alienation and crime. Instead of being unemployed, many poor American young men are in gaol. In Europe wages have held up better, even for the unskilled, but rates of unemployment are very high and, in many countries, continuing to rise.

One thing is clear: we cannot rely on market forces alone to solve our problems, either of unemployment or of low pay. It may have been excusable twenty years ago to think that the market on its own could produce a socially acceptable outcome; it is not so today. All countries in one way or another use the powers of the state to alter the outcome of market forces, for example regulation or public ownership or a combination of taxation and public expenditure. These powers have been at the disposal of successive governments in our countries, but they have not been used successfully to prevent the increase in unemployment and relative poverty.

The Failures of Government Policy

Unemployment in Britain has increased both under a Labour government in the 1970s and under a Conservative government in the 1980s. The policies followed to reverse that increase have been quite different in these two periods, but neither approach achieved its goal. On more than one occasion in the 1970s measures were taken to expand demand. This approach could not be followed consistently because inflation speeded up and the value of the pound fell. In answer to these threats the government relied on prices and incomes policies to hold back inflation and on financial controls both to support sterling and to limit the expansion of credit at home. Neither proved sufficiently robust in the face of inflationary pressures from the world economy and from the domestic labour market. As a result the British economy experienced both rising unemployment and very high rates of inflation at the same time. The 1970s also saw the introduction of a multitude of special employment measures. Some involved the direct use of public expenditure to subsidise employment. Others were introduced to train or retrain the unemployed. A good number of people were helped in this way, but the schemes never operated on a sufficient scale to reverse the rising trend in unemployment.

The Conservative government in the 1980s believed that demand management should concentrate on reducing inflation, even if that required a temporary rise in unemployment. The policy was expressed in terms of monetary control, that is to say preventing the money supply from expanding too rapidly, but it was generally recognised that this policy would also involve reducing the demand for labour, at least for a short period. They thought that, within a few years, this new strategy would overcome the inflationary tendencies of the British economy and hence it would actually result in lower levels of unemployment than had been typical of the 1970s. Events proved them wrong. Far from resulting in a fall in unemployment the change of approach was followed by a further large increase in unemployment up to the mid-1980s. Some economists think that the monetarist, free-market, approach is at last beginning to work in the mid 1990s as unemployment in Britain is currently falling, but compared with earlier decades it is still very high and the fall may be no more than a cyclical response as activity recovers after the recession at the beginning of the decade.

Special employment measures under the Conservatives in the 1980s included a major commitment to employment creation through the Community Programme as well as a variety of training measures. More recently they have concentrated less on subsidies for work or training, more on identifying those not seeking work effectively and providing help with interview preparation and similar skills. The 'Restart' interviews typical of this approach persuaded or helped significant numbers to find work in the relatively good years of the late 1980s when in some parts of the country there were plenty of jobs to be found. They also persuaded some unemployment benefit claimants to stop claiming. To that extent they saved public expenditure, without necessarily addressing the problem of unemployment itself.

Government ministers in Britain from Denis Healey to Kenneth Clarke would claim that reversing the rise in unemployment has been the aim of policy ever since the upward trend began. Some observers question this. Certainly ministers and their advisors have taken the view that a temporary rise in unemployment has on more than one occasion been the necessary cost - 'a cost worth paying' - of bringing inflation under control. Some commentators would go further and say that a permanent increase in unemployment was an undeclared objective of policy. They see unemployment as serving the interests of the rich and powerful, holding back the growth of real wages, increasing the profit share in national income and undermining the political power of organised labour. In other words they would question the true motivation, conscious or unconscious, of those responsible for economic policy in Britain and elsewhere. There may indeed be some of the rich and powerful who regard the rise in unemployment as a bonus for them, although we cannot claim ourselves to have heard such opinions expressed. Even a purely selfish calculation, however, ought to lead the rich and powerful to a different conclusion. High unemployment is very expensive for society as a whole, not least for the rich and powerful. There would surely be very widespread political support in all sections of the community for policies which really did produce a lasting fall in unemployment.

Why then have Governments, in Britain and Ireland and elsewhere, not taken more effective action to combat rising unemployment? In this report we shall argue that there is a great deal that can be done, by creating better incentives for firms in the private sector, by expanding labour-intensive services in the public sector, by helping the long-term unemployed to overcome the obstacles they face. These ideas are not totally new, and some of them have been tried out already on a small scale. What have been lacking have been the vision and determination to take measures on the scale made necessary by the size of the problem.

There has been substantial disagreement, especially in Britain, about what measures should be taken and how well the market will cope on its own. Economists have been divided, and in the past the political parties have adopted radically different programmes. It has been difficult to build a coalition of beliefs and interests behind one set of policies with reducing unemployment as their sole objective. Public opinion, although it consistently expresses the belief that unemployment is a great evil, has not been mobilised effectively by the political process to demand a remedy. In practice there has been, and still is, widespread fatalism or complacency about unemployment amongst those not directly affected by it. Most politicians of all parties have felt unable to promote remedies which match the scale of the problem.

We must face the fact that effective policies to combat unemployment will be costly. By one route or another funds must be made available to pay for the extra work that needs to be done. Politicians are reluctant to accept this, or to spell it out clearly. They seek instead for palliatives which are cheap or even costless. This reflects a dim view of what public opinion will accept, a view which we, in preparing this report, have quite deliberately set aside. We will argue that policies to promote employment should be given much higher priority than they have been to date.

Behind the economic and political failure to respond adequately to the changing nature of work, there is a more fundamental social failure. The issue must be addressed at that level as well. In their recent statement on social teaching, the Catholic Bishops of England and Wales had this to say about the 'common good':

> 'Public authorities have the common good as their prime responsibility... The common good cannot exclude or exempt any section of the population. If any section of the population is in fact excluded from participation in the life of the community, even at a minimal level, that is a contradiction of the concept of the common good and calls for rectification.'

A contract of employment is a social as well as an economic relationship. The time it takes for an unemployed worker to find a job depends, not only on his or her qualifications and pay expectations, but also on a circle of friends and acquaintances and their willingness to help. Another consideration is the attitude of society to unemployment. Is it perceived as a socially-acceptable way of life? Do family and close friends care one way or the other, given that it is the state which provides the safety net, not them? Different societies regard these matters differently, and our own society has changed over the years. It is arguable that the underlying reason why full employment could be maintained for two decades after the war was that the shared experience of wartime had produced an unusually strong sense of community. Since then social cohesion has weakened; individuals have become more individualistic and economic relationships have become less personal and more remote.

The process of economic and industrial development is itself destructive of local and regional communities. People have to move to find work. In some towns and villages social as well as economic life once centred on a single industry - mining, steel, shipbuilding or the docks for example - which has contracted or closed down. New industries do not operate on the same scale. We inevitably met many situations of this kind on our travels as a working party. In some cases, nevertheless, Merseyside for example, we also realised that local identity still remains very strong and is seen as the basis for possible strategies of economic regeneration. At a meeting we held in Liverpool with business and community leaders, the suggestion from one of them that emigration from the region might be encouraged, was met with general hostility as if it were a bit of an insult to local patriotism. One of the consistent themes in the campaign for Scottish Home Rule, and the reason for the inclusive nature of the arrangements proposed by the Scottish

Constitutional Convention, has been the belief that in Scotland there remains a strong sense of community that can be harnessed for economic as well as social advantage.

The relationships between economic and social life are considered in depth in *Community and the Economy: the Theory of Public Co-operation* by Jonathan Boswell. He writes:

> 'For people to be left out or marginalised, whether they are long-term unemployed, disadvantaged ethnic groups, immigrants, single-parent families or, more generally, the chronic poor, is offensive to community. Their integration demands both redistributive taxation and voluntary, decentralised forms of action. In terms of fraternity, associativeness and participation, the efforts to 'include them in' would be seen as a never ending challenge, but one spurred on, above all, by the search for associativeness in liberty.'

Another book which throws light on the relationship between society and poverty is *The Culture of Contentment* by John K Galbraith. He describes a society in which the comfortable majority feel no moral obligation to help the poor. 'In past times in the United States' he writes

> 'many experienced a certain sense of unease, of troubled conscience and associated discomfort when contemplating those who did not share the good fortune of the fortunate. No such feeling,' he claims, 'emanated from Ronald Reagan; Americans were being rewarded as they so richly deserved... That appeal was widespread; it allowed Americans to escape their consciences and their social concerns and then to feel a glow of self-approval.'

In Britain at least that feeling is not as glowing as it was a few years ago. The culture is one of anxiety rather than contentment for most people since the experience of the last recession. Whether that makes people more or less self-centred is a matter of opinion. We have not ourselves met people who express a willingness to write off the poor and the unemployed, but that may reflect only the attitudes of people who choose to speak to a churches' enquiry.

It is a matter of debate whether the poor and underprivileged in Britain or Ireland constitute a distinctive class which is identified by its own members and others as separate from the rest of society. This would mean that a 'class consciousness' had grown up, separating some individuals, families or communities from the mainstream of economic, social and political life. This would have profound implications for society as a whole, with the danger of social breakdown and instability. We find the whole idea deeply disturbing.

This report is a plea to society not to let such a separation happen. It would be unjust, unwise and also profoundly unchristian.

From our own experience we would say that the unemployed and the employed, the rich and the poor are all members of the same society, friends and relations of one another. Almost everyone faces the risk of unemployment and poverty. If they do not have such experience themselves, they may well have close relations who do. There **is** such a thing as society. There **is** a belief that we are all members one of another and responsible for each other's well-being. The sense of an inclusive community needs re-affirmation and expression in practical action.

Chapter Three

National and Regional Variations

The working party held residential meetings in various parts of Britain and Ireland. In addition several visits were made by one or more members to other cities or countries. We are very grateful to the many people who gave up so much of their time to help us. In this way we were able to discuss the main issues of our enquiry with a large number of people, with very different points of view. In the process many of us felt that our eyes were being opened for the first time to the real gravity of the problem which our enquiry was set up to address. These conversations are reflected throughout the report. But we also learnt about the different circumstances of different nations and regions, and these impressions provide the subject matter for this chapter. We were not able to visit all the areas we would have wished to cover, and the visits we did make were very brief. There is not space in one chapter to record much of what we saw or much of what was said to us. All that we can do here is to convey, from each visit, a little of the message we took away with us. Nevertheless we think it right to include some account of our travels because for some of us at least this was a mind-changing experience.

The contrasts we saw were quite dramatic, both between regions and also, more especially, within them. What follows is not an account of unrelieved gloom; on the contrary we saw much evidence of economic strength and success. Indeed it was the growing gap between those who do well and those who do badly which we feel the need to stress throughout our report.

London

The contrast between riches and poverty is nowhere more vivid than in central London. We visited a project for training the long-term unemployed right on the borderline between the City itself and the beginning of the East End. Some of the finance for the project comes from the banks in the shining new glass-fronted office blocks within a few hundred yards of the old warehouse in which it operates. One of the recent successes of the project was to train maintenance staff for the drinks-dispensing machines that have made all the tea-ladies in those office blocks redundant.

The contrasts are also extreme in London's Docklands. The old sources of local employment have all gone since the docks themselves closed down and local people are said to be reluctant to venture into neighbouring boroughs to look for work. We were told that office staff could not be recruited locally and that when training schemes were advertised the local people did not seem keen to take up the opportunities on offer. There was certainly some work which the local people could do, servicing the buildings that housed the head offices of multinational companies, but the jobs were not secure. Everything seemed to be sub-contracted, with no-one taking responsibility for the pay and conditions at the bottom of the chain. We were told, although we had no way of checking this, that many of the unemployed people in central London were working illegally.

In Peckham we heard a rather different account of unemployment. There we were told of large numbers of people from ethnic minorities, some of them immigrants, speaking little or no English and often too frightened or depressed to go out of their houses or flats. The only way to recruit people into job search or training programmes was to go round from door to door with a personal invitation.

It was suggested that there was no real shortage of jobs in London, although they would not be jobs of the traditional kind. Most of them were created by small firms, some were quite precarious, many were part-time. It was possible, in fact advisable, for the long-term unemployed, once they had built up enough confidence in themselves, to look around and choose a job carefully, not necessarily accepting the first one they found.

The North-East

On Teesside we saw the effects of downsizing. The steel and chemical industries both seemed to be prospering and, in many ways, the region was benefitting from that success. But there were not many jobs to be had. There was clear evidence of a society developing in which unemployment had become accepted as a way of life, with some imaginative ideas being put forward by unemployed people themselves as to how that life could be made more bearable. One sharp contrast we saw was between a training centre preparing young men for the good skilled jobs which remain and the drop-in centre, no great distance away, which provided a little comfort for the young men who had no such opportunities.

We heard of a housing estate in County Durham which had a male unemployment rate of over 30 per cent. Close by there was an industrial estate where there were vacancies for unskilled work; but supply and demand were not being brought together. We visited one firm which seems to exemplify all the good features of modern management. New technology was much in evidence and the workers were taking more and more responsibility for their own methods of production. The influence of foreign-owned firms was resulting in a great improvement of productivity and job satisfaction. But overall the forecast was that employment in the region would continue to contract.

One foreign-owned firm was reporting difficulties in recruiting skilled labour, even though men with those skills had recently been laid off in large numbers. Were they actually unwilling to go back to work, even at excellent

rates of pay? Part of the trouble seems to be the lack of security of employment with the new firms. Perhaps they did not want to leave a relatively
secure job which they had found in the meantime, even if it was less well
paid, for something much more demanding and also very short-term. A
survey showed that 47 per cent of the new jobs created on Tyneside were
temporary.

South Yorkshire

The divorce rate shot up after the end of the miners' strike. Once the pits
closed the earning power of the men was lost and women stood a better
chance of supporting themselves on their own. The old pit villages have not
regenerated even now. Those who can do so move away. We were told that
some estates are now run by gangs, with fierce dogs, and most of the work
done is illegal.

Yet there is economic growth in the region as well and those who enjoy
nationally negotiated rates of pay benefit from the relatively low cost of
living. Unemployment in the region as a whole is falling faster than the
national average, but rates of pay are often very low. Many of those who
lost their jobs in the last two recessions are classified as sick rather than
long-term unemployed - but it amounts to the same thing. Some people still
say that the only 'real' jobs are in coal and in steel, but of course there are no
such jobs, or very few, being created now.

It was suggested to us that a new crisis was in the making just in the last
few years. After the job losses of the 1980s, people had settled into a way of
life which was wretched enough, but familiar. They knew that they could
survive, on some combination of Income Support and casual work. Now
things were changing, because the conditions for receiving benefit were
getting tougher all the time. The patience of the long-term unemployed was
being stretched to the limit. The truth of the matter was that, in their local
area, there simply were no good jobs to be had, so the efforts of the benefit
agency and the employment service could never succeed. They just added
to the hardship of communities which had already suffered too much.

Merseyside

Some people told us that Merseyside is the victim of prejudice in the
media. It was not nearly as grim as it is portrayed. Certainly there were some
very clear signs of recovery and improvement in the centre of Liverpool
itself. Business and community leaders expressed a strong local patriotism
and commitment to the regeneration of the city. We were taken to visit
a manufacturing firm which was recovering its share of the world market,
providing well-paid employment for a skilled workforce and good profits
as well. The improvement in employee relationships and better access to

capital for investment were the explanations we were given. That was one side of our visit to Liverpool; but there was another side which was very bleak indeed.

One person said to us that it was the buildings that were being regenerated, not the people. In one area of Merseyside we were told that half the working population was either unemployed or surviving on very low paid or casual work. About two-thirds of the jobs vacant at a local Job Centre paid £3.50 an hour or less. On one of our visits it was said that society has broken down. What remains was described as the 'Giro culture'. There was little community spirit or political awareness; people were shut in on themselves and living from day to day. There was a great deal of suspicion about any attempt by the government to help the unemployed. People on benefit were not allowed to study, we were told, because the government did not want them to be educated. This reflects the impact on the unemployed of the notorious 12-hour rule. Training schemes were invented, we were told, not for the benefit of the unemployed, but for the benefit of 'the training industry' itself.

In 1993 Merseyside was granted Objective One Status under European Union regional policy. This status opens access to additional funding for economic development and renewal and is given to regions which are seen to be lagging behind the rest of the EU in terms of economic growth. This recent development is expected to have a significant impact on the regional economy both in the Programme Period, 1994-99, and beyond.

Merseyside is eager to attract new businesses to the area, especially those who will provide employment for local people. There is now keen competition between cities for the location of financial services operations. With new communications technology office support for national or world markets can be moved very readily from one part of the country to another, or indeed to anywhere in the world. There is also keen competition between cities to attract government funding or support for projects from the European Commission. But in Merseyside, and elsewhere, we were also told that there are dangers in relying on external sources for economic growth. Local initiatives were more reliable. People said that power should be given back to the community.

Birmingham

As a centre of manufacturing industry the West Midlands is enjoying a period of recovery. The collapse in the 1980s had been a devastating blow to the region and it could not expect to rebuild to the scale of employment it provided before then. Nevertheless, thanks partly to inward investment by large multi-nationals, engineering was again doing well. There remained a substantial number of small components manufacturers who were not up to world standards of production or cost, and these still needed to reorganise or perish. But a great deal had already been achieved.

This was the only visit on which the availability of capital was raised as a serious handicap for British industry. Everywhere we went we met people who could quote arguments about short-termism which they had read in books and newspapers; here we met people who claimed to have suffered from its effects themselves. Banks and institutional investors were expecting quite unreasonably short pay-back periods. The 'performance' of firms was being managed from day to day, instead of from year to year. The Continental pattern, where bankers take an equity stake and hold it for many years, would be much better for small businesses who were doing well and wanted to grow.

Despite the economic upturn there were parts of Birmingham in which unemployment rates were over 30 per cent. Many of the new jobs were going to people who lived outside the city and commuted in each day. The ethnic communities in the West Midlands suffered from the effects of discrimination in the labour market. They had the highest rates of unemployment and the lowest rates of pay. Attempts at economic revival in inner city areas would be successful only if the ethnic communities themselves were involved in the process and given a real say in what was proposed.

One incident on our visit illustrated well the national problem of low pay and employment incentives. A young man who had been unemployed for a long time described his difficulty in even getting short-listed for a vacancy. An employer at the same meeting with us then offered to interview him for a job in the next week. We subsequently heard that the young man was offered a job at the going rate, but turned it down because, as a married man living in a hotel, he was better off unemployed.

Cambridge

In and around Cambridge there are shortages of people with the right level of skill for employment in some very successful high-tech businesses. Despite all the automation, or sometimes because of it, there is a need for technicians and staff with qualifications at NVQ level 3 or above. These are the people it is hard to find. There is not the same difficulty in recruiting graduates, who may of course come from anywhere in the country - or indeed in the world. It was suggested that government-funded training schemes were not flexible enough to meet the needs of different regions. What employers needed in an area like Cambridgeshire was bound to be quite different from the national average. The lack of trained staff, including managers, was holding back the competitiveness of British industry relative to the Continent.

At the same time there was still a problem of unemployment in the area. Perhaps 3 per cent of the population, it was suggested, were effectively unemployable, at least in the present labour market. Claimants need more advice, as soon as they become unemployed, about the training they need if they are to get a decent job. There were not enough full-time jobs in the area, too many were part-time and did not pay enough to replace Income Support. There were not many jobs suitable for young men with no qualifications. We visited one estate in the area where rates of unemployment were high even by national standards. It was not well-situated for employment opportunities. Some of the local unskilled work on offer was too physically exhausting for any but the most fit young men to take on.

Exeter

Devon is an area of relatively low unemployment. Although wages in Devon are below the national average, incomes are above, as many well-off people retire to the county. There are few large employers, but many small ones. Industrial and business premises are expanding around Exeter. Communications with London and the Midlands are relatively good.

Yet, even here, we met the same contrasts between growing affluence and ingrained poverty. In Devonport, we were told, the official rate of youth unemployment was as high as 40 per cent, and the true figure was much higher than that. As elsewhere, we where told of people who had effectively given up hoping to get work. At one church 96 per cent of the worshippers were either unemployed or retired. If the unemployed could not have work then it was essential for them to find something else to fill their lives. Even on this visit we were made aware just how empty some lives have become.

Cornwall

Rates of unemployment are high in parts of Cornwall (10½ per cent for example in the Redruth and Camborne area in October 1996). On top of the decline in employment in agriculture and fishing, the county has lost jobs in mining and manufacturing industry. The tourist industry provides some work, but it is generally seasonal and not well paid. Cornwall has been neglected by government policy and it has not been able to attract inward investment of the kind that has helped Wales or Scotland.

It was suggested that the contrasts between riches and poverty are particularly acute in a rural setting, where they may exist side by side in the same village. Certainly there is some quite severe poverty in Cornwall. The cost of living is relatively high and wages relatively low - driven down, it seems, by the informal economy. At one local school the pupils were asked what they hoped to do when they grew up; three-quarters said that they would have to move away from Cornwall if they were to find a job.

One problem worth special mention arises from the temporary and seasonal nature of many of the jobs in this area. If benefit claimants take on a temporary job there is a sense in which they get sent to the back of the queue by the benefit system when that job is over and they have to sign on again. Some special schemes are limited to people who have been unemployed for a long time, and new claimants face new and tougher conditions as the regime gets tighter. Seasonal work is also a problem, if earnings in the good months mean that entitlement to benefit is reduced in the bad months as well.

Scotland

The working party held a residential meeting at Scottish Churches House in Dunblane, as well as paying a visit to Glasgow. Contacts were also made with the Scottish Office.

We were very conscious of visiting another country, with a strong sense of its own nationality, and considerable uncertainty about its future relationship with the rest of Britain. Important elements of economic policy are the responsibility of Scottish departments, although these must operate within the overall strategy of the United Kingdom Government.

The average unemployment rate for Scotland in October 1996 was 7.8 per cent, compared with 7.2 per cent in the United Kingdom as a whole. Within Scotland there are some very wide variations with 14 out of 60 travel-to-work areas having rates in excess of 10 per cent - the highest is Cumnock and Sanquhar with a rate of 15.9 per cent, the highest anywhere in Britain. But it would be wrong to characterise Scotland as a whole as economically depressed; in fact its position relative to England and Wales has improved over the past ten or twenty years, thanks partly to the effects of North Sea oil.

Some important differences were pointed out to us between the economies of Scotland and England. The public sector is still very important in Scotland, despite central government policies of privatisation. This is reflected in housing, education and employment policy as well as industrial planning. It was suggested that Scotland has a better tradition of working together for the common good than any English region. Employers, trade unionists and local government officials in Scotland share many of the same objectives. No one is more than two hand-shakes away, we were told. This may account for the effectiveness of some Scottish initiatives for economic development.

We visited Yarrow Shipbuilders who build warships on the Clyde. Their experience illustrates very well the successes and the problems of much of British industry. They are competing well for orders at home and abroad, using technology at the frontier of development. But their success depends on keeping costs as low as possible, and that creates problems for employment. In an uncertain market it is especially important to reduce fixed costs and overheads. It is no longer possible, as it once was, to provide continuity of employment for a large workforce of skilled and semi-skilled workers. Demand fluctuates according to the state of the order book and the stage of production of the ships being built. The only way to cope, we were told, was to distinguish the core workforce from the periphery. The swings in activity had to be accommodated by giving temporary contracts of employment to a large proportion of the staff they employ. This left some anxieties about the training needs of the workers. There was not the same pool of skills to draw on in Scotland that there would have been a generation ago. They felt that more public money was needed to support training which would benefit the economy as a whole. Shortly afterwards we heard senior officials of the Scottish TUC saying unequivocally that there had to be an end to the two-tier workforce.

Also in Scotland we learnt about the development of intermediate labour markets to help the long-term unemployed, particularly from the Wise Group. This has contributed a great deal to the ideas we put forward later in this report, and it has lessons for national policy and all regions of the economy. It may be significant nevertheless that these ideas were pioneered, by the Wise Group and others, in Scotland. They undoubtedly drew on the traditions we have referred to: co-operation in the public interest, partnerships between the private and public sectors and the initiative to seek practical solutions, with or without the encouragement of a rather remote central government in London.

Wales

In Wales administration of government, if not government itself, is devolved. The Welsh Office in Cardiff now has responsibility which includes health, education and local government. We were very aware on our visit that Wales is a separate country from England with its own traditions and way of life. About one eighth of the population speak Welsh as their preferred language and that proportion is higher in the rural areas. During recent years there has been a steady increase in the use of the Welsh language. For public bodies the use of Welsh is no longer an option but a statutory requirement.

In June 1996 CYTUN, the ecumenical body which brings together most of the churches in Wales, published a report called, *Wales: A Moral Society?* The group which wrote the report was chaired by Rowan Williams, the Bishop of Monmouth, who also spoke with our working party about the theology of work. Although that report is addressed primarily to the situation in Wales, its discussion of work and economic policy in particular is of more general relevance, drawing attention to 'some of the morally unacceptable consequences of the way the [economic and industrial] systems operate' and appealing for remedial action.

On our visit to Cardiff, we learnt about the Wales Rural Forum, chaired by Eleanor James who is herself a member of our working party. The problem of unemployment in rural areas cannot be separated from social and environmental concerns, and the preservation of a unique cultural heritage. What is being attempted was described as a 'bottom up' approach with local action plans based on consultation with local communities. This led to a discussion about the role of local government and democracy in coping with economic problems which relate to particular communities.

In rural Wales regular employment with fixed full-time hours throughout the year is less common than it is in urban areas. Self-employment and part-time work are both very important. Measured unemployment levels are similar to those of the United Kingdom as a whole, but the social effects are quite different. Many women, for example, who are unemployed in fact keep themselves very busy doing good work in the community on a voluntary basis. Their quality of life does not suffer to the same extent as would be the case in an urban setting.

South Wales is well known for the very sharp contrasts between the growth of new manufacturing industries based on inward investment and the dereliction of whole communities resulting from the loss of the old industries, especially mining and steel. Overall unemployment levels in Wales are not much above the UK average, but there are still very serious local problems, for example in Aberdare (nearly 13 per cent unemployment) or Merthyr (about 11 per cent). It was on this visit in fact that we heard some of the most moving accounts of the social, psychological and spiritual damage caused by long-term unemployment. The 1930s have come back so far as the South Wales valleys are concerned. 'Unless you have been there you will not know.' One of the main anxieties must be that young people growing up in such a community have no experience of regular work. The link between the generations, which should be based on the shared experiences and pride of achievement in work, has been broken. Young people spend their time in their own groups with only limited contact with older generations. The traditions and values of the community are not being passed on.

The trade union movement in Wales, as elsewhere in the UK, is campaigning for full employment. This, we were told, would in their view correspond to a figure for unemployment of at most 4 per cent. The main need identified was for more and better training. There is concern that the firms which have been attracted to the area by regional policies and by relatively low pay do not have a firm commitment to the Welsh economy. It was even described to us, half seriously, as a 'colony of Korea'. The sense of government in London as remote and unsympathetic came over even more strongly in Wales than it had in Scotland. On the other hand we missed the sense of unity and common purpose within Wales that we had experienced so strongly on our visit to Dunblane.

Northern Ireland

The working party visited Belfast and met representatives of industry, the churches and government agencies as well as experts on the economy of the province. We were made aware of some striking contrasts between the labour markets of Northern Ireland and Great Britain. The unemployment rate in the province was 10.7 per cent in October 1996, compared with 7.1 per cent in Great Britain. Moreover long-term unemployment was as high as 5.7 per cent in Northern Ireland, compared with 2.6 per cent in Britain. As many as 2.3 per cent of the workforce in Northern Ireland had been unemployed for more than 5 years; this compares with just 0.5 per cent in Britain.

In other respects the economy of Northern Ireland appears to be performing well, with output rising relatively fast and a significant increase in employment. We were told that it has the potential to grow faster than any region of comparable size in Europe. The reasons given for the continuing high levels of unemployment were of broadly three kinds. The first was demographic, citing the relatively high birth rate and the inflow of migrants in response to new job opportunities. The second explanation was in terms of economic structure, in particular the insufficient number of small enterprising firms of the kind which have been creating many of the new jobs elsewhere in the United Kingdom. The third, and most disturbing, explanation was in terms of motivation and community pressure. It was suggested to us that the unemployment problem would never be solved on its own; there needed also to be a redirection of community life and political involvement. The two reforms need to be made together. Job creation was necessary, but not sufficient, as a cure for the social problems of the province.

With a few exceptions, there seemed to be no real shortage of money to promote employment in the province. This was in striking contrast to our visits elsewhere in the United Kingdom where again and again we heard of local initiatives that could not be developed for lack of government or other finance. In Northern Ireland the attitude seems to be quite different, partly one assumes because of the ever-present threat of violence, but also in recognition of the greater need for economic development. The economic policies of the UK government do not seem to be as much driven by free-market liberalism in Northern Ireland as they are in Britain. Moreover the European Union and indeed private charities worldwide are very active in support of community and employment projects in the province. The lesson has to be drawn that sometimes money is not enough.

We were impressed by the community workers that we met, both Protestant and Catholic. The churches are well aware of the denominational basis for social divisions and are making great efforts to make their communities more open and tolerant. This means that they must oppose the influence of paramilitary groups, which they see as increasing in the Belfast area. One Protestant minister described the 'Theology of Peace' which is the basis for his work in a divided community. It means avoiding the temptation of making Christianity itself a divisive issue, but instead sharing power with any group that is motivated by the same compassion, irrespective of their faith. One Catholic priest also described how the more successful members of the community, who had moved out of the more deprived areas of Belfast, were now offering their time and money to help those who are less fortunate.

One of the main issues we discussed on this visit was discrimination in the labour market. The laws against discrimination on grounds of religion in Northern Ireland are much tougher than any laws against discrimination in Britain, or perhaps anywhere in the world. The 1976 Act outlawed direct discrimination, but this was substantially extended in the 1989 Act which outlawed indirect discrimination as well. This means, for example, that it is no longer allowable to fill job vacancies by 'word of mouth' through friends or relations of the existing workforce. Vacancies have to be advertised in ways which make them equally accessible to people from all communities. It also means that there can be no expression of allegiance to one community rather than another at the place of work. The wearing of sportswear that implies support of one football team rather than another for example is interpreted as indirect discrimination. The damages payable under the law are a real deterrent and the Fair Employment Commission can in effect impose severe fines as well.

There is no doubt that the law has changed behaviour quite profoundly. The commitment to it from major employers seems to be complete. They say it has required them to do many things which are in fact in their own interest. By Short Brothers we were told that the composition of their intake of new recruits now reflected the composition of the population much better, but that it would be a long time before the same could be true of the workforce as a whole. In judging the success of the legislation it has also to be borne in mind that a huge difference remains between the rates of unemployment for different communities. About 11 per cent of Protestant men are unemployed, but about 22 per cent of Catholic men. This can only be explained to a limited degree by the different demographic structures of the two communities. The ratio has not changed very much since the 1970s. A study by the Northern Ireland Economic Research Centre estimated how that differential should change if the fair employment legislation were implemented effectively. The process would necessarily be slow as it depends on the speed of turnover of the existing workforce. They reckon that over a five-year period the ratio of Catholic to Protestant male unemployment could be expected to fall from 2.5 to 2.1. In fact a fall of comparable magnitude has taken as long as twenty years (see the article by David Armstrong on Northern Ireland in *Unemployment and Public Policy in a Changing Labour Market* published by PSI in 1994).

Republic of Ireland

Our visit to Dublin coincided with the Social Partnership meetings between Government, employers and unions to negotiate a new agreement on pay and on economic and social policy. Coming from the United Kingdom we were fascinated to learn about the more co-operative approach to policy-making in Ireland. Since the 1980s there have been three agreements, for three years each. The wage norms are voluntary, but we were assured that compliance is almost universal. The first agreement was reached at a time of national economic crisis, with unemployment at 17 per cent and the national debt rising out of control. Since then the consensus approach to policy making has continued against a background of exceptionally rapid growth in output and employment with unemployment falling towards the European average.

The debate over economic policy in Ireland is conducted in more pragmatic terms than it is in Britain. The political parties are not far apart on economic and social issues, and for most of the last decade coalition governments have been in power. The accounts of the Irish economic situation which we heard from representatives of government, employers, unions and the unemployed were all within the same framework of agreement about objectives and even about policy instruments. To an audience accustomed to the controversy surrounding economic policy in Britain it all seemed exceptionally good tempered and undogmatic. One explanation may be that the economy of the Republic is now growing so fast that no-one is being asked to make sacrifices. Another explanation may be the small size of the country, which means that the main participants in the policy debate may know each other personally and relate to one another well. We asked whether a third explanation might be the influence of the Catholic Church, but that suggestion met with a mixed response, some saying that the direct influence of the Church on economic policy was nowadays very slight, others saying that its indirect influence on the climate of opinion and the sense of national community remains very important indeed.

Certainly the Republic of Ireland is the fastest growing national economy in Europe, one of the fastest growing in the world. The manufacturing sector is being strengthened by inward investment, supported by a very low rate of company tax. The main growth of employment is in private sector services and tourism in particular is doing very well. Ireland is a very open economy in which the growth of output depends, not on domestic demand, but on competitiveness and the strength of demand overseas, especially in the United Kingdom. It illustrates very well one of the main concerns arising out of our enquiry: it is possible for an economy to grow and progress exceptionally well, but at the same time to experience high levels of unemployment and poverty.

We were not in the country long enough to see this for ourselves, but we were told that the contrasts between the areas benefiting from the boom and the areas suffering from long-term unemployment are becoming more and more a cause of national anxiety and dismay. Rates of unemployment in Ireland have been high relative to the UK ever since the Second World War, thanks partly to the continuous decline in agricultural employment.

The high level of unemployment, and especially of long-term unemployment, is a clear sign that something is still very wrong with the Irish economy, much as we may admire other aspects of its performance. The figure for the claimant count, or live register, is significantly higher than the figure derived from the Labour Force Survey. Some commentators are suggesting that this is because a significant proportion of claimants are not actively seeking work and some are actually claiming fraudulently when they have a job. This suspicion has been strengthened following a special survey of claimants conducted by the Central Statistical Office, but its significance remains uncertain and controversial. What can be said is that unemployed people who claim benefits in Ireland have never been subjected to the same degree of questioning and surveillance as has been in operation in Britain since the mid 1980s.

In October the total number of the registered unemployed in the Republic was 267,586. Of these about one half, 134,324, had been unemployed for more than a year, and about one quarter, 68,323, for more than three years. The long-term unemployment rate in the highest in Europe. Whilst the total register is falling, the long-term proportion is rising.

The level of unemployment benefit is higher in the Republic than it is in Britain and the conditions for claiming are not so severe. One effect of this is that people of Irish origin who lose their jobs, or their benefit entitlement in Britain, may choose to return to Ireland and claim benefit there. For unemployed people with dependants the replacement rate (that is the ratio of benefits paid to previous earnings) is around 70 per cent. Moreover people who are unemployed may be entitled to secondary benefits such as free health care, which is not universally available in Ireland, and to a supplement for rental costs for which those in full time work would not be eligible. As in Britain there is debate as to the adequacy of benefit rates, especially for the long-term unemployed. Unlike Britain however the aim of policy is to increase the real value of benefits, indeed to raise them gradually relative to the take-home pay of those in employment. The 'minimum adequate level' of benefits recommended by the Commission on Social Welfare in the mid 1980s has not yet been reached for all types of payment, but steady progress towards it has been made. It would be surprising if these relatively high replacement rates had no effect on the level of unemployment at all, but the size of the effect is a matter of speculation. The relatively easy benefit regime must help to explain why the percentage claimant rate is higher in Ireland than in the UK. What effect the benefit regime has on the percentage actually in work is much more difficult to judge.

The Irish government has introduced a variety of employment measures to help reduce unemployment. Two seemed to us of special interest. Community and voluntary groups can receive funding to employ people over the age of 35 who have been out of work for more than five years at a weekly wage of £180. Another striking difference from the British system is that people who can only find part-time work are able to claim benefit for the days that they are unemployed. This may be another aspect of the Irish situation which merits study in Britain.

How do the Irish manage to combine a relatively expensive system of social security with relatively low rates of company tax to attract foreign investment? The answer is a high rate of tax on expenditure and personal incomes. Many workers in Ireland pay the highest rate of income tax at 48 per cent. We were told that pressure was beginning to build up for tax cuts, and that the consensus in favour of redistribution was not as rock solid as it had been in the past.

We should mention one Irish institution which we particularly admired. The Irish National Organisation of the Unemployed (INOU) acts as an advocate for unemployed people, representing their interests in local, regional and national debates. It also provides information and advice. It is a federation of around 100 local centres, community organisations and branches. It is well funded and employs twelve full-time staff.

The importance of EU funding deserves mentioning more generally, as it makes a very significant contribution to social action of all kinds. The attitude of the Irish to Europe is, of course, very different from that of the British government. There is general support for European social policy and also for the proposed economic and monetary union. The constraints on public sector borrowing required to meet the criteria for membership of the

Chapter Four

Work and Income

It was never intended that means-tested benefits should be the source of livelihood for a large part of the population. When the social security system was set up in Britain after the second world war it was fully recognised that it would function properly only in a society close to full employment. Unemployment insurance without a means test was intended to be the main form of support, with National Assistance, a benefit like Income Support, only for a very small number of hard cases. In 1950 1.3 million people claimed National Assistance, of whom only 73,000 were unemployed; in 1993 as many as 5.6 million people claimed Income Support, and of them 1.9 million were unemployed. The number of people (claimants and their families etc) dependent on Income Support in 1993 is estimated at 9.8 million (Figures from *Making Welfare Work* by Frank Field, 1995). In 1996 the figures were virtually unchanged.

This situation cannot continue. Either we must provide more benefits as of right without a means test or else we must ensure that more people are able to support themselves. Long-term dependency on means-tested benefit offends human dignity, can undermine moral values and it threatens to produce social instability. Meanwhile the cost of providing benefits on this scale is proving intolerable, creating unacceptable pressure for cuts in other areas of public spending and provoking opposition to taxation in most sections of the community. The need for radical change is accepted right across the political spectrum. There are divergent views however as to what form that change should take.

In this chapter of our report we shall be comparing two different broad approaches to unemployment and the future of work. One seeks the solution in finding acceptable alternatives to paid work for a substantial proportion of the population, in the belief that there will simply not be enough good jobs to go round. The other approach says that paid work should be created to match the needs and abilities of everyone, in the belief that there is plenty of work which needs to be done. We see the choice between these two approaches as fundamental to our enquiry. Both have advantages and disadvantages. Neither offers an easy way out. Men and women of good will and practical wisdom appear on both sides in the debate. Whilst making our own views clear, we wish also to pay due respect to the views of others with which we find ourselves in disagreement.

The Value of Work

The main purpose of work is, of course, to produce something of value, which meets some human want or need. But the activity of work also has psychological, social and spiritual significance in its own right. It can be seen as a part of human nature, fundamental to the way in which our identities, both individual and collective, are built up. According to *The Social Psychology of Work* by Michael Argyle,

> 'forms of work and social behaviour similar to those of humans are found in higher mammals and birds. Work among apes and monkeys is in fact remarkably similar to work in the most primitive human societies, suggesting that there may be innate factors in human work-patterns also.'

This implies that work, and the social relationships of working, are on a par with other kinds of innate social behaviour like language or morality or family life. The form which work takes varies from one culture to another, but some kind of organised work seems to be universal.

Michael Argyle also writes about the motivation of work in our own societies. He writes,

> 'Not so long ago... it was widely believed that people disliked work, and only did it because it led to rewards... Many psychologists believed that activity was motivated by 'deficits', like those of hunger and thirst, to reduce 'tensions' and that rest and satiation were the goals of activity. These views have been considerably revised. Surveys have asked workers if they would carry on working if it were not financially necessary: one survey found that 31 per cent of men and 34 per cent of women would stay in their present job, while 35 per cent of men and 29 per cent of women would work but try to change their jobs. A number of surveys in different countries have found that having interesting or challenging work, and a good work environment, are more important than pay.'

Standard economic theory argues that workers regard work as a cost and leisure as a benefit. Otherwise it would be in danger of predicting that work would go on twenty-four hours a day. This theory seems to conflict with the psychological evidence, but must be correct nevertheless at the margin - in other words the longer and harder one works the less the enjoyment and the greater the cost in terms of boredom, fatigue or damage to health, as well as in terms of the opportunity lost for enjoyment of other kinds. But, although this is true at the margin, it does not mean that people would be happier if they had no work to do at all.

The ancient Greeks thought that work was best left for their slaves to do. The good life for the free man or woman might involve intellectual effort or administrative tasks, but not manual labour or household routine. In contrast to this, the Bible places a much higher value on work, even acknowledging that God works as well as men and women. The work ethic of modern industrial society owes a great deal to its Christian origins.

In the Middle Ages the monastic life combined together prayer and manual work, both being seen as service to God and the community. The leaders of the Reformation developed the idea of daily work as part of a Christian's calling and as a sign of faith. The Protestant churches have been famous for their encouragement of thrift, hard work and responsibility. Some have seen in this the origins of changed attitudes to enterprise and wealth creation which made possible the Industrial Revolution of the eighteenth century. Certainly the development of both Catholic and Protestant Christian teaching for several centuries past has emphasised ordinary paid work as one way in which human beings can co-operate with the purposes of God.

The work of God is both creative and redeeming. As children of God it is our privilege to share in that work, knowing that such labour is never altogether in vain. If we seek to follow the example of Jesus we will serve one another, and our daily work is one part of this service. There is nothing inconsistent with human dignity in helping other people - on the contrary it is the highest calling of all. At the same time Christians proclaim liberation. God has set us free from slavery; that applies to our everyday work as well as our spiritual life. Liberty is perfectly compatible with service, provided that the service is freely chosen. The Christian work ethic has never suggested that human salvation or fulfilment can be earned by hard work. If some Christians have given that impression they are not true to the religion they profess. What Christianity does say is that one way of showing our gratitude for the free gift of salvation is by working to serve God and our fellow human beings.

God has given us gifts of many different kinds, making it possible for us each to play a part in the life and work of the community to which we belong. These gifts are intended for use, and they are not to be wasted. That is part of the tragedy of unemployment, one reason why we believe that it is offensive to God. The purpose of God for an individual, and for society as a whole, is being thwarted. Society as a whole suffers if the gifts of God are wasted, because they are meant to complement one another. No-one can achieve their full potential unless we all do so together.

There is a fuller historical account of Christian teaching about work in the paper by Peter Sedgwick in Annex A. Given this view of the relation of work to human nature and society, we must conclude that work of some kind is both a right and a duty for everyone who is capable of doing it. This applies to old and young, male and female, rich and poor. We accept the view put to us that unemployed people have a duty to seek work, although we will want to explore further what kind of work that might be. Equally we would argue that the rich, who do not need to work to earn their living, should nevertheless work in some way for the good of others as well as contributing financially. No-one should be left out of the common task. No-one should be told that their contribution is not wanted. Everyone should share in production as well as in consumption. The fact that some people, according to a conventional calculation, are more productive than others, is beside the point. We are not valued for our productivity, and our membership of society does not depend on it.

It is important to emphasise that, in order to be creative and fulfilling, work does not have to be paid. We want to affirm, in exactly the same way, the value of unpaid work, for example the work involved in looking after a family or the work that is done on a voluntary basis. By work we mean any human activity whose purpose is to produce something of use or intrinsic value. Having recognised this essential point, we need then to ask how work should in fact be organised for different groups of people, and how it should be rewarded. It is very important to most people to be able to say that they have 'earned' something in their lives.

Redefining Work

About ten to fifteen years ago a succession of books appeared in Britain which prophesied the transformation of work, even its abolition. Several of them were written from a more or less explicitly Christian point of view, the most famous being *The Future of Work* by Charles Handy, published in 1984. Despite the passage of time, the issues raised in these books are central to our enquiry - hence its title. They brought together the perception of technology as accelerating ahead with the observation of a sudden sharp rise in unemployment that was catastrophic for individuals and communities. They asked the question, which many thought too painful to ask, whether full employment could ever be achieved again. They began to explore alternatives.

The Future of Work begins by saying: 'the signs are, to put it bluntly, that there are not going to be enough conventional jobs to go round'. In a chapter on 'Rethinking Work' Handy went on to ask some related questions. 'What do we mean by work?' 'Do members of the younger generation see work as central to their lives?' 'Is work going out of fashion?' He ended up with two options. In the positive option the supply of labour is reduced by early retirement, longer holidays and shorter hours. Workers will build up 'portfolios' of work, some of it paid, some of it given in voluntary service, some done to please or serve oneself. The negative option includes the same numbers of hours worked, but it will be divided up less equally. There will be a strict stratification of society, with the 'knowledge people' at the top having most of the work and much of the wealth, whilst the rest live in idleness, supplemented by 'barter and brigandry'. Obviously we would prefer the positive option to the negative one, but first we have to ask whether this really is the choice we face. Why cannot everyone work as long as they want?

David Bleakley, in several books published in the 1980s, saw a potential for good in the decline of conventional employment. His 1985 book *Beyond Work - Free to Be* is dedicated 'to those who have discovered the difference between good work and mere employment - and who share their vision with others'. His vision was that the young, the retired and the unemployed would pioneer a new kind of work independent of the conventional 'capitalist' job market. He saw the beginnings of this movement taking place as some young people chose simpler lifestyles and more self-sufficiency, as some of the unemployed worked on community projects or bartered work informally between each other, and as people made redundant enjoyed a new lease of life without so much stress or anxiety.

On our visits we have met numerous people who share this vision today. For some it is a matter of accepting reality. They have been unemployed for long periods or work with people in that position. However society may be reformed in the future, they face the problem of what to do in the present. They say that the unemployed should be allowed, indeed should be encouraged, to react positively to their situation. The unemployed should spend their time creatively, in study, voluntary work, handicrafts and hobbies, physical training, social activities and sport. They should not have to waste their time looking for paid work which they are not going to find.

The dilemma of voluntary work and the unemployed was drawn to our attention on more than one occasion. If you take the view that there will never be enough paid jobs to go round then it makes good sense to encourage people who are unemployed to do voluntary work instead. It is much better, we entirely agree, for people to be doing voluntary work than doing nothing at all. But suppose that there is in fact an alternative which would create more paid jobs, perhaps jobs of the same kind as the unemployed would like to do, or have done in the past on a voluntary basis whilst drawing Income Support. Then the question to ask is why unemployed people should be expected to work for nothing, and why society as a whole should support them while they do. Voluntary work may be very worthwhile, enabling unemployed people to contribute to the community whilst maintaining their skills or developing new ones and acquiring work experience that may help their re-entry into employment. That much should be common ground. The hard question is whether voluntary work should actually be a substitute for paid work. On that there is not the same agreement.

A man who had both experienced unemployment and made an academic study of its psychological effects wrote as follows:

'Personally I have been able to achieve something of a sustainable state by engaging in voluntary work, which has enabled me to develop relationships and many useful contacts within the local voluntary community work sector. This provides some structure to my time, which also helps to reduce the stigma attached to an inactive lifestyle. It also provides a means of social support, as well as a way of using existing skills.'

We learnt about the development of Local Employment Trading Systems (LETS) in several different places. Members of LETS work for one another and are paid in accounting units instead of money, building up positive or negative balances. Such arrangements create a multilateral barter economy operating in parallel with the conventional market economy and the benefit system. They give members who are unemployed a way of using their time and talents constructively, whilst at the same time benefiting from some services which they could not afford to buy. The organisers are, naturally enough, indignant when the officials of the Department for Social Security suggest that work and income of this kind will result in a deduction from means-tested benefits. Two quite different work ethics have come into conflict at this point.

The issue is not just about the quality of life for those in long-term unemployment. The founder of the 'Impasse' initiative in North-East England describes it as 'a wider concern for purpose and meaning in life whether we have paid employment or not'. This is contrasted with the aim of full employment.

'The problem is wider than one of job creation with economic growth as the main focus. It is to do with human growth... Many stories can be told of lives changed simply by releasing resources, both human and material; by removing the boundaries and releasing the creative human spirit.'

The question being asked here is not just whether full employment is possible, but whether it is actually what we want.

There is much in this questioning approach which we commend. As we have said, good work in harmony with the purposes of God in creation is often unpaid and insufficiently recognised by the society in which we live. It is right to question whether the conventional contract of employment is the right way for most work to be organised. It is certainly right to question whether success in the market for labour is the right way to value people and the work that they do for one another. But the questioning cannot stop there. If work is to be redefined, we must also ask how it is to be paid for. If people are to go 'beyond work' and to be set 'free to be', who is to provide them with a livelihood? Is it possible to separate income from work?

Separating Income from Work

In *The Future of Work* Charles Handy recognised that this 'new agenda' required a source of income independent of work available to those who could not find conventional jobs, or who chose not to have one. This is an essential point. Any acceptable alternative to full employment must include a payment, out of taxation, to everyone at a level adequate to sustain a decent standard of life. He wrote:

'If the state cannot guarantee a job which provides a livelihood, then, say some, the state should guarantee livelihood directly. After all, in most modern states today the state provides, as a universal right, access to education and health care. Why not, then, access to the basic necessities of life such as food, clothing, shelter and heat, by the means of a straight cash payment?'

He goes on to quote estimates of the cost of such a guarantee. In the long run the required rate of tax is difficult to estimate because there would be changes in the levels of income and expenditure which would raise or lower the revenue from existing rates of tax. But, to quote Handy again

'in the short term taxes would have to be raised enormously to collect enough money to redistribute. VAT rates of 100 per cent have been mentioned and basic income tax rates of 50 per cent or more.'

The idea of an unconditional income paid by the state to all citizens has been in circulation for at least seventy years, with names such as citizen's income, basic income, social wage, social dividend, negative income tax and child benefit for grown ups. The campaign for such a payment in Britain is led by the Citizen's Income Research Group. Its supporters and advisers include leading economists and political commentators from both left and right. It does not now, however, campaign for the introduction of a basic income at anything like the level needed for subsistence or to replace Income Support. Its immediate objective (in July 1996) is a Transitional Basic Income of £17.75 a week for every man, woman and child. If this replaced personal tax allowances it could be introduced at little extra cost, that is it would be broadly revenue-neutral. It would however be a very long way from providing the guarantee of a livelihood described by Charles Handy in *The Future of Work*.

The implications of providing a basic income to all citizens were studied very thoroughly in the Republic of Ireland by the Expert Working Group on the integration of the tax and social welfare systems, which reported in June 1996. They calculated that the cost of a full basic income system, adequate for subsistence, with an adult rate of £60 a week and £17.40 a week per child, would imply a tax rate on all earned income of 68 per cent. This was their main reason for rejecting the idea. They also drew attention to the problems which might arise from the incentive to migration within Europe if some countries paid a basic income and others did not. The group also looked at a much more modest proposal for a partial basic income at a much lower rate. They also rejected this option, but suggested that it 'could be reviewed in the future'.

The Commission on Social Justice (CSJ), set up by the British Labour Party, which reported in 1994, looked at the principle behind the Citizen's Income proposals, and not only at the transitional kind which could be revenue-neutral. The Commission recognised both a moral and an economic case in its favour, but also three 'severe difficulties'. The first was the lack of the 'broad-based consensus' necessary for such a fundamental change. Popular opinion would not support an unconditional payment to those who chose not to work. The second was that such a payment could lead to more social exclusion rather than less. An unconditional benefit might encourage people to drop out of society rather than to contribute more effectively. The third was the effect of much higher rates of tax on participation in the labour force, especially amongst women.

The first and second objections raised by the CSJ were countered by the proposal for a 'Participation Income' put forward by one of the Commission's members, Tony Atkinson. This would be paid without a means test, but only to those who were, in some sense, 'active citizens'. The definition of participation would include, not only those working or looking for work, but also those in approved education or training and those caring for young, elderly or disabled dependents. Although this variant on the Citizen's Income proposal goes far to meet some of the objections raised, it creates other difficulties. Who would decide what constitutes 'active citizenship'? Who would approve the education and training which qualified for support? Experience with the availability-for-work condition applied to current benefits suggests that in practice such conditions can be seen as oppressive and interfering.

The Commission summarised its attitude as follows:

'We believe that in present conditions our new social insurance scheme is more likely to win popular support and to provide an effective foundation on which people can build through their own earnings and savings. It would be unwise however, to rule out a move to Citizen's Income in the future: if it turns out to be the case that earnings simply cannot provide a stable income for a growing proportion of people, then the notion of some guaranteed income, outside the labour market, could become increasingly attractive.' (p263)

Our concern in our own enquiry is not with the modest proposals now being put forward by the Citizen's Income Research Group. An income of £17.75 a week is obviously not intended to bring about the radical change in the organisation of work foreseen by Handy or Bleakley or the Impasse initiative. The rate of Income Support for a single person aged over 25 in 1996/97 is £47.90 and that is widely regarded as too low. If an effective separation of work and income were to be achieved, that is the minimum level that could be contemplated. As we have seen the implications of that for tax rates could be quite dramatic. That is not to our way of thinking a knock-down argument against the idea, since we as a group are quite happy in other contexts to contemplate tax increases where the need can be demonstrated. The point is rather that other calls on taxation and public spending might deserve a higher priority - and that in our view, would apply especially to taxation that financed job creation. In any case, setting on one side the implications for taxation and political acceptability, we have to ask whether a separation between income and work for some people along these lines is actually what we would like to see achieved.

Gifts and Wages

One of our members, Erik Cramb, whose childhood in post-war Glasgow was lived in a tenement typical of its day, gives us this parable which illustrates life in a close-knit community:

'If I shut my eyes, I can still remember almost all the people who lived up that stair - I can even put names to most of the faces. I recall how every adult had the right to reprimand me if I were being naughty and I think at one time or another, every adult did! The other side of the coin was that every adult would also look after me - if for example I got home from school and my mother wasn't in, I could knock on any neighbour's door and be taken in till my mum got home - and I think at some time or another I had a biscuit or a drink in every house in the stairs. That is a model of social cohesion that, without wanting to get romantic about the old crumbling tenements that were rightly swept away, still shines for me like a beacon.'

In a family, or amongst friends and neighbours who know one another well, work and income can be shared out quite informally. There is no need to earn your daily bread: it is given to you without condition. Equally there is no need to reward those who work for the common good; they do it freely from the goodness of their hearts. 'From each according to his ability, to each according to his need.' This ideal has not been put into practice by socialist or communist states, but it has always been followed, on a small scale, in religious communities, as well as some contemporary secular communes. We need to ask how an alternative economy on these principles might conceivably be organised on a larger scale.

In the absence of a market system, economic activity often takes the form of gift exchange. In such a society one may question whether the giving of gifts is purely altruistic. There may be no immediate reciprocation, but an obligation is created that is more or less clearly defined. The sense of owing or being owed a favour is, of course, very familiar from all walks of life. It requires a level of mutual trust much higher than that needed for market transactions. Somewhere in the background there are likely to be sanctions against those who seek to exploit the system for their own individual benefit. These may even involve expulsion from the sharing community - a sentence of death in some circumstances. So gift exchange as opposed to a market system does not necessarily go with a more loving or forgiving attitude between members of the community.

As Christians we believe that the love of God is freely given to all humanity. Our sins are forgiven as an act of grace, not because of any merit or effort or achievement of our own. We are called to act with generosity and to come to the needs of anyone we meet, like the Good Samaritan in the story which Jesus told (Luke 10:30-37). Jesus also told the story of the labourers in the vineyard (Matthew 20:1-16). Some worked all day in the heat of the sun; others, who had previously been unable to find employment, worked only for the last hour of the day. Yet all were paid the same wage. This is how we believe that the grace of God is given to us. How best can we express such grace in our relationships with one another?

The early church supported widows and orphans out of common funds, but not those who chose a life of idleness. St Paul put it quite bluntly when he wrote to the Thessalonians: 'Those who will not work shall not eat' (2 Thessalonians 3:10). When he said that he was not, of course, legislating for a modern welfare state. Nevertheless he gave his response to a problem which can arise in any community which treats the right to an adequate income as unconditional.

The 'free-rider' problem is not in fact the only one which should give us concern. There is also the problem of dependency or humiliation for those who are given grudging support by a society with little love or fellowship. The essence of gift exchange is that it is reciprocal. There is a duty to give and a right to receive; but equally there is a right to give and a duty to receive. The community is not compartmentalised into one group that gives and another that receives. Even in the context of marriage, one partner may wish not to be wholly dependent on the other in financial terms. Each might want to have something of their own to contribute to the common funds. Those who are poor but nevertheless able to contribute to society will lose self-respect and the respect of others if they are treated in a way more appropriate to those who cannot help themselves.

We live in a market economy and the question we face is how best the Christian vision can be realised in that context. We are particularly anxious to avoid a partition of society into those who always give and those who always receive. That situation is bad enough in a close community; it would be disastrous in a modern nation state. One can see it beginning to happen already in communities where unemployment is becoming the expected way of life. It cannot be right to say to these communities that the nation as a whole has nothing better to offer them. Yet if the state simply abandons all conditionality and says that the unemployed can have Income Support as of right, will that not in effect mean that all hope has been abandoned of integrating them with the rest of society? We see a real danger that separating income from work in fact means separating non-workers from the labour force.

The writings which we have reviewed in this section, which speak of redefining work and breaking its link with income, seem to us most relevant to the more fortunate and productive members of society. They are the ones who can choose to work less, to work for nothing or to build up a 'portfolio' of different jobs all running concurrently. They may have savings or sources of unearned income; they may have few if any dependants. They are in a position to pioneer new life-styles and new organisations of work.

Most of those now unemployed are not in this happy state. What they want and need is paid work, in most cases full-time and reasonably reliable work for a decent rate of pay. The whole 'Future of Work' literature is based on the premise that this is something that can no longer be given to them. We question that assumption. For us the real challenge is to find means of increasing the number of good jobs available, not means of coping with only the number we have now

The Challenge to Society

We have heard nothing to convince us that decent paid work for all is an impossible dream. Certainly the nature of work is changing, but there is still plenty of work to do. If the needs of our own society were ever to be fully satisfied, there would still be plenty of needs unmet elsewhere in the world. There is work which can only be done by human effort, despite the sophistication of new machines. There is work to be done in our own country, despite the globalisation of the world economy. As we enter a post-industrial society we will leave the industrial organisation of work behind, but work itself is so basic to human nature and society that it will continue indefinitely in one form or another.

The twentieth century has been the age of the consumer. Cheaper goods and services, in greater variety, have been made available to all those who can afford to buy them. A standard of living, and a choice of life-style, once open only to the aristocracy has been extended to much of the population. Choosing and spending have become our great preoccupations. Culture and commercial advertisements have become closely intertwined. As consumers we have learned to demand our rights - safer products, accurate information on labelling, reliable independent tests of quality and so on. Increasingly we can express our values as well as our tastes in the shopping mall, by refusing to buy products which do not meet our ethical criteria. The power of the consumer is being used to political ends.

The twenty-first century will have also to be the age of the producer. We can no longer take work for granted, as individuals or as a society. As individual workers we will face more choices and have to accept more responsibility for the work we do and how it is done. As a society we shall need to treat good working conditions as an objective quite as important as higher productivity. The pressure that has been exerted to win rights for consumers, will need to extend itself to win rights for producers as well. Individuals will express their personalities by the work that they choose to do, as much as by the products that they choose to buy.

The idea that work has no future does not appeal to many economists. Most economists believe that the problems of unemployment and low pay can be solved, although the solutions may take time and be costly. The true pessimists we have met are some businessmen and some of the unemployed themselves, who may generalise too much from their own experience, and assume that present economic and political conditions cannot be changed. Society does not, in our view, give a high enough priority to the creation of good jobs. If opinion shifts in that direction, as we think it should, then the pessimists can yet be proved wrong.

In 1996 the International Labour Office published a report on *World Employment 1996/97* which included a considered reassessment of the prospects for achieving full employment. It reviewed the standard reasons for long-term pessimism, including the effects of globalisation and new technology. It concluded:

'Full employment is still feasible and highly desirable. The current high unemployment level in industrialised countries has human costs of the utmost severity for those directly involved and breeds crime and other social pathologies from which everyone in society suffers. There is thus a very strong economic as well as moral case for reinstating full employment as an important policy objective. The objective of full employment is still highly relevant in spite of the rise in non-standard forms of work and other recent changes in the labour market.'

The challenge to society is to create good work for all. This means more than just the theoretical opportunity to work, more than just access for all in principle to the work that is on offer. It also means an outcome in which people actually do have work to do, appropriate to their abilities, preferences and other responsibilities. We could call it a right to work, or even a right to earn, but it is equally a duty to work and to support oneself. A better way of putting it would be to say that we all have a calling to serve one another and no-one should be denied the opportunity to carry it out.

Such phrases will remain empty slogans, however, unless some means can be devised to put them into effect. It is all too easy, especially for the churches, to denounce the present organisation of society, bewail its tragic effects and then leave it to someone else unspecified to put the world to rights. We understand our remit to be more ambitious than that. We are also asked to 'evaluate the policy options from a Christian standpoint'. This means considering what is possible, as well as what is desirable.

The second part of our report is about what society could do to respond to the challenge we have described. We must resist two opposite temptations. At one extreme we could take the existing agenda of public debate as given and concentrate on marginal changes to public policy which would offend no-one, but would make little difference for good or ill. At the other extreme we could ignore all the obstacles that stand in the way of virtue in a fallen world and simply recommend unrestricted freedom, justice and love. Instead we aim to be ambitious but not unrealistic. We do call for a change of heart, that is for repentance, but we address ourselves to men and women, not to the angels of heaven.

PART TWO: THE CHOICES WE CAN MAKE

Chapter Five

Expanding Employment

The challenge to society, as the nature of work changes, is to find good work for everyone to do in the economy of the future. In responding to that challenge the first, and most obvious, need is to expand employment (or self-employment), so that we are not constrained by a scarcity of jobs. In this chapter of our report we shall be arguing that this can be achieved, provided that it is given a high enough priority in the choices of individuals, and also most importantly in the conduct of public policy.

As a group appointed by the churches, we are aware of two difficulties we face in addressing policy issues. The first is the obvious risk that (especially in an election year) our views will be misinterpreted as partisan support for one political party or another. That is certainly not how we wish our report to be read as should be abundantly clear to anyone reading it in its entirety. Another difficulty is that the design of economic policies to increase employment is in part a technical matter on which a church enquiry would not normally be expected to offer a view. However, we would argue that the issues involved are not just technical ones. The questions of fact about how the economy functions and the questions of value about how its functioning should be improved are very closely related to one another and cannot be discussed satisfactorily if they are kept totally separate.

It is important to understand why people are unemployed, their objectives and the constraints they face; equally it is important to understand the aims which motivate employers and how they see their own social obligations. Labour market behaviour expresses social values, which economic policy must either counteract or reinforce. Economic policy is not just a kind of engineering, it must be based on a sympathetic interaction between different groups of human beings, including the policy makers themselves. But it also requires its own variety of expertise. There is no merit in well-meaning people suggesting impractical solutions. But equally, if there is no real commitment to the objectives of expanding employment, practical obstacles will all too easily be seen as insuperable.

We begin by asking what kinds of employment could most readily be expanded. Then we shall ask what kinds of action governments can take to increase employment in the context of a market economy with a large public sector. We need to be clear, or as clear as we can be in the present state of knowledge, about how creating a higher level of employment risks increasing the rate of inflation, and what that implies for the longer-term effectiveness of different kinds of policy action. This is plenty of ground to cover in one chapter; we postpone for later chapters discussion of other aspects of government policy such as labour market regulation, special schemes for the long-term unemployed and the provision of education and training.

What Kind of Employment could Expand?

In 1994 the Organisation for Economic Co-operation and Development (OECD) concluded its extensive review of unemployment in advanced industrial countries, called simply *The Jobs Study*. We do not find ourselves in agreement with all its policy recommendations, but it provides an authoritative summary of what might be called the 'conventional wisdom' amongst economists and policy makers, not just in our own countries, but worldwide in the early 1990s. We begin with two quotations from the summary report called *Facts, Analysis, Strategies* (p33).

> 'The basic answer to unemployment problems lies in creating more jobs. Although it is impossible to predict what these jobs will be, they are likely to share some basic characteristics. New jobs are likely to appear in the service sector, which already accounts for more than half of total employment in most OECD countries. The service sector is producing a higher proportion of new jobs as the demand for new services increases. Some of these are new types of jobs. Others are activities that formerly were performed within manufacturing enterprises, but are sub-contracted'.

The 'service' sector of the economy includes all activities which consist of 'doing' rather than 'making', for example private sector activities like catering and banking or mainly public sector activities like health and education. Employment in activities which produce 'goods' rather than 'services', for example manufacturing or agriculture, has declined and is unlikely to increase in the future. This much is uncontroversial. The next quotation is not quite such plain sailing.

> 'Many new jobs are likely to be low-productivity, low-wage jobs. From one point of view, this is intrinsically undesirable. Yet at the same time there are also calls explicitly to foster the creation of low-productivity jobs, especially in the non-tradeable sector, in order to absorb significant numbers of low-skilled unemployed workers. Policy has to find a balance between these two considerations.'

On this question, we would comment first that some (but not all) service jobs which are called 'low productivity' as measured by market valuation may be very worthwhile in terms of human relationships. We would also question whether such jobs need to be as low-waged as they commonly are. (The privatising and contracting out of public services may have reduced costs, but often by reducing the bargaining power of employees who in any case include many who are low paid.) However, the reference to the 'non-tradeable sector', that is to activities which do not compete with imports or try to sell on a world market, must surely be correct.

We would wish to see employment expanded in all sorts of directions if that were possible , but given the growth of competition with developing countries and the introduction of new technologies, we are more likely to see net job reductions in manufacturing, transport or 'high-tech' services. Our particular concern, given the threat of unemployment, is to see a very substantial increase of employment which does not require an initial level of education and training beyond the reach of most of the existing labour force. Many such jobs will fall within the definition of the service sector, but others will be elsewhere in the economy, for example in construction and the maintenance of existing buildings and works.

The record of job creation in Britain in recent decades is not good compared with other advanced industrial economies. In Britain the decline in employment in manufacturing has been particularly sharp: from 1970 to 1990 the number of manufacturing jobs halved (see Chart 3). It has been a feature of relatively successful industries like chemicals, as well as others like motor vehicles where, until quite recently, output was also falling sharply. By contrast employment in services has been rising. Between 1970 and 1990 there was a substantial increase in employment of women in that sector, while employment of men also held up well. However, comparing the growth of service sector employment in Britain with other countries over the same period, suggests that growth could well have been more rapid. In America employment growth in services through the 1970s was twice as fast as in Britain. In banking for example, new technology may actually have increased rather than decreased employment in America, as the range of services on offer has been widened. In health services the rise in employment in America has been truly spectacular, whilst in Britain it has been held back severely by the lack of funds for the NHS.

It is unlikely that the new jobs which can be created will be in the same sectors as continuing job losses occur. There is a natural and understandable reluctance to move from one industry, which has been traditional in a family or a community, to work of a quite different kind. We have already mentioned the view expressed to us in South Yorkshire, that the only 'real' jobs are jobs in coal or steel. This is not an attitude that we can encourage or condone. There has to be mobility and the acceptance of change. Old forms of employment need to be run down, but at a pace which takes account of the human as well as the economic costs. New forms of employment need to be created, jobs of which in due course we can be at least as proud.

CHART 3: EMPLOYMENT IN MANUFACTURING AND NON MANUFACTURING

Thousands

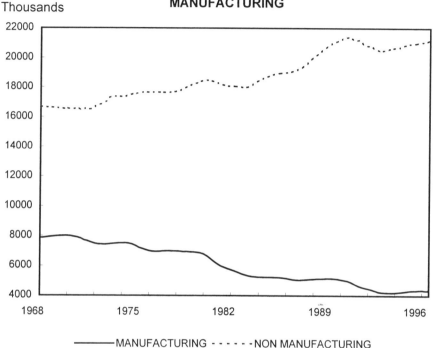

——— MANUFACTURING - - - - - - NON MANUFACTURING

At one time those who could not find work in their native place were expected to migrate, either within their native country or abroad. In the nineteenth century there was massive emigration from both Britain and Ireland to America, Australia and elsewhere. Within Britain there was also massive internal migration, typically from rural to urban areas. Migration is still of major significance to the economy of Ireland and to several regions of England, Scotland and Wales. We do not see it, however, as playing an important role in solving the problems of unemployment identified in this enquiry.

Migration is an expensive solution to a regional unemployment problem because it requires the old infrastructures of housing, roads and amenities to be written off and a new infrastructure built. It is usually cheaper, in purely economic terms, to bring the work to the people rather than vice versa (as communication becomes cheaper this argument is becoming stronger).

85

Private firms will not take account of infrastructure costs in making their decisions where to locate production. It is worthwhile therefore preserving, and perhaps increasing, the tax and other incentives to create jobs in areas where they are most needed.

Economics apart, it is also a strong argument against migration that it destroys local communities, separates families and weakens the link between generations. In the process people are pulled up from their social roots, and perhaps their moral and religious roots as well. For some this may be stimulating or even liberating, but for many it is a confusing and isolating experience.

What can Governments do to Expand Employment?

Twenty years ago the OECD published a report called *Towards Full Employment and Price Stability*. This was at a time when unemployment in the OECD area was about 20 million, compared with about 35 million today. It said 'The fundamental aim of policy is to return to reasonable rates of growth and high levels of employment'. It was assumed that governments could reduce unemployment to tolerable levels, if they went to the task with sufficient determination and skill. Now people are not so sure. *The Jobs Study* of 1994 included many policy recommendations to improve employment prospects. It said 'there is no single recipe for full employment, but a menu of measures that can help move OECD economies towards higher employment with good jobs'. This nicely dodges the question of whether full employment can be achieved at all. The OECD as an organisation is not as certain about that as it was twenty years ago. It also says that its recommendations 'do not apply to governments alone. In many cases responsibility for action to improve employment performance lies most directly with employers, trade unionists and individual workers'. That is certainly true, but we need to press the point that governments do have the power to act decisively if they choose.

One limitation to the powers of governments results from the growth of international markets, which has accelerated since the 1970s. The global market for capital is especially active and can frustrate national economic policies if exchange rates or interest rates become unstable. This was true even in the 1970s, as the sterling crisis of 1976 demonstrated, and it has become even more true since the abolition of exchange controls throughout Europe. This certainly restricts the ability of national governments to conduct independent monetary policies or to borrow on a scale that 'the markets' believe to be imprudent.

The international mobility of production itself also has implications for the taxation of profits and investment income. The Republic of Ireland for example has been very successful in attracting firms to locate in that country by offering them a relatively generous taxation regime. To a lesser extent Britain is doing the same. Within Europe as a whole there is pressure to harmonise as many rates of tax as possible so as to avoid a competition to attract investment which would ultimately undermine the tax-raising powers of all the governments concerned. These are real limitations to the powers of national governments, meaning that some economic policies now have to be conducted by governments jointly in agreement with one another. That much is true about internationalisation and globalisation, but it does not mean that governments in Britain or Ireland have no powers to create jobs or encourage job creation.

Most labour is not internationally mobile at all. Labour markets, except for some special highly-skilled occupations, are national or even local in extent. Regulation and the structure of taxation falling on labour does not have to be the same in different countries. The systems are in fact very different in Britain and Ireland. If the Irish government decides for example, to pay a higher rate of social security benefit than the British government, the British unemployed cannot migrate en masse to take advantage of it. There is a real choice here to be made by each government separately, for which each government must take the responsibility. A similar point could be made in relation to the taxation of domestic property, earned income and household expenditure, as well as most forms of public expenditure.

According to the ILO report already quoted:

'It is not true that globalization is an overwhelming supra-national force that has largely usurped national policy autonomy. There is still considerable policy autonomy and national macroeconomic, structural and labour-market policies are still the dominant influence on economic and labour-market outcomes in any country'

It is to national governments therefore that we would look mainly for policy action to expand employment. There is however an important role for local government as well as national. On our visits we have learnt much about the concern at local or regional level to devise economic programmes which will stimulate local employment as well as economic activity. It is sad to see their efforts often frustrated by their lack of real authority, or by their inability to generate enough revenue to have a large impact on their own labour markets. On the other hand we appreciate the need for an equitable sharing of resources between regions and local authorities at a national level, which must be the responsibility of national government. We have been led to believe that competition between local authorities for shares in both private investment and public funding can be wasteful and unfair in its results, however good it may be at stimulating local initiatives. We certainly see a vital role for local government in the process of employment expansion, but it must be within the framework of a national strategy to achieve that end at a national level as well.

Cyclical and Structural Unemployment

A quite different limitation on the powers of government arises from the nature of the market economy itself. If the pressure of demand rises too high then inflation will accelerate. This happens whatever the reasons for the increase in demand - it does not have to be an increase deliberately engineered by an act of policy by a government which wants to see unemployment fall. The nature of this constraint is the subject of continuing debate amongst economists. It depends on how much unemployment is interpreted as cyclical and how much as structural in its origins.

Unemployment rises and falls with the pressure of demand in the economy. This accounts for most of the movement in unemployment from year to year. In Britain for example the unemployment rate reached 12½ per cent in the aftermath of the recession at the beginning of the 1980s, but fell to 7 per cent after the boom at the end of the decade and then rose to over 10 per cent again in the next recession. These are very large swings, creating and destroying millions of jobs. Clearly it would be very attractive to keep the pressure of demand high all the time, so that jobs were always at least as easy to find as they were at the peak of the last boom. It is also clear however, that this cannot be achieved simply by expanding demand. When the economy 'overheats' the result is accelerating inflation, which must sooner or later halt economic growth and push unemployment back up again.

We recognise that this relationship between unemployment and inflation does limit what governments or central banks can do to expand employment by stimulating demand. This does not mean, however, that the management of demand and the conduct of monetary policy are purely technical matters on which the experts should be given a free hand. The variations from year to year in the demand for labour or the swings in unemployment and vacancies which result are themselves a cause of social as well as economic upheaval. Greater stability in the pressure of demand for labour is itself a very worthwhile policy aim.

It has become almost uncontroversial to say that the objective of monetary policy should be low inflation or price stability. This will be the declared aim for the European central bank if monetary union goes ahead as agreed in the Maastricht Treaty. It is, of course, a necessary aim for any central bank to adopt. But, consistent with that aim, policy can and should also seek to limit the variation from year to year in the pressure of demand, especially as that affects the labour market. It seems to us that this very important function of monetary policy has not, in recent years, been given as much emphasis as it deserves.

The main challenge to economic policy however, is to reduce the level of unemployment which is sustainable and consistent with low inflation or price stability in the longer term. This level is variously described as the 'natural' rate, the 'equilibrium' rate or the NAIRU (non-accelerating-inflation rate of unemployment). Alternatively it can be called structural unemployment, as opposed to the component of unemployment which is merely cyclical. The distinction is very helpful in theory, although the figures corresponding to it are always uncertain and controversial. It may be helpful again to quote the OECD *Jobs Study* report (p 32): 'an often discussed aspect of the unemployment problem is how much is cyclical and how much is structural... In practice, however, there are many definitions of structural unemployment, and there is no unambiguous way of providing a decomposition, especially as there seems to be strong interaction between the two. Factors that increase structural unemployment will often exacerbate cyclical unemployment; while cyclical unemployment, if it persists, may well lead to an increase in structural unemployment.' In other words, no-one knows for certain how much unemployment is due to the ups and downs of the economy from year to year, and how much is due to more lasting causes; and anyway the ups and downs themselves may have lasting effects. This last point certainly reinforces the need to avoid sharp cyclical contractions of demand as a means of repressing inflation. The effect of a recession on unemployment may be long-lasting or even permanent.

The level of structural unemployment is not constant over time and it seems to be very different in different countries. There is no simple well-defined cause and no simple obvious cure, but there are many different factors influencing structural unemployment, and many of them could be altered by government policy.

Obviously the existence of social security benefits must have an influence on the level of unemployment, and especially the numbers of claimants unemployed. In poor countries which cannot afford social security systems recorded unemployment percentages are often very low. In America, where there is no equivalent to Income Support, unemployment has usually been lower than in Europe. In America more poor people have work than they do in Europe, but that does not mean that they are necessarily better off as a result.

For a significant group in Britain, mainly parents with several dependent children, the relationship between benefit levels and wages is such that it is difficult to find work which does not involve an actual loss of weekly income. This situation could certainly be improved by government policy, as indeed it has been in recent years through the provision of benefits to people in work - an issue discussed in chapter 8. We also discuss in chapter 6 below the case for introducing a national minimum wage.

It is very likely that the structure of taxation also affects unemployment, although the magnitude of its influence is debatable. It is generally recognised in Continental Europe that the high level of taxes and social security contributions which have to be paid by employers is a disincentive to job creation. When these charges are lowered the result will be either more employment or higher wages, or some combination of the two. Again this is something which is directly under the control of national governments.

A less tangible, but very important, influence comes from what is called 'mismatch'. The pattern of demand for labour does not match the pattern of supply, and relative wages and salaries do not move to clear the market. There can be mismatch between regions, industries, possibly genders and certainly between skills. In a time of rapid technical change these mismatches get worse. There can be an excess of demand over supply for some kinds of labour alongside an excess of supply over demand for others. Retraining and relocating the labour force takes a long time and is expensive. There may be a good social reason why it cannot happen at all. It may seem, at first sight, that there is not a great deal that governments can do to correct mismatch, but we hope to show that it would not be impossible to shift the pattern of demand significantly whilst acting on the supply side as well.

Finally, many economists, notably Richard Layard who addressed one of our meetings, believe that the level of unemployment which is sustainable depends on the average duration of unemployment itself. The higher the proportion of people who have been unemployed for long periods, the more difficult it will be to reduce unemployment in total. It is as if the long-term unemployed have been cut off altogether from access to jobs, and for that reason play no part in the labour market at all. The market settles down, according to this view, at a level of short-term unemployment which is the equilibrium or point of balance between supply and demand. Then the long-term unemployed have to be added on to that equilibrium of short-term unemployment to arrive at the level of unemployment in total.

Looking at it this way suggests an important conclusion. If special measures can be devised to overcome the problems of the long-term unemployed then this will be a means of reducing total unemployment and not just of reducing its average duration. We shall devote chapter 7 of our report to considering measures of this kind. We continue in this chapter looking at measures to increase the demand for labour, first in the private and then in the public sector.

Employment growth in the private sector depends directly on the decisions made by employers (or the self-employed) to maintain and to increase the size of the business that they run. Public policy can influence that decision, but it is the entrepreneur who takes it, and who takes the risk that goes with it. The success of any economic strategy in a market economy like our own depends on the courage and the hope in the future shown in the actions of large numbers of individual owners and managers. The economy will flourish and employment expand only if these qualities are nurtured and supported by public opinion and by public policy. This point has been made to us frequently in our enquiry - and not only by representatives of the business community itself. What is needed in the future is not so much growth in private sector output, profits and dividends, as growth in private sector jobs. The risk which entrepreneurs seem most reluctant to take is the risk of creating employment - yet it is on this most of all that public support for entrepreneurship rests.

Christians too easily fall into the error of thinking that enterprise and personal greed are the same thing. In fact the motives of entrepreneurs, as described for example in Peter Sedgwick's book *The Enterprise Culture*, are often at least in part idealistic. They value freedom and creativity at least as much as the purely material rewards of business success. Some of them would say - and quite rightly say - that their hard work advances the Kingdom of God.

In several of the regions we have visited the economic regeneration and employment growth we have seen have been the result of inward investment, that is the decision of foreign firms to locate new production in our country. It seems crucially important to the expansion of employment in the private sector that this inflow should continue. (Moreover, it is inevitable, and not always a matter of regret, that domestically-owned firms choose to locate some of their production overseas.) One key decision is where a multi-national allocates its centres of research, development and innovation. It has been suggested to us that this matters more even than the location of its head office. Our countries have a good reputation for the quality of their higher education and, in many fields for the quality of their scientific research as well. In the long run the quality of the academic research base is critical to the wealth of the whole community and hence its ability to create employment either in the public or in the private sector.

One means of increasing the demand for labour in the private sector would be to change the structure of taxation to encourage more labour-intensive methods of production. Firms, when they decide to hire or to fire look at the effects of that decision on their own profitability, not at the wider social costs or benefits of what they do. At present the structure of taxes encourages labour saving which is not cost effective in social terms. When an employer takes on an additional full-time employee the cost includes not only the gross wage but also some social security contributions. The employee receives a net wage which excludes some more social security contributions as well as income tax. The cost to society is much less than that, because society as a whole has use of the contributions and taxes paid both by the employer and the employee. Moreover society as a whole pays for the benefit income which some at least of the workers would receive if they were unemployed. It would make more sense to subsidise employment than to tax it, because then employers would be encouraged to do what it is in the social interest for them to do - that is to use more labour, when they have that option, and less capital and other scarce resources.

Reducing the burden of taxation and insurance contributions that fall on employment would, as we have suggested above, either increase jobs or pay, or both. We believe that there is a strong case for reducing the costs of employing labour and also the taxes and insurance contributions paid by workers themselves on employment income. But the case is most compelling in relation to relatively low skilled jobs. These are the jobs held by people most at risk of unemployment, and the jobs which most unemployed people have the best hope of securing. The effects of reducing taxes and charges on low skilled jobs in particular would be either to create more jobs of the right kind to cut unemployment or else to raise the take-home pay of relatively poor people in work. Either way it helps to achieve social aims.

The European Commission favours such a change in the structure of taxation in the White Paper mentioned above. It refers to 'statutory charges' on labour, including taxes as well as social security contributions. These amount on average in Europe to 40 per cent of Gross Domestic Product (GDP) to 37 per cent in the Irish Republic, 34 per cent in the UK and 30 per cent in the USA (1991 figures quoted in the White Paper). 'In order to help maintain employment and create new jobs without reducing wage levels,' the White Paper states,

'steps must be taken to reduce non-wage costs, particularly for less skilled labour... The reduction of statutory charges on labour should apply as a priority to the lowest earnings. This would make it possible to limit the budgetary cost of the measure per job saved or created while responding to the scale of unemployment among the least skilled workers'.

Inevitably the question then arises as to what taxes should be raised to compensate for the loss of revenue. The European Commission very properly does not duck this issue. The White Paper considers options to raise the taxation of energy use, or consumer spending (VAT) or income from financial capital. It quotes estimates of the effects of a tax switch throughout Europe. Suppose that employers' social security contributions are reduced by just 1 per cent of GDP, 'targeted on categories of workers with a low level of skills' and the revenue is recouped by an energy tax. The econometric model used shows a reduction in the unemployment rate of 2½ percentage points over four years (White Paper, p 150).

We do not attach any great significance to these precise numbers. If the policy is as effective as is claimed then why stop at switching only 1 per cent of GDP of revenue from one tax base to another? Why not actually replace the tax on labour by a subsidy? Is there not a case for higher taxation of the top ranges of earned income, rather than raising indirect taxes which could fall most heavily on those who are relatively poor? Even approximate estimates of the effects of such changes are very uncertain, since everything depends on the model of the economy that is used. Nevertheless the idea looks a very promising one; possibly it could have a really substantial effect on employment in any country where it was introduced. It illustrates very well the general point we wish to make in this report - that there are areas of the private sector in which the expansion of employment is perfectly possible, and where straightforward government action can help to make it happen.

Expanding Employment in the Voluntary Sector

Before moving on from the private sector to the public sector we should draw attention to the very important sub-sector, which in some senses lies between the two. The 'third sector' as it is sometimes called includes voluntary and charitable activities, organised in a variety of ways, often involving trusts and non-profit companies. Although the activity takes place in the private sector, its funding is a mixture of private donations and public expenditure. There would appear to be scope for expansion here, but it will be necessary to address some of the problems which have arisen in relation to public funding. By 'expansion' we mean an increase in paid employment, jobs which carry similar expectations and similar rewards to those of the other sectors of the economy.

The nature of funding for the voluntary sector has changed considerably over the last twenty years, and with it the kind of work being undertaken and the relationship with the statutory sector. Twenty years ago many voluntary sector organisations (whether large or small) saw their role as providing services which were not provided by the statutory sector, often because there was no statutory requirement to do so. This might be the development of a community-based adventure playground or the provision of group homes for ex-psychiatric patients. Sources such as Urban Aid often provided funding for the initial few years, and where projects were successful they were usually taken onto mainstream funding. (Funders would in these cases provide post-related funding, so that increments and inflation were covered, as were other costs such as maternity cover.)

With the advent of employment-creation schemes such as the Community Programme many voluntary sector organisations became involved in administering 'schemes' of various kinds. The withdrawal of funding regimes such as Urban Aid and the introduction of competitive regimes such as City Challenge (where local authorities have to bid for urban renewal money) meant that it was increasingly difficult for voluntary sector bodies to rely on consistent mainstream funding. In recent years they have had to turn to bidding for contracts to provide services; most grants have now been changed to contracts. Post-related funding is a thing of the past. Some voluntary sector organisations have been ruined by becoming involved in employment-creation schemes with short-term funding dependent on outputs. For others the contractual nature of funding means even more bureaucracy and often extensive annual negotiations to secure funding for the following year.

Many of the areas in which employment could be expanded are covered by the voluntary sector. We see scope for local groups being funded to provide local jobs which are of immediate benefit to local communities. Similarly, much work with the most vulnerable in society (such as the homeless and the mentally ill) is done by the voluntary sector and should be expanded. The balance to be struck between creating employment in the public sector and in the voluntary sector is a difficult one. The voluntary sector should not be expected to provide what are effectively statutory services. The voluntary sector should not be seen as a cheap way of providing such services through ever more tightly drawn contracts. Much employment creation in people-related services should be within the public sector. We would, however, favour creating more employment through voluntary organisations in those fields where they have particular expertise, especially in local communities and in innovative social, health and educational projects. Currently however many voluntary organisations lack the resources to be good employers, providing proper equipment and training for their staff.

Drawing the borderline between the voluntary sector and the public sector also requires reconsideration of the best means of involving local communities more actively in the planning and provision of services. The Centre for Theology and Public Issues at the University of Edinburgh recently published the report of a conference on *Work, Worth and Community* (edited by John Hughes and Andrew Morton). They concluded both that 'Whatever the scope for locally based measures, they should include close collaboration between the public and the private sectors with strong leadership from the local authorities' (page 59) but also that 'policy making to meet local community needs is a task for the community itself and not for professionals alone'. We agree with both objectives, but also recognise that in some areas of the country they seem to be difficult to reconcile.

Jeremy Rifkin's recent book *The End of Work*, mentioned above, ends up with a chapter on what he calls 'the third sector'. This is the one chapter in which he shows any optimism at all about the expansion of employment. Rifkin has little faith in government expenditure, but he recognises the need for 'community-based organisations' to meet social need and provide worthwhile work opportunities. As he himself acknowledges his solution also involves higher levels of taxation - and he has some imaginative suggestions as to how the revenue should be raised. This provides us with our answer to a question many of our readers may want to ask. Suppose that Rifkin is right, suppose that for many, even most, of the population paid work will not be available in the competitive market sector, what happens then? The answer must be that paid work can still be made available, to meet real needs, but on a not-for-profit basis in the community. It could be financed in part by taxation of the high incomes earned in the competitive market sector. If Rifkin is right the 'third sector' will have to grow vastly bigger than it is now.

Expanding Employment in the Public Sector

Up to this point we have said nothing which is seriously out of line with the 'conventional wisdom' amongst economists who advise governments as exemplified by the European Commission or the OECD Secretariat. Now we do part company. In describing where new jobs could be created the OECD *Jobs Study* said 'new jobs must certainly be generated by the private sector, because in nearly all countries budget deficits and resistance to tax increases rule out significant expansion of the public sector'. We need to ask whether this is really the case. In the OECD report it is asserted rather than argued.

So far as budget deficits are concerned the conventional wisdom may be generally right. The Irish government learnt this lesson in the 1980s. In the long term a country cannot allow its public sector debt to rise indefinitely as a proportion of its national income. Otherwise the interest on that debt will use up more and more of its tax revenue, until ultimately the debt has to be eroded either by an unexpected burst of inflation or else by outright default. In an emergency, for example in wartime, countries always have borrowed in excess of what is prudent in the long term. To meet a temporary crisis of employment similar behaviour would be justified, but the problem of unemployment is not just a temporary one. To counter that problem by unsustainable borrowing might just be to push it into the future.

The case with tax revenue is very different. The OECD Secretariat are right to refer to taxpayers' resistance, but that is a constraint of very different kind to the iron laws of economics or accounting. So far as the economics is concerned, taxes could certainly be increased to pay for a higher level of public spending.

There are two economic arguments against raising taxes to fund employment creation, but neither of them seems to us to be a serious objection. The first is that raising taxes will reduce demand, for example for consumer goods, and hence offset the effect on employment of the increase in public spending. But virtually all the extra public spending will go to expand employment, whilst most of the tax revenue will come out of savings or the purchase of imports, materials and fuels or the profit content of the goods which taxpayers would otherwise have bought. The net effect on employment creation will still be very substantial.

The other argument is about the supply side, about incentives and costs. It would, of course, be very foolish to finance job creation in the public sector with a tax on job creation in the private sector or by taxes which undermine the international competitiveness of the economy. That is not what we propose. Ideally, from the point of view of job creation, all the extra tax would fall on factors of production which compete with private sector jobs, such as income from capital, imports, materials, fuels and so on. That would actually reinforce the expansionary effect on employment of the extra public spending. An increase in general taxation of domestic income and expenditure, if that was the preferred method of finance, would fall in some degree on all factors of production. But, again, this offset to the effect of the extra public expenditure would be relatively small, leaving a substantial net positive effect on employment in total. We believe therefore that the case for extra public spending to raise employment holds good whether it is viewed from the demand side of the economy or the supply. We could put it another way. No-one would doubt that an increase in spending on health care in the private sector, paid for by the customers through charges or private insurance schemes, would stimulate employment. Why should the same not be true of a similar increase in spending on health care paid for by society as a whole through the medium of taxation?

Compared with the rest of Europe, Britain has a relatively low ratio of taxation to GDP. In 1994, current receipts of General Government were 36.4 per cent of GDP in the United Kingdom. This compares with only 31.5 per cent in the USA, but as much as 46.5 per cent in Germany and 48.9 per cent in France.

We are not suggesting that taxes should be raised to German or French levels in a one year's Budget. It would be possible however to add several percentage points of GDP to taxation in Britain over a run of years, making possible a gradual expansion of labour-intensive public service expenditure.

At the same time economies might be found in other areas of public spending which do not have a high direct labour content. We were advised by Andrew Dilnot of the Institute of Fiscal Studies that there is indeed scope to raise that percentage in Britain by judicious changes to the tax system, without causing serious harm to the economy or treating any taxpayers with flagrant injustice. In our view there is scope to widen the tax base to include some categories of expenditure or income which are now untaxed and also to increase the rate of income tax on higher levels of earnings. It would not, of course, be popular with everybody, but that does not mean it could not be done. It seems to us absurd to constrain policy action by saying that it must make no-one at all worse off. A great deal could be done without hitting the incomes of people who are already poor. When policies change there will always be winners and losers. If taxes went up there would indeed be some losers - we would hope they were people well able to afford to pay more. If the revenue was used to create jobs there would be some very significant winners as well.

It is worth recalling how the unemployment problems of the 1930s were eventually solved. It was not by making labour markets more flexible, or by tightening the eligibility conditions for welfare benefits. It was by a massive increase in public expenditure, directed at rearmament and ultimately at war. Obviously the economics - and the politics - of different forms of public spending are not the same, but the point is worth making nevertheless.

We have been aware in travelling round the country that the reduction in military spending now under way or in prospect is hitting employment in some localities very hard. We saw this in Belfast, on the Clyde, in the South West and in the Medway towns. The preservation of the armaments industry has been given a particularly high priority by Government and the effective rate of subsidy is very high indeed, according to a recent report by the Campaign against the Arms Trade (*Killing Jobs: The Arms Trade and Employment in the UK*, published April 1996). Politicians and the public seem willing to accept that government expenditure must increase and taxes must be raised when the purpose of that expenditure is seen as essential to national security. Whatever we may think about the morality of defence spending - and that is an ongoing debate in the churches - there is a lesson here about government spending and employment policy. What is needed today is a similar sense of urgency in relation to the issues of employment and social cohesion which are the subject matter of this report.

It is generally agreed that the greatest scope for employment expansion is in the service sector, especially services which are not subject to foreign competition or technological innovation. It so happens that many such service activities are to be found in the public sector, for example health, education and community care. If we keep these services in the public sector then we will distort the natural growth of activity and employment if they are not adequately funded. Job losses in manufacturing industry or coal mining may be defended as an appropriate, even an inevitable, response to economic change. Job losses in the health service or the care of the environment cannot. Of course the resources devoted to these activities need to be used efficiently, with proper accountability and the most effective management techniques. This may mean contracting out work to the private sector or it may mean direct employment by the public sector itself. This is not a matter on which we would claim expertise. The main point is that, by one route or another, employment could be expanded and good work done.

There is no reason to doubt that employment could, indeed, be expanded and good work done by the public sector if more funds were available. We asked some local authority leaders and officials what unmet needs they were aware of in their region and, as we expected, they had no difficulty in providing examples. Moreover some of the examples they gave were tasks which people now unemployed could very readily do with only a limited amount of training. They mentioned for example the imbalance that now arises when new money is made available for high-profile investment projects, but not for the subsequent, less newsworthy but equally necessary, costs of maintenance and repairs. They also mentioned social work where cuts have put an unreasonable burden on both professional and support staff.

It has been suggested to us that giving a green light to the expansion of employment in the public sector would not be compatible with maintaining financial control and accountability within government. We do not accept this criticism at all. We believe in the good use of resources, not least in the public sector - 'stewardship' is the word used for this in the Christian tradition. Moreover, everything we have said about the need to create real work, which makes a real contribution to society, implies that the real value of the work done in the public sector should be subject to continual and rigorous scrutiny. We certainly do not propose signing a blank cheque so that public sector employees can go ahead and spend taxpayers' money on any programmes that they fancy. The point we are making is that taxpayers actually want better services than they have been receiving over the past twenty years and that the drives for economy in the public sector have been conducted in such a way that they are actually preventing taxpayers from getting what they want.

We have referred to 'mismatch' as one of the underlying causes of structural unemployment. Expanding employment in the public services can be seen as a means of tackling that problem. The composition of employment growth in the private sector can only be influenced indirectly and very imprecisely by public policy. If public expenditure is increased, the resulting job growth can be matched much more closely to the skills that are available in the labour force. We are not talking now of special schemes for the long-term unemployed - a subject we will address in chapter 7 below - but of the level and composition of public spending as part of their normal budgeting process, on a permanent basis and not as a temporary expedient.

In assessing the cost of such expansion it is, of course, important to take account of the resulting saving in social security payments. At the same time society as a whole would benefit from better public services, such as health and education facilities, care for children and the elderly, and so on. There would be real, and very visible improvements in the quality of life for all. The taxpaying public would be getting good value for their money. To win support for tax increases the link with improved services as well as job creation should be made as explicit and direct as possible. The more that tax payers can see and approve the way in which public money is spent the better.

Expanding Employment in Ireland

Most of what we have said in this chapter so far is addressed to the situation in Britain. The policy choices faced in the Republic of Ireland are similar in many respects, but different in others. The very rapid growth of the Irish economy illustrates well how an expansion of activity helps create jobs, but also that it does not of itself solve the whole of the unemployment problem. Unemployment in Ireland is falling, but it is still unacceptably high, higher indeed than it is in Britain. Part of the explanation is a reversal of the emigration which took place some years ago before the economic expansion got under way. But there is a further explanation, which indicates a need for policy action: the increase in the demand for labour is failing to reach the regions of the economy and the people whose need for new opportunities is greatest.

The recent history of Ireland illustrates very well the dangers of increasing public expenditure without raising taxation. However an increase in some areas of public expenditure, properly financed by taxation, could have a part to play in solving the problems of unemployment in Ireland. As we have argued above the expansion of the service sector, both public and private, provides the best hope of creating more jobs. Moreover in the public sector such expansion can be targeted to the regions and the occupations where the demand for labour is deficient. We also believe that, in Ireland as in Britain, demand for labour in the private sector should be increased by shifting the burden of taxation and insurance contributions away from relatively low-paid labour. Steps in that direction have been taken in Ireland, but we suggest that a great deal more needs to be done before the problem of unemployment is solved.

The Irish government has been imaginative in addressing the issue of financial disincentives to work. As indicated in chapter 3 above these are more genuinely problematic in Ireland than in Britain as social security provision is more generous. We would emphasise however that these financial disincentives do not form the only, or even the most significant, barrier to overcome. Unemployed people need to be aware of what job opportunities are open to them and the various measures that have been introduced in recent years to help the transition back into employment, for example the possibility of retaining some benefits for a period after recommencing paid work. The approach of those helping the unemployed should be active, based on a perception of the right of everyone to appropriate work, as well as the duty of everyone who can to participate in the work of the society to which they belong. It may well be that the approach in Ireland in the past has put too much emphasis on the purely passive task of making sure that people who are unemployed receive the benefits to which they are entitled. This does not mean of course that we favour a policy of 'harassment'. We repeat what we have said in relation to the UK: no-one should be written off as unemployable, even if they have few educational qualifications and even if they have been out of work for many years. It is up to the society as a whole to ensure that appropriate and rewarding work is there for everyone to do. To quote the well-chosen words from the Pastoral Letter of the Irish Catholic Bishops' Conference, we believe in 'an economy that needs everyone'.

A Question of Priorities

We do not think that there is a quick and easy way of expanding employment on the scale which the situation demands. We do believe however that such expansion would be possible over a period of time if it were given a much higher priority in the conduct of public policy. We have given some examples, which involve making employment creation an explicit aim and not just the by-product of economic growth.

The Report of the Commission on Social Justice in Britain, published in 1994, was very influential in the formation of Labour Party thinking at that time. It deals with many of the same issues as we have addressed in this chapter and it comes to some of the same conclusions (see especially pages 151 to 170). It recognises the potential of the service sector, both private and public, as the main area for job creation. It also recognises the need for 'the wealth created in a dynamic tradeable sector to be used to employ other people in services which enrich the quality of all our lives'. In other words the parts of the economy which are growing faster and competing successfully in international markets must provide the income which pays for other, less competitive but equally important, parts of the economy like childcare and hospitals. In another passage it refers to finance for such services 'whether through taxes, charges, partnerships or other means'. We agree that charges and 'other means' may be worth exploring, but in practice we think that the main source of funding will have to be taxation. Since so much of the service sector is supported by public spending it is difficult to see how employment creation can take place on a large scale in that sector without increasing the level of taxation. It becomes a question of priorities: job creation as against low taxation. Sacrifice is necessary in seeking the common good. We do not think that the deep running sores of unemployment and poverty can be healed without some sacrifice on the part of those of us who are better off.

It was suggested to us at one meeting that it is becoming increasingly difficult to collect taxes. Certainly there was a scare during the course of our enquiry when government receipts of revenue appeared to be coming in well below forecast. It was suggested to us that both tax avoidance and tax evasion have become more socially accepted. It was also suggested that in a flexible market it may be easier to conceal tax liabilities. If this really is a growing problem - and we are not certain that it is - then the answer is not to reduce taxation, but to devote more resources to collecting it. It may also be necessary to simplify the tax system, removing exemptions which are open to abuse. But it would also help if political leaders were to encourage the belief that paying taxes is a social obligation to the common good and not an arbitrary extortion.

We have argued, as Christians, that job creation should be given a very high priority for reasons which are social and spiritual as well as economic. The priority to be given to low taxation is a different question, on which Christians differ. One view, with which we sympathise, is that paying taxes is a way of discharging (in some part) our obligation to meet the needs of our national community as a whole, and especially the needs of its less fortunate members. The origin of that obligation can be attributed either to love or to justice - to compassion for those in need or to a duty to share God's gifts more fairly. A case for redistributive taxation can be constructed on either base. These arguments are not heard often enough today.

This does not tell us, of course, what is the optimal rate of taxation, the rate which is neither too low nor too high. Neither does it tell us how the burden of taxation should be shared out between different groups in the community. To answer such questions would involve a review, not just of employment creation but of all the other objectives which public expenditure may serve. Perhaps savings can be made in other programmes. This would take us well beyond the remit of this enquiry. Our plea is simply that the aim of low taxation should not automatically be given the highest priority of all. There are other aims that matter far more than that one.

Chapter Six

Fair Pay and Conditions of Work

The challenge is not just to expand employment but to expand good employment, to produce more work and better work at the same time. This is an essential part of the message we seek to convey in this report. As well as the growth in unemployment over the past twenty five years, we have also seen, especially in the last five years, an increase in jobs which pay unfairly low wages and involve disgracefully poor conditions of employment. This is what we have been told again and again on our visits. At the same time, therefore, as we call for a substantial change of policy to promote the growth of paid work, we must also call for a new attitude to the quality of the employment relationship and for new policy measures where they are needed to support it.

To illustrate the issues which cause us concern we cannot do better than draw attention to a paper published by the William Temple Foundation. It is called *Invisible Hands - Contract Cleaning: a Theological Reflection* by Margaret Halsey, an industrial missioner in South Yorkshire. It describes a process, typical of recent times, by which an important service, school cleaning in this case, was transferred from stable direct employment to competitive tendering by independent firms. It is about low paid work becoming even more low paid, about women being treated with less consideration then men, about risk to health and safety and about temporary contracts and job insecurity. This does not mean, of course, that the desire to secure greater flexibility in the labour market has all been misguided, but it does draw attention to some side-effects of the process which we find unacceptable.

Work is rightly seen as a form of service to one another, to the community and to the well-being of the world. All those who are called to such service should accept it. But willing service should never become a kind of servitude. The wish to do useful work, indeed the need to earn a living, should never be exploited by employers offering pay and conditions which are unfair and offensive to human dignity.

In this chapter we shall try to translate these grand words into more concrete suggestions for changes in employment rules and practices. But whatever the law and the conventions, there is a prior question about human feelings and motivation. Employment is not just a contract to be negotiated under terms dictated by market forces, it is also a relationship between human beings. Even if the employer is a large and remote corporate enterprise, the manager is a man or woman dealing day-by-day with men and women who work together and know each other, perhaps very well. So good employment practice is not just a matter of abiding by the rules and being fair, it also requires human understanding, sympathy and fellowship. Moreover the rules which govern employment practice will never themselves be right unless they express something of these same human qualities.

The least we should expect of the employment relationship is that it should be fair. This means several different things. It means that procedures for recruitment, promotion, setting pay and conditions of work should all be free of coercion, prejudice or deceit. It also means that the outcome should be equitable and meet certain ethical criteria. The same word 'justice' is used to cover a great variety of moral considerations, about some of which reasonable and well-meaning people will hold different views. We do not claim, as Christians, to have unique access to the principles of justice in the workplace, although the Bible does contain some exceedingly telling examples of injustice and some powerful expressions of concern that the strong should not exploit the weak, or the rich exploit the poor. We shall make use of one of these below.

In a market economy we need to use all the means we can to ensure that the market works in favour of fairness. It is true that a competitive market in itself, under conditions of full employment, can sometimes act as a curb on the worst forms of unfair treatment. Workers who suffer from harrassment or discrimination, for example, may be able to leave their jobs to find a better employer who will pay the same or better wages, if the labour market is competitive. But conditions of perfect competition are not often to be found in practice. The best safeguard therefore for humanity and fairness is usually for employees to be organised and well-informed to make their case, and to bargain collectively with their employers.

Market behaviour is commonly based on self-interest and many companies see it as their duty to pursue corporate, meaning shareholders', self-interest as far as is practicable and legal. For employees to speak, and occasionally to act, collectively from strength provides a necessary countervailing force. The freedom of management to manage must be respected, but also constrained by the possibility of resistance on behalf of the workforce. In particular the weakness of demand in the labour market must never be allowed to drive wages down to levels that are evidently unjust. It is not in fact necessarily in the interests of employers collectively, or the economy as a whole, that wage levels should always be pushed down and down.

Fairness in the market also requires regulation, and the less reliance can be placed on good collective bargaining, the more far-reaching regulation may have to be. The outcome of competition in an open market may be unjust, for example by encouraging child labour in unsafe or unhealthy conditions, as is common now in many parts of the world. Even the most enthusiastic supporters of the market would outlaw some practices, even if they are entered into 'voluntarily' under pressure of hardship or destitution.

But we must also recognise the limitations of the law, especially in the field of employment. Laws must be enforceable, or they should not be enacted. There must be some means of establishing when the rules are broken and making those concerned answer for what they have done. There must be sufficient support from public opinion for the principles involved. It must be demonstrable that the social benefits of regulations justify the interference and expense. This usually means supporting the practices of good employers, and enlisting their help in reforming, or eliminating, the bad.

Fair Pay

The dispersion of wages has widened significantly in Britain in recent years, more so than at any time in this century. The Joseph Rowntree Foundation Inquiry into Income and Wealth reported changes between the late 1970s and the early 1990s. Hourly wages for the lowest paid men hardly changed after allowing for price inflation, medium wages grew by 35 per cent and high wages by 50 per cent. The Gini Coefficient, which measures income inequalities, after a long period which it remained almost constant, increased dramatically by 10 percentage points between 1977 and 1991. At the same time the proportion of the population in receipt of low pay increased because more part-time jobs were being created, especially for women, and often at very low hourly rates indeed. In terms of household earned incomes the dispersion was further widened by the increasing numbers of two-earner or no-earner, rather than one-earner, households. Employment was declining in traditional highly-paid occupations (skilled work in manufacturing for example) and increasing in lower-paid occupations (security guards for example).

The current position in relation to low pay can be summarised by looking at the percentage of workers earning less than £3.50 an hour. For men working full time the percentages are low (5½ per cent for manual workers, 2 per cent for non-manual). For men working part-time they are considerably higher (38 per cent for manual and 18 per cent for non-manual). Low pay on this definition is much more common for women, even when working full time (24 per cent for manual, 4 per cent for non-manual) but highest of all for women working part-time (40 per cent for manual and 15 per cent for non-manual). These figures are taken from the New Earnings Survey, which is likely to underestimate the numbers on low pay, especially those doing temporary or casual work.

In the context of unemployment it is important also to look at the job vacancies being advertised, not just the pay of those now in work. In February 1994 a national survey showed that 58 per cent of vacancies at Job Centres, more than half the jobs on offer, were for £3.50 or less; only 15 per cent were for more than £4.50 an hour. (For a rather more comprehensive picture of low pay see the paper by Gabrielle Cox reproduced as Annex B below.)

Many reasons can be given for the increase in the prevalence of low pay. Two very obvious ones are the revoking of the Fair Wage Resolution applied to government contractors and the abolition of Wage Councils in 1993. Privatisation or subcontracting has contributed to low pay in what is or was the public sector. The weakening of trade union power is another factor, as well as the insecurity of individual employment rights. The high level of unemployment together with pressure on the unemployed to accept low paid jobs is no doubt another very important factor. We have also heard it suggested that competition from the unemployed who work illegally helps to drive wages down. More fundamentally the lack of well-paid jobs reflects the same factors as we have considered in relation to unemployment - the mismatch between the skills that are in demand and the skills which most of the working population can offer.

It is against this background that we have to assess the proposals in Britain for a national minimum wage. The economic arguments, for and against, have been well presented elsewhere. There is very real uncertainty what the effects would be. We have heard an atypical employer arguing that it would be beneficial because it would make firms spend more on training. We have also heard an atypical trade unionist saying that, in the public sector at least if expenditure levels stay the same, it can only result in the loss of more jobs. In some parts of the country we have visited, the suggestion of a minimum over £4 an hour is met with a mixture of alarm and incredulity, not just by employers but by the unemployed as well.

The debate about the minimum wage does not turn on such calculations alone. Even if the level was initially set relatively low, the issues of principle are important in their own right. The prevalence of very low pay has increased rapidly in recent years. Legislation now would at least bring that process to a halt, and signal public concern that it was going too far.

We are convinced that some rates of pay are now too low in relation to the cost of living. A national minimum wage is one means of limiting poverty. As such it is, we recognise, a blunt instrument: it would be impossible now to set the rate so high that one earner alone at that rate could support a family. We have to recognise that many households have more than one source of income. Even so purchasing power is a proper consideration in setting pay, as good employers have always recognised. The recent statement of the Catholic Bishops of England and Wales said that 'Employers who pay only the level of wage that the labour market demands, however low, are avoiding their responsibilities for the welfare of their employees'.

In a wealthy society like ours it is scandalous that some people in full-time employment should be living close to the margin of subsistence. The process of bargaining is itself sometimes grossly unfair. Many of the lowest paid workers have no trade union to represent them. Workers do not know enough about the business of their employer to claim a reasonable share of the proceeds of their labour. Frightened of losing their jobs, they accept pay which results in an unduly high rate of profit for the shareholders (or remuneration for the directors) of the firm. Individually they have no bargaining power, and employers will sometimes go to great lengths to prevent them bargaining collectively. These facts about the contemporary labour market convince us of the need for a counter vailing force. A national minimum wage would prevent the worst abuses.

We have also looked at low pay from the viewpoint of the man, or more likely the woman, who receives it. What does it mean to her to be told that her value to society is only £2 an hour? Of course we should say that the pay on offer is not really a true measure of what she is worth to society. She may or may not believe that; but all the rhetoric there has been recently about the need for 'market-testing' and 'performance-related pay' will have conditioned her and her friends to take her value in the market seriously as a measure of her worth. To be unemployed and hoping for a job at say £4 an hour is damaging enough to one's self-esteem. To be obliged to accept a job at half that rate could be much more so. The signal that we would want to send is different. The offer of a job should be a mark of confidence and respect, the beginning of a relationship of co-operation and mutual support. That requires that the rate of pay offered is not insultingly low.

For these reasons we support the introduction of a national minimum wage. To ensure that it is effectively enforced the law should be kept very simple. This may mean that the rate should be the same in all regions and occupations, although the possibility of a lower rate for trainees merits consideration. The point has been made to us that a minimum wage per hour is difficult to reconcile with piecework or payment by results. Our response is that the incentive element in pay should refer only to the part which is above a decent minimum. Even a worker of limited productivity deserves to be paid an adequate wage.

If the rate is set by a Commission, we would suggest that representatives of the unemployed should be included on it as well as employers and employees. Obviously it will need to be reviewed every year to preserve its relationship with other incomes and to reflect experience of its initial impact on employment as well as pay in general. If a national minimum wage is introduced it will be essential that workers who now receive pay above that level do not seek to maintain their differentials. The likelihood of this happening varies from one sector to another, with the main risk of 'knock-on' increases being in the public sector. Provided that such effects are avoided, the consequences of a minimum wage for cost inflation in the economy as a whole should be small.

So much for pay at the lower end of the distribution. We need also to react as a society to what is happening at the upper extreme. Is it fair that the rich are getting so much richer? Or is this also a process to which society should call a halt? The Catholic Bishops' Statement includes the words

> 'There must come a point at which the scale of the gap between the very wealthy and those at the bottom of the range of income begins to undermine the common good. This is the point at which society starts to be run for the benefit of the rich, not for all its members.'

The issue is somewhat complicated by the need to examine the whole package of remuneration, to look at shareholdings as well as pay, and so on. This makes the actual figure work difficult, but it hardly changes the initial observation. Certainly the market is rewarding the hardworking, the able and the fortunate, not to mention the ambitious or the unscrupulous, to a much greater degree than it did even ten years ago. Should this be a cause for concern?

We do feel concern for two reasons. First, we are concerned that public recognition of service to the community is being given in a purely financial form. Maybe the directors and chief executives of large companies, or the most expert professionals in banking and commerce, do deserve our gratitude for their contributions to general prosperity. It does not follow that the best way of expressing such gratitude is to allow them to enjoy riches which for most of us are 'beyond the dreams of avarice'. The satisfaction which comes from doing a demanding, stimulating and responsible job is itself a reward. Do they really need to be paid vast sums of money in order to make such jobs attractive? Avarice or greed is a real danger to the spiritual wellbeing both of the rich and of the poor. We do not believe that society should encourage or applaud it.

The second reason for concern is that paying directors or senior management vast salaries can destroy the sense of community within a company. The workforce gets the message that the bosses are in it for what they personally can get out of it, whatever they may say about team spirit or community service. This is especially true when, as has happened in many cases recently, enormous increases in pay at the top coincide with massive redundancies or pay cuts lower down. This betrays insensitivity or indifference towards the feelings of those whose livelihood has been destroyed in the process of corporate reconstruction, whether that reconstruction was necessary for survival or not.

There have been many examples recently of quite clearly excessive pay, not only in industry and commerce, but also in sport and entertainment. We do not think, however, that this is something which can be put right by legislation. Regulation in this area would be relatively easy to avoid or evade. Minimum wages can be enforced if those who are paid less than the minimum are prepared to stand up for their rights. The enforcement of a maximum wage would have to depend on the vigilance of shareholders and auditors whose interests would not be so clearly at stake. The two proposals are not really measures of the same kind. Instead we would like to see a voluntary national code of practice established with the backing of share-holders, employee and consumer representatives as well as responsible directors themselves. Firms could then take pride in publicising their adherence to its principles.

Fair Conditions of Employment

There is a story in the Bible about the way in which the Egyptian task-masters treated the Israelites working on their construction sites.

> 'Pharaoh ordered the people's overseers and their foremen not to supply the people with the straw used in making bricks, as they had done hitherto. 'Let them go out and collect their own straw, but let them produce the same tally of bricks as before. On no account reduce it. They are a lazy people... Keep the men hard at work; let them attend to that and take no notice of a pack of lies!' (Exodus 5:6-9).

Such oppression brought the judgement of God down on the Egyptians, and the Israelites were set free.

The drive to increase productivity and reduce labour costs in our society today can result in situations not altogether different from that described in this story. There is the same incremental tightening of conditions which are already onerous; expectations are raised beyond what is really achievable; hours of work are progressively increased; the results which were once achieved for a brief period as a result of an all-out effort are expected to be repeated every day. Employees who are in a weak bargaining position are unable to protest.

We cannot, in a report of this length, document all the examples of bad employment conditions and unfair treatment of workers that have come to our notice. We would commend a publication prepared by one of our members, Gabrielle Cox, from the Greater Manchester Low Pay Unit and called *Workers' Voices: Accounts of Working Life in Britain in the Nineties*. It allows twelve workers to describe in their own words what they have experienced at what might be called the cheap end of the labour market. It is an account of hardship and injustice which many people will recognise, but which others would prefer not to know about.

The labour market generally is in a state of turmoil in which people are unsure what constitutes good practice. The decentralisation of personnel management means that responsibility for conditions of work may fall to line managers with little or no experience in this area. The decline in the influence of trade unions has left individuals to fend for themselves, often without the benefit of any professional advice at all. Many businesses and individual workers do thrive in this less formal environment, but it also results in a multitude of individual disputes, which cause personal unhappiness as well as interfering with the running of the business itself.

One indicator of conflict at work is the number of individuals' conciliation cases handled by the Advisory, Conciliation and Arbitration Services, ACAS. These have risen from 52,071 in 1990 to 91,568 in 1995. The largest part of the caseload is formed by allegations of unfair dismissal. Similarly the Citizens Advice Bureaux report that they are dealing with increasing levels of employment problems. Employment enquiries numbered 839,816 in 1993/4. Over a five-year period in the late 80s and early 90s the case load increased by 31 per cent (although it appears to have eased back somewhat since the end of the recession).

One category of workers who seem to be getting a particularly raw deal are homeworkers, whose rate of pay is often under £1 an hour. One of the members of our working party, Dian Leppington of the Leeds Industrial Mission, has observed their conditions of work closely over a period of many years. Often the work is organised locally by sub-contractors, but the firms for whom it is done may be well-known high-street stores, or indeed national charities. That firm may not know, indeed may prefer not to know, about the conditions of work for the people who actually make or assemble the products they sell. In most cases it would be much better if the 'middlemen' were cut out. Apart from the very low rates of pay, there are many other ways in which the organisation of home working is unacceptable. Frequently there is no written agreement at all, so rates of pay or required standards of performance can be changed unilaterally without notice. The work is often unsafe and unhealthy.

Work processes which could be carried out safely in a factory become potentially dangerous when undertaken at home where space is limited and shared with children and other family members. The flow of work is unpredictable and the receipt of any payment at all is by no means certain. The lack of available and affordable childcare is the reason given by many women who work from home. Yet women often find trying to combine homeworking with childcare a difficult and stressful combination, as they are unable to give attention to the needs of the child and at the same time to their work. Good quality, affordable childcare is a priority for many people who want to be part of the mainstream labour market.

The increase in the numbers of those combining family responsibilities with paid work, as well as the development of facilities for 'teleworking', probably mean that more and more work will be done at home. This will raise issues for many aspects of employment conditions. We believe that home-workers should be treated like the rest of the workforce, and that the law should be amended if necessary to bring this about. They should, where possible be given employee status, with proper contracts of employment, entitlement to National Insurance benefits, paid holidays and protection from unfair dismissal. Most homeworkers now have none of these. They occupy a position on the margins of the labour force and their plight is only a little better than that of the long-term unemployed.

The growth of temporary work and self-employment has excluded a substantial proportion of the workforce from various employment rights. Many temporary jobs are for less than two years and thus deny workers the right to claim unfair dismissal or redundancy pay. Although there has been a recent decision to the contrary, agency workers have customarily not been considered to be employees of either the agency or the hiring business, and thus are excluded from all employment rights. Some employers are now claiming that workers who by any objective test should be regarded as employees are actually self-employed, again excluding them from employment protection.

We regard as unacceptable the way in which the rights of all workers to claim unfair dismissal have been eroded. During the 1980s the length of service required before an unfair dismissal claim could be lodged was raised from six months to a year and then to two years. This means that all workers with less than two years' service can be dismissed at an employer's whim without redress of any kind. (There are some exceptions to the two-year service rule, mainly in relation to sex and race discrimination and trade union activity.) We have heard of workers being dismissed just before their second anniversary of engagement and taken on again just after it. The government recently undertook a consultation on the proposal that the right to claim unfair dismissal should be removed completely from employees of small firms. We are encouraged to note that employers have overwhelmingly rejected this proposal. We would support moves to give all employees protection against unfair dismissal after a short probationary period.

There is no legal right in Britain to any paid holidays, whether annual leave or Bank Holidays - a situation which is unique in Europe. Increasing numbers of workers have no contractual right to any holidays. We therefore welcome the Working Time Directive which when implemented should give all workers the right to three weeks (and ultimately four weeks) paid holiday per year. The Working Time Directive is also important in relation to its provisions for limiting working hours and ensuring that workers have breaks.

This is a vital area given that few workers (drivers are an exception) have any statutory right to breaks during the working day, and indeed such statutory rights as used to exist (for example under the Shops Act) have been removed. We are concerned that in 1990 the prohibition on 16 and 17 year olds working at night was removed, along with a 44 hour limit on the hours they could work each week. We would support a reintroduction of the ban on night-work and a non-negotiable limit to the working week for young people.

Some employers are adopting increasingly exploitative 'penalty' clauses within contracts. The law needs to be strengthened to protect workers from such punitive contractual terms. Whilst it is unlawful for employers to change employees' contracts without their agreement it is usually difficult for employees to have any legal redress for such changes unless they involve a monetary loss, and even then the onus is on the employee to take individual action to claim illegal deductions from wages at either an Industrial Tribunal or a Small Claims court. We would welcome a strengthening of employment law to ensure that unilateral changes in employment conditions could be penalised through a system of fines and compensations.

Trade Unions and Employment Law

We have already emphasised the importance we attach to trying to strengthen the bargaining position of the weak in the market place. During 1996 an enquiry reported to the Fabian Society on employment relations in a changing labour market. Clive Brooke, who is a member of our working party, also took part in that enquiry. We support what is said in their report about the need for consultative arrangements which are 'efficient, consistent, adaptable, clear in their purpose and have the commitment of all those workers in their implementation'. We also agree that such arrangements 'are likely to be enhanced by trade union mediation'. Indeed we think that in most circumstances arrangements for employee consultations and negotiations over pay and conditions should include representation by one or more trade unions.

Trade unions in Britain now seem uncertain about their role. They represent some 30 per cent of the workforce, a significant proportion, but a minority. They have been under sustained attack from government and many employers for nearly sixteen years. The structure of the economy, with the decline of heavy industry, large employers and the public sector, has changed in ways which would, in any case, have required a new style of unionisation. According to a survey reported in *Social Trends 1996*, employees now look to their unions to protect existing jobs rather than to improve their pay or conditions. Their ambitions, both in terms of negotiating power and political influence, are now much more modest than they were a generation ago. It is possible in fact that they have become **too** modest.

One way in which pay and conditions of work for the least-well-treated workers in Britain could be improved would be for the union movement to organise them and negotiate on their behalf. Obviously this is a great challenge to the unions, since it would involve dealing with very large numbers of small employers, in an environment which might well be hostile to them. But in many ways this is a more attractive route than the alternative of detailed regulation and enforcement of individual rights through the courts of law. In any case a network of trade union representatives should be the best and least cumbersome means of bringing pressure to bear on employers to ensure that they abide by whatever regulations there are.

There is a long tradition of support for responsible trade unionism in the churches. The spirit of co-operation has a strong appeal to Christians, provided it is not just the solidarity of one group to improve its own position at the expense of others. Very recently this support has been confirmed by the Roman Catholic Bishops of England and Wales in their statement on *The Common Good*. In particular we align ourselves with the following passages:

'The Church's social teaching has always deplored an 'us and them' attitude between managers and workforce. Industrial relations should not be organised in a way that fosters such confrontational attitudes. On the one hand, it is possible for employers to be unfairly disadvantaged by an imbalance in the relative economic strength of each side in negotiation, for instance when a trade union exploits a monopoly control of the supply of labour. On the other hand, trade union activity is sometimes a necessary corrective to managerial policies which are devoted purely to profit, regardless of the interests of workers. There can be a substantial imbalance of economic power between an isolated individual employee and a large employer, and this imbalance is not corrected merely by the fact that the employee has entered into a contract. Contracts between unequal parties are a potent source of structural injustice.' (para 93)

'Trade unions have a role in correcting this imbalance, and membership of a union is a right the Church upholds as a manifestation of the principle of solidarity and the right of association...We do not think the decline in union membership in recent years is necessarily a healthy sign, and we note that it is paralleled by a high degree of dissatisfaction with their working lives that many ordinary people express.' (para 94)

'Employers are not entitled to negate the right to join a union by refusing to have any dealings with union representatives. Where a majority of employees in a particular work group opt to be represented by their union for collective bargaining, it is unreasonable of an employer to refuse that demand. In certain circumstances the law may have to intervene to protect these rights.' (para 95)

'At the same time, unions which are granted legal protection or a special legal status have a duty to conduct their affairs in accordance with the common good...They must also take a responsible view of the profitability and financial viability of their employer.' (para 96)

We support the view that employers should be required to negotiate with a union where a majority of the workers concerned wish it. At the same time we recognise that the form of negotiation adopted should take account of the rights of those workers who are not union members and whose views or interests may be different. We think that it is of the essence of the working person's human dignity, that he or she have means to express views and negotiate terms and conditions as equally as possible with their employer.

The Fabian Society report also makes the point that employment law needs to be clarified and made more easily comprehensible to both employers and employees. People want to know where they stand. In some cases a fixed-term contract of employment is the right solution. Sometimes it would be imprudent or unrealistic for an employer to offer permanent work, for example where the continuation of the job is dependent on raising new finance - a very common situation today. Equally the employee may have no intention of staying for more than a brief period and that fact should not be concealed from the employer.

It is a matter of dispute amongst labour economists whether employment protection increases or decreases the number of jobs in the economy. Clearly it makes it more difficult for firms to lay-off staff in a recession, but it also makes them less eager to take on staff in an upturn. A recent paper by Julian Morgan of the National Institute of Economic and Social Research based on the study of seven European countries concludes that on balance employment protection increases the level of employment on average over the cycle.

Many firms cover the dismissal of employees who do not perform well by stretching the definition of 'redundancy' almost to breaking point. This causes distress and leads to unnecessary disputes. Well-defined but limited rights to security of tenure for the duration of a contract would seem more fair to both sides. The old days of the 'gentleman's agreement' have long passed away. Part of being a considerate employer is to be open and explicit about the extent of the commitment one is able to take on.

Meanwhile, until the law is comprehensively revised we feel that the existing rules should be applied more firmly. When a dispute arises over dismissal, the job could be frozen until it is resolved. A more effective means should be found of monitoring and enforcing all aspects of employment law so as to reduce the number of disputes which end up in Industrial Tribunals. One possibility would be the setting up of a Labour Inspectorate which would also oversee the implementation of a statutory minimum wage. We believe that this and other options require urgent consideration.

Discrimination at Work

Throughout this report we have emphasised that people should treat one another fairly, and even generously, simply by virtue of our common humanity. In the first place it is a matter of justice; but beyond that it is an expression of concern for the good of the whole community and every individual in it. This is especially true in relation to divisions of society by age or sex, disability, race or religion. It is an acute problem for ex-offenders and those with a history of mental illness. Discrimination is to be found in most aspects of life, but discrimination at work has proved especially difficult to root out. A free and flexible labour market ought in principle to give everyone an equal chance of success. But that is not how things work out in fact. Market behaviour reflects the prejudices of the people who make up the market.

Good employers are aware of the need to monitor the composition of their workforce and ensure that no-one is excluded from the workplace or denied access to training and promotion because of prejudice and stereotyping. The Institute of Personnel and Development has recently launched an initiative on 'managing diversity' to draw attention to the many possible dimensions of such unfair discrimination. We applaud such voluntary action, but question whether, on its own, it is enough.

Unfair discrimination by age is an increasing problem, which makes it virtually impossible for the many who lose their jobs in middle age to find any comparable paid work at all. The convention used to be that workers who were past their peak in physical strength or in mental agility were given less arduous tasks by the employer that they had served in their youth. Now they are more likely to be 'let go' with a small pension. The Carnegie Inquiry into the Third Age has demonstrated that the middle-aged make good employees, better in many respects than their juniors. It has also documented how difficult it is to get that message across to employers. We do not believe that putting pressure on older workers to retire early is an appropriate or effective way of creating jobs for the young. The message of this report is, of course, that there should be enough good work for all. Laws against 'ageism' in the United States may have helped in that country to slow down the trend towards premature and involuntary retirement. Some progress is being made in this country with voluntary codes of practice especially in the advertising of vacancies. But the option of legislating should also be seriously considered.

Discrimination in employment between men and women is against the law, but still widespread. In low-paid work men may now feel that employers are choosing women in preference to them, but when it comes to promotion the old prejudices die hard. There is evidence of a 'glass ceiling' in many professions which even the most able women cannot often break through. In visiting some firms ourselves where skilled engineering is done we were struck by how, even today, so few of the better-paid staff were female.

This is one of the issues to which we wish that we could have devoted more time in the course of this enquiry. Another is discrimination in employment against people with physical or mental disabilities. This is topical in Britain because of the Disability Discrimination Act which came into force in 1996. The first point made to us by a member of Church Action on Disability was that the churches' own record, as employers and as 'service providers' leaves a great deal to be desired. The second point was that the churches need to develop a theology which learns from the experience of people who find themselves disabled. The third point was that discrimination is shown, not just in individual prejudice but in the social system itself: for example, people whose mobility is impaired become disabled if society choses to live and work in buildings with no level access.

The Employers' Forum on Disability, an organisation with over 200 members, employing some 16 per cent of the workforce in the UK, promotes equal opportunities for disabled people. It helps employers to set new standards in best practice and promotes the business as well as the social benefits which result from employing people with disabilities.

The Disability Discrimination Act creates a 'right of non-discrimination' in employment. Its main weakness is that people who are disabled must seek their own remedy in the courts. There is no agency like the Equal Opportunities Commission which will take action on their behalf. Employers have a duty under the Act to provide a 'reasonable' adjustment to working conditions or the working environment to overcome the practical effects of a disability. The Act does not apply to organisations with fewer than 20 employees. No financial provision is made to help employers meet the costs of complying with the Act, which many will claim are prohibitive.

This new legislation replaces the quota system under which organisations had a duty to have at least 3 per cent of their workforce registered as disabled. The main problem was that it was not enforced. Moreover people with moderate but increasing impairment were often reluctant to register themselves as disabled. It remains to be seen whether the Disability Discrimination Act will be any better enforced and whether it will in fact make the quota system redundant - we doubt if it will.

In 1995/96 11 per cent of the working age population (3.9 million) in Britain were disabled. Of these 40 per cent were economically active - that is either employed or looking for work. The unemployment rate for people with disabilities was 21 per cent, compared with 7½ per cent for the rest of the workforce. This is a very large difference which we believe could be narrowed substantially if the intention to eliminate discrimination were actually carried out.

We are particularly concerned about access to work for people who have suffered from mental illness. Their needs are not just the responsibility of the health and social services, but also of government, employers and the whole community. Work is crucial in the process of re-integrating people who are recovering from mental illness back into their society, but too often prejudicial attitudes from the public and employers exclude them from employment. A number of voluntary organisations have projects which help with the process of re-integration but they need the active support of employers as well if they are to succeed.

Racial Discrimination

Discrimination by race is a very serious problem in Britain, actually getting worse in recent years. It is associated with racism, an ideology fundamentally inconsistent with Christian belief. Racial justice depends on access to employment. Nothing will change for people from the black and ethnic minority communities until they have an economic stake in society.

An article in the official publication *Labour Market Trends* for June 1996 gave unemployment figures by ethnic origin for men and women. At that time the latest figures were 9½ per cent for white men and 6½ per cent for white women; the corresponding figure for men and women from ethnic minorities were 20 per cent and 17 per cent - a vast and shocking difference. For Bangladeshi men and women the unemployment rate was extraordinarily high at over 40 per cent.

To learn more about this important aspect of our enquiry we held a meeting with members of the Churches' Commission for Racial Justice (CCRJ). They are encouraging companies to support the Wood-Sheppard Principles, named after the Bishop of Croydon, Wilfred Wood and the Bishop of Liverpool, David Sheppard. These principles were drawn up by Race Equality in Employment, a project of the Ecumenical Committee for Corporate Responsibility. They are a model for 'positive action' to give people from ethnic minorities fair and effective access to work and not 'positive discrimination' which would be against the law. In brief companies should:

i)   adopt a detailed Equal Opportunity Policy
ii)   declare an intention to increase employment of black and minority ethnic workers where they are under-represented
iii)   undertake positive action to offset any imbalance
iv)   monitor the ethnic composition of the workforce regularly
v)   use fair recruitment and selection procedures
vi)   provide training for employees and potential recruits
vii)   where equal opportunities are not fully in place, designate an Equal Opportunities Manager
viii)   make racial and religious harassment serious disciplinary offences
ix)   publish an annual employee profile with the Annual Report
x)   seek actively for a professionally qualified minority ethnic board member.

It is important that senior management should take direct responsibility for implementing these principles. Otherwise it is far too easily delegated to some-one in a junior position, who may be over-burdened with other routine tasks and who does not have the status or 'weight' in the firm to overcome opposition or inertia.

The meaning of 'positive action' was spelt out by Paul Riddell of the Commission for Racial Equality (CRE) to a conference on the 'Economic Empowerment of the Black Community' organised for the British Council of Churches in 1990. He said:

'The term 'positive action' is a concept of equality held on the belief that racial discrimination and disadvantage are and have always been a fact of life for ethnic minorities in Britain... The White Paper on Racial Discrimination, which introduced the 1976 Race Relations Act (RRA) recognised these facts and therefore the Act needed to contain measures to both stop discrimination and redress inequalities between members of different racial groups... The RRA contains three provisions that directly relate to positive action, all of which may be used at the discretion of an organisation.'

These three provisions allow companies to encourage employees and potential employees from particular ethnic groups to apply for jobs and promotion. They also allow companies to provide training to people who are members of racial groups that have been under-represented in particular areas of work. We have heard of employers who are concerned that black people are under-represented in their workforce and who have used pre-recruitment courses as a way of solving that problem. We wish that the practice was much more widespread.

Members of the CCRJ said that the market does not work fairly for people from ethnic minorities. Young black people ask what is the point of education when many black people have achieved educational qualifications and still have no jobs. They need to believe that there is something in society to which they can aspire. Richard Crowson of the Church of England Board for Social Responsibility, and a former local authority race equality officer, said that the attempts made to combat racism in employment, especially in local authority employment in the 1970s and 1980s were not generally successful and political support for effective action was now lacking. The black communities, especially young black men, are becoming more alienated and, although the problem in Britain is not as serious as in American cities, it is getting worse all the time. A Government report in early 1995 showed 62 per cent of young black men, aged 16 to 24, in London, out of work.

Members of the CCRJ drew our attention to the legislation against religious discrimination in Northern Ireland as a possible model for tougher laws against racial, as well as religious, discrimination in the United Kingdom as a whole. On our visit to Belfast we learnt about the implementation of the 1976 and 1989 Acts and the role of the Fair Employment Commission (see chapter 3 above). It is clear that this very tough approach to discrimination has made a real difference to the behaviour of some large employers in the province. The direct costs of compliance are said to be low and often the actions taken by firms to reform recruitment and promotion procedures are no more than good management practice anywhere would prescribe. We also heard however that some firms were adopting the letter rather than the spirit of fair employment. It was suggested that some employers found the required procedures burdensome and bureaucratic. If mishandled such comprehensive regulations could actually make community relations worse, rather than better.

The lessons to be learnt for race relations in Britain from this experience deserve more detailed study. One problem could be the geographical coverage of any new legislation. Would it be right for example for the same monitoring requirements to apply throughout the country irrespective of the racial composition of the population? Would the law apply to all minority groups collectively or each group separately? The principles behind the Northern Ireland legislation seem to us right, and they could apply to race as well as religious discrimination. The issues which require further study concern the best means of implementing these principles in a very different context. The CRE has proposed ethnic monitoring of the workforce of larger employers, as the law requires for example in Holland. That might be a sensible first step to take. Some new initiative is required or discrimination will continue, and its consequences may get worse.

The Good Employer

In 1996 the European Christian employers' organisation, Uniapac, published a report called *Committed Entrepreneurial Action against Unemployment.* It contained ten guidelines, aimed at generating more and better jobs.

'i)   Stimulate greater commitment and imagination to securing employment for the young;
ii)   Recognise continuous training as a necessary personal investment and promote it;
iii)   Provide more comprehensive information so as to secure acceptance of realities and safeguard jobs;
iv)   Introduce new types of organisations and partnership in the workforce so as to increase productivity;
v)   Secure agreement on flexible working times and flexible remuneration as a means of preserving, and even increasing, the number of jobs;
vi)   Examine all feasible solutions before resorting to dismissal: see dismissal as a solution of last resort;
vii)   Make available all information on immediate job opportunities so as to minimise short-term unemployment;
viii)   Involve the labour authorities in a new tripartite 'supporting labour contract' that gives the long-term unemployed a fair chance;
ix)   Change labour laws to ensure that they help to promote employment rather than constitute barriers to the creation of new jobs;
x)   Encourage entrepreneurship at all levels of society.'

As one member of our working party put it:

'Social justice, provision and maintenance of employment must be seen as part of an organisation's goals. It cannot be at any cost. However firms will and quite legitimately can seek to maintain employment levels.'

We shall return to some of these issues, especially the provision of training, in later sections of this report. But the main point to emphasise here is the recognition in the Uniapac statement of the employer's responsibility to provide more good jobs and not just to make money for the shareholders. It is not just a responsibility to safeguard existing jobs, which many employers would recognise, but also a responsibility to increase the number of jobs with a special concern for the young and the long-term unemployed. There has been much debate in Britain in the last few years about the objectives and governance of companies. Strictly the law is that directors should serve the interests of the company, which is interpreted to mean the shareholders. Fortunately, few companies are in fact run in accordance with that precise interpretation of the law, but there is no doubt that the interests of shareholders have been given far higher priority recently than they were say twenty years ago.

If the challenge that we see in the future of work is to be given an adequate response, then employers must play the major part. They are the ones who can actually create good jobs and we believe that they should see that as one of their most important social functions. Many do so now and they need affirming in that belief and practice in the face of pressure to be less good employers if that would produce better financial returns. It is, of course, a perennial subject of debate whether being a good employer also serves the interests of shareholders in the longer term. In many cases it clearly does, so that there is no conflict of interest to be resolved. It has been said recently that 'downsizing' has been taken too far and is now destroying the expertise and teamwork within companies on which corporate growth depends. This may well be true and we hope that more companies will take this warning seriously. All the same we would like to comment also on the more difficult cases where a conflict of interest really does arise. The Uniapac guidelines say that dismissal should be 'a solution of last resort'. Yet when redundancies are announced by a firm its share price often rises. We would want to support Uniapac in this case against the stock market. Firms should not see their function in purely financial terms and sometimes they should do things which do not maximise their profits, either short-term or long-term. Firms have moral responsibilities as well as legal ones.

In saying this we recognise that competition between firms, for markets and for capital, both at home and abroad, can mean that putting the public interest first would threaten their survival. To be a good employer is usually in the long-term interest of the firm. It reinforces the loyalty of the staff and helps to attract high quality recruits. But this is not the whole of the story. Sometimes hard choices do have to be made. Sometimes employees do have to be made redundant, for example, even in firms which would much prefer to be good employers. The alternative, sometimes, really is for the whole business to collapse. Those who have to carry out such decisions deserve our sympathy - as well, of course, as the people who lose their jobs as a result.

Whenever possible firms should not be put into such positions. The system of taxation and regulation should be such as to bring the public interest and the conditions for the survival of good employers as closely as possible into line. This will require regulation in some areas to prevent the bad employers stealing a march on the good. In other areas it is unlikely to be achieved without a strong trade union presence. When the threat comes from international competition however, a contraction of employment in this or that industry may well be inevitable. What those who are made redundant in such circumstances most need is the hope of a good new job. That is something which we as a society should provide for them, when their old employer has done all that can be done to help.

The good employer of the future will not be quite the same paternal figure as has been associated with that term in the past. Workers accept more responsibility nowadays and expect more freedom of action. Long-term stable employment relationships are still right for some occupations, but not for all. Employers who offer short-term contracts have a different relationship to their employees from employers for life, with different expectations on both sides. It is not a case of one being good and the other bad: either can be a good relationship in its own terms.

Similar points could be made about regulation of the labour market more generally, including the national minimum wage. These are costs which fall on employers and risk destroying jobs by making the goods and services they produce too expensive. As we indicated in chapter 5 above the structure of taxation should be changed so that employers pay less of it and consumers or those on high incomes pay more. There would be justice in that too.

Chapter Seven

Work for the Unemployed

The main reason why there is so much unemployment is that there is not enough demand for labour, or at least for labour of the kind most people can supply. The main cure for unemployment, as we have suggested in chapter 5, is to expand employment, concentrating on particular sectors, regions and occupations. An expansion of that kind is necessary, but it may not be sufficient. The problem almost certainly needs to be tackled from the supply side as well. Even when employment opportunities have increased there will still be some people who, for one reason or another, are unable to find good jobs. These are the people most at risk of long-term unemployment. Moreover the fact that people have been out of work for a long time is itself a serious handicap in the labour market. In this section we consider what could be done to help them.

Long-term Unemployment

Too often society blames the victims of unemployment. Certainly some of the long-term unemployed blame themselves for their situation and many feel themselves stigmatised and rejected. Such attitudes are totally wrong. They are wrong because long-term unemployment is a trap into which anyone could fall and it is the fault of the system that this trap is there. They are wrong also because even those who have contributed in some way to their own misfortune would in any decent society be given a chance to start afresh. There is a vigorous debate under way at present in our countries and around the world about how best to cope with the problem of long-term unemployment. What is needed is imagination and generosity of heart.

The emphasis of recent policy initiatives in Britain and elsewhere has been on helping the long-term unemployed to look for work. They are being given advice about such things as writing CVs and preparing for job interviews. No doubt that is important, but it clearly is not enough. In fact the offers of help are all too often seen by the long-term unemployed as society putting pressure on them to look for jobs which do not exist or apply for jobs that they have no realistic prospect of getting. What we would like them to be given instead is an offer of real work on reasonable pay which they could be confident of doing well.

We are talking about real work, not just 'work experience'. There should be a real need to be met as well as a real chance to use one's abilities. It should also provide a real chance to move on to more permanent work and full integration into the labour force once more. We certainly do not want to perpetuate a kind of 'second-class' employment outside the mainstream of the economy. Many jobs today are for a fixed period, so it is not unreasonable for job offers to the long-term unemployed to be for a fixed period as well. But for those who do need job offers created especially for them again and again, there should be plenty of opportunities to come back for more.

No doubt some of the work provided for the long-term unemployed will be at the expense of work for others. It would, of course, be totally unacceptable for employers to lay off staff deliberately so as to benefit from special inducements to hire the long-term unemployed. It should be possible to stop that happening. More indirect effects will occur however which it will be impossible in practice to trace or to prevent. For example an expanding business may choose a long-term unemployed worker in preference to other candidates for a new job because the state makes it worthwhile to do so. Moreover a business that takes on labour on preferential terms may then compete successfully against other rival businesses which do not. If all that help for the long-term unemployed could do was to shorten the average duration of unemployment that would in itself be worthwhile. However it can almost certainly do more than that. As we said in chapter 5 above many economists believe that reducing the average duration of unemployment is a means of reducing unemployment in total.

People who are long-term unemployed are a very varied group. It is unlikely that the same kind of help will be appropriate for them all. The situation is also very different in different regions. In some parts there really is no general shortage of work on offer; elsewhere there are almost no vacancies at all. So some of the help might consist of enabling the long-term unemployed to take up jobs which are waiting for them, and some of the help would have to involve creating jobs which would not otherwise exist at all. Similarly the situation will change from year to year and it is necessary to plan ahead. Under conditions of boom it should be possible to place virtually all the long-term unemployed in work. It would be rash to say that the same could be done in the lean years at the tail-end of a recession. We are not trying to design just one 'scheme' that will solve all our problems. What is needed is a variety of measures brought together to give the long-term unemployed a fresh start.

All the evidence suggests that most of the long-term unemployed are able and willing to work. The Wise Group, based in Glasgow, described to us their considerable experience of providing work, mainly maintenance and construction on public sector housing estates. They find that roughly three-quarters of the people they take on are perfectly capable of doing the jobs they are given. About half find more permanent employment later on. Some are quite as effective at work as the average manual worker in employment, and need only to overcome the real or imagined disadvantages that result from a long period out of work; others are perfectly employable but need their skills upgraded. Of the quarter who did not manage to complete the tasks satisfactorily some had health problems or addictions to drugs or drink. Most of them needed help of some other kind in addition to offers of work.

We also learnt a great deal about the problems of the long-term unemployed from talking to people in churches and Christian organisations who give them counselling or operate some of the existing schemes with statutory funding. The same message comes from many different regions. The long-term unemployed suffer from depression and loss of self-esteem. They have experienced repeated rejection and come to believe that they will never succeed. If someone is able to give them a sympathetic hearing and encouragement, they are themselves astonished at what they can do. The first need is to make contact, because many of the long-term unemployed are effectively housebound and unlikely to respond to anything except a well-judged personal approach. This may be more effective coming from a church or a voluntary organisation than it would be coming from an official of a government agency.

We have tried to find out whether there are many amongst the long-term unemployed who actually prefer not to work. It is not an easy question to answer. Certainly there are people who will not, or can not, accept work which pays less than their benefit entitlement. (We discuss the so-called 'unemployment trap' in the next chapter of this report.) We have also come across cases of people who are probably being rather unrealistic in looking only for work of a kind that they are unlikely to find. It was suggested to us that people in some communities have now adjusted to a way of life in which paid work has almost no part. They have learned to compensate to some degree for not having the sense of purpose, social contact and achievement which most of us get from our job. This is not at all surprising, nor should they be criticised for it. It is unrealistic to imagine that people could devote themselves full-time to looking for work after years of failing to find it. It does not at all mean that they would reject offers of good work if they were made to them.

Measures to Help the Long-Term Unemployed

The detail of measures is important as well as their strategic design. The way in which schemes to help the long-term unemployed are implemented is important as well as the wording of the legislation. In this area of policy especially, the Christian imperatives for justice and for compassion apply to the small print as well as the large, to the junior official as well as the Government minister. That is why we feel it right to cover some issues in this enquiry which may seem too 'technical' to have a place in a report by a church working party.

The state and its officials acting on behalf of us all should treat people who are long-term unemployed as we would all wish to be treated ourselves should we be in the same position. That, according to Jesus, sums up the teaching of the Law and the prophets (Matthew, Chapter 7 verse 12). The job offers should be offers of work we would be willing in the same circumstances to take on ourselves. The pay on offer should be such as we would ourselves think it right to be paid. Not all of the schemes that have been implemented in Britain by successive governments would pass that test. Some of the schemes now being proposed would certainly fail it.

Several people who we have met speak with regret of the passing of the Community Programme. This was a scheme in the 1980s which offered work to the long-term unemployed on projects run by local authorities and voluntary organisations. It built up to a quarter of a million places in 1987, of which three-quarters were part-time. Many churches and Christian organisations were heavily involved in its implementation. It paid 'the rate for the job' and some work of real value to the community was carried out. It is now criticised by some as being too expensive. Some of the projects were not well run and some of the work done was not really needed, but it did provide a stepping stone back into regular employment for many unemployed people at the time.. Reports we have heard of Government training schemes for the long-term unemployed in the past are generally less favourable. They are seen as leading nowhere, of raising false expectations of skilled employment. Some say that they have been no more than a means of disguising the true level of unemployment.

'Project Work' is being tested out during the period of our enquiry. It involves projects rather like those of the Community Programme, but instead of the normal wage participants receive their benefit payments plus a small premium. It is seen therefore as a way of working for benefit rather than a way of getting off benefit altogether. Moreover participation in the projects is compulsory and those who fail to turn up for work will be penalised. It is seen not so much as a way of getting necessary work done as a means of identifying the 'workshy' and excluding them from claiming benefits. We know of many charitable organisations who have refused to become involved with the project for precisely that reason.

The Labour Party has made job creation for young people and the long-term unemployed one of its priority commitments if it wins the general election. Under the slogan 'A New Deal for a Lost Generation' it has put forward a programme to reform training for 16 to 18 year olds and to provide four options for those aged 18 to 24 who have been unemployed for more than six months. The options are: full-time education; employment with a tax rebate for the employer; a voluntary sector job or a placement with the Environmental Task Force. There will be no 'fifth option' of benefit. The cost of these measures will be met either by running down existing programmes or from the proceeds of a 'windfall tax' on the privatised utilities.

As earlier chapters of this report have already implied, we do not regard this on its own as an adequate response to the challenge which we face as a society to find good work for everyone to do. In the particular context of this chapter, the programme certainly has some merits, building on the experience of current schemes and making use of ideas developed by several research groups described below. However one aspect of the Labour Party proposals themselves causes us serious concern. This is the lack of the 'fifth option', after just six months of unemployment. We discuss the issue of compulsion in a more general context below.

Of the many other proposals to solve the problem of long-term unemployment now being discussed in Britain, we will comment on four. The first is the 'Right to Work' Bill introduced into parliament by Sir Ralph Howell and Frank Field; the second is the scheme published by the Institute for Public Policy Research (IPPR) and supported by the TUC; the third is called *Regeneration through Work* published by the Centre for Local Economic Strategies; the fourth is the less well-known programme put forward by the Movement for Christian Democracy (MCD) in 1994. A very useful summary of many of the schemes introduced or proposed in Britain can be found in the report of the House of Commons Employment Committee, February 1996, called *The Right to Work/Workfare*.

The Howell-Field proposal is in two parts. The first is relatively orthodox and broadly along the same lines as the existing Workstart scheme. It offers a temporary subsidy to firms who take on the long-term unemployed (in this case those who have been unemployed for just six months would qualify). The more radical proposal involves the abolition of all benefit paid to the unemployed. Instead they would be able to work at a special 'work centre' at the rate of £3 an hour. Those who preferred not to work would not be compelled to do so, but they would be paid only £30 per week, which is only a quarter of what they would be paid for working a 40-hour week. The claim that this scheme would actually save the Government money is based on the assumption that large numbers of people are now defrauding the system by drawing unemployment benefits whilst actually in paid work. The official view is that the scheme would be costly, partly because many of those who were working in the scheme would otherwise have found work for themselves in the private sector.

These proposals were considered in the course of an enquiry by the House of Commons Employment Committee, which recommended in February 1996 that they should be given 'serious attention by Government and others'. The Prime Minister agreed with Sir Ralph Howell that there should be an independent study made of the costings of his schemes. The study was undertaken by National Economic Research Associates, who published their report in December 1996. Two points from that report deserve emphasis. First: 'Sir Ralph's costings assume that 25 per cent of those who would otherwise have been claimant unemployed disappear from the register when confronted with RTW - 'The right to work'.' In other words the scheme is based on the assumption that a quarter of the unemployed do not really want to work, a view which we do not share. Second: 'Sir Ralph emphasises that conditions on RTW would not be attractive, and the vast majority would feel a strong incentive to find a regular job.' In other words the scheme is cheap because no-one would stay on it for a moment longer than they had to.

Our main objection to this and similar schemes is that it could produce a kind of marginalised employment, almost as alienated from the world of real work as unemployment itself. It would be seen as a scheme to 'teach the unemployed a lesson' rather than a means of giving them real assistance. The concept of the 'non-worker' seems particularly objectionable. We do not think that anyone should be written-off in that way, or be allowed to write themselves off either. In effect the scheme is made compulsory for most of the unemployed. For some participants, that alone will transform what might have been good work into a form of servitude. In making these criticisms, of course, we do not underestimate the difficulty of devising any scheme which escapes them.

The IPPR proposal is for half-a-million places on a part-time scheme in the local government sector. The justification for providing only part-time work is one of cost, since the rate for the job is to be paid. It has also been suggested to us that participants would need time off from the scheme to continue looking for a 'real' job. It may be that another reason was that the authors wanted to make a clear distinction between those 'scheme-based' jobs and the jobs done by the ordinary employees of the local authorities or their contractors. Clearly there is a real possibility of conflict here if the regular employees (and trade union members) fear that their jobs are being taken away from them and given to the long-term unemployed. But the existence of a sharp demarcation line would also reduce the perceived status of those who were only employed because of the scheme. Again this is a real dilemma with no obvious solution, which any such scheme must face.

The paper by Dave Summers and Mike Emmerich of the Centre for Local Economic Strategies has similar objectives and makes all the right points about the need to pay proper wages and create real work. It draws on the experience of initiatives in the intermediate labour market like those of the Wise Group which we met on our visit to Scotland. It considers how projects of this kind could be organised on a national basis. It shows great ingenuity in devising a financial framework for such a programme. The whole point of the exercise is to demonstrate how much could be done 'using existing government resources', in other words by transferring money from one budget heading to another. The authors accept this limitation, we assume, because of the prohibition put on new public spending commitments by the leadership of the Labour Party. We do not think that the generosity of our response to the needs of the unemployed should be curtailed in this way. With more money, a larger and better programme could be devised, and we think that would be money well spent.

The Movement for Christian Democracy (led by David Alton MP) published a pamphlet in 1994 called *An End to Unemployment!* by Philip Truscott and others (foreword by John Philpott of the Employment Policy Institute). It argued strongly, from a Christian standpoint, that high levels of unemployment are unacceptable and went on to propose a comprehensive set of policy measures to remedy the situation. We cannot comment on the whole package in this report, but two measures aimed directly at assisting the long-term unemployed are very relevant to this section. Both are variants of ideas which have appeared elsewhere, but the MCD discussion is commendably clear and concise.

They propose an Employment Compact Scheme under which employers in the private sector would accept the long-term unemployed on placements similar to those often given to trainees. There would be a job preparation course as well as a pre-recruitment assessment by the employer and a subsidy 'in the region of £1,000'. This differs in spirit a little from the similar formula of Workstart in that the employer is being asked to take more responsibility for helping the recruit to get over the barriers to full participation in the labour force. It would include an element of training on the job.

The more radical second proposal is for a Job Guarantee Scheme open to anyone unemployed for more than a year. In effect the public sector would act as 'the employer of last resort'. In this variant on that theme the proposed pay is set at the Income Support level plus £60 per week, which would result in some participants being rather well paid compared with many employed by subcontractors to the public sector. The costings are done on the basis of ¾ of a million such jobs, but if this really is a job guarantee then of course the commitment is open-ended and the cost would be indeterminate. The concept of a guarantee is certainly attractive, but we would want to be certain that it could be honoured. It is not just a matter of cost but of administrative feasibility as well. Would the scheme be able to cope with a sudden sharp recession? The aim to eliminate long-term unemployment is surely right, but the term 'guarantee' implies a promise which might not in all circumstances actually be kept.

A Fresh Start for the Unemployed

In discussing the whole range of measures to help the long-term unemployed the working party has benefitted greatly from the advice of David Price who retired recently from a senior position in the Employment Service. The paper he wrote for us is included as Annex C to this report.

On our visits to the different regions of our country we have met a number of people who have themselves been unemployed for many years. We also held a consultation with a group of people from different parts of Britain with experience of long-term unemployment. This meeting was arranged by Church Action on Poverty, an organisation set up with support from all the churches to campaign on behalf of the unemployed and other groups of people in need. They submitted a paper as evidence to the enquiry called *The Future of Work* which is reproduced as Annex D below. We found this exchange of views extremely helpful.

We do not see it as part of our remit to put forward our own 'scheme'. Indeed we think that something more radical than just another 'scheme' is needed. A new approach is required, building certainly on previous experience and adapting the best features of previous 'schemes', but also being considerably more ambitious in what it tries to achieve. It should include both the subsidising of employment in the private sector and also the development of what has been called the 'intermediate labour market'. These are not mutually exclusive alternatives. In fact we favour both of them.

The long-term aim is that no-one should be unemployed for long periods ever again. Through the Employment Service, or some similar Government agency, the Government should accept responsibility for finding, or if necessary actually creating, appropriate job opportunities to offer anyone who has been out of work for say twelve months (or say twelve months out of the last fifteen months). These should be good jobs, reasonably well paid, which the unemployed people could do without loss of self-esteem. They should match the actual or potential skills of the individual workers and make use whenever possible of their previous work experience. A number of different offers should be made so that the unemployed can choose between a variety of opportunities in different occupations or places of work. The only 'positive outcome' in the first instance is a job offer which the unemployed person is pleased to accept. At the end of that first job strenuous efforts would be made to help in the search for further work or training so as to prevent anyone from slipping back into long-term unemployment once more.

Universal coverage of the long-term unemployed would be difficult, perhaps impossible, to achieve fully in present labour market conditions. Set in the context of the other measures discussed in this report, however, these aims are not unrealistic. If the demand for labour in general were increased as we have argued in chapter 5 above that it could be, then the number of people at risk of becoming long-term unemployed would be much lower. There would be far more vacancies, in both the private and the public sector, for which the unemployed could apply with the help, if need be, of a temporary subsidy or a period of appropriate training. If there were a national minimum wage, more equal bargaining and better enforcement of employment rights then there would be more good jobs to be had and less pressure to take bad ones. There would not be the same resentment from the 'working poor' if society treated the unemployed with decency and even generosity. We see the new deal for the unemployed as just one part of a programme to change the labour market quite fundamentally. It should not be judged in isolation from the other policy changes which ought to be taking place at the same time.

Most of the unemployed people who spoke to us during the enquiry were clearly quite capable of doing paid work. They had just been in the wrong place at the wrong time, or had some small disadvantage in the labour market which needed to be overcome. They needed help, to find their own feet and make their own way. There should be someone to share with them the responsibility for finding work. In some cases this will not require an enormous amount of time or expenditure by the agency concerned, but we believe that the commitment should be there to provide what resources it takes. At present the government seems to be obsessed with the drive to achieve small savings in the cost of administration. Helping the unemployed is itself a labour-intensive service activity, and should be expanded accordingly.

The estimates of cost for existing or proposed schemes are very uncertain, but typically quite moderate in scale. For example David Price in his paper suggests that a programme to assist about half a million long-term unemployed people might have a net cost of around £2 billion a year. This would be around one per cent of total public expenditure, a considerable sum of course but not at all a large price to pay for the good which it could do. (It would be roughly equal to the yield of a penny on the basic rate of income tax. This is the cost of the special measures to help the long-term unemployed described in this chapter. The exchequer cost over a run of years of raising the demand for labour more generally as described in chapter 5 above would, as we have indicated, eventually be much greater than that but, as we have also indicated, the social benefit would be much greater as well.)

It has been suggested to us that many of the things which people do when they are unemployed are quite as worthy of recognition and reward as the jobs which they are likely to find in the market economy. For example they look after their own children or elderly relatives and perhaps the children of their friends as well. They may do some voluntary work in their community, and might do more if the rules for benefit entitlement allowed them to. Some may be active in local churches or community organisations. Some do small jobs for their neighbours in return for similar favours. Some do craft work or sporting activities. The question arises whether this is not good work which should be encouraged rather than penalised or driven underground.

Taxpayers' money, we accept, cannot be used simply to pay for any activity which people choose to call work. Neither should the Employment Service or a similar agency be asked to say which activities merit support and which do not. There does need to be an objective assessment of the value of what is being produced, not just of the satisfaction people feel in producing it. Having said that, we also recognise that some of the community activities in which some unemployed people are involved probably do merit public support. They may serve as a model for one kind of paid work in the 'third sector' which could expand and provide employment for people who would otherwise be unemployed - see chapter 5 above. To give just one small example, some unemployed people became very expert at advising other unemployed people how to survive on Income Support and what benefits they can claim. In a perfect world such advice would not be needed, but if it is needed then either a charitable organisation or an agency of government ought to be training and paying people to provide it.

The Issue of Compulsion

Society faces a very difficult dilemma in dealing with those few people who really do not want to work. The issue, in our view, plays too large a part in the discussion of employment policy, because the numbers of people involved really are very small. The element of compulsion in current policy towards the unemployed is being increased all the time. Unemployment is sometimes discussed, at a popular level and too often in political speeches, as if the unemployed were all 'workshy'. That is grossly unfair to the great majority of unemployed people, who would be overjoyed to accept an offer of good work if it were made to them. But the issue of compulsion should not be ducked all the same.

In recent years the centre-left in Britain, as well as the right, has put increasing emphasis on the obligations of benefit claimants as well as on their rights. In a recent paper, Alan Deacon, one of the members of our working party, offers three explanations. One is the importance attached to 'character' by the very influential Communitarian Movement in America. Another is Christian Socialism, which is profoundly egalitarian but also insists that everyone should be treated as a responsible moral agent. The third influence, less often acknowledged, is from American writers who fear the growth of benefit dependence amongst what they see as an urban and often criminal underclass.

In Christian teaching there is a duty to work as well as a right to work. It is wrong to expect the community to support you when you could perfectly well support yourself. That is the easy point to make. The more difficult question is how society should treat its members who do not appear to accept this obligation. Christian teaching also urges us to be generous, patient and forgiving, so that no-one is beyond the reach of our concern and compassion. No-one can actually be left without means of support.

At present the law requires unemployed people, or job seekers as they are now called, to be 'actively seeking work' as well as being available to do it. That would be a perfectly reasonable condition, if the state were prepared, as we have suggested, to share with them the responsibility for finding work of an appropriate kind. We do not accept the concept of the 'non-worker' as defined in the Field-Howell Bill. We do not think however that any of the offers of work made to the unemployed should be compulsory. People should never be told that a particular job is the only alternative to disqualification from benefit. This in effect turns them into conscripts. There should always be a choice. However, if over a period of months or years, someone turns down a range of different good job offers, then it would be reasonable to conclude that they were not really looking for work at all. Inevitably, the process of making good offers will make it easier for such people to be identified. Even though that is not the purpose of the exercise, it will nevertheless be an inevitable consequence of it. Given the character of the fresh start we describe, we would be very disappointed and surprised if more than a tiny fraction of the long-term unemployed did not accept the work they were offered.

There is no altogether satisfactory answer to the problem posed by that tiny fraction, which is one of the oldest in social policy. If the demand for labour generally was strong, and if a succession of job offers were made available to all those who were out of work for a long time then clearly the problem would be very much less serious than it may appear today. In those circumstances there would come a time when, after adequate warnings were given, it might well be right to refuse benefit to anyone who was simply trying to exploit the system. They would then be obliged to accept work, or else to depend on private charity, for which the rules are not the same.

In the next chapter of the report we shall look at the benefit system more broadly and especially at the way it interacts with employment policy. Some of those who are reluctant to accept employment stand to gain little or nothing financially from doing so. This suggests a need to reform the system as it applies to people both in work and out of it.

Chapter Eight

Work and the Benefit System

We could not possibly in this enquiry cover all the aspects of the benefits system which are in need of reform. Frank Field, the chairman of the Commons Social Security Select Committee begins his book *Making Welfare Work* with the following paragraph:

'Britain's welfare system is broken-backed: the number of claims escalates and so, therefore, does the welfare bill. Yet independence is not encouraged. Already half the population lives in households drawing one of the major means-tested benefits. Means tests paralyse self-help, discourage self-improvement and tax honesty while at the same time rewarding claimants for being inactive or deceitful. Means tests are the poison within the body of the welfare state.'

There are grave problems related to retirement pensions, benefits for children and single parents and the sick or disabled as well as the unemployed. These problems are all made worse by the condition of the labour market which encourages premature retirement, and prevents many people from accumulating savings or pension rights. It also denies opportunities for employment to many mothers who would like to work, as well as to people with sickness or disability which is not incapacitating. Each of these issues merits study in its own right. We must concentrate our attention however on a more limited range of questions, about the benefits available to those seeking work and to those in work. The relation between these benefits is crucial for the incentives facing many of those who are long-term unemployed.

In preparing this section of our report we have been greatly helped by a second paper from David Price called *Social Security and Unemployment*, reproduced as Annex E below. A general point needs to be made first about the adequacy of the levels of most benefits in Britain, both contributory and means-tested. Both kinds of benefit have increased broadly in line with prices since 1980 and have therefore fallen sharply in relation to average earnings. (They are now lower in relation to average personal disposable income than they were in 1948.) This has been a major reason for the growth in income inequality over that period and especially for the increase in the number of children in poverty. Estimates of the cost of an 'adequate' budget, based on what survey respondents regard as necessities, indicate that Income Support levels are too low to maintain a minimum standard of living as commonly understood in Britain today. This is, of course, one factor behind the anxiety over benefit fraud so often expressed today.

We do not believe however that the right approach to reform of the benefit system is simply to increase the rates of benefit paid, attractive though that would be. The only satisfactory solution we can see is to reduce substantially the numbers dependent on benefits. The way to do that is not to limit eligibility but to increase employment. It will also involve re-designing some aspects of the benefits system. Only then will it be possible to raise the general level of benefit without creating even greater problems for work incentives. We are not afraid to recommend a substantial increase in public spending overall, but we would prefer to see it concentrated on job creation, since that is in our view the only satisfactory solution to the problems of the unemployed.

The Insurance Principle

Unemployment is a hazard of life to which we are all exposed. In that respect it is like ill health, accidents and premature death. As for other misfortunes, we naturally seek some form of insurance to provide an income for ourselves and our dependants when we are out of work. That was the original idea behind the national insurance systems which operate in all advanced industrial countries. As the labour market becomes more flexible and more competitive the need for such insurance becomes ever greater. Periods of unemployment between jobs are becoming more and more common as part of a working life.

Universal insurance against unemployment cannot be provided by private sector companies for several good economic reasons. One problem is that the people most eager to buy such insurance would be those most at risk of unemployment, typically people who could not afford to pay high premiums. Another problem is that contributors may have an element of choice as to whether they become unemployed and how soon they find a new job. This is what insurance experts call 'moral hazard'. A third problem is that the risk of unemployment will increase for everyone at the same time during a general downturn in economic activity. For a private unemploy-ment insurance scheme a recession would be like an epidemic of a fatal disease hitting a life assurance company. The funds needed to cover such a risk would be truly vast. A national insurance scheme solves (or reduces) these problems by making contributions universal and compulsory, with the relatively good risks in effect subsidising the relatively bad risks and the whole system underwritten by the commitment to make good any deficit from general tax revenue.

The great merit of the National Insurance system is that it does not require a means test for those who claim benefit. The right to claim rests on the contributions that have been made. This is not the same as the right to benefit from a private insurance scheme which is purchased by paying premiums calculated on a strict actuarial basis. It is more like the social recognition of a right based on the contribution that has been made to the work of the community as a whole. It is not enough to be a citizen or a taxpayer, one has to have been a worker to earn the right to benefit from this form of insurance. The fact that the well-paid now receive no more benefit than the poor, despite their larger contributions, underlines the social significance of the scheme. It is recognised as being redistributive within the working community.

The assumption underlying unemployment insurance is that work can be found within a matter of months. It is meant to enable unemployed workers to search the labour market for rather longer than they could otherwise afford, with the expectation that they will find a better or more appropriate job as a result. It cannot cope with a situation where there are simply not enough jobs to go round, nor give an open-ended commitment to pay out benefits to the unemployed for an indefinite period. There was always meant to be some pressure on claimants to search actively, knowing that their rights to benefit would run out. In America, where contributory benefits are the only benefits paid on account of unemployment, a large number of claimants go back into employment during the last month of their entitlement. That is what one would expect in an insurance-based system. Its incentives work in the right directions.

The Jobseeker's Allowance (JSA) was introduced in Britain during the time of our enquiry. It reduced from twelve months to six the period for which non-means-tested benefit was paid to the unemployed on the basis of their contributions record. In effect it halved the period of entitlement to any benefit for those with any savings or redundancy payments and those living in households with other earners. In our view this aspect of the legislation has not been criticised as vigorously as it should have been. It seems unjust to us for the rights of contributors to the scheme to be curtailed quite drastically in this way. It has undermined any trust that remained in the commitment of the Government to the principles behind the National Insurance system. In very different circumstances the question of the optimum duration of benefit entitlement could reasonably be a subject of debate. Six months ought to be long enough to find another job, but that would require a very large increase in the demand for labour. As things are now twelve months is not too long a period for contributory benefit to be paid. We believe that this change in the law should be reversed.

The basis of national insurance is also being undermined by the increasing proportion of the workforce who are not covered by insurance contributions. This means that they are excluded, not only from unemployment insurance but from the national pension scheme and sickness benefit as well. They are not covered by insurance because they are classed as self-employed or because they work part-time (perhaps in fact doing more than one part-time job) or because they have inadequate records of contributions in the past. The aim should be to make the system as universal in its coverage as it can be, so that eventually almost everyone in the workforce is included.

At the same time the structure of contributions also needs to be reformed. This follows directly from what we have said in chapter 5 about the structure of taxation in relation to job creation. Employers' contributions to national insurance operate like a tax on employment, and employees' contributions like a tax on earned income. We are attracted by the proposals put forward in the paper by the Movement for Christian Democracy referred to previously in this report. They suggest employers should contribute at an increased rate in proportion to their total wage bill, but receive back a 'Job Credit' in proportion to the number of employees - measured, presumably, as 'full-time equivalents' (Truscott and others: *An End to Unemployment!* Movement for Christian Democracy, 1994, p22). This would give employers an incentive to create or maintain jobs rather than increase pay or hours of work. It would provide an element of subsidy to relatively low-skilled labour, as suggested in chapter 5 above. The rates of contributions would have to be set so as to provide an adequate flow of contributions to maintain the social insurance scheme. Also, like many commentators, we see no reason why employees should not contribute in proportion to their total earnings, with no upper limit.

An even more fundamental reform is worth consideration. The problem with most proposals to revive or expand the insurance basis of social security is that national insurance contributions have much the same economic effect as a tax on employment. As we have said, the right to national insurance benefits does not, and should not, depend on the amount of contributions made by, or on behalf of, the claimant. The right in effect follows from the record of work. If, as seems right, more of the cost of the national insurance scheme was shifted over a period of years from employers and employees to general taxation (including expenditure as well as income tax), then entitlement to benefit could eventually be based on having worked (or sought work) for some minimum period of time, rather than on some minimum record of contributions.

Means-tested Benefits for the Unemployed

It would be possible to provide financial help on a temporary basis to a small minority on the basis of need in a way which combined generosity of spirit with reasonable economy in the use of public funds. That was what Supplementary Benefit was originally intended to do. We do not think however that it is possible to devise an acceptable regime for giving adequate means-tested benefits on a long-term basis to very large numbers of claimants. That is what we are trying, but failing, to do now. Income Support has become the livelihood of millions of people in Britain and its petty rules and regulations have come to dominate their lives. Children are born and brought up on Income Support, expect to live their adult lives on it, and to grow old and die on it as well. As the cost escalates, the restrictions become tighter and more complicated; some claimants learn to manipulate or dodge the system and the number who depend on it continues to rise.

Recent reforms have been directed mainly towards containing the cost to the taxpayer. For example budgeting loans instead of grants are now given to those in receipt of Income Support from the Social Fund to meet exceptional expenditure, such as buying a replacement cooker or a bed for a child who has grown out of a cot. The effect is to reduce income below the level which is believed to be adequate in subsequent periods as the loan is repaid. Since the fund is cash-limited, loans may not be available; applicants may be turned down on the grounds that they will not be able to repay the debt. Income Support is no longer paid to young people aged 16 or 17. The theory may be that they should be supported by their families, but that is clearly not possible in many cases. Of course Income Support should be the last resort, but it should be there when it really is needed. Increasing numbers of young people are becoming homeless and some are turning to prostitution and crime.

During 1995/96 over 300,000 people had their benefits cut for contravening the requirement to seek work or for failing to attend compulsory programmes. There is a massive increase compared with 1993/94 when the figure was not much more than 100,000. The regime is being made stricter and the Employment Service is setting performance targets for its staff, measured by the number of cases submitted for adjudication.

It is worth pausing for a moment to reflect on this example of the way in which the issue of unemployment is being addressed by current government policy. The staff who are responsible for administering benefit payments are being given a financial inducement to ensure that as many claims as possible are disallowed. We said in the Introduction to this report that Christianity is about the detail of administration as well as its guiding principles. This is an excellent example. We find this particular performance target morally indefensible.

For the unemployed Income Support has been renamed as the Jobseeker's Allowance, but the conditions remain much the same. The Social Security Act of 1989 already required unemployed claimants to make 'all reasonable attempts to seek work every week' for example by making written applications for vacant positions. The Restart interviews for the long-term unemployed had already been in operation since the mid 1980s. The unemployed people we spoke to said that they felt more help should be given to them when they first sign on, before motivation is weakened by the experience of failure. They also said more help should be given to those aged 50 or over. They expected the pressure on them to be increased following the introduction of the Jobseeker's Allowance. They expected, for example, to be told that they must get their hair cut and smarten up their appearance so that prospective employers would not be put off. They expected new restrictions on the time they could devote to voluntary work or leisure activities.

Officials we have spoken to seemed to expect little change unless and until the job market became more buoyant. As a result of the JSA, they would devote rather more resources to interviewing and advising claimants, but the results would depend on the availability of work. They did not expect to require claimants to accept jobs paying less than their benefit entitlement. It is too early to be certain what effect the JSA itself is having on unemployment and on the lives of the unemployed. Early indications are that it represents a significant further tightening of the regime and that significant numbers of people may be deterred by it from claiming benefits. These will probably include some who have been, in effect, frightened out of claiming what is in fact their due.

The tendency of some recent reforms has been to suggest that if life on Income Support can be made sufficiently unpleasant then the problem of unemployment will solve itself. If this is what the public at large, which pays for the system through taxation, really does believe, then we must respond that it is an uncharitable belief, and also untrue. The first requirement is that the jobs exist; the second is that the long-term unemployed are given some help in securing them. Without those two conditions no amount of harassment will actually succeed.

Benefits and Work Incentives

The benefit system can create a serious disincentive to work, or to work harder. Claimants have always been criticised for choosing to remain unemployed at the expense of the taxpayer. For a small proportion of claimants however it may be very difficult to find a job which will leave them as well off financially as they would be on Income Support. They may want to work, but not be prepared to do so if it takes them and their dependants below a level of income which society (in setting the level of Income Support) has decided is at best, barely enough to keep them. The disincentive effect is most significant for lone parents and the partners of people who are unemployed. Their benefit entitlements are relatively high; their income in work is likely to be relatively low; and they may well need to pay someone to look after their children if they take a job. Complications also arise for those with mortgages or high levels of rent. For anyone on Income Support there is a strong disincentive against taking part-time work. After the initial 'disregard', which varies between £5 and £15 a week, income is deducted pound for pound from benefit entitlement. Working more than the maximum number of hours, paid or unpaid, irrespective of income, can result in the loss of all benefit for that week on the grounds that the claimant is not available to take a job.

It is partly in order to increase the incentive to accept employment that a range of benefits has been introduced in Britain which are payable to people on low incomes in work. The most important ones are Family Credit, Housing Benefit and Council Tax Benefit. Without these additions to income it would be much more difficult for unemployed people with children to find jobs which are worthwhile in purely financial terms. This is an important gain, although it has created problems of another sort.

The introduction of Housing Benefit to replace rent subsidies seems, in retrospect, to have been a mistake. The idea was to concentrate help on those most in need, that is those on low incomes. The result has been a sharp rise in rent, but this has failed to produce the expected increase in good affordable housing. Meanwhile, with the increasing problem of low pay, the costs of the benefit itself have risen enormously.

One effect of in-work benefits is probably to reduce the wages offered for relatively unskilled jobs. There would be far fewer takers for jobs at £2 or £3 an hour if that was all that the workers had to live off. In other words some of the money spent on Family Credit, Housing Benefit and so on goes in effect to the employers of people on low wages. The other way of looking at it is to say that the existence of these benefits is increasing employment, making some jobs viable which would not otherwise have survived or been created in the first place. In any case the introduction of a national minimum wage would prevent employers from gaining unreasonably from the in-work benefits.

Another effect of in-work benefits is to reduce the net gain to a worker who moves to a better job, works longer hours or earns a bonus. When income tax and national insurance contributions are also taken into account many families face a 'poverty trap'. At one time the resulting loss of net income at the margin could actually have been over 100 per cent. Changes in the last ten years mean that this can no longer happen, but losses close to 100 per cent are not uncommon.

The 'obvious' solution would be to reduce tax rates or the rate at which Family Credit and other means-tested benefits are withdrawn as income rises, but that is likely to prove very expensive indeed. For example increasing personal tax allowances would take many of the poorer families out of the tax system altogether, giving them an increased incentive to raise their earnings. But the whole population, even the richest, would also benefit from the measure, as everyone would see their taxable income reduced. The gain could only be concentrated on relatively poor taxpayers if there was an offsetting increase in rates of tax paid higher up the scale. Similarly reducing the taper on Family Credit would mean that it was paid to more families, including some who are not really very poor; and the families who would benefit most would not be those who are poorest. Simple arithmetic dictates that any means-tested benefit which is concentrated on those most in need will also reduce the financial incentive to escape from poverty by any other means. No amount of ingenuity will change that fact.

Benefit Fraud

Everyone has heard stories about benefit fraud and the House of Commons Social Security Committee has assembled some evidence of its magnitude. As a church-sponsored enquiry we would be expected to take this aspect of unemployment very seriously, as indeed we do. We are deeply concerned about the problem of benefit fraud as well as fraud in relation to taxation. Both kinds of crime are the theft of public money. Both undermine respect for the law more generally and contribute to a culture of lawlessness that threatens social cohesion. In terms of saving public money, we would guess that the returns would be vastly greater from pursuing people who evade tax rather than people who cheat the benefit system. But that does not mean that people, especially employers and landlords, who cheat the benefit system should be allowed to get away with it. We would certainly applaud a drive against both kinds of fraud in the context of a programme which created realistic job opportunities for those now excluded from the 'legitimate' market.

We have also come across examples of people who manage quite heroically year after year to resist the temptations to cheat which the benefit system places in their path. They do not receive the popular acclaim which they certainly deserve. There are people on Income Support who choose to work part-time for a variety of reasons and who do declare this income, even though they might well escape detection if they did not. When a taxpayer is honest about declaring small sums of income he or she surrenders at most 40 per cent; when someone on Income Support does the same he or she surrenders the lot.

On one visit it was suggested to us that claimants who are active in the informal economy are demonstrating exactly the qualities which our society most admires. The implication was that this kind of activity should be left alone and allowed to flourish. Better a few tough weeds growing in the wasteland than no green shoots at all! In other places we met a different attitude altogether. Paid work done on the side by benefit claimants stifles the growth of legitimate businesses. It drives wages down. It destroys the market for many forms of self-employment, like painting and decorating, which the unemployed could most readily take up. It could lead to intimidation. These two pictures are not, of course, inconsistent with one another. The best answer to benefit fraud is to create more and better legitimate jobs. In a better labour market environment it would also be much easier to tackle fraud of the kind which is organised by criminals.

There is something rather unpleasant about the moral indignation of the rich over the dishonesty of the poor. John Chrysostom, a fourth-century archbishop of Constantinople, put it very well in the sermons he preached to lambast the rich people of his day:

> 'You who fatten yourselves and enjoy your ease. You who drink well into the night, and then cover yourselves with soft blankets...you dare demand a strict account from the needy who is little more than a corpse, and you fear not the account you will have to render before the court of Christ, terrible and frightful. If the poor fake, it is out of need that they fake, for it is your merciless inhumanity and your cruelty that forces them to do so.'
> (Quoted in J L Gonzales: *Faith and Wealth*)

Some Options for Benefit Reform

The benefit system is extremely complex and it keeps changing. We have ourselves found it difficult to understand and we sympathise deeply with those who have to understand it in order to claim what is due to them. We are pleased to learn that some churches and Christian organisations are offering to help unemployed people and others establish what their benefit rights really are, and that some new computer programmes are available to help them. It is a shame that the DSS is doing less to ensure that everyone who should claim benefit actually does so.

There is a need for reform just to make the system simpler and to reduce the paperwork and administrative confusion. Three much more radical changes should be considered at the same time. One would be to integrate the benefits available in work and out of it, so that claimants did not need to re-establish eligibility every time they move from one situation to the other. (Perhaps there could be a form like the P45 document used by the Inland Revenue when a taxpayer changes jobs.) The second option would be to change from the household to the individual as a basis for benefit entitlement. The third would be to pay benefits to part-time workers to cover the days when they are not at work. All are discussed by David Price in his paper at Annex E. Here we shall consider each briefly in turn.

The case for a single benefit was put to us by unemployed people themselves. They said that people who had established a claim to Income Support could be very reluctant to give it up in order to take on a job which was unlikely to last for very long. Apart from the anxiety and inconvenience caused by making a new claim, some of the conditions applied to new claimants were less favourable than those for existing cases. The treatment of mortgage interest payments was quoted as a particular example. It was only after six months of continuous eligibility that interest was paid in full.

There would clearly be some technical problems to overcome in making a change of this sort. Family Credit is assessed on a six-month period whilst Income Support is assessed by the week. If Income Tax was to be assessed at the same time that would be even more complicated as it depends on income over a full year. The case for merging Income Support with the other means-tested benefits is much stronger. The information required about the income and other resources of the household or individual is quite similar.

Some of the worst features of the Income Support system result from the household assessment of means. There is a strong incentive for couples to split up and live apart, so that one can claim benefit whilst the other is working. Divorce is a common consequence of unemployment and sometimes the motive may well be partly financial. Long-term cohabitations are also at risk, even where the household includes young children. There has been an increase in the numbers of households with no earners or many earners, and a decrease in the numbers of households with just one earner. This trend may have several causes, but one of them is probably the operation of the household means test. For example a wife who works part-time may actually gain by giving up her job when her husband loses his. Undoubtedly the household means test is also a powerful incentive to tell lies, particularly about cohabitation. Attempts to detect such dishonesty are bound to be intrusive and distinctly unpleasant for all concerned. There does seem to be a pressing need for reform.

The White Paper published by the Australian Government in May 1994, *Working Nation: Policies and Programmes*, proposed a personal entitlement to a Job Search Allowance. The spouses of unemployed people would be entitled to benefit only if they were over 40 or looking after dependent children below the age of 16. Otherwise it would be up to them to claim benefit in their own right on the grounds that they were themselves unemployed and actively seeking work. The effect of this reform is that childless couples are in the main treated as two individuals with independent entitlement to benefit when they are out of work. For couples with young children however one partner will still be entitled to benefit on the grounds that the other partner is unemployed or has a low income. This is a step towards individual means assessment, but obviously it does not go the whole way.

This Australian reform has much to recommend it. A childless couple with one partner in work and the other unemployed would no longer be better off if they divorced or separated. The other side of the coin is that the partner of someone who is unemployed will not necessarily receive benefit unless they are looking for work themselves. The issue of benefit entitlement clearly raises very important questions about the relation of work to marriage and family responsibilities. We do not see much scope for the benefit system to actively encourage marriage and stable relationships, but we are concerned that it should not actually discourage them.

More and more of the new jobs being created are part-time. For the person who is unemployed and living off Income Support this is a serious problem. It would often require two or more such jobs, whether they are done by one or more household member, to guarantee an income for the household as a whole above its benefit entitlement. It is rather unlikely that more than one such job will happen to turn up at the same time. There is a good case for paying benefit, as in Ireland, whether means-tested or not, at a proportionately reduced rate to those who are 'part-time unemployed'. On the other hand it would not seem appropriate for the state to pay benefits to the millions of part-time workers who have other means of support and little prospect of working full time. The requirement that they were actively seeking full-time work would have to be quite rigorously enforced. One suggestion is that benefits would be payable on a part-time basis only to those who had been employed full-time in the recent past.

A much more modest reform, easier to implement, would be to raise significantly the income which is 'disregarded' in the means test for Income Support. Currently that figure for some households is only £5 a week. We support the suggestion in David Price's paper that this might be increased to £20 a week.

Chapter Nine

Education and Training

By far the most attractive solution to the twin problems of unemployment and low pay would be to raise the levels of education and training in the workforce. If everyone could be made more productive, then living standards could rise, as a nation we could compete more successfully in international markets, we would make more effective use of new technology and no-one would lack opportunities for interesting and rewarding work. It has become part of the conventional wisdom that the remedy for our economic and social ills can be found in better education and training. This area of policy is being made to carry a frighteningly large weight of public aspiration and expectation.

The European Commission, for example, in its White Paper *Growth, Competitiveness and Employment* writes:

'There can be no doubt that education and training, in addition to their fundamental task of promoting the development of the individual and the values of citizenship, have a key role to play in stimulating growth and restoring competitiveness and a socially acceptable level of employment in the Community.' (p133)

An even greater emphasis is given to education and training in the report of the Social Justice Commission in Britain. It states:

'The first and most important task for government is to set in place the opportunities for children and adults to learn to their personal best. By investing in skills, we raise people's capacity to add value to the economy, to take charge of their own lives, and to contribute to their own families and communities. 'Thinking for a living' is not a choice but an imperative. Lifelong learning is at the heart of our vision of a better country.' (p120)

We entirely agree that better education and training offer the best hope of combining higher living standards with greater equality of opportunity - if not of actual achievement. But this must be a slow process, taking decades or even generations to be completed. Moreover it is an uncertain process since the experts do not agree on what reforms to education and training will help the most. Certainly it is not just a matter of spending more resources in these areas, although that would no doubt be helpful. For all these reasons we have given these policies emphasis in our enquiry, but not exclusive emphasis; we do not expect too much from them on their own.

The economist's model of education is a process of investment in human capital. Knowledge and skills are built up like a stock of productive equipment by a process of learning which is costly in terms of effort, time and money. The return on the investment comes from the higher productivity of the skilled workers for the remainder of their working lives. The worker benefits from a higher wage or salary; the employer may benefit too if the increase in value added is greater than the increase in pay; society as a whole may benefit if the higher skill level of one worker adds to the productivity of others. Human capital, like the value of machinery or buildings, depreciates over time: workers forget what they have learned, grow old and die; knowledge itself becomes obsolete as technology advances. The highest return is earned from investment in human capital when workers are young, quick to learn and with a long working life still ahead of them. After that it is a matter of maintenance, repair and occasional updating to keep the human capital in active use as long as is financially worthwhile. As for any other capital equipment there comes a time when it is right for it to be written off and scrapped.

Although this model offers some useful insight into the process of education and training, we would not for a moment accept it as adequate to deal with all aspects of the subject. The process of learning should itself be enjoyable and, in itself, a worthwhile use of human capacities. Human beings have an innate drive to learn, just as they have an innate drive to work. We take pride in our achievements, the new skills and competences we acquire. We feel the better for them, even if they do not contribute to our economic well-being or make us more productive and better paid. The purpose and justification of education should continue therefore even into old age. There is a growing awareness in our society that human beings will only be at their best, to speak very broadly, if they go through life in a spirit of learning and enquiry. This has always been true, but it becomes more and more true in a society which itself goes through so much change in the course of just one lifetime.

There is also a religious case for education and training. It is no accident that churches and Christian organisations have played such a large part in teaching at all levels for two thousand years. Of course our relationship to God and our value in his sight do not depend on our abilities and knowledge, but that does not mean we should make a virtue of weakness or ignorance. God has given us potential which he wants to see us use. Knowledge of the truth brings us closer to God. The better we understand the world in which we live the more we will praise the God who made it. Equally the more skills we acquire, the more actively we can share in God's work of creation and preservation. Religion, at its best, is a spur to enquiry and a patron to scholarship as well as the arts.

The system of education and training expresses the values of society, and also helps to perpetuate them. Children should know from an early age that they are valued as individuals by the society to which they belong, as well as - one hopes - by their parents and close friends. Education and training should identify and develop the natural gifts which all young people have and encourage them all to make their contribution to the wider community.

A divided education system helps to perpetuate divisions. Too often the system reinforces the differences which already exist between regions and social groups. In Britain these differences are sometimes magnified by the split between the public and private sectors. The fact that some parents are prepared to pay substantial fees rather than send their children to a state school demonstrates some of the weaknesses of the system, but it also helps to perpetuate them. As part of a complete overhaul of the education system, the tax advantages of private schools might be removed. But that of itself would not produce equality of opportunity. Young people who have a good start in terms of parental support, character and upbringing do well, whilst the more difficult pupils are too easily abandoned as unteachable at an early age. National competitiveness has its place, but our vision of a good society, consistent with our Christian faith, is one in which everyone is included and in which the strong give help to the weak. A good school should be a society of that kind. The existence of good schools and colleges, accessible to all, is our best hope of realising more of that vision in the whole of our society at some time in the future.

Schooling as a Preparation for Work

Employers in British industry are unanimous that they will have few jobs for the undereducated in the future. As universities expand a growing proportion of their recruits, at various levels, will be graduates. Where that is not appropriate they may still look for more than one A level or equivalent, or just possibly for five good grades at GCSE. This is a new situation, reflecting developments both in technology and industrial organisation. The lower skilled jobs, if they are done at all, are often done by sub-contractors and temporary staff, where rates of pay are low, and getting lower. Those with relatively low educational attainments are being pushed to the margins of society and find it increasingly difficult to escape relative poverty, except perhaps by means of self-employment.

We risk deepening divisions within our society. To avoid this danger a pincer movement is needed. More and better jobs are needed for those with relatively low education and skills, as proposed in earlier sections of this report. But at the same time we need to devote far more attention to raising the potential both of new entrants and existing members of the workforce. The aim should be universality. This should be given priority over the ambition to do even better for the most able minority. It means taking special care of those who tend to be disadvantaged, not using the education system as a sieve; it means resisting the pressure to select the most able and discard the rest.

Both Britain and Ireland have a good reputation for educating their most able young people to a high standard. This helps attract international businesses to locate in our countries and is the basis for success in some highly advanced sectors of manufacturing and financial services. Education for the majority is not so good: standards realised by the average pupil in British schools do not compare well with those on the Continent.

Sig Prais in his recent book *Productivity, Education and Training* quotes the scores of 13 year-old pupils in an international test of mathematics carried out in 1990. The average score of English pupils was behind that of pupils in France, Italy and Switzerland, but ahead of those in America. The score of the highest decile (the top tenth) in England was much the same as that of the highest decile in the three other European countries; but the score of the lowest decile (32 per cent) was well below that in France (37.5 per cent) in Italy (36.5 per cent) and Switzerland (51 per cent) and not much better than that in America (29 per cent).

What stands out in these international comparisons is the variability of performance within British schools. In a subject like mathematics this is particularly damaging as failure to master one year's syllabus can make it impossible to understand the next year's syllabus at all. Thus the variability of attainment within the class must get progressively wider. It is difficult and inefficient for teachers to give adequate instruction to a class with a very wide range of understanding in a subject of this kind. International comparisons tend to focus on mathematics teaching partly for this reason and partly because it is obviously easier to compare across different cultures than literary subjects would be. Moreover a basic mathematical understanding is a necessary grounding for many kinds of technical training after pupils have left school.

It is a very common complaint from employers that many school leavers cannot do simple arithmetic and require remedial teaching in it before they can embark on any vocational studies. Complaints are also common that too many pupils leave school unable to read or write. We have heard many such complaints from employers to whom we have spoken in the course of our enquiry. Public opinion and the government now seem to be well aware of the situation and efforts are being made to improve it.

It has been suggested that the problem begins at an early stage. It does not begin in the secondary schools or even necessarily in the primary schools. Levels of attainment at age five already show marked divergences, due in part to differences in parenting and early socialisation. The involvement of parents in their children's education seems to be an important determinant of success at every level. This points to one respect in which educational practice could be improved, but it also points to the inter-generational aspect of the problem and hence the very long time-scale over which reforms will have their effects.

Employers also emphasise other qualities which school-leavers often seem to lack, such as the ability to communicate with adults, the motivation to succeed and the willingness to work as part of a team. The key skills which everyone needs also include problem-solving and learning how to direct one's own development - learning how to learn. These subjects are only beginning to appear on the school curriculum. It is not only in school that young people can learn them; they are nevertheless an essential part of education, for work and for adult life as a whole. Such abilities ought to characterise a society growing to be more human, in which work is seen as a collaborative endeavour.

Schools are being asked to make up for the weakness of other institutions, including the family and the local community. This is not, of course, a totally new situation: schools have always performed these functions, especially in communities which are relatively poor and disadvantaged. The new dimension of the problem is that more children now seem to grow up without much community life at all.

The return of mass unemployment began in the 1970s. This was the period when the confident expectation of a job for life began to fade away. The children born at that time are now adults. The recession of the 1980s saw the end of many more working communities and the acceptance by many people of unemployment as a way of life. The children born at that time are now at school. The damage done by mass unemployment cumulates over time and across generations. Some of the price for the failures of economic policy in the 1970s and 1980s is being paid today.

One of the most powerful incentives for young people to succeed at school should be the prospect of a good job. The collection of papers submitted to the enquiry by the Baptist Church included a note by Doreen Landriau based on the 1987 Young People's Leisure and Lifestyles report. She comments:

> 'There were significant gender and class-based differences in relation to education and employment. Young men were more likely than young women to place a high priority on starting work as soon as possible and were less keen to pursue further full-time education. Males were more likely than females to consider much of their experience of school as being a waste of time... Almost half of the young people who came from a home background where the head of the household was unemployed, regarded starting work as soon as possible as a priority, despite the fact that they were more likely than any other group to feel they lacked confidence and ability to do so.' (p66)

The better performance of schools on the Continent seems to be linked to the availability of apprentice training and skilled employment for those who do well at school. A similar motivation applies in Britain to children with the prospect of university entrance and academic success, which still opens up the prospect of a progressive career in the long term. But for those with less academic ability or interest there is nothing comparable on offer. We were told on our visit to Merseyside that children as young as twelve will say that they expect to be unemployed when they leave school. It was even suggested to us, how seriously we do not know, that schools should be preparing young people to accept such a fate, rather than raising expectations of employment which were bound to be disappointed. That was one of the most shocking things that we heard during the whole of our enquiry.

What is needed is the exact opposite of that recommendation. There should be more guidance given to pupils about the jobs to which they can aspire and the educational qualifications they will need to achieve their ambitions. There should be more teaching of practical subjects related to the world of work, with emphasis on the standards expected in the workplace. Local employers should continue to be encouraged to take an interest in schooling, explaining to both teachers and pupils what skills and abilities are likely to be in demand in the future. The movement for school-industry links has made great progress and we hope it will continue. Pupils should be encouraged to think for themselves about what their future employment should be.

None of this makes any sense, of course, unless there are in fact jobs to be had when the pupils leave school. Better schooling is often prescribed as the potential cure for unemployment. In fact the converse may be nearer to the truth. In areas of high unemployment there needs to be some provision of employment opportunities before we can expect any marked improvement in the achievements of school leavers. The problem needs to be tackled from both ends, but the increase in the local demand for labour may have to come first.

Recent educational reform has concentrated on improved testing of pupil attainments, on giving schools more control of their own policies and expenditure, and on introducing more explicit competition between schools, in imitation of a market system. The emphasis on raising standards and encouraging excellence is of course very necessary and very welcome. Competition between schools is one way of achieving these ends, and it has always existed whether it was encouraged by educational policy or not. The need for a businesslike use of scarce resources in schools is readily accepted, but notions of a market for schooling within the public sector are unrealistic, since parents and pupils do not often have much real choice. What in fact happens too often is that financial resources are taken away from areas, for example in inner cities, where they are most needed. The brightest children and the better schools attract each other, so that there are built-in tendencies for the weakest to fall by the wayside. In any case we would question whether a market would be an appropriate way of organising such an essential social service.

We have argued that employment should expand particularly in service activities where there is growing demand, which are not exposed to international competition, and where human involvement could not be replaced by new technology. Education is, of course, an excellent example. It is also, properly in our view, an activity mainly in the public sector, financed out of general taxation. There should be more and better jobs for teachers, technicians, administrators and maintenance staff, educational social workers and psychologists. Despite all the public professions of support for education as the solution to all our ills, many of those actually involved in running schools lament how underfunded the system still remains.

Vocational Training

The value of skilled work is not just economic. In the Bible, the second book of Chronicles describes how King Solomon built the temple of God in Jerusalem. It describes the workforce of craftsmen that was assembled, with skills in felling and preparing timber, working in 'gold and silver, copper and iron, and in purple, crimson and violet yarn'. The dimensions of the building are recorded with loving care, together with its rich and splendid ornamentation. This was all done 'because our God is greater than all gods'(2 Chronicles 2:5). The same care and pride went into the building of our great cathedrals, and the tradition is maintained by the churches on a more modest scale today. Excellence in workmanship and expertise in performing work of every kind does not need justification in financial terms. Neither should training which enhances human capabilities and fulfils individual potential be seen simply as a means of increasing pay or profit.

The book by Sig Prais mentioned above also gives figures for the percentage of the workforce in Britain and Germany at the end of the 1980s with various levels of qualification. The proportion with university degrees or similar qualifications was 10 per cent in both countries. The proportion with craft and technical qualifications was 27 per cent in Britain as against 64 per cent in Germany; those with no vocational qualifications at all were 63 per cent in Britain and 26 per cent in Germany. These figures confirm that a far higher proportion of workers in Germany have recognised skills than in Britain. The same is true of other countries on the Continent. Some allowance might be made for skills acquired on the job in Britain, which are not recognised by any form of vocational qualification at all, but it is unlikely that this goes very far to close the very wide gap shown in the figures. The implications of relative skill levels for relative productivity in Britain and Germany have been demonstrated in some detail by Sig Prais and his colleagues in a variety of case studies of both manufacturing and service industries. There can be little doubt that the level of vocational training in Germany makes a big difference to the level of wages and the standard of living in that country, as well as the level of youth unemployment.

These figures and case studies reflect the skill level in the workforce as a whole. In recent years employers and Government have made a considerable effort to improve matters. More qualifications are being awarded as a result, although many of them are at such a low level of skill that they would not be awarded any certification at all in Germany. Sig Prais also provides figures for the numbers passing vocational examinations at craft level in the late 1980s in Britain and Germany. Mechanical, electrical and building trades are all covered. The grand totals are 45,000 in Britain as against 139,000 in Germany. It could be said in mitigation that the need for craft training in Britain is much less, because the size of the engineering industry is so much smaller than in Germany. To this one could respond that the British engineering industry has contracted in large part precisely because it has neglected in the past to train its workforce to an adequate standard to meet the foreign competition.

The changes in the nature of work which we have identified in this report pose serious problems for the provision of training. New technology requires new skills; without those skills workers will not be employable; thus training has to be a continuing activity for most of a working lifetime. A more flexible labour market also raises questions about who it will be that pays for this training to be done.

The economic theory of training is straightforward. If a skill is transferable from one job to another and the labour market is competitive, then employers will have no incentive to pay for their workers to be trained. If they do not give the whole benefit of the productivity increase to the workers as higher pay, then the workers will all leave to work for someone else. The only case, in theory, where employers have an incentive to pay for training is when the skills are not transferable, otherwise the workers will have to pay for their training themselves. One way for this to happen would be for workers to receive lower pay during the period when part of their time is spent learning on the job. Not many workers can afford actually to take time off unpaid and pay the cost of their tuition as well. Even if it were worth their while to do that, because of the higher pay they would receive after completing their training, they would not have access to the funds to support them in the meantime.

In 1994 the Confederation of British Industry carried out a survey of its members asking about their experience in training workers in a flexible labour market. They found that firms did in fact provide training even for temporary staff (despite what economic theory would predict) and that some employment agencies were taking on the responsibility for training staff whose services they would contract to their clients. At the same time they found an increasing willingness amongst individuals to invest in their own training and development. The report suggested that a number of policy measures should be examined, including individual training accounts and a return to the old idea of a training levy.

The Chairman of the CBI Education and Training Affairs Committee, Dominic Cadbury, in his foreword to the report wrote: 'The CBI remains convinced that the responsibility for training a company's employees rests with the employer'. When he spoke to the working party at one of our meetings he said it was difficult to draw the line between the responsibility of the employer for training and that of the state, but he was convinced that employers should do more. He said that highly successful companies tended to be the ones which trained well and that this fact was now recognised by institutional investors.

It is not just a matter, however, of recognising that educating the workforce is good for company profits. Employers do, and should, accept responsibilities to their employees and to society at large. This will often include giving people the chance to learn throughout their working lives. In manufacturing industry for example, Ford, Rover and Lucas have schemes which offer all their employees time and money for educational courses. In some cases the employer does not demand that the learning have any direct relationship with the learner's job, or the employer's interest at all. The company's understanding is that people work better, gain confidence, take initiatives, and are readier to retrain, if given the chance of continuing education.

In a more flexible labour market, with the prospect of more frequent job changes for some if not all employees, the best employers are also asking how they can now discharge the obligation they still feel to provide some kind of security for all their staff. If they cannot offer a guarantee of employment, perhaps they can at least offer a guarantee of employability. This can only be achieved by continuous updating of knowledge and skills. Prudent employees who are in a strong bargaining position will insist that their employer enables them to keep abreast of all developments in their field of competence or expertise.

It is good that leading employers take this attitude, but we must beware of expecting too much from firms which operate in very competitive markets. It may really pay them only to train their core staff on whose expertise and loyalty their success depends. It may not be so much in their interests to train the workers on the periphery. On our travels we visited some firms who seemed to be living off their past investments in training, with a skilled workforce that was ageing and not being replaced. We were also told that many small employers, who are unlikely to be members of the CBI, do not spend anything on training at all.

We agree that both individual learning accounts and the levy system need further study. At one of our meetings we were joined by Carolyn Hayman who was a member of the Dahrendorf Commission which reported on *Wealth Creation and Social Cohesion* in 1995. That report includes an interesting discussion of individual learning accounts. The proposal is that employers and employees should both contribute to such accounts on a compulsory basis. 'Such a system recognises the need for employees to develop their skills continually in order to build their careers, and also recognises that while employers cannot offer lifetime employment, they have a responsibility to promote lifetime employability.' (p80). The suggested contribution is 1 per cent each by both parties 'with the state making its contributions in the form of tax relief and interest-free lending against future payments'. The report says that the use of individual learning accounts 'must be in the hands of those who contribute', which presumably means both employers and employees, although it is not made clear how that joint decision would be made.

For those on relatively low pay a contribution of 2 per cent a year would not buy very much training. It is arguable that more resources should be made available to train the low paid, as they are precisely the people who need it most. On the other hand it would be wrong for the contributions paid by employers to be the same amount for all workers, as this would add disproportionately to the costs of job creation. If there are going to be individual learning accounts we would expect the state to subsidise the accounts of those whose resources would otherwise be inadequate.

A training levy certainly has attractions. Under such a scheme firms which spend a prescribed minimum on training are exempt, whilst the rest are obliged to contribute to the scheme's cost. Where training is specific to one industry, and skills transferable between firms, the levy arrangements look like the text-book answer to the problem of training finance.

This was the justification for introducing a scheme in Britain where each industry was covered by a separate Industrial Training Board. Except for the building and engineering boards, however, which still survive, the scheme was abandoned in the early 1980s. It gained a reputation of overheavy bureaucracy and of encouraging companies sometimes to maintain courses that were not cost-effective. This history suggests that practical experience may belie theory here and that it would now be unwise at least to reintroduce a comparable system.

The theoretical solution to the question of payment is not so neat when the training is transferable anywhere in the economy at all - for example remedial training for literacy or numeracy. In that case all employers ought in principle to pay the levy, but it would be simpler in fact to collect it out of general taxation. Again we must state a preference for policies which do not add to the costs of employing labour. That, after all, is the main thing we should be trying to encourage. If training helps to reduce the costs or improves the quality of everything we consume, why not pay for it out of a tax on all expenditure? It would still be possible to give employers more of an incentive to train by a more generous treatment within company taxation.

In Germany, where training is more comprehensive and better organised than it is in Britain, a significant share of the cost of initial training is borne by the apprentice, as trainee wages are below the going rate for unskilled work. That is not unreasonable given the advantages which come to the individual later on in better pay and prospects for employment. The apprenticeship system has never been as well developed in Britain, and it is now in urgent need of revival. The modern apprenticeship scheme recently introduced by the Government seems to be one of the best features of current training policy.

We visited a training centre where engineering courses to craft and technician levels were being provided in an area of relatively high unemployment, on what seemed to us very traditional lines. (The students were told to mind their language as well as to work hard.) The courses were very popular with students, we were told, and most of them found appropriate jobs at the end. Sadly, the funding for this centre, which had been provided for several years by two large local employers, had just been sharply cut back.

In recent years Government training policy has centred on developing the role of Training and Enterprise Councils (TECs). They appear to have been successful, in some areas at least, in reconciling the interests of local businesses, the existing workforce, the tax payers and the unemployed. There has been considerable progress in the last few years and TECs are originating and co-ordinating innovative training projects. They are now able to lead bids for funding from government in their geographical areas together with local authorities, business leaders and community associations. We heard some complaints that TECs did not have sufficient funds at their disposal to make it worthwhile for firms to co-operate with them. It was also suggested that more local autonomy in the design of training schemes would produce better results. It was claimed that the LECs in Scotland worked better, because they were not so much subject to central direction. But there is a fundamental conflict between the priority of meeting the skill needs of employers, which were rather specific and often quite demanding, and the priority of helping the unemployed back into work, which requires some very basic training of a much more general kind. Greater clarity of aim would help the TECs give priority to those whose need of training is greatest.

In discussing education we have stressed the aim of universality. The same applies to vocational training. Richard Layard and his colleagues at the London School of Economics have proposed that all young people in employment between the ages of 16 and 19 should be trainees, with at least one day a week of vocational training provided free. It would be an obligation on employers to see that this training was undertaken and the costs of tuition would be paid by the state. This would be coupled with a trainee wage well below any statutory minimum that might be in force. They also favour the free provision of vocational training to adults, on conditions similar to those which now apply to university students. Maintenance costs would be financed by loans.

This general approach seems right to us. At present the actual target is that 80 per cent of young people should attain at least the equivalent of a National Vocational Qualification at level 2. This corresponds to a quite modest academic achievement for most young people and still leaves 20 per cent with nothing to show for their education and training at all. We think the aim should be virtually 100 per cent at that level or above.

The objectives of education and training in the key years 16 to 19 remain incoherent in England except for the minority who are taking A level courses. As Alan Smithers and Pamela Robinson concluded in a recent study, 'there is effectively no mainstream post-16 education for most of the school population'. The solution must be to build a less narrowly academic path of education and training alongside the academic path. This involves widening, rather than narrowing, the breadth of vocational courses. (The experience of educational reforms in Scotland may well be valuable.) As our chairman, Patrick Coldstream, has put it, when he was director of the Council for Industry and Higher Education: 'what is needed is a broad and liberating education which nonetheless is related to the activities and concerns of the world outside education, not least the world of work'.

Most of the people we spoke to were generally pleased with the system of National Vocational Qualifications (NVQs and SVQs in Scotland) to which there had been much opposition when they were first introduced. They clearly provide a good framework for improving, and certifying, the competencies of existing employees. It is more doubtful whether they provide the best introduction to skilled work for young people leaving school. For that purpose tests of more general education and capability are required, possibly along the lines of the GNVQs and GSVQs recently introduced in Britain. Another criticism we heard came from someone working with a group of unemployed people. He told us that the achievement of NVQs did not seem to make it any easier to break into employment.

We met a number of organisations acting as training providers with statutory funding, some of them supported by churches or other Christian groups. They suggested to us that the provision of training was becoming more of a commercial business, and that as a result the people who most needed training were losing out. The issue most often raised was that of 'output-related funding'. This means that providers get most of their funds when their students achieve vocational qualifications or obtain employment. Clearly this presupposes very rigorous supervision of the testing procedures. But the main objection is that trainers are obliged to select the students who already have the best chance of passing the test or finding work. In the extreme they would recruit students who did not need to be trained at all. Commercially-motivated training organisations certainly go in for 'cherry picking', rather than accepting those whose need for training is greatest. To be fair a system of output-related funding should take full account of the 'input' as well. But we remain unconvinced that any form of output-related funding is really appropriate to the provision of training.

We are particularly concerned about access to training for people who are unemployed. Many of them wish to spend a significant part of their time acquiring new skills or improving existing ones, as well as looking for a job. It is surely right that they should be able to do this, subject to some requirement that the courses they take are appropriate to the jobs they can expect to get.

The regulations governing eligibility for benefits now prevent claimants from studying for more than 16 hours a week. Some of them might apply for a discretionary grant, but these are not easy to secure. We recognise the difficulty of devising appropriate rules to deal with the thoroughly unsatisfactory state of the labour market. But it seems to us, nevertheless, absurd that people who cannot find work should be prevented from using their time productively.

There is one fundamental point to be made in conclusion about both training and education. There is an understandable wish to reward success in schools and colleges, to make educational and training institutions more accountable and encourage them to aim at ever higher standards of achievement. The effect is like that of a market. Average performance does improve, but the variation of performance widens at the same time. The most able press ahead, leaving the least able further and further behind.

A school should be answerable, not just for the average performance of its pupils, but also specifically for the performance of the tail-enders. In the same way a training establishment should be assessed on its contribution to placing in work the most disadvantaged people in its area, as well as to raising skill standards in the population as a whole. It would not be impossible to devise performance measures which took this priority into account.

Chapter Ten

The Work Ethic and Full Employment

When our enquiry was launched, in September 1995, we issued a Press Statement which included a list of questions we hoped to address. We reproduce a shortened version of some of them below, together with the answers offered to us by a 22 year old man who was himself unemployed.

- **Is it still true to say that everyone has a right and a duty to work?** It's better to create things that help the community, that people want to do, rather than telling them it's their duty.

- **How can the idea be expressed that all good work is service to God and our neighbours?** To say that working on a vegetable packing line is a service to God sounds ridiculous.

- **What degree of loyalty do employers owe to their employees, and vice-versa?** Most businesses are geared to make as much profit as possible. People don't matter to the equation in today's society.

- **Should we be prepared to accept low pay if that enables more people to work?** Accepting low pay encourages people in business to exploit even more. Wouldn't it be better to teach employers, especially big business, not to be so greedy?

- **Should life on benefits be more, or less, comfortable?** Life on benefits is not comfortable, but we are lucky in this country to be supported. If more varied options and training were offered it would be more constructive.

- **Should the unemployed be allowed, even encouraged, to take unpaid work?** Yes, I think so, with government-funded, recognised training in a placement of a recognised standard, in the field of their choice.

- **Is full employment still a realistic and appropriate objective today?** Not really. I don't think there are enough jobs for everybody, because of the IT revolution. You would either have to sacrifice technology, or create opportunities for different ways of life, such as community farms. If these could be made to work, and support themselves, I think it would be a very good idea, as a lot of people would prefer an alternative to today's way of life, and it would reduce unemployment. Then you would be left with sorting out the tax!

We have already offered our own answers to some of these questions, which in some cases differ significantly from those given by the young man we quote here. It seems right nevertheless for these views to be expressed, as well as our own, in our report.

In earlier chapters of this report we have described what we see as the challenge to society presented by the changes which are taking place in the world of work and we have considered some quite specific ways in which society might respond. In this chapter we bring together two more fundamental questions about individual and social values in relation to work and its future. The first concerns what is called 'the work ethic'. How should we now understand our work as giving purpose and meaning to our individual existence? The second concerns the social objective of 'full employment'. What obligation should our society as a whole accept to make sure that we all can in fact have work to do which does offer some purpose and meaning to our lives? We think it appropriate that these two questions should be addressed together, because the answers one gives to each of them must surely affect the answer one gives to the other.

Faith and Work

The Christian work ethic is widely misunderstood. Some people think Christians believe that if they work hard God will reward them in heaven. That is not at all what Christians in fact believe. We believe that our eternal life depends on the free gift of God, not on anything which we can do to deserve it. In recognition of that free gift we offer our life and work to God, as a token of our love and trust and worship. The result may look much the same, in that either could be the motive for good work, but the difference in our relationship to God, and hence in the meaning of our own lives, is fundamental.

Something similar can be said about the relationship of individuals to one another and to the community. We could imagine a society in which people were valued only for the work that they did. Husbands and wives would value one another because they earned a lot of money or were good at looking after the children. Old people would be valued for the work they had done in the past, young people for the work they would do in the future. But that is clearly not enough. In a good society people are loved and valued in their own right, not just for their achievements or their contributions to the common prosperity. Membership of the community does not have to be earned. We might want to say that people should work because they are members of society. We would not want to say that they are members of society only if they do work.

The work ethic which we would commend is, in part therefore, a grateful recognition of what we have been given. That gratitude takes the form of co-operation, joining in the activities from which we ourselves derive benefit. This means working with, and for, God as well as working with, and for, the society to which we belong. Michael Bourke, as chairman of the

Anglican Industry and Economic Affairs Committee, sent us a paper on *The Concept of the Work Ethic* (see Annex F). In it he says:

'The purpose of work is not just to maintain the existing order of things, but to transform the world... The new creation is not a human achievement but the gift of God; nevertheless the human project waits for God's transformation of the existing order not passively, but actively ... Even when we are found wanting, God is working with the raw material of human history.'

So our work ought to be to make the world a better place. This does not apply only to work which is done in a Christian setting. The work which we do in any community to which we belong can be part of the process of redemption, if it is done in accordance with the will of God. This could even, we maintain, be true of work on a vegetable packing line. God made the vegetables for people to eat, and if the vegetables have to be transported to where the people live then they will need to be packaged!

Michael Bourke also writes about an ethic which requires 'an attention to quality, reliability and detail', even 'a certain obsessive perfectionism': 'If the quality of goods and services is neglected, the result is not only a loss of competitiveness, but also a lowering of the quality of life, sometimes with serious results'. If we are to offer our work to God then it must be the best that we can do. So religious faith can inspire us to the highest possible standards of service or design and production. Obviously this is not the only possible spur to excellence. Some will say that they seek high standards to fulfil themselves, to satisfy their customers or for the pure joy of creation. Certainly we would want to commend a work ethic which is not purely selfish or purely financial. The aim of a valid work ethic cannot just be to become less poor or more rich, necessary though that incentive may be. The aim must transcend, or go beyond that, so that work becomes, in a sense, 'an end in itself' or rather an activity which produces something which is good 'in its own right'.

In 1995 the Committee for the World of Work of the Roman Catholic Bishops' Conference of England and Wales issued a discussion document called *A New Community of Work*. The opening section sets out the ethical understanding of work in Catholic social teaching. It 'points towards a new kind of society in which moral considerations rule over the purely commercial, and people see themselves as stewards of creation with wide social and ecological responsibilities'. In this vision work may be paid or unpaid. Its first priority is to meet basic needs - food, clothing, shelter and health, with basic education only a little less urgently required. The document goes on to say:

'These considerations should define society's priorities. It is wrong that some should indulge themselves in material luxury, whilst others have insufficient to meet basic needs... Above a certain level, the acquisition of material goods inhibits people's higher moral and spiritual development... Beyond this point the accent of human development should be on being rather than having, the object of work should be seen increasingly in a less material way, and the fruits of progress taken in a less material form..' (pp3-4)

Another paper submitted to the enquiry was written by Andrew Shanks and quotes from the writings of Simone Weil (see Annex G). She wrote:

'Workers need poetry more than bread. They need that their life should be a poem. They need some light from eternity. Religion alone can be the source of such poetry'.

She did not necessarily mean the religious life to be found in a church. Neither did she mean necessarily the poetry that expresses itself in the creative arts. She also meant the faith which keeps the human spirit alive even when work is no more than drudgery, and the poetry that finds beauty in the harshest of suffering. Work, even mindless work, must be transformed so that it transcends the wages that would otherwise be its only justification. Only then can the lives of the workers be given meaning. When we speak of the need for a Christian work ethic we mean something like that as well.

Vocation and Choice of Work

Whilst the work ethic respects the value and dignity inherent in all good work, the concept of calling or vocation usually refers to some specific task. As one member of the working party described it 'each and every person is a piece of the jigsaw of society. The whole picture is the Kingdom of God'. It was common at one time for Christians to refer to a calling, not only to church ministries or life in a religious community, but to other occupations like teaching or nursing, or for that matter book keeping or carpentry. The implication was that God had chosen an individual to do some ordinary paid work 'for the Lord', just as someone else might be called to be a missionary or an ordained minister. The word 'calling' is not so often used in that sense today. Nevertheless the idea that a particular kind of work is right for each person is as important now as it ever was in the past.

Christians still, of course, seek the guidance of God as to what occupation or career is right for them, as they would in any such important decisions they need to make. We are all born with different aptitudes and potential. We have certain gifts or talents, whether they are inherited or acquired when we are young. They can be developed and put to use, or they can be

161

neglected and ignored. Sometimes they may never be discovered at all. We also have preference for one kind of work rather than another, which may or may not match the talents which we actually possess. This will point us in the direction of one occupation rather than others.

This emphasises the importance of giving people a real choice as to how they participate in the world of work. That means breaking down the remaining barriers which prevent some people from doing some kinds of jobs. It also means creating more jobs in total, so that people's choice is not restricted to the few poor jobs that are actually on offer. The whole idea of a vocation or calling will seem quite unrealistic to many people who are now unemployed. That is another reason why unemployment is so abhorrent to the Christian understanding of work and society.

The changes which are taking place in the nature of work should open up all kinds of opportunities which did not exist in the past. Totally new jobs are being invented every year. (A newspaper picked at random contained advertisements of vacancies for an Oracle Analyst Programmer, Openmail Support, NT Engineers, Database Administrator and Business Analysts with Derivatives and Risk Management experience.) It is no longer expected that children will follow in their parents' footsteps, or continue in the occupations of their local community. During a working life in the future many people will change their occupation many times. Somehow any sense they may have of being dedicated to their work will have to survive such upheavals. Perhaps that dedication will be to some kind of work rather than to a single job - dedication to art, to design, to business efficiency or the needs of young people would all be examples. Perhaps it will simply be dedication to work as such.

Working too Hard

According to the account of creation in the Old Testament, God made the world in six days. 'And on the seventh day God finished the work which he had done, and he rested on the seventh day from all his work which he had done' (Genesis 2:2). The fifth of the ten commandments given by God to Moses on Mount Sinai was

> 'Remember the Sabbath day, to keep it holy. Six days you shall labour, and do all your work; but the seventh day is a Sabbath to the Lord your God; in it you shall not do any work, you, or your son, or your daughter, your manservant, or your maidservant, or your cattle, or the sojourner who is within your gates; for in six days the Lord made heaven and earth, the sea, and all that is in them, and rested the seventh day; therefore the Lord blessed the Sabbath day and hallowed it.' (Exodus 20: 8-11).

Even the work of God is complemented by rest. Certainly human work cannot be uninterrupted. The work ethic suggests a duty to work; but there is also a duty to rest. There may be a right to work, but only a right to enough work; it is not a right to as much work as anyone might want to do. We note also that the requirement to rest applied to everyone in the community, including even the servants and the foreign visitors. It was a social obligation as well as an individual one.

We are not, of course, suggesting that the Sabbath rules in all their strictness should be applied to everyone today. We are not even at this point reopening the campaign to 'Keep Sunday Special'. We are using the institution of the Sabbath to make a much more general point about the need to balance work with rest and other activities, including family life, leisure, sport, recreation and the worship of God. This is not just a matter of individual choice, because work is a social activity and so are many of the other ways in which we use our time.

Overwork is a sign of individual or social malfunction. According to *Social Trends*, 1996 the average weekly hours worked by male employees in the United Kingdom were 43½, as against a European average of 40. Average hours for women were much lower, because many work part-time: 30½ in the UK, as against 33 in Europe as a whole. We have all heard plenty of anecdotal evidence of an increasing problem of over-work in Britain. It may be managers and professional people working late every evening, and at weekends as well. It may be bosses who insist that their staff are instantly available to work at any time of day or night. It may also be very low-paid staff or homeworkers who have to work up to 100 hours a week to earn a living wage. There have been reports of increased stress and illness directly attributed to excessive hours of work. A doctor wrote to us as follows:

'I feel very strongly about the problems of stress at work. As a GP I have had to recommend early retirement for far too many able, conscientious and gifted people. One of the common denominators in the stress was the inability to lower standards... to keep the personal load within reasonable volume'.

Some of this frenetic effort may really be voluntary, due to enthusiasm for the job or ambition for a high standard of living. Much of it is probably not really a matter of choice for the individual. In a firm which survives through over-work, it is not really open to an individual employee to say that they will work their contracted hours and no more. With high unemployment, lack of trade union support and job insecurity, employees can easily be told that they must work for as long as they are needed, or else look for easier work elsewhere.

The increase in the practice of working long hours reverses a long

163

established trend. Between the 1960s and 1970s average hours worked in manufacturing fell by 10 per cent (4 hours a week). By 1992 however the average hours worked fell no further. The standard working week was reduced from 40 to 39 hours, but in fact the proportion working in excess of 45 hours (according to the General Household Survey) rose from 16½ to 26½ per cent for men and from 2½ to 5½ per cent for women. So despite the marked increase in part-time working, the average hours worked have not gone down. One reason may be the shift to self-employment, where people have always tended to work longer hours than as employees. Another is the increase in employment of managerial staff and the increase in hours worked by this group.

Why do they do it? This was the question asked by Paul Gregg in an article in New Economy. He suggested that 'the answer is probably related to the growth during the 1980s of the rewards associated with successful career development and promotion'. He also mentions the reductions in higher rates of income tax and the expansion of performance-related pay. He quotes the results from the British Social Attitudes Survey. Asked whether they would prefer to work more or fewer hours per week: 65 per cent of full-timers said they were content as they were; 5 per cent wanted to work more hours and 30 per cent to work less (including 25 per cent who would choose to do so even with a corresponding cut in pay).

On one of our visits to a manufacturing company we asked both management and staff, who were working very long hours, whether they would be prepared to cut down on their overtime to create more jobs in what was an area of high unemployment. Their union representatives said that this would be in line with their national policy. Management said that it was more economical to employ a small staff more intensively than to meet the overhead costs, including training, of increasing the workforce. The workers themselves, who were mainly married men, were quite clear that they preferred the long hours and good pay. Asked how their wives felt about their absence for much of the weekend, they said that their wives liked the good pay too.

It seems to us absurd, and also altogether unjust, that some people should be working so long and so hard, whilst other people have no paid work to do at all. We believe, as we have said in earlier chapters of this report, that the total amount of paid work being done could be increased to provide good work for the unemployed to do. But we are concerned about the distribution of work as well as the total amount that is done. Would it not be helpful if those who now overwork were to work less, creating more opportunities for others who now work too little or not at all?

If the total amount of work being done remains the same, then clearly a reduction of average hours will increase the number of jobs. On the other hand, if the average rate of pay per *week* cannot be reduced and the total wage bill cannot be increased, then a reduction in *hours* per week will not create any more jobs. In general the situation will be more complicated than either of these simple examples, especially in the longer term, because the level of output will be affected and so will wages, prices and profit margins. We suppose that the full effects will be different in different industries and occupations.

The case for limiting hours of work does not turn only on calculations of this sort. Independently of its effect on employment we feel that no-one should be required to work longer than is good for their health or their wellbeing more broadly defined. In some cases this is really an issue about the rate of pay per hour, which we have already discussed in chapter 6 where we support the introduction of a minimum hourly rate. But in other cases it is a separate issue, which may indeed require separate regulation of maximum hours, as is the practice in Continental Europe.

The economic effects of such regulation, or of deals negotiated between employers and trade unions, might well be beneficial for society as a whole in creating more jobs. Just how beneficial it would be, and in what circumstances, are matters which need further investigation. British economists seem particularly reluctant to accept that this might be one means of increasing total employment. We would like to see the question investigated in more depth as it may have important implications for policy.

Work and the Family

Poverty and unemployment have a corrosive effect on family life. They make people unable or unwilling to take on the commitment of marriage or any stable relationship. They can damage self-esteem and mutual respect - they should not do so, but in practice they do. In communities where young men have little hope of finding work they cannot take on the responsibilities traditionally associated with fatherhood. Moreover, as we have seen, unemployment has been identified as a cause of divorce and family breakdown. Relations between parents and children are often made much more difficult if either or both are out of work. Politicians seeking measures to support the family would do well to turn their attention towards the labour market.

We are very conscious that the relationship between employment and family life is one aspect of our enquiry which we have not been able to cover in the depth which is required. Although some valuable studies have been done, it is an area which would probably benefit from further study by social scientists. It is one of the most serious questions we face as a society. How can the participation of both parents in the labour force be best reconciled with the stability of marriage and the upbringing of children? Should single parents be encouraged to return to work at the first opportunity? How can the skills of parenting be enhanced and passed on to each new generation? What responsibilities rest with the family for the well-being of the elderly and the disabled? We do not claim to have the answers to these questions, but we do see the need to ask them. Part of the solution must be a more active involvement of fathers in the upbringing of their children than the work place as it is now organised usually allows.

The provision of childcare in Britain lags far behind what is available in much of Europe. This makes it much more difficult than it need be for parents, especially single parents, to combine the care of children with paid work. Moreover the quality of childcare varies so much that it is impossible to generalise about its effect on the lives of the children. As a society we are deeply ambivalent about the role of childcare and its place in the economy. Is it part of a modern welfare state? Or is it a luxury that only the well-paid parent should be able to afford? It would certainly be one sector of the economy where lots of good jobs could be created. But who should pay for them? If we want parents to work, and especially parents who would otherwise be dependent on state benefits, then that issue has to be resolved one way or another.

Attitudes to the working lives of men and women still reflect the traditions of a male-dominated society. The obstacles which this puts in the way of women seeking to work on equal terms with men are described in a paper by Anne Borrowdale called *Sex and Sexism in the Workplace* published by the Scottish Churches' Industrial Mission in a volume called *A Woman's Place...?* She writes:

'It still seems to be the case that women need to be better than men to succeed, yet they are blamed for being unfeminine if they do. Nevertheless a lot of women put a great deal of energy into trying to have both a successful job and a fulfilled family life - and that is why so many women feel under pressure. Women are often associated with the gentler virtues of caring and tenderness, and this leaves men free to pursue success in a harsh competitive world. But if women too are only seeking fulfilment, wealth and ambition, society seems doomed...The answer is not to discourage women from having careers, so that they may continue to be the carriers of virtue, but to challenge damaging patterns of work and encourage men to change their behaviour.' (p78)

The question then arises whether encouragement of new working patterns needs to be reinforced by changes in the law. Shirley Dex in her paper 'Employment and Caring within Households' included in the volume on *Building a Relational Society* edited by Nicola Baker makes three very concrete suggestions. The working hours of **all** parents with children under 10 (fathers as well as mothers) should be restricted. Those who care for young children should be paid a sum by the state equal to the annual value of the personal tax allowance. There should be a legal entitlement to (unpaid) parental leave in the form of reduced hours for parents. Of these, the third is clearly the easiest one to implement.

We learnt something of the problems of combining work with family responsibilities from Lucy Daniels, the director of Parents at Work. In 1996 that organisation was conducting a campaign against long hours from an office located, appropriately enough, in the heart of the City of London. It culminated in a national Go-Home-on-Time Day which achieved some coverage in the press. She said that in her view the ideal solution for families would be for both fathers and mothers to have paid work for four days a week, each looking after the children on one weekday. The other three weekdays would be covered by a childminder. She thought that a good childminder, and the company of other small children, might well provide better child care than a mother could do on her own.

We also received a report prepared by the Liverpool Diocesan Board for Social Responsibility on work and families in Warrington called *A Family Affair?*. As well as bringing together some national statistics, the report described research carried out in 13 local organisations. They found that

'of all the working time arrangements in operation in the case study organisations, flexitime appears to be viewed most favourably by employees... The perceived advantage of flexitime over more informal arrangements for altering starting and finishing times is that the element of managerial discretion is removed.'

This agrees with the other findings that

'three-quarters of employees in the case study organisations stated that they were sometimes or often asked to work additional or different days. This could prove disruptive to child care arrangements if employees feel unable to refuse such requests.'

This survey illustrates quite vividly the practical difficulties which working mothers still face. One way of describing the situation is that most women have chosen to enter the labour market, but that they have not given up their other job of looking after the children and doing most of the housework. The combination can be quite unreasonably stressful and exhausting. It seems that we are in a process of transition to a different way of organising work and family life, but there are serious tensions still to be resolved.

It is not only children who are affected by these changes in family life.

The role of the older generation is also called into question. An interesting point was made to us about grandmothers. In the current period of transition, some working mothers are able to rely on their own mothers to look after the young children. But this will not be so true in the future because the grandmothers themselves will have jobs.

The report on the family of a working party appointed by the Church of England Board for Social Responsibility, published in 1995 with the title *Something to Celebrate*, touched on the relationship of work to marriage and the upbringing of children. It said, for example that

'it is possible to see the participation of women in the labour force as a consequence of feminism, or of changes in the character of family life, but it is at least as convincing to consider change in the economic environment as the cause, and the social revolution of the late twentieth century as the result.' (p61)

Undoubtedly the opening of access to employment for women has been associated with a fundamental change in the internal economy, and one might say the internal politics, of the household. In the process the economic rationale for a lifetime commitment to marriage has been seriously weakened. This brings into greater prominence the other purposes of marriage, including the moral and spiritual rationale for a lifetime commitment.

The main purpose of marriage and family life is not, of course, economic. To quote again from *Something to Celebrate*:

'The modern view of the family is sometimes dominated by economic concerns, according to which the home is either an escape from work or a base from which people do other work or go out to work. The Christian understanding is different. The role of the family is not, in the first instance, to produce workers. Rather the role of the family is to produce healthy, mature and creative human beings who have learned that, in a quite profound sense, our true work as human beings is to love God with all our hearts and to love our neighbour as ourselves.' (p79)

One very important component of the traditional work ethic has been the responsibility of husbands to support their wives, and fathers to support their children. The nature of that obligation is now changing, but that does not mean it has disappeared. If the relationship were to become fully symmetrical, then wives would need to accept a responsibility to support their husbands, as indeed some are doing already. The alternative is to make the two partners in a marriage economically independent of each other, but that would surely destroy one essential element of the relationship, that is the sharing of 'worldly goods', for better or for worse.

We have not been able to resolve the many very difficult dilemmas which we have identified. We are clear on one thing: parenting is among the most important tasks that women and men ever undertake. On their success rests the future wellbeing of our whole society. This fact needs to be recognised more widely, not least in relation to employment. Whatever their employment situation may be, mothers, and fathers as well, have a prior commitment to their children. But the upbringing of children is not just a responsibility for their parents: it involves us all. That fact also needs to be recognised. Ultimately we would foresee the need for changes, both in the law and in accepted employment practices. That is as far as we can take the debate ourselves; it would be particularly appropriate, in our view, for a church working party like our own, but with a different mix of expertise, to try to take it a stage further.

Enough Good Work for Everyone

Work is a social activity. Indeed, from one point of view, it is work which makes society possible. That is why discussion of the work ethic cannot be separated from discussion of full employment. Work is one of the most important ways in which we all relate to one another, the quality of our relationships reflecting the ways in which work is organised. Many of the values on which the existence of society depends - self-discipline, honesty, co-operation, mutual trust - can be learned in the workplace. That is why unemployment destroys the fabric of society as well as individual lives.

Bishop David Sheppard delivered a lecture to the Royal Society of Arts in London in March 1995, with the title *Count us in: The Quest for Unity in Britain*. On the subject of employment he had this to say:

'In some areas, where mass unemployment is two or three generations deep, rhetoric about bringing back full employment will be greeted with hollow laughter. The objective needs to be spelled out more accurately'.

Hence this enquiry.

We have heard some very different reactions to the expression 'full employment' during our enquiry. The trade unionists we have spoken to made it clear that in their view this was the right objective. Indeed they urged us to reaffirm it. Some people in business and industry said quite explicitly that they thought such an objective was unrealistic. They thought we should concentrate on measures to combat long-term unemployment, since that was what caused the greatest hardship. Some people in church organisations, and others with first-hand knowledge of conditions in areas of deprivation, assumed that mass unemployment would persist for the foreseeable future. Their most urgent concern was to make the life of unemployed people easier to bear.

In March 1996 the International Labour Office (ILO) organised a seminar in London in collaboration with the Employment Policy Institute on the theme 'Choices and Trade-offs - the Political Economy of Full Employment'. The speakers were four well-known economists: Patrick Minford, Dennis Snower, Andrew Glyn and Andrew Britton, the executive secretary of our own working party. Minford proposed further deregulation of the labour market together with lower interest rates; he believed that there would be political support for such a package from the floating voters. Snower proposed employment subsidies for the long-term unemployed and the replacement of unemployment benefits by 'negative income taxes'. These would go a long way to meeting employment objectives. Glyn favoured a mix of job creation measures including tax-financed public spending. He said he did not accept the conventional wisdom that increased taxation is not politically feasible. This very disparate group of economists each prescribed a different cure for the same disease; but none said it was incurable.

As we have made clear earlier in this report, we do not think that society must, or should, accept the continuation of mass unemployment. The social ills to which we have drawn attention will continue, and indeed get worse, until there is a substantial increase in paid employment. Moreover we are very concerned with the quality of employment, as well as the quantity. That is one significant difference between the problems we face now and those of earlier generations. We must resist the temptation to follow the American solution which creates more jobs at any price.

It is all too easy to imagine that the future might be a return to the past. Those who talk of reviving the work ethic too easily assume that this means restoring the work patterns of say the 1950s. Those who talk about regaining full employment too easily assume that the economic and social conditions which made that possible in the past can be brought back to life today. In fact we are moving on beyond the economies of the 1980s and 1990s to something quite different again, which we cannot see at all clearly at this stage.

For all these reasons we cannot summarise all we want to say about job creation simply by setting a target for the percentage rate of unemployment. If we said nothing about that percentage however, we might give the impression that a rate not very different from that prevailing in Britain and Ireland today would be acceptable. We must make it clear that such an impression would be totally wrong. Of course unemployment cannot be eliminated altogether, especially in a flexible economy subject to rapid technical change. Of course the highest priority must be to tackle long-term unemployment. All the same we do not think that society should rest content until the unemployment percentage overall in our countries is substantially, and permanently, lower than it has been in the last twenty-five years. Given the problems of measurement and definition it is difficult to set an arithmetic target, but the figure of 4 per cent, suggested to us by the Wales TUC, at least points quite firmly in the right direction.

The right slogan for today might be 'Enough Good Work for Everyone'. That avoids the danger inherent in the words 'Full Employment' of suggesting a return to the conditions of the past, for example to full-time jobs for all men but not for women. It also avoids the danger inherent in the word 'opportunity' which now appears very often in the rhetoric about employment policies. The theoretical opportunity to work is of little value unless there is enough actual demand for labour in the economy. Moreover some people need more than just the opportunity to work; they need positive help in finding work as well. The qualification 'good' before the word 'work' sums up one of the most important messages we want to convey. Work may be good in itself; but some jobs are not good at all. Finally the words 'for everyone' convey the original sense of 'full' employment and emphasise that one of the main reasons for setting this objective is an abhorrence of social exclusion. As David Sheppard put it: 'Count us in'.

A Sense of Common Purpose

Charles Leadbeater and Geoff Mulgan of the policy institute Demos wrote an article in 1994 called *The End of Unemployment, Bringing Work to Life.* They said,

> 'Unemployment is not just an issue of economics. Effective job creation would dramatically improve the quality of life for millions of people without jobs. It would also help the overworked and over stressed, and the many millions trapped in unskilled, unfulfilling jobs. Above all it would help our society regain a lost sense of vitality and common purpose. That is why this is now the central issue facing Britain today: the litmus test of political leadership.'

This is, of course, precisely what we have been saying in this report. The creation of enough good jobs for everyone would make a big difference to the lives of everyone in the community, not just those now out of work. The whole economic life of society would be driven more by hope and less by fear. There would be more hope of personal and social improvement in the quality of life as well as private consumption; there would be less fear of individual failure and hardship or of social conflict and disorder. As things are now we cannot be a society which is at ease with itself.

Politicians of all political parties in Britain today have failed to give the lead which is needed to win support for the change of policy which is required. We have found that many people would in fact be prepared to support a radical approach and do accept that there are costs which have to be paid if the problems of the labour market are to be tackled effectively. This seems to be particularly true of people in the churches, and we hope that they can use their influence on public opinion as a whole to good effect.

There needs to be, as we have indicated, a change of heart. This will be necessary to bring about the policy changes that are needed. It is equally necessary to raise the priority given to employment issues in the decisions of business and industry. The promotion of good employment should be central to the mission and values of all companies and all public authorities. Trade unions should press for more and better jobs, and not just for their own membership. There needs to be a change of climate, as well as some new economic policies.

The 'sense of common purpose' to which the Demos article refers may need some new institutions to express it. In the Republic of Ireland regular consultations take place between representatives of government, employers and employees to discuss the performance of the economy, the policies which might improve it and the implications for prices and pay. The suggestion is under discussion that representatives of the unemployed should also take part in these talks. That would seem to us an excellent idea.

These Irish consultations no doubt remind many British observers of the various phases of prices and income policies in Britain from the 1950s to the 1970s. We have considered whether an institutional setting of this kind could or should be revived as part of the changes of climate we have described. In particular we are concerned that the maintenance of high levels of demand for labour should not result in a return to high levels of inflation. As in the past the sense of common purpose might need to express itself as restraint in increasing both prices and wages. John Cole, a member of our working party, with his long experience of successive phases of incomes policy in Britain, has reminded us of the benefits which resulted from voluntary agreements in the days of Cripps in the 1940s, Macmillan in the 1950s, Wilson for a time in the 1960s and Callaghan briefly in the 1970s. At different times the same tripartite approach has worked well in West Germany, Austria, Holland, Norway, Sweden and Denmark. We all recognise the attraction of these examples, whilst seeing the risks and the headaches they would bring as well. Ideally we would look for a way of reviving the concept of partnership in a new institutional framework appropriate to the 1990s and beyond.

We have to emphasise again that the future cannot be a return to the past. The TUC, amongst others, have told us that the structure of pay bargaining is now so fragmented that there is no way of imposing controls or 'delivering' an agreement reached at national level. So it cannot now be a matter in Britain as it is in Ireland of centralised bargaining adopting a 'formula' with confidence that it can be applied locally. Something quite different would be needed.

There is a good case, as a start, for some kind of national employment forum in which questions of job creation, pay and conditions of work could be debated. It could have a broad remit, as broad perhaps as the coverage of this report. It would include representatives of interested groups, not just employers and employees, but consumers, investors, central and local Government, and of course the unemployed. It would advise, not only government, but all the other interested groups as well. It should not itself make policy for anyone, but it could have a powerful influence nevertheless.

Work is the Key

In our enquiry we have been particularly influenced by the Pastoral Letter of the Irish Catholic Bishops called *Work is the Key* published in 1992. It was introduced to us by one of our members, Margaret Burns of the Council for Social Welfare. The bishops ask what seems to us the right question about unemployment:

> 'How can we live so complacently with it? Only an intense and practical indignation, undiluted by rationalisation, by selfishness, or by the kind of excuses which sound weak and unacceptable to unemployed people themselves, can generate the kind of resolve that the present situation demands. This indignation is not a transient emotion nor a self-righteous anger but a real, continuing, concrete determination to overcome the evil.' (p20-1)

We agree that work is the key. It is not only the key to new hope for individuals suffering poverty and social exclusion; it is also the key to social harmony and a better life for us all. We do not believe that any other key will fit.

The Irish Bishops, in the introduction to their Pastoral Letter, say that their competence is 'religious and, therefore, ethical and human, not economic'. They say that they do not offer a 'blueprint for job creation'. The aim of our enquiry is rather different, in that we have been asked to produce a report which 'analyses the various emerging trends, and evaluates the policy options from a Christian stand point'.

Our main findings could be summarised as follows:

* New technology, economic globalisation and changes in the structure of employment offer great opportunities for human creativity and well-being. They also present very serious challenges to society, because of the increases in both unemployment and poverty.

* The problem is not just one of creating more jobs, but providing enough good work for everyone to do. By this we mean jobs which produce something of real value, and jobs with decent pay and conditions of work. This will call for some sacrifices, but given the right priority, we believe that the problem can in fact be solved, over a period of years or perhaps decades.

* The combination of policies most likely to achieve this aim includes:

- reform of the tax system to encourage much more employment in the private sector;
- much more employment in the public sector, financed by higher taxation;
- a programme creating good jobs for the long-term unemployed;
- a national minimum wage;
- better conditions of work and fairer bargaining over pay;
- reform of social security benefits to reduce reliance on means testing;
- giving priority in the education system to basic skills for all young people;
- a national employment forum at which such policies could be debated by all interested parties.

The problem is not just a technical one of finding clever solutions to economic problems. The spirit in which policy measures are implemented is as important as their design. At every stage there must be both justice and compassion. Without them, we may be sure that the evil in society will simply reappear in some other form.

PART THREE: WHAT THE CHURCHES CAN DO

Chapter Eleven

Christian Mission and the World of Work

In his Preface to the Statement by the Catholic Bishops' Conference of England and Wales, *The Common Good*, Cardinal Hume wrote as follows:

'Religion is always personal, but never just a private affair. Discipleship involves seeking God in this world, as well as preparing to meet Him in the next. The Gospel imperative to love our neighbour entails not only that we should help those in need, but also address the causes of destitution and poverty, the deepening of the spiritual life must go hand in hand with practical concern for our neighbour, and thus with social action.'

On our visit to South Yorkshire we were met by civic leaders with the comment that they were pleased to hear that the churches were taking an interest in unemployment and the future of work. They said they were pleased but not surprised. This is an involvement that they had come to expect of the churches in their part of the country.

Individual Christians witness powerfully to the social implication of the gospel in the way that they live their lives as workers, employers or consumers and in their giving to help those in need. They also serve the community through their involvement in secular organisations, such as trade unions, professional associations, charities, pressure groups and political parties. The Christian allegiance of British political leaders is becoming more visible and is receiving more public attention. One of the most important tasks of the churches is to equip their members to respond in this way. But we are concerned in this enquiry with the witness of the churches themselves and of other groups or bodies which are explicitly Christian in their allegiance or objectives. In this third and final part of our report we consider what they might say and what they might do in response to the challenge and opportunities facing society as a whole outlined in the chapters above.

The paper by Peter Sedgwick (Annex A) describes how Christian teaching about society and the world of work has developed from its Biblical foundation. In our enquiry a great deal of very helpful material has been provided to us by churches and Christian organisations and we have also been able to draw on a number of publications and reports by church groups large and small concerned with the issues of unemployment and the future of work. We are very conscious that we are building on the work of others and we have not attempted to repeat what has already been done well.

The Future of Work study group of the Baptist Union sent us a set of six papers as their contribution to the enquiry. The introductory essay by Simon Jones is reproduced as Annex H below. The other papers, by Albert Richards, Robert Paul, Paul Allen and Doreen Landriau, have all been of great value to us. The papers submitted by the Industrial and Economic Affairs Committee of the Church of England included the paper by Michael Bourke, reproduced as Annex F below. We have made use of several other papers prepared by that committee, of which our executive secretary has been a member. (It merged in 1996 with the Social Policy Committee to form the new Social, Economic and Industrial Affairs Committee.) Our debt to the publications of the Roman Catholic Churches will be very evident from the quotations in our report, especially *Work is the Key* by the Irish Bishops, *A New Community of Work* by the World of Work Committee in England and Wales, and most recently *The Common Good*. From the Methodists we received *Our Daily Labour*, a very helpful reflection on employment, growth, conservation and the environment. Looking further afield we are particularly aware of the publications of the World Council of Churches, notably the July 1996 issue of the *Ecumenical Review* which is devoted to *Work in a Sustainable Society*. The Work and Economy Network in the European Churches held a consultation in September 1996 and the valuable papers prepared on that occasion are available from the William Temple Foundation at Manchester Business School.

We are aware that this literature raises many theological issues about the nature of work and society which we have not attempted to cover in this report. Malcolm Brown of the William Temple Foundation sent us a very interesting paper on issues of method raised by an enquiry of this sort - see Annex I below. We have not answered these questions, except perhaps implicitly by the way we have done our theology in preparing this report. Our priority was to devote time to policy issues. Nevertheless we hope that this is not just yet another report about the economy which might just as well have been written by an economics institute.

At an early stage of the enquiry members of the working party were asked to write down what values they thought our report should express. One response was as follows:

'I believe that love is the foremost value which should run throughout our report. This should distinguish uniquely the Churches' Enquiry into Unemployment and the Future of Work from the several others currently under way.'

We hope that we have achieved that aim.

The churches should have something to say which is different from the message of any political party or interest group. They cannot, for example, unequivocally support either the free market or a planned economy. If we lived under state socialism the main targets to attack, if we were so bold, would be coercion, corruption and waste. Living as we do under triumphant capitalism, we should be more concerned with private greed, social exclusion and exploitation. This does not mean, of course, that all Christian or church leaders have a duty in our present society to speak for the left of the political spectrum. Christians should write their own political agenda, which cuts across the familiar party differences. That agenda, as we hope this report has demonstrated, is not a compromise between familiar political positions. In the words of John Atherton, 'Christian social vision has to offer a radical framework to ensure that the rejection of the two opposing ends of the spectrum does not become an excuse for a centrist Laodicean moderation which is neither hot nor cold. For that will never remove poverty or grave divisions from Britain' *(Faith in the Nation, p67)*.

The churches have no special expertise to offer in the solution of economic problems. As Archbishop Temple wrote many years ago on the subject of unemployment, 'Christian faith does not by itself enable its adherents to foresee how a vast multitude of people, each partly selfish and partly generous, and an intricate economic mechanism will in fact be affected by a particular economic or political innovation'. This is clearly right, and very relevant to an enquiry like our own. We may conclude that a particular set of policy measures holds out a good hope of creating more and better employment, but requires the sacrifice of other objectives if it is ever to be put into operation. Economics being such an uncertain science, we may be right or wrong about that; it cannot be a matter of religious faith. Political as well as economic judgement is involved. We hope however that the churches will endorse our view that measures to promote employment should be given much higher priority than they have been so far.

The Churches and the Policy Debate

The initiative of the churches in launching this enquiry was welcomed in talks with us by politicians of all parties, by officials and representatives of the many organisations which we have consulted. Appendix A describes the process we have followed and mentions many of those who have been of assistance to us. We have been very pleased that so many people in positions of great responsibility in government, industry, trade unions and the churches have felt able to talk with us about the momentous issues with which we have been concerned. The involvement of the churches in the national debate over the future of work is seen as appropriate particularly by those who are themselves active church members, but also by many others whose connection with the church is slight or non-existent. This may be partly because the churches can raise issues and suggest remedies which political parties and interest groups regard as out of bounds.

According to a recent study - *Changing Perspectives: Christian Culture and Morals in England Today* by Rosalie Osmond - the majority of people believe that the stand taken by the churches on moral and social issues does have an influence on society as a whole. This view was actually held more strongly by atheists and agnostics than by Christians. It applied to issues of public as well as private morality, specifically to unemployment, but more strongly to poverty and racial discrimination. It seems as if the churches can sometimes speak, not only on behalf of their active membership, but also for the Christian beliefs which still underlie the attitudes and ideals of many people today. This gives church leaders an influence beyond the size of their immediate 'constituency'.

One leading politician who has directly asked the churches to contribute to the debate about poverty in Britain is Peter Lilley, the Secretary of State for Social Security. He gave a public lecture in Southwark Cathedral in June 1996 on the theme of 'Equality, Generosity and Opportunity - Welfare Reform and Christian Values'. He began: 'I am not one of those who deny the right, indeed the duty, of the Church to speak out on political issues. Christianity affects every aspect of life and therefore must encompass politics. On the issue of poverty the Church has always played a supremely important role.' He ended with the words: 'There is no bigger challenge than helping people off welfare and into work. The Church has always, and properly, concerned itself with the least well off. But the greatest good we can give them is to help them help themselves. So I would welcome the Church's contribution to the debate on how this can be achieved.'

Church leaders have been able on occasion to speak in national policy debates on behalf of the powerless, whose voices might not otherwise be heard. This was one reason for the impact of *Faith in the City*. What can be achieved in this way is also illustrated many times by Bishop David Sheppard in his book *Bias to the Poor*. During the course of our enquiry the national organisation, Church Action on Poverty, organised a series of 'hearings' in many parts of Britain at which people living in poverty, including many who were long-term unemployed, had the opportunity to describe their way of life to an audience of leaders in church and community. This process culminated in a national hearing in the Assembly Hall of Church House in Westminster, attended by the national leadership of the main Christian denominations as well as members of Parliament and representatives of business, the trade unions and many other organisations. It was a memorable and moving occasion, and a powerful demonstration of how the churches can act to stir the conscience of the whole nation.

The churches also have influence because they include in their member-ship many in positions of power and responsibility in government, business, trade unions and other organisations. This means that they can draw on a wide range of experience and expertise to ensure that their contribution to debate is not based on misunderstandings of the situation. Nevertheless the churches as institutions - even the established churches - are no longer identified with the political 'establishment', and are free to raise protest against injustice or inhumanity.

The role of church leaders in responding to social problems is not just to articulate the views of church members. Nevertheless there is a danger of disunity, and very visible disunity too, if church leaders, and national enquiries like this one, speak only for, and to, an active minority in church circles with an interest in social affairs and not for the church membership as a whole. There is a continuing need for wide consultation or accountability using the different structures that exist in each denomination.

Provided that these processes are taking place in each member church of the Council of Churches for Britain and Ireland, there are great advantages in the churches speaking collectively on the issues discussed in this report. Clearly this was recognised when the enquiry was set up, but we would urge that collaboration should continue as a matter of course. This could avoid duplication of effort in relation to issues, like unemployment and the future of work, which do not appear to raise any serious issues of doctrine or practice that divide Christians on denominational lines.

Statements made on behalf of all the churches on social issues where sufficient agreement exists will carry much more weight with public opinion than a number of similar statements by individual denominations. This does not mean, of course, that there will be no disagreement or debate within the churches on these issues. On the contrary we hope that the vigorous discussions which we have heard taking place, and in which we have taken part, will continue and will attract public interest. If anything our anxiety is rather that the debates within the churches are conducted in terms which mean little to those outside, and which do not hold out much hope of reaching a conclusion.

A report of this kind may hope to have some impact when it is published. But experience suggests that this will soon be lost if no follow-up activity is planned. The ideas which we develop in this report are radical and they should be the subject of continuing debate and controversy. There are areas of our very wide remit which we have not been able to explore at all thoroughly. As one example we might mention the issues surrounding retirement and the provision for an adequate income for pensioners. Another is the role of local initiatives in building communities and fostering local enterprise. Yet another is the care of those with mental or physical disabilities, including their access to work whenever appropriate. We have already mentioned the relation between work and family life as a crucial issue to which we think the churches should return. These, and other related topics, could usefully be taken forward by study groups, including experts in the relevant secular disciplines as well as theologians and also people who are directly affected in their own lives. As with this enquiry the aim would be to 'evaluate the policy options from a Christian standpoint' as well as to 'offer a theological exploration of the issues'.

The Carnegie Inquiry into the Third Age offers an interesting model for the follow-up to a study of a major social issue. After the main report was published in 1993, a programme committee was set up for a further three years, recently extended to six. This meant that the conclusions of that report could be tested and refined by further debate, could be kept up to date with subsequent developments, could be expanded into new areas and above all could be promoted vigorously in the media and kept high on the policy agenda. All these aspects of a follow-up are at least as relevant in the case of the present enquiry.

In the nature of church structures, especially when many different churches and several different nations are involved, it is not immediately obvious where responsibility for such a follow-up would lie. There is a danger that no organisation will feel it appropriate for them to take it on. We would suggest that our own sponsoring body should remain in existence after the enquiry is complete and after this working party has disbanded. Its next task might be to decide how best the work could be carried forward, either by the sponsoring body itself or by some other group of church representatives within the framework of the Council of Churches for Britain and Ireland.

Mobilising Our Resources

The churches themselves are deeply involved in the world of work and with the social issues which have been the concern of our enquiry. We will concentrate in this chapter on employment projects and industrial mission in Britain, but many other Christian activities and organisations take part in mission to the world of work. We should also mention the Catholic Young Christian Workers, the Social Responsibility Boards, the Justice and Peace Committees, the William Temple Foundation, the Industry Churches' Forum, the Von Hugel Institute, the Jubilee Centre, the Hinksey Centre, St George's at Windsor, St William's at York and too many more to list them all. There is a great deal of excellent work going on, indicating a high level of interest and commitment.

We are also conscious that these efforts need some co-ordination to make them fully effective. Someone remarked to us that the churches' activities to help the unemployed were impressive but patchy. In some places churches seem to be falling over one another to obtain support for employment projects; in others no-one is doing very much at all, so far as we could tell. Much depends, as it must do, on the initiatives of individuals, acting as catalysts to promote activity in the church as a whole.

We, as a working party, were not asked to review the use of resources within the churches or to recommend how the best results could be obtained. We do feel however that we have identified the need for a rather different sort of enquiry to which such a remit could be given. It would need first to map the current situation in all the relevant church and Christian organisations. Then it would ask where existing resources (human and financial) could be better deployed. Having done that it would be well placed, if it saw fit, to make a strong case for more resources in total to be provided by the churches. Our overall impression is one of dwindling resources leading to defensive reactions. Unless some action is taken by the churches together there is a danger that the potential for effective mission in the economy will gradually be diminished, and both church and society will be poorer as a result.

There are some areas of the world of work where the churches need to lead by example as well as words. The employment practices of the churches themselves may not be altogether above criticism. We have been aware that some of the clergy and other church employees with whom we have been discussing pay or employment conditions may not have always been treated very well themselves. 'Down-sizing' is not unknown in the churches and it has not always been as well handled as it should be. Many employees of the churches, including the clergy, are encouraged to overwork. Some churches are copying the secular world in discriminating against applicants for jobs simply on the basis of age. Ethnic minorities and the disabled are under-represented in church employment. Some lay people employed by the church as well as the clergy themselves are paid very low wages indeed. Church leaders and officials have in recent years been striving, quite rightly, to make more efficient use of church funds, adopting some of the management practices being introduced in competitive firms or in the public sector. But in the churches above all, the search for efficiency surely cannot be given priority over giving fair and even generous treatment to all those in their employ.

One reason why the churches will be listened to when they talk about unemployment and contribute to a national debate is that many Christian organisations are known to be active locally in helping people in poverty and unemployment in a variety of practical ways. In the course of our enquiry we have visited a number of such projects and organisations, to observe their work and discuss its impact with them. We have been impressed again and again by the dedication and enthusiasm we have seen, and by the success which many groups have achieved. The churches are determined to stay in the inner city centres and on the toughest estates, where many other national institutions and professional groups have given up trying to help, or offer help only from a safe base located at a distance.

The activities which we have seen, or heard about, cover a wide range. They include counselling and pastoral care of the unemployed, training and careers guidance, community development and organisation, care for the homeless and ex-offenders. Often it is difficult to draw the line between help with employment problems and help with related problems of education, morale or discrimination. Christian organisations are concerned with the whole person, not just with their potential contribution to the workforce.

We have been able to observe industrial mission, in which several members of the working party are involved, in action at a local level. This also encompasses a wide variety of activities: pastoral care of individuals in the workplace, mediation in industrial disputes, advice and counselling in relation to redundancies, study groups and prayer in a workplace setting, bringing local economic issues to the national agenda or taking part in local or regional economic planning.

Most local Christian initiatives in the world of work face some of the same problems in relation to funding, to partnerships with government agencies, to the involvement of local churches and to the perception of Christianity in the communities they seek to serve. Below we give some examples of these problems as well as the various solutions which have been found to them. We are very grateful to all the organisations which have provided us with valuable information.

Employment Projects

The **Peckham Evangelical Churches' Action Network** (PECAN) in South London is a good example of a Christian-based employment project. It began in the late 1980s with the observation that shortages of skilled and reliable staff persisted in an area with up to 30 per cent unemployment. The answer was to go from door to door personally inviting unemployed people to attend an employment preparation course. PECAN now trains over 1000 local residents each year and has total annual income and expenditure of over £350,000, of which the bulk is from statutory grants and a Jobclub contract. Its example and assistance has contributed to the foundation of similar projects in other locations, including the Hackney Employment Link Project (HELP) which has grown rapidly in the last few years.

Also in London we visited **New Life Electrics**, one of several projects run by Quaker Social Action. This is unusual in that it is entirely independent of statutory funding, relying on donations and trading income. It provides training and work for unemployed people and at the same time reconditions cookers and other electrical equipment for families in need.

We obtained a more comprehensive picture from the London Churches' **Employment Development Unit**, an ecumenical body, funded by the London Borough Grants Committee, which provides advice to churches on how to set up and manage church projects for unemployed people. In their report *Into the Lion's Den* they describe 21 such projects active in 1993, which between them had 1470 'clients' with 37 paid staff and 358 volunteers.

No such organisation exists nationally but projects are nevertheless abundant in most parts of Britain. Special mention should be made of the **Christians' Unemployment Group** in South Yorkshire (CHUG) which in 1995 was in contact with over 20 community projects in that area related to unemployment, poverty and community development. It has been involved in campaigning and practical work since the early 1980s.

As an example of Christian involvement in vocational training we visited Training for Employment Ltd, in Exeter, a subsidiary company of **Christian Care Training**. This is a successful training provider offering courses for NVQ levels 1 to 3 and modern apprenticeships. It grew out of an initiative by local church leaders in the 1980s and retains its link with them although it now operates as a quite separate organisation. The profits generated by its business activities enable it to pursue social objectives, for example in giving more individual advice and guidance to trainees than could be provided using statutory funding alone.

To illustrate the link between pastoral work and employment advice we could quote the example of the **St Ignatius Housing and Advice Centre** in South Tottenham. The project was set up about twelve years ago, and grew out of the help given by a Catholic parish church to people who were homeless and asking for food or money. It became clear that there was also a need for advice in seeking work and a volunteer was found with experience of working for the Employment Service. The centre is open on Sundays so that people can call in for advice before or after attending mass. The organisers believes that spirituality cannot be divorced from the rest of life.

Right at the beginning of our enquiry we were told that one of the organisations we must certainly visit is **Respond!** on Teesside. We did so and we were impressed by what we saw. It was established in 1984 as the response of the major church denominations in the region to the crisis of unemployment. It was asked to discover 'new patterns of living and working'. It 'provides a space for people to share their ideas and visions, their concern and problems, and supports them in making a response'. It has organised workshops, national conferences and meetings between church leaders and successive Secretaries of State for Employment. It shows how thought and action can be integrated, helping individuals to cope with their own problems but also asking what is wrong with the society in which such problems arise. We are convinced that Christians should do all these things, and do them together so that the way they all relate to Christian faith is clearly expressed.

In many communities programmes for economic regeneration and employment creation should rightly be organised on an inter-faith basis. We met with the organisers of **Linking-Up**, a 'multi-faith led' project development agency run from an office of the Board for Social Responsibility of the Anglican Diocese of Manchester. It arose out of the *Faith in the City* report and existed to foster community development in deprived city areas and to advise groups based in churches or other religious communities. The philosophy was that regeneration depends on the people themselves taking the initiative, with religious leaders sometimes proving to be the key to such action. The aim was not to spread religious belief - whether Christian or otherwise - but rather to provide the help that is needed for people to improve their own lives. That can itself, of course, be an excellent example of Christian service and witness. Sadly we learnt towards the end of our enquiry that the project is now in abeyance as funds cannot be raised to keep it going.

We also made contact with a different approach to urban renewal in the form of the **City Life** initiative being developed by the Relationships Foundation associated with the Jubilee Centre at Cambridge (which also ran the Keep Sunday Special campaign). What they aim to do is to rebuild the relationships on which the strength of the local economy rests. In this way the enthusiasm, the enterprise and the finance can all interact together if the right catalyst is present to get the reaction going.

Various different strands of Christian involvement in the world of work have come together to draw up the **Teesside Employment Initiative**, a proposal for action supported by Shape Training, Respond!, Teesside Industrial Mission, the Relationships Foundation and the Anglican Diocese of York. This is an ambitious programme to create jobs in the social economy for people who are long-term unemployed, drawing on the experience of other projects in the intermediate labour market, such as Glasgow Works and the Wise Group, described in chapter 7 above. After six months of development a concrete proposal was put to the relevant agencies of national and local government. At the time of writing the outcome of this submission was still awaited.

During the period of our enquiry we learnt of the launch in London of **UK Action**. This is a new venture by Tear Fund, the evangelical Christian organisation best known for its work in helping poor communities overseas. In the words of the UK manager 'when people at the bottom of society's heap are treated with dignity and respect, their spiritual needs start to be addressed.' The work includes help with training and in looking for employment as well as many other social and individual needs. It is a sign of the times that charities set up to help the poorest people in the 'Third World' are now turning their attention to people in all too similar circumstances in Britain as well.

In financial terms a very significant contribution to urban regeneration, and to addressing the problem of poverty and unemployment in inner-city areas has been made by the **Church Urban Fund**. This fund was set up by the Church of England, following the publication of *Faith in the City*; it is a sign of the church's own commitment to meeting the challenge identified in that report. The total of church money given through that fund in response to unemployment and the problems associated with it has amounted over ten years to more than £2.6 million.

The European Contact Group on Urban Industrial Mission has collected together the experience of churches in several countries in responding to the challenge of unemployment. A report is available from the William Temple Foundation with the title *Working Models: Unemployment and Church Action*.

Some more general conclusions emerged from the many examples we met. Firstly the churches have been heavily dependent on public funding to support their voluntary action. That funding was relatively abundant in the 1980s, most notably through the Community Programme. We have met both critics of that era and enthusiastic supporters of it, as indicated in an earlier section of this report. Whatever its merits as a programme, it certainly created opportunities for many churches to take direct action in the face of a social disaster affecting the communities they served. Some church projects ran into acute financial difficulties as public funding was withdrawn and some memories of that period are still bitter. Other projects survive to this day, having changed course to secure new sources of public finance, either as training providers or as providers of Job Clubs and similar schemes. This history raises difficult questions about the proper relationship between Christian service to the community and the changing policy framework laid down by the government of the day.

The point is well illustrated by the experiences of churches with Project Work as it was piloted in Kent and Yorkshire during the time of our enquiry. This programme involves compulsion in that people who refuse to take part, or fail to co-operate, lose 40 per cent of their entitlement to Income Support. For this reason several church based groups refused to take part in the programme.

One could argue the case for compulsion either way and we have made our own views clear in an earlier section of this report. The point to make here is that Christian groups must be prepared to take a stand on principle if they believe that any schemes introduced by government are unfair or ungenerous. In the last resort they must be prepared to reduce their scale of operation to that which can be financed from other sources, especially from the donations of church members themselves. It is the existence of such donations, and especially the gifts of time by volunteers, which enable church projects to have their special character and merits. There would be little point in the churches or other explicitly Christian groups running projects on a purely commercial basis delivering what the state as sole paymaster prescribes.

Churches and other Christian organisations who decide to set up projects designed to help unemployed people would usually be well advised to draw on the experience of existing groups and copy the features of their projects which have been most successful. We are keen that the enthusiasm of church members should be channelled into effective action, and also that what the individual group can achieve is set in the wider context of action by the church as a whole.

Industrial Mission

The history of Industrial Mission in Britain goes back more than forty years with the appointment of the first industrial chaplains commissioned specifically to work with people in industry and commerce. It could be seen as a natural development of the role played by chaplains in the armed services, in hospitals or in schools. But it was also a reaction to the neglect of large sections of the population by the mainstream churches ever since the first industrial revolution. It was not just opening up a mission to work, but also a mission to the working classes, as they would then have been described. The situation is well described in the writings of Ted Wickham, who was the pioneer and inspiration of the movement in the post-war period, notably in *Church and People in an Industrial Society* published in 1957 when he was an industrial missioner in Sheffield.

The Industrial Mission Association handbook for 1995 lists over 300 members in England and Wales, most of whom are engaged in mission to the world of work either full-time or part-time in conjunction with parochial or similar responsibilities. Most of them are ordained ministers, with a majority of Anglicans but good representation of all the main Protestant denominations. There are IM teams in England, Scotland and Wales, but none in Ireland, North or South.

Industrial Mission, now sometimes called Mission in the World of Work, or Mission in the Economy, involves both workplace visiting and helping local churches to take an active interest in the economic life of the local community. It seeks to understand the nature of working relationships by patient listening to many different points of view and by close involvement in the life of the workplace community. Ultimately its objective is to transform work in the light of the Christian Gospel. In the guidelines prepared by the Churches' Commission on Industrial Mission in the 1980s its goal was described as follows: 'Industrial Mission works for the reordering of the relationships, methods and goals of industry and commerce, in the light of the Christian hope for justice and community, and through the process of participation, reflection and evaluation'. Increasingly, in the 1990s, there is emphasis on the local economy as a whole, not just industry and commerce but housing, health, education and welfare as well. Some Industrial Missioners are becoming what is known as 'social entrepreneurs' offering advice and leadership to communities in need of economic development.

Some examples may illustrate the range of IM activities taking place during the period of our enquiry.

* The South Hampshire IM prepared study material for use by churches and other groups on the implications of a statutory minimum wage. This was done in relation to Christian teaching. It gave examples based on concrete employment situations in the local economy showing what kinds of jobs would be most affected.

* Leeds IM held an international conference on home-working, bringing home-workers from several other European countries to Yorkshire to talk to local people and to share ideas for more effective organisation and campaigning.

* South London IM appointed a pastor of a black-majority Pentecostal church as a missioner with special responsibility for issues of racial discrimination in employment, seeking commitment from firms to the Sheppard-Wood principles described in chapter 6 above.

* Merseyside and Region Mission in the Economy kept in contact with leaders of both sides in a long-running industrial dispute at the docks. Industrial chaplains briefed and supported church leaders acting together in attempted initiatives towards a settlement.

Industrial mission has been a focus for controversy ever since its foundation. A vivid, but also balanced, account of the disputes surrounding the Sheffield Industrial Mission, as well as its notable successes, is given in the history *The Church beyond the Church* by Paul Bagshaw. There have been disputes over theology, arising from the fear that traditional Christian teaching was being compromised in an attempt to be more relevant or more appealing in an irreligious culture. There have also been disputes over politics, because of the perceived close alignment of some missioners with political movements and parties of the Left. Some disagreements of this kind are, in our view, inevitable and indeed healthy. It is far better that the issues be discussed openly with mutual respect within the fellowship of the church, than that they should be a hidden source of mistrust and disunity.

An additional source of dispute, in some parts of the country in recent years, has been the finance and funding of Industrial Mission. It would not be too much to say that some missioners feel they have been let down by the churches which have supported them in the past. As one of our members put it:

> 'Much of the story of industrial mission has been one of frustration, with constant problems of the wider church not fully 'owning' its work, or of industrial mission failing to get itself 'owned' by the church. And now it is threatened by complete disappearance.'

This is mainly a reflection of a general shortage of resources, which has led to cut-backs in all forms of sector ministry. Like many corporations, churches have seen the need to concentrate resources on their 'core business activities'. This has been taken to mean local congregations. Our view is that mission to the world of work is central to the effective preaching of the gospel, as well as Christian service and witness in the world.

A review of Industrial Mission in England was commissioned by a committee of the Anglican Board for Social Responsibility in 1987, the report being published with the title *IM - An Appraisal*. The Chairman of that working party was Bishop Peter Selby who is also a member of our working party. The closing words of the report are:

> 'It is the responsibility of the whole Church to ensure that its missionary policies in the industrial and economic field are properly integrated with all other aspects of mission and ministry. Industrial Mission needs to feel that it really belongs and is properly located in appropriate church structures, where its voice can be heard.'

Alongside this quotation could be set one from *Front Line Mission: Ministry in the Market Place* a recent book by Denis Claringbull, National Moderator of the Industrial Mission Association. He writes:

> 'The Christian Gospel proclaims how Jesus became incarnate in the front line in a carpenter's workshop in Palestine two thousand years ago, and that the Church is called to be the Body of Jesus Christ incarnate in the workshops of the world today. The Church must not therefore behave as if it were a private holy club for religious people, or a safe refuge from the 'naughty' world. The Church proclaims God's love for the whole world. The focus of

the Church's ministry should therefore be those who are engaged in the secular world and to provide support and affirmation to those who are in the 'front line' in public life.'

Various schemes have been devised to shift the financial cost of Industrial Mission off the churches and onto someone else. There have for example been experiments in sponsorship by businesses or trade unions. This is clearly not intended to be a payment for services rendered, but it nevertheless runs the risk of being seen as such. If church-based groups are offering counselling services, careers advice to individuals or even business consultancy to management then it is only to be expected that the 'customer' will pay. There is a close parallel here with the use of statutory funding by church groups involved in employment projects and Job Clubs. But if Industrial Mission is also, as it should be, part of preaching the gospel, then it is the responsibility of the churches, in financial as well as in spiritual terms.

Several ideas are being tried out in different regions to integrate more closely the activities of Industrial Mission and social responsibility. This seems very appropriate given the emphasis within Industrial Mission today on taking care of the casualties of economic life, especially those who are hit by redundancies. On our visit to the North-East we saw the Churches' Regional Commission in action. Its overall aim is 'to enable the Churches in the North East to engage purposefully, creatively and strategically with the economic, social and cultural life of the Region'. It was very clear from our visit that this aim is, to an increasing extent, being achieved. The projects we visited involved Christians from many different denominations, and their work was being enhanced by the resources which the Commission could provide. They covered a wide range of activities, some essentially pastoral, others undoubtedly prophetic. The different kinds of ministry, drawing on different experience and traditions, were being successfully brought together. No doubt more needs to be done, for example to involve local congregations more fully with the project work, but we felt we were observing an experiment that showed every sign of success. It may have lessons for the organisation of similar activities in other countries or regions.

Industrial Mission is organised on a local or regional basis, and that is one of its strengths. Nevertheless it needs some co-ordination and management at a national level. In England a new body called INDEM, the Churches' Co-ordinating Group for Mission to Industry and the Economy, was set up in 1996. It has no executive authority, but will co-ordinate action and maintain a strong link with the supporting churches. This new organisation may be the means of reviving IM where it is not fully effective and reforming it where that is necessary. We hope it will also ensure that the supporting churches make adequate funds available to the very important missionary tasks that face us all in the world of work.

Work and the Local Congregation

Most people experience the Church, not as a national organisation engaged in policy debate, not as ministry in their place of work or training, but as a local gathering of a few dozen, or at most a few hundred, people who worship and pray together. The clergy who lead and minister to these congregations often determine the role that the churches play in the wider society in which they are set. It is the voluntary service of committed lay members of these congregations that makes church life possible. Church mission to the world of work must be founded on belief and action at this local level, on prayer, on praise and on fellowship in Christ.

It is a continuing complaint, however, of many lay people in all denominations that the local churches to which they belong give them little or nothing to support them in the work that they do for a living most of the week. Many of the clergy, and the active lay leadership as well, still seem ignorant and uninterested in issues of business, employment or economics. When 'work' is discussed in church it too often means only work on church committees or working parties. Congregations expect to be asked to support organisations like Christian Aid or CAFOD which help the poor in other parts of the world, they do not expect to contribute directly to industrial mission, or employment projects in this country or the Young Christian Workers. Little reference is made to everyday work in the course of public worship, in prayers or sermons. This supports the model of religion as an escape from the problems of the world, not as a means of addressing them. Lay people who attend church only irregularly see it as a suitable place to celebrate 'rites of passage' in family life, but a world away from their everyday occupations or the difficult transitions they must make in work and inactivity.

A postal survey of churches was undertaken by Church Action With the Unemployed (CAWTU) in 1992/3 asking them what they were doing about issues related to unemployment. The response rate was discouraging, but the replies included some examples of zealous commitment.

Some individual responses indicate the range of views expressed:

* '[Our Centre] for the unwaged and unemployed has existed since 1984.... In a large church hall over 80 people a week gather for classes and activities. Those who are unemployed share their skills with others... Many people have found new confidence which has helped their re-entry into the labour market. It is a very significant partnership between the local authority and a voluntary organisation, improving the quality of life in the inner city.'

* 'Our church is an open centre - unemployment is amongst other needs that come up... We do provide odd jobs etc involving unemployed people in the work of our church centre so giving them some dignity etc. Volunteers (often unemployed) man the desk.'

* 'We have an Action for Community Employment Scheme which is currently employing 23 persons with two managers and has been able to create two full-time posts as a direct result of the scheme.'

* 'As we are an enclosed, contemplative order our contribution to Unemployment Sunday is mainly in the form of prayer and solidarity...'

* 'I tried to start a club for unemployed folk, but there was nil response. People do not want to be labelled. Many are moonlighting and don't trust each other.'

* 'I think you are wasting time and money. Village churches can't do anything about unemployment except pray.'

* 'I am myself unemployed having been ordained as an NSM (non-stipendiary minister). I now describe myself as a MSU, Minister in Secular Unemployment. I shall be preaching on 21st February, the anniversary of my redundancy notice.'

Many of the responses to the survey refer to counselling and pastoral work with the unemployed. In the course of the enquiry we have received mixed reports about the support which church members who are unemployed have received from their local church. Some have spoken warmly of the help and encouragement given by individual ministers or congregations; others felt neglected and undervalued by the church just as much as they were by society as a whole.

The experience of unemployment is, of course, very different in different parts of the country. At a public meeting in Hackney we heard a clergyman pour scorn on the idea that the church might turn its back on the problem of unemployment. It was an unavoidable issue. At the other extreme a curate in the Winchester diocese sent us a report he had written in which he said that he did not know whether there were any people unemployed in his own local church. He estimated from the local percentage that at most there might be one or two. 'Because of the sensitivity which some people feel at the stigma of unemployment, there is no real way of knowing whether this is the true figure, or just a statistical probability.' He did not think however that this made the issue irrelevant to that congregation and he had chosen 'ministry to the unemployed' as the topic for his post-ordination training project.

We have not in this enquiry been able to devote as much attention as we would have wished to the vast range of moral or spiritual issues which arise all the time for individual Christians in relation to their own situations at work. What jobs should a Christian refuse to do? When does a clever business manoeuvre become an immoral deception? Is there a right way to respond to a notice of redundancy? Is there a right way to present one? How can pressure of work be reconciled with family life? The list is a very long one. Numerous books are available which do offer some guidance as to how these questions can be addressed, either by individuals on their own or in small discussion groups. We give some examples in the bibliography which is Appendix B of this report.

Some excellent study material, books and pamphlets have been prepared by various church groups in different places to help the unemployed and those who are advising them. Two examples illustrate what is available. The Unemployment Group formed by the Board for Mission and Social Responsibility of the Diocese of Newcastle have produced the *Hopeseeker Pack*. It is divided into five sections (Listening to Each Other; Behind the Headlines; Work and Worth; Unemployment and Faith; Action) together with a list of further resources and suggested reading material.

The Churches' Support Group on Unemployment in Surrey and NE Hampshire has recently produced a handbook for leaders and helpers of support groups for the unemployed. It describes how to form a group in very practical terms, with an appendix called 'Notes for Guidance for the Newly Unemployed (or Those Confused by the System!)'.

In some churches there needs to be an initial leap of understanding and sympathy before there can be any perception of what it is actually like to be poor or unemployed for any length of time. This could be helped by meeting people who are unemployed directly and by role play activities in which the choices open to the unemployed are realistically assessed. This will help to break down the antagonism to the poor and the jobless which undoubtedly exists in some congregations.

Unemployment Sunday is celebrated each year on the Sunday before Lent by churches of all denominations. Suggestions for prayers, hymns, readings and other activities are provided by Church Action on Poverty. In 1996 they distributed about 2,000 copies of their pack, which brought together the themes of unemployment and low pay. Although it is certainly welcomed by many churches, the attempt to turn this into a recognised festival in the yearly cycle of worship by the whole Christian community has not so far been successful. It is seen, by those churches who know of its existence, as an optional extra not a 'day of obligation'. That is not enough to fulfil the need we see for due recognition of human work, or lack of it, right at the heart of Christian worship.

We would strongly support an annual focus in every church on the issues covered by our enquiry, not just on unemployment, but on all the issues summarised by the 'future of work' concern. Use could be made of published material, such as pastoral letters, local or national reports, if the local church itself does not have the resources to provide its own input. One particularly useful publication which was sent to the enquiry is *The Merseyside Churches' Unemployment Book* which includes stories, readings, liturgies and prayers. Plenty of scope should be given to the local congregation to decide what kind of event is most appropriate to the area they live in and the circumstances of their active membership. We would hope that most churches would adopt Unemployment Sunday for this purpose. Another approach might be to widen the traditional Harvest Festival service to include the fruits of human labour and divine providence more broadly defined than just agricultural. It could become an annual rededication of the whole working life of the church community.

Differences of tradition and churchmanship will certainly result in differences of style in such services as well as content. The different political allegiances of church members must also be respected. This is not an occasion for preaching socialism to the middle classes or patient humility to the workers! If it is ever to be adopted by most churches, rather than just a few, in the way that Remembrance Sunday or Harvest Festival have been in the past, then it must be allowed to vary a lot from place to place. The result could be a vivid illustration of the unity despite diversity which is the great strength of the churches to which we belong.

But an annual celebration is not the only way for churches to express this side of their faith. Study groups, prayer groups and home groups may be founded with a particular focus or experience in the labour market. This could lead to mutual support or outreach as well as social action. In some circumstances it could well lead to protest against some injustice in the local economy.

It would seem appropriate for churches of different denominations in the locality to work together on issues of this kind. As at the national level, there are few issues of doctrine dividing denominations, and the impact on public opinion would be all the greater. Where local ecumenical co-operation is languishing, for example because of differences amongst the local clergy on strategies for evangelism, this could be an occasion for reviving it.

It was suggested to us when we visited South Yorkshire that every local church in the whole country should be involved in some way with the running of a community employment project. We agree that this should be the aim. Some of the contribution will be financial, supporting projects in more needy areas, but money is not a good substitute for more personal involvement. Even in prosperous suburbs there are many people who need practical help in finding work or overcoming poverty. We have met several cases where members of the local congregation were said to resent the time devoted by their clergy to social work outside the church fellowship. That attitude strikes us as dreadfully narrow. Clergy in that position should surely be asking their congregations to share more actively in the work that they are doing and make that an important part of their Christian service and their common life.

Our main concern is that the world of work should be taken right into the heart of Christian life, which is the main Sunday service that most church members attend. This is when we all pray together, every week in most churches, for peace and justice in the world, for those who are sick in body or mind and for the coming of God's Kingdom here on earth. We should also pray, every week as a matter of course, for God's help in our daily work, for economic justice and prosperity, and for the poor, the overburdened and the rejected.

In many churches the main service on Sunday morning is a celebration of the Eucharist or Holy Communion. This is the point at which all the great themes of Christian belief and worship come together. One such theme is 'the work of human hands'. The offering of bread and wine to be transformed into the body and blood of Christ is a symbol of the offering of all our lives - God's gifts to us given back to God. With this we also offer the work that we have done, knowing that God can transform it so that it will become part of a new creation. Having been given power by the Holy Spirit we are then sent out into the world to live and to work to God's praise and glory.

A CONCLUDING REFLECTION

Working Still

The rush hour traffic jams, and people packed into buses and trains, give a clear message: people are going to work, more or less willingly, for more or less money, with better or worse prospects for the future. Most people are still working, making a contribution to the common good, the common wealth. They draw from the stock of 'jobs', of work which people will pay to have done.

Such full-time workers continue to be the majority; most of us who have served on this enquiry belong to that majority in one way or another. As we join our own train, it is easy to feel that the future of work is like the past: toiling through the week for a pay packet at the end of the month.

Yet even as the majority of us crowd into our trains we know that 'working lives' are changing around us: the 'future of work' is already part of the present. Some have an exciting sense of how their work has changed: they find themselves on the technological frontier, part of the information revolution that has produced challenging jobs for some and unemployment for others as certain jobs are made unnecessary, and with the jobs the people are made unnecessary too. Some work in the expanding sectors, service industries or financial services, often working a different pattern of hours, perhaps participating in the economy 'online' from home.

At the same time, though, we sense a new 'labour force' growing around us, working 'part-time' or 'more flexibly', with contracts, if they are lucky, that have limited benefits and hardly any security. We know that work in the public sector has been put out to tender, and for some that has meant doing the same work for less money, or responding to the threat of unemployment by accepting work they would far prefer not to do.

As members of the enquiry we are conscious of living in that changing world of work even without the searing experiences of exclusion from society which are the lot of those who have no paid work. We have sought to do justice to the experience of those who have spoken to us from that situation.

We recognise that while we are all aboard the 'train' of work now, or have been for most of our lives, along with the majority for whom this is a 'working life', even if a different one from what they had once expected, others are not on the train at all, often for short periods but in some cases for years, and in many communities for generations. They are 'the unemployed', or as we should want to say, unemployed people; and it is their situation that has concerned us most both in our debates and on our visits. We have written most about them in our report because, being denied a place on the train they sense themselves to be abandoned to a twilight existence on the edge of society. We have been confronted again and again with the low priority they occupy in most of the political programmes about which this year's general election campaigns are waged.

We have met unemployed people on our visits and have been confronted by their ingenuity and resilience in the face of circumstances that would (we often felt) defeat most people who have jobs and incomes. We have been amazed at the determination of so many of them to seek work come what may and to accept wages which scarcely exceed what their benefit entitlement would be - in some cases not even matching it. We have been moved by the commitment of many to pioneer initiatives that enable creative opportunities to open for people who are unemployed. They set an example of endeavour motivated by compassion, often empowered and encouraged by their Christian faith. They are working still, seeking to change as much as they can and to support those whose situations appear beyond change.

In the midst of this experience we have found ourselves united in a sense of outrage that such a proportion of our population should be ignored. We have been determined to regard the issue of unemployment, massive numerically and of long duration, as one not to be forgotten, and to communicate to our fellow-Christians, and to all our fellow-citizens in these islands, what we have observed both of injustice and of hope. Many people who are unemployed are 'working still', seeking change in their communities and our society, drawing others alongside them in working for what is just.

In all of this we have pressed ourselves constantly with the question how the dynamic of Christian faith can energise an approach to these issues. What do we expect to get from the tradition of faith which has itself confronted the issue of work? And what specific remedies, if any, do persons of faith seek to offer? And if the Bible and the body of Christian teaching cannot bring any remedies to bear, other than providing texts to justify the shame which many people of goodwill feel anyway, does that not undermine the credibility of faith itself?

To be a member of this enquiry has involved a constant movement back and forth between our inheritance of faith and our experience of the plight of the unemployed and the ill-treated. The Bible does not speak of public sector borrowing or job creation, of a benefit system, of the respective merits of direct and indirect taxation, of world markets and industrial competitiveness; that might suggest either that it is simply reduced to silence in the face of this massive human problem, or that we need some complex system for 'deducing' economics from biblical texts.

Yet we have not found ourselves faced with such a choice. Time and again we have found ourselves driven back to the Bible, to our common experience in worship and to the teaching of our churches, by the experiences and conversations we have had. And when we return to the resources our faith offers us, what we find is something very specific to drive our search for remedies: the vision, backed by stories of actual history, of a human society reflecting the shape God gave to the world; a society where money and wealth and land are there for sharing, and where for that reason the firstfruits of the harvest, the first portion of all wealth, is to be set aside, a sign that all wealth comes from God.

So in the search for solutions, the Bible is working still, and calling us to work in quite specific directions that challenge the common assumptions of the societies of these islands. This, the body of teaching and experience of God's people, is not merely the rhetoric that can say, confronted with unemployment, that 'we are against it'. It is a word that directs our attention to the how and the why of our present political climate, and calls for specific changes of attitude as absolutely necessary for the devising of the remedies we need.

We believe that the remedies we propose are just and feasible; but even more we are clear about what changes of attitude are needed, especially in the understanding of the nature of our wealth, where it comes from, what it is for and whose needs have highest priority in the shaping of human community. We have found the movement between the experience of unemployment and work as our society has allowed it to be and the resources of faith a powerful tool as well as a direct encouragement in our search for solutions.

Part of what we have found, too, is something about work that is not connected with money: the rhythm of work and rest, of shared recreation as part of the basis of society, are, on the one hand, grounded in the Sabbath tradition of faith and, on the other, demonstrated as absolutely essential by the serious consequences we see in a society where work is so unequally shared. On the part of those who have no employment, we have seen a real longing for the place a job gives; on the part of many who have work, a grave forgetting of the way in which our personal and social health depend on our sharing Sabbath celebration and restfulness and on a balance between work and play.

This report is meant as a call to be working still against the tide that accepts this inequality of work and rest. Society seems to have taken a false Sabbath of complacency from action against injustice in place of the promised Sabbath rest that is promised to God's people when they have worked for God's commonwealth of justice and peace. That is the desire of a God who will not rest till all the children of God's love are included.

Appendix A

THE CONDUCT OF THE ENQUIRY

The proposal for an enquiry into unemployment and the future of work arose out of discussions held within many different church organisations in the late 1980s and early 1990s. For example, CAWTU (Church Action with the Unemployed) which was an ecumenical body concerned both to give practical help to unemployed people and with campaigning on their behalf proposed a 'high level commission…consisting of people who can command the respect and confidence of all sections of the community and all political parties'. An independent initiative about the same time brought together church leaders on Merseyside, including the Anglican Bishop of Liverpool, David Sheppard and the Catholic Archbishop, Derek Worlock. The proposal was also discussed by the informal Anglican Urban Bishops' Group, which was formed following the publication of *Faith in the City* in 1985.

These and other concerns about unemployment and the future of work were brought together in the Social Responsibility network, which meets under the umbrella of the Council of Churches for Britain and Ireland. The Revd Ermal Kirby, the Public Affairs Secretary of CCBI, convened a 'shadow' Sponsoring Body, which prepared the ground for putting forward a plan for an enquiry: the Churches Representatives Meeting of CCBI agreed that this should be an independent enquiry conducted under the auspices of the CCBI. The different churches nominated members of the formal Sponsoring Body, which was given the task of raising the finance, setting the terms of reference and appointing the Working Party. An appeal for funds was sent out during the course of 1995 with the support of the Archbishop of Canterbury, the Cardinal Archbishop of Westminster and the President of the Free Church Federal Council.

The enquiry was launched on 29 September 1995 with a press briefing and the mailing of an information pack to several hundred addresses. The aim was described as producing a report which:

- offers a theological exploration of the issues
- analyses the various emerging trends, and evaluates the policy options from a Christian stand point
- will attract the general approbation of the Churches
- will be of real service to both Church and Society.

The Sponsoring Body

Archbishop Derek Worlock was a member of the Sponsoring Body until his death in February 1996, when his place was taken by Bishop John Jukes. The members were:

Rt Revd David Sheppard, Bishop of Liverpool - Chairman
Ruth Badger - Secretary
Marion Beales (Free Church Federal Council)
Rt Revd M Bourke, Bishop of Wolverhampton (Church of England)
Ruth Clarke (United Reformed Church)
Ven John S Davies (CYTUN - Churches in Wales)
Lady Marion Fraser (Church of Scotland)
Revd Robin Hutt, Chairman of the Newcastle District (Methodist Church)
Revd Simon Jones (Baptist Union)
Rt Revd John Jukes OFM Conv, Bishop of Strathearn (Roman Catholic Church)
Rt Revd Dr Gordon McMullan (Church of Ireland)
Hugh Mellor (Society of Friends)
Revd Mark Nicholson (Black Majority Churches)

The **chairman** of the working party at the time of the launch was Sir Geoffrey Holland, Vice-Chancellor of Exeter University. Unforeseen pressure of work obliged him to resign in May 1996 and he was succeeded by Patrick Coldstream CBE, Director of the Council for Industry and Higher Education. The **executive secretary**, who worked full-time on the enquiry, was Andrew Britton, formerly Director of the National Institute of Economic and Social Research. An **assistant**, Katie Lane, worked for the enquiry half-time. The sixteen members of the working party covered a wide range of experience and expertise, and belonged to a variety of different denominations. One member, Brandon Gough, resigned in August 1996 due to pressure of other commitments. Anthony Stoughton-Harris was appointed to replace him. At the end of the enquiry the membership of the working party was:

Patrick Coldstream - Chairman
Andrew Britton - Executive Secretary
Revd Bill Allen, Director of Pastoral Studies, Spurgeon's College, South Norwood, London
Clive Brooke, Joint General Secretary, Public Services, Tax and Commerce Union
Margaret Burns, Roman Catholic Council for Social Welfare, Dublin
John Cole, formerly Political Editor, BBC
Gabrielle Cox, Co-ordinator, Grater Manchester Low Pay Unit
Revd Erik Cramb, Industrial Mission in Scotland
Ricky Davies, Director of Management Services of Associated Church Clubs and formerly
    National President of the Young Christian Workers
Alan Deacon, Professor of Social Policy, University of Leeds
Kumar Jacob, Criterion Software Ltd
Dr Eleanor James, Chair of Wales Rural Forum
Revd Dian Leppington, Industrial Mission in Leeds
Rt Revd Dr Peter Selby, Professorial Fellow in Applied Christian Theology, University of
    Durham and Bishop-designate of Worcester
Anthony Stoughton-Harris, Deputy Chairman of Southern Electricity and formerly Chairman
    of Northants TEC
Dr Ntombenhle Protasia Khoti Torkington, Dean of Hope in the Community, Liverpool Hope
    University College

The office for the enquiry was set up at the South London Industrial Mission, 27 Blackfriars Road, London. Administrative help was provided by the staff of CCBI, and secretarial help by Deborah Cunningham.

Terms of Reference

The terms of reference for the Working Group were:

a)   to develop a theological framework for the Enquiry
b)   to evaluate existing work
c)   to collect examples of good practice and practical experience within the Churches
      concerning both unemployment and employment
d)   to examine the changing nature and patterns of employment, noting the impact and
      influence of polices of the European Union
e)   to discover and describe the effects of such changes on the well-being of all people,
      identifying the particular effects on men and women, the young, the disabled and the
      members of different ethnic and religious groups
f)   to give early and careful attention to the best means of communication of the findings.

Joint meetings of the Sponsoring Group and the Working Party were held in London in January, September and December 1996 and in February 1997. Day meetings of the Working Party were held at SLIM in October 1995, March, May, August, October and December 1996, and in January 1997. Presentations to London meetings of the Working Party were made by:

Mr Dominic Cadbury, Chairman of Cadbury Schweppes
Mr Andrew Dilnot, Director, Institute for Fiscal Studies
Mr Frank Field MP
Prof Richard Layard, London School of Economics
Mr John Monks, General Secretary, TUC
Rt Revd Rowan Williams, Bishop of Monmouth

At the August meeting, David Price, recently retired from a senior position in the Employment Service, presented a paper on policies to help the long-term unemployed. At the October meeting the Working Party met with a group of people with experience of long-term unemployment. A report was presented by the group, prepared in co-operation with David Cross and Paul Goggins of Church Action on Poverty. At the same meeting there was a consultation with employers and experts in human resource management.

The first residential meeting of the Working Party was in **Exeter** and organised by Sir Geoffrey Holland in January 1996. Presentations were made by clergy, community workers, and representatives from training organisations and the Employment Service in the region.

The second residential meeting was held at Dunblane in **Scotland** in April. It was organised by Erik Cramb, a member of the working party. A visit was paid to Yarrow Shipbuilders on the Clyde where the group met Murray Easton, the Managing Director and Ian Jackson, Director of Personnel. Presentations were made to the working party on behalf of the Scottish TUC, Unison and the Wise Group.

The third residential meeting was in **Liverpool**, co-ordinated by Randell Moll of 'Mission in the Economy'. For the first session, with the theme 'Training for What?' the Working Party divided into four groups and held discussions with 24 representatives of industry, local government, trade unions, churches and the unemployed. Members also joined a breakfast meeting of the Michaelmas group, an informal consultation group chaired by the Bishop of Liverpool. Visits were made to a centre for the unemployed, a manufacturing company, training organisations and a drop in centre for people with mental health problems. There was a discussion meeting with members of the local 'Future of Work' project, chaired by Hilary Russell and introduced by Paul Skirrow.

The fourth residential meeting was at **Durham** in September, co-ordinated by Chris Beales of the Churches' Regional Commission in the North-East and Tony Attwood of Teesside Industrial Mission. The programme began with a visit to Teesside to see the Cleveland Trade Union resource centre and meet members of the action group Respond! as well as the OK4 drop-in centre at Redcar and the Teesside Training Enterprise College. Presentations were made by representatives of Tyneside TEC. The working party split into groups to visit: South Tyneside Training and Enterprise Network, Bonas Machine Company, Northumbria Churches' Training Consortium, Project North East and the Durham University Arts and Recreation Chaplaincy.

The final residential meeting involved visits to Ireland both North and South. In **Belfast** the programme was organised by Rt Revd Gordon McMullan, a member of the sponsoring body. Presentations were made by local clergy, community workers and academics. The working party met Bob Cooper, the Chairman of the Fair Employment Commission as well as Roy McNulty, Chairman and Brian Carlin, Vice-President of Short Brothers.

In **Dublin** the programme was organised by Margaret Burns, a member of the working party. Presentations were made by representatives of the Irish Congress of Trade Unions, The Irish National Organisation of the Unemployed, the Irish Business and Employers' Confederation and the Department of Enterprise and Employment. The working party also met John Bradley and Brian Nolan of the Economic and Social Research Institute as well as John Sweeney SJ from Leuven University.

In addition to these residential meetings of the whole working party, sub-groups made one-day visits to a number of other cities and regions.

In **South Yorkshire** the meeting of the group was hosted by Mike West of the South Yorks Industrial Mission. It visited the Highway project in Conisbrough, the Rotherham District Council and the Lower Don Valley Economic Development Project. A discussion took place with the Churches Together in South Yorkshire Unemployment Strategy Group.

In **Birmingham** the meeting was organised by Denis Claringbull, the National Moderator of the Industrial Mission Association and chaired by Rt Revd John Austin, Bishop of Aston. Consultations were held at the Bank of England and the executive secretary of the working party gave a lunchtime lecture in the Cathedral. About 30 representatives attended from local business and industry, trade unions, church organisations, and centre for the homeless and the unemployed.

The visit to **Cornwall** was organised by Alan Chesnay of the Council for Social Responsibility of the Diocese of Truro. The executive secretary met church leaders and unemployed people at Lis Escop, before visiting St Austell College, the St Austell Job Centre and the Community Centre at Hayle.

The visit to **Cardiff** was organised on behalf of CYTUN, Churches Together in Wales, by Richard Kilgour and James Hall. Presentations were made by Welsh trade unions and employers organisations, unemployed people and community workers, a local government official, and representatives of the Wales Rural Forum, the Welsh Development Agency and the Prince's Business Trust.

The visit to **Cambridge** was arranged by Geoff Pearson, a chaplain to people at work. The executive secretary visited the Cambridge Job Centre and the Cambridge TEC. On the Cambridge Science Park he called on Chiroscience Ltd, a pharmaceutical company. He also visited a community service project in Huntingdon and the Cambridge career guidance centre.

Consulting and Collecting Evidence

The executive secretary and other members of the working party have consulted very widely, in a series of informal meetings with individuals and representatives of organisations, including the following:

Political leaders:	Rt Hon Gillian Shepherd MP, Secretary of State for Education and Employment
	Rt Hon Peter Lilley MP, Secretary of State for Social Security
	Rt Hon Dr Gordon Brown MP, Labour Party front-bench spokesman.
	Mr Michael Meacher MP, Labour Party front-bench spokesman.
	Mr Don Foster MP, Liberal Democrat front-bench spokesman
	Sir Ralph Howell MP, Conservative Party back bencher.
Officials:	Department of Social Security, Department for Education and Employment, Scottish Office.
Church and Christian Organisations:	The Archbishop of Canterbury, The Cardinal Archbishop of Westminster, The Moderator of the Free Church Federal Council, William Temple Foundation, Church Action on Poverty, Linking-Up, Jubilee Centre,

Evangelical Alliance, Churches' Commission on Racial Justice, Church Action on Disability, Luton Industrial College, Baptist Union, Plater College.

Industrial Mission and
Employment Projects: Leeds IM, Norfolk and Waveney IM,PECAN (South London), London Churches' Employment Development Unit, Quaker Social Action, Christian Care Training (Exeter), Hackney Employment Link Project, St Ignatius Housing and Advice Centre (Tottenham), Cambridgeshire IM, Medway Unemployment Centre, Home Counties South IM, Merseyside Mission in the Economy.

Other Individuals and
Organisations: Confederation of British Industry, Parents at Work, Institute of Directors, Cariocca Enterprise Park (Manchester), London Docklands Development Group, Centre for Local Economic Strategies, The Post Office, Christian Association of Business Executives, Advisory Conciliation and Arbitration Service, BT, ICI.

Other Activities

The Executive Secretary has carried out a number of engagements related to the work of the enquiry, including the following:

- Address in Lichfield Cathedral for the celebration of industry in the Midlands
- Address to Black Country Urban Mission
- Radio interview on Analysis Programme about unemployment
- Talk to Association of Christian Economists about the enquiry
- Workshop at SLIM Economic Forum
- Paper on 'Full Employment' at seminar of Employment Policy Institute
- Presentation to St George's, Windsor, Consultation
- Talk at Chatham House Seminar on Unemployment in Europe
- Address to Industrial Mission Association Conference on Mission to the World of Work
- Address to URC National Gathering at Birmingham on the Future of Work
- Paper presented to annual conference of the Society for the Study of Theology at Cambridge on Economics and Christian Belief
- Talk to seminar on unemployment at South Bank University
- Lecture on Economics and the Gospel in Manchester Cathedral
- Paper to Cambridge Econometrics on economic and employment policies of three political parties
- Lecture to St Lawrence Roman Catholic Church, Sidcup
- Presentation to South-east Institute for Theological Education
- Workshop at ecumenical gathering at Stowmarket in Suffolk.

Finance

The total budget for the enquiry was over £80,000. Contributions were made by churches, companies, trusts and individuals including the following:

Central Church Fund, Bishops of London, Liverpool, Birmingham, Manchester, Wakefield, Ripon, Leicester, Southwark and Lichfield, United Reformed Church, Methodist Church, Religious Society of Friends, Catholic Bishops' Conference of England and Wales, Church of Ireland, Churches Together in Wales, Free Church Federal Council, St Martin-in-the-Fields.

Richard Attenborough, Holt Trust, ICI, Mercers Company, North West Water, Nuffield Foundation, TUC, Unilever, Carnegie Foundation

Appendix B

BIBLIOGRAPHY

At the end of an enquiry with as broad a remit as this one it is impossible to list all the publications which are relevant to the subject matter of our report. In this bibliography we concentrate on books, papers and other resource materials which have influenced us, either directly or indirectly. Most of those listed here are recent and the great majority are published in the UK. We have not attempted to be comprehensive even within that scope, but readers of the report may find it useful to be pointed towards sources where they will find the topics we have addressed in this report described and debated at greater length.

The bibliography is in six parts, but inevitably some items really span more than one area. It may be advisable therefore to look through more than one section when collecting material on a particular topic.

1.   The Future of Work

Barley, S. R.: *The New World of Work*, British North America Committee, 1996.

Bloch, S and T Bates: *Employability - Your Guide to Career Success*, Kogan Page, 1995.

Bridges, W: *Jobshift*, Brealey, 1995.

Britton A: *Changing Jobs*, ICF Quarterly Papers, Winter 1994/5.

Dicken, Peter: *Global Shift*, Chapman, 1992.

Fabian Society: *Changing Work* - Report of an Enquiry, 1996

Handy, Charles: *The Empty Raincoat*, Hutchinson, 1994.

Handy, Charles: *The Future of Work*, Blackwell, 1984.

Keesler, I and R Undy: *The New Employment Relationship*, IPD, 1996.

Leadbeater, C and J Lloyd: *In Search of Work*, Penguin, 1986

Leadbeater, C and G Mulgan: *The End of Unemployment - Bringing Work to Life*, Demos Special Employment Issue, 1994.

Meadows, P (ed): *Workout - or Work in?* Joseph Rowntree Foundation, 1996.

Rifkin, J: *The End of Work*, Putnam, 1995.

Robertson, James: *Future Work*, Gower, 1985.

Robertson, James: *Future Wealth - A New Economics for the 21st Century*, Cassell, 1990.

Royal Society of Arts: *Redefining Work* - Seminar Report, 1996.

Schumacher, E: *Good Work*, Abacus, 1980.

Stanworth, J and C: *Work 2000*, Paul Chapman, 1991.

Stevens, B and W Michaelski: *The Future of Work and Leisure*, OECD, 1994.

2.   Unemployment and Economic Policy

Alogoskoufis et al: *Unemployment, Choices for Europe*, Centre for Economic Policy Research 1995.

Atkinson, A and G Mogensen: *Welfare and Work Incentives*, OUP, 1993.

Barrell, R (ed): *The UK Labour Market*, CUP, 1994.

Beveridge, W H: *Full Employment in a Free Society*, Allen and Unwin, 1944.

Blanchflower, D and R Freeman: *Growing into Work*, OECD, 1996.

Bradley, J et al: *Stabilization and Growth in the EC Periphery*, Avebury 1993.

Britton, A: *The Goal of Full Employment*, National Institute of Economic and Social Research, 1996.

Campaign Against Arms Trade: *Killing Jobs*, 1996.

Cantillon, S et al: *Economic Perspectives for the Medium Term*, Economic and Social Research Institute Dublin, 1994.

Confederation of British Industry: *Tackling Long-term Unemployment - A Business Agenda*, 1994.

Department of Enterprise and Employment (Ireland): *Growing and Sharing our Employment - A Strategy Paper for the Labour Market*, Stationery Office, Dublin, 1996.

European Commission: *Growth, Competitiveness and Employment*, 1993.

Employment Policy Institute: *Choices and Trade-offs - The Political Economy of Full Employment*, Policy Report, June 1996.

Employment Policy Institute: *Employment Audit, 1 and 2*, 1996

Employment Policy Institute: *What Works? Jobs for Young People*, 1997.

Freeman, Charles and L Soete: *Work for all or Mass Unemployment*, Pinter, 1994.

Gregg, Paul: *Share and Share Alike*, New Economy, 1995.

Glyn, A (ed): *Unemployment*, Oxford Review of Economic Policy, Spring 1995.

Gold, M and D Matthews: *The Implications of the Evolution of European Integration for UK Labour Markets*, DfEE, 1996.

Grieve-Smith, J and J Michie (ed): *Unemployment in Europe*, Academic Press, 1993.

Grieve-Smith, J: *Full Employment - A Pledge Betrayed*, Macmillan, 1997.

Holtham G and K Mayhew: *Tackling Long-Term Unemployment*, Institute for Public Policy Research, 1996.

House of Commons Employment Committee: *The Right to Work/Workfare*, 1996.

International Labour Office: *World Employment*, 1996/97.

Layard, R (ed): *Britain's Training Deficit*, Avebury 1994.

Layard, R: *What Labour Can Do*, Warner, 1997.

Layard, R, Nickell S and R Jackman: *Unemployment*, OUP, 1991.

Marris, R: *How to Save the Underclass*, MacMillan, 1996.

Morgan, J: *Employment Protection and Labour Demand in Europe*, National Institute of Economic and Social Research, 1996.

Morgan, J: *Labour Market Recoveries in the UK and other OECD Countries*, Labour Market Trends, Dec 1996.

National Economic Research Associates: *'Right to Work' Assessment*, 1996.

OECD: *Towards Full Employment and Price Stability (The McCraken Report)*, 1977

OECD: *Jobs Study Report*, 1994.

Philpott, J (ed): *Looking forward to Full Employment*, Employment Policy Institute, 1994.

Philpott, J (ed): *Working for Full Employment*, Routledge, 1997.

Pollard, S: *Jobs and Growth*, Fabian Society 1994.

Prais, S: *Productivity, Education and Training*, CUP, 1995.

Simmonds, D and M Emmerich: *Regeneration through work - Creating Jobs in the Social Economy*, Centre for Local Economic Strategies 1996.

Stoneman, P: *The Economic Analysis of Technological Change*, OUP, 1983.

Truscott P (ed): *An End to Unemployment!* Movement for Christian Democracy, 1994.

US Department for Labour: *What's Working (and What's Not)*, 1995.

Wales TUC: *Unions Work for Full Employment*, 1995.

Worswick, D: *Unemployment, a Problem for Policy*, CUP, 1991.

Wood, A: *North-South Trade, Inequality and Unemployment*, OUP, 1994.

3. **Social Conditions**

Arendt, H: *The Human Condition*, Chicago University Press.

Argyle, M: *The Social Psychology of Work*, Penguin, 1989.

Atkinson, A B: *Income Distribution in an International Context*, South Bank University, 1996.

Baldwin, S and J Falkingham (ed): *Social Security and Social Change*, Harvester Wheatsheaf, 1994.

Boswell, Jonathan: *Community and the Economy*, Routledge, 1990.

Bradley, J: *An Island Economy - Exploring the Long-term Economic and Social Consequences of Peace and Reconciliation*, 1996.

Brown, P and R Scase (ed): *Poor Work*, Open University Press, 1991.

Bryson, Alex and John Jacobs: *Policing the Workshy*, Avebury, 1992.

Carnegie Inquiry into the Third Age: *Life, Work and Livelihood in the Third Age*, 1993.

Carnegie UK Trust: *The Third Age - The Continuing Challenge*, 1996.

Confederation of British Industry: *A National Minimum Wage - The Employers' Perspective*, 1995.

CBI: *A Skills Passport*, 1995.

CBI: *Flexible Labour Markets - Who Pays for Training?* 1994.

Coldstream, P: *Higher Education, Industry and the Journey of Learning*, Hull University Press, 1991.

Commission on Social Justice: *Strategies for National Renewal*, Vintage 1994.

Commonwealth of Australia: *Working Nation - The White Paper on Employment and Growth*, Australian Government Publicity Service, 1994.

Dahrendorf Commission: *Report on Wealth Creation and Social Cohesion in a Free Society*, 1995.

Deacon, A: 'Welfare and Character' in *Stakeholder Welfare*, Institute of Economic Affairs 1996.

Deacon, A: *Should we Worry about the Character of the Poor?* Beckly Lecture, 1996.

Etzioni, A: *The Spirit of Community*, Simon and Schuster, 1993.

Expert Working Group (Ireland): *Integrating Tax and Social Welfare*, Stationery Office, Dublin, 1996

Field, F: *Making Welfare Work*, Institute of Community Studies, 1995.

Ford J, Kempson E and J England: *Into Work?* Joseph Rowntree Foundation, 1995.

Galbraith, John K: *The Culture of Contentment*, Penguin, 1992.

Gallie, D et al: *Social Change and the Experience of Unemployment*, OUP, 1994.

Giddens, A: *Beyond Left and Right*, Polity Press, 1994.

Giles, C et al: *Living with the State*, Institute for Fiscal Studies, 1996.

Greater Manchester Low Pay Unit: *Workers' Voices*, 1995.

Hutton, W: *The State We're In*, Vintage, 1996.

Industrial Society: *The Disability Discrimination Act 1995*, 1997.

Institute of Directors: *The Minimum Wage - No Case for Complacency*, 1996.

Irish Business and Employers Confederation: *Social Policy in a Competitive Economy*, 1996.

Joseph Rowntree Foundation: *Inquiry into Income and Wealth*, 1995.

Kempson, Elaine: *Life on a Low Income*, J Rowntree Foundation, 1996.

King, Desmond: *Actively Seeking Work*, University of Chicago Press, 1995.

McLaughlin, E: *Flexibility in Work and Benefits*, Commission on Social Justice, 1994.

Moon, J D: *Constructing Communities*, Princeton University Press, 1993.

National Council for One Parent Families: *Returning to Work*, 1996.

Office for National Statistics: *Social Trends 1996*.

Ransome, Paul: *Job Security and Social Stability*, Avebury, 1995.

Real World Coalition: *The Politics of the Real World*, Earthscan 1996.

Royal Society of Arts: *Tomorrow's Company*, 1995.

Sly, F: *Ethnic Minority Participation in the Labour Market*, Labour Market Trends, June 1996.

Scottish TUC: *Beyond Enterprise - Shaping the Future for Economic Development and Training in Scotland*, 1996.

Smithers, A and P Robinson: *Beyond Compulsory Schooling*, Council for Industry and Higher Education, 1991.

Stocpol, T: *Social Policy in the United States*, Princeton University Press, 1995.

Trinder, C et al: *The Role of Work in the Third Age*, Carnegie UK Trust, 1992.

Trades Union Congress: *Arguments for a National Minimum Wage*, 1995.

Unemployment Unit: *Unemployment and Training Rights Handbook* (4th edition), 1996.

Weil S: *Oppression and Liberty*, Routledge, 1958.

Weil S: *The Need for Roots*, Routledge, 1952.

Weil S: *Gravity and Grace*, Routledge, 1952.

Walzer, M: *Spheres of Justice*, Martin Robinson, 1983.

White, M (ed): *Unemployment and Public Policy in a Changing Labour Market*, Policy Studies Institute, 1994.

Youthaid: *Guide to Training and Benefits for Young People*, 1996.

4. Christianity, Work and Society

Addy, Tony: *The Future of Work - Reflections from Europe*, Crucible, October/December 1996.

Atherton, John: *Faith in the Nation*, SPCK, 1988

Atherton, John: *Christianity and the Market*, SPCK, 1992.

Atherton, John (ed): *Social Christianity, A Reader*, SPCK, 1994.

Bagshaw, P: *The Church beyond the Church*, Sheffield IM, 1994.

Baker, Nicola (ed): *Building a Relational Society*, Arena, 1996.

Bellah, R: *Habits of the Heart*, University of California Press, 1985.

Bleakley, D: *In Place of Work - The Sufficient Society*, SCM, 1981.

Bleakley, D: *Beyond work- Free to Be*, SCM, 1985.

Borrowdale, A: *A Woman's Work*, SPCK, 1989.

Breailly et al (ed): *Faith in the Future (The 1991 Malvern Conference)*, ICOREC, 1991.

Brierley, P: *'Christian' England*, Marc Europe, 1991.

CAWTU: *Action on Unemployment*, 1994

Claringbull, D: *Front-line Mission*, Canterbury Press, 1994.

Clark, D: *Christians at Work - A Survey*, Christians in Public Life, Westhill College, 1993.

Clarke, Roger: *Work in Crisis*, St Andrew Press, 1982.

Daly H and J Cobb: *For the Common Good*, Beacon Press, Boston, 1989.

Davie, G: *Religion in Britain since 1945*, Blackwell 1994.

Davies, J (ed): *God and the Marketplace*, IEA, 1993.

Dow, G: *A Christian Understanding of Daily Work*, Grove, 1994.

Duchrow, U: *Alternatives to Global Capitalism*, Kairos Europa, 1995.

Fox, M: *The Reinvention of Work*, Harper Collins, 1995.

Gay, C: *With Liberty and Justice for Whom?*, Eerdmans, 1991.

Gonzalez, J L: *Faith and Wealth*, Harper and Row, 1990.

Gorringe, T: *Capital and the Kingdom*, SPCK, 1994.

Gray J: *The Moral Foundations of Market Institutions*, IEA, 1992.

Greene, M: *Thank God it's Monday*, Scripture Union, 1994.

Greenholm, C: *Protestant Work Ethic*, Uppsala Studies in Social Ethics, 1993.

Griffiths, B: *Morality and the Marketplace*, Hodder and Stoughton, 1982.

Grundy, M: *An Unholy Conspiracy*, Canterbury Press, 1992.

Halsey M: *Invisible Hands*, William Temple Foundation, 1996.

Hay, Donald: *Economics Today*, Apollos, 1989.

Hobgood M: *Catholic Social Teaching and Economic Theory*, Temple University Press, 1991.

Hughes J and A Morton (eds): *Work, Worth and Community*, CTPI Edinburgh, 1996.

Industrial Mission Association Theology Development Group: *The Gospel and its Competitors*, 1990.

Kuhn J and D Shriver: *Beyond Success*, OUP, 1991.

Liverpool Diocesan BSR: *A Family Affair? - Balancing the Needs of Employment and Families*, 1996.

McOustra, C: *Love in the Economy - Social Doctrine of the Church for the Individual in the Economy*, St Paul Publication, 1990.

Meeks, D: *God the Economist*, Fortress Press, 1989.

Moltmann, Jürgen: *On Human Dignity*, SCM, 1994.

Mulholland C (ed): *Ecumenical Reflections on Political Economy*, World Council of Churches, 1988.

Novak, Michael: *The Spirit of Democratic Capitalism*, Simon and Schuster, 1982.

Ormiston, H and D Ross (ed): *New Patterns of Work*, Scottish Churches' IM, 1990

Osmond, R: *Changing Perspectives*, DLT, 1993.

Preston, R: *Religion and the Persistence of Capitalism*, SCM, 1979.

Preston, R: *Religion and the Ambiguities of Capitalism*, SCM, 1991.

Richardson, A: *The Biblical Doctrine of Work*, SCM, 1952

Ryken, Leland: *Work and Leisure in Christian Perspective*, Inter-Varsity Press, 1987.

Santa Ana, J de, Raiser K and U Duchrow: *The Political Economy of the Holy Spirit*, WCC, 1990.

Schluter, M and D Lee: *The R Factor*, Hodder and Stoughton, 1993.

Schumacher, C: *To Live and Work*, Marc Europe, 1987.

Sedgwick, Peter: *The Enterprise Culture*, SPCK, 1992.

Sheppard, David: *Count Us In*, Edward Boyle Memorial Lecture, 1995.

Sheppard, David: *Bias to the Poor*, Hodder and Stoughton, 1983.

Sheppard, David et al: *God at Work*, Grove Books, 1995.

Simons R: *Competing Gospels - Public Theology and Economic Theory*, Dwyer (Australia) 1995.

Storkey, A: *Transforming Economics*, SPCK, 1986.

Stott, John: *Issues Facing Christians Today*, Marshall Pickering, 1984.

Suggate A: *William Temple and Christian Social Ethics Today*, T and T Clark, 1987.

Sweeney, J et al: *Work and Poverty, Ethical Perspectives*, European Centre for Christian Ethics, April 1996.

Temple, W: *Christianity and Social Order*, Penguin Books, 1942

Templeton, Elizabeth (ed): *A Woman's Place?* St Andrew Press, Scottish Churches' IM, 1993.

Volf, Miroslav: *Work in the Spirit*, OUP, 1991.

Webley, S: *Codes of Business Ethics*, Institute of Business Ethics, 1993

Westcott, D: *Work Well, Live Well*, Marshall Pickering, 1996.

Wickham, E R: *Church and People in an Industrial City*, Lutterworth, 1957.

Wogaman J P: *Economics and Ethics*, SCM, 1986.

5. **Church Reports**

Catholic Bishops' World of Work Committee: *A New Community of Work*, CTS Publications, 1995.

Catholic Bishops' Conference for England and Wales: *The Common Good*, 1996.

Church Action on Poverty: *Speaking from Experience* (Voices at the National Poverty Hearing) 1996.

Church of England Archbishop's Commission on UPA's: *Faith in the City*, Church House Publishing, 1985.

Church of England Bishops' Group on Urban Priority Areas: *Staying in the City*, Church House Publishing, 1995.

Church of England Board for Social Responsibility: *I.M. An Appraisal*, 1988.

Church of England Board for Social Responsibility: *Perspectives on Economics*, 1984

Church of England Board for Social Responsibility: *Growth, Justice and Work* 1985.

Church of England Board for Social Responsibility: *Something to Celebrate*, 1995.

Church of England Board for Social Responsibility: *Not Just for the Poor*, 1986.

Church of England Board for Social Responsibility: *Church and Economy*, 1989.

Church of Scotland Committee on Church and Nation: *Changing Patterns of Work in a Global Economy*, 1995.

Church of Scotland Committee on Church and Nation: *Personal Taxation*, 1995.

CYTUN (Churches Together in Wales): *Wales - A Moral Society?* 1996.

Evangelical Church in Germany and the German Bishops' Conference: *On the Economic and Social Situation in Germany*, 1994.

Irish Episcopal Conference: *Work is the Key*, Veritas, 1992.

John Paul II, *Centensimus Annus*, CTS, 1991.

Methodist Church Division of Social Responsibility: *Our Daily Labour - A Methodist Reflection on Employment, Growth, Consumerism and the Environment*, 1994.

National Conference of Catholic Bishops, Washington DC: *Economic Justice for All*, 1986.

Second Vatican Council: *Gaudium et Spes*, 1965.

UNIAPAC: *Committed Entrepreneurial Action Against Unemployment*, 1996.

Work and Economy Network of the European Churches: *The Future of Work in Europe*, William Temple Foundation, 1994.

World Council of Churches: *Work in a Sustainable Society*, The Ecumenical Review, July 1996.

World Council of Churches: *Will the Future Work?* 1985.

6.   Additional Resource Material

The list below is by no means comprehensive of all the written material which has been submitted to, or obtained by, the enquiry. For a fuller list please contact Katie Lane at South London Industrial Mission, 27 Blackfriars Road, London SE1 8NY until September 1997.

*ACAS, (1989) *Hours of Work*, Advisory Conciliation and Arbitration Service

*Attwood, A.N. (1994) *The Interaction of Faith and Economics*, The Coal Crisis 1992/3

*Ball, L. (1995) *Guide to Training and Benefits for Young People*, Youthaid

*Baptist Union Future of Work Study Group (1995) *Unemployment and the Future of Work*

*Beattie, N. (1996) *Future of Work*, Kent Industrial Mission

*Brain, P. (ed.) (1996) *Some Views on Economics*, United Reformed Church

*Britton A. (1996) *The Future of Work*, Crucible July-September 1996

*Brown M. (ed) (1994) *The Other Side of the Economic Coin - A Letter of Faith on the Economy; DISK- Industrial Mission in the Netherlands*, William Temple Foundation

*CHUG, (1996) *My Testimony: Stories from Christians about Unemployment*, CHUG

*Church Action on Poverty *Unemployment Sunday Packs* 1995, 1996, 1997

*Churches Together in South Yorkshire, Unemployment Strategy Planning Group: August 1995, *A Strategy to Help South Yorkshire Churches Respond to High Unemployment*

*Citizen's Income Trust (1995) *Aspects of Citizen's Income Papers 1-5*

*Citizen's Income Trust (1994) *Discussion Notes of Citizen's Income and the Trade Unions*

*Clements, R. (1996) *Basic Income for Beginners*, Citizen's Income Bulletin No.22

*Community and Race Relations Unit, British Council of Churches, (1990) *Account of Hope: Report on a Conference on The Economic Empowerment of the Black Community*, Community and Race Relations Unit, British Council of Churches

*Community and Race Relations Unit, British Council of Churches, (1989) *Future Investment: The Economic Empowerment of the Black Economy*, Community and Race Relations Unit, British Council of Churches

*Community and Race Relations Unit, British Council of Churches (1991), *Towards Economic Justice for the Black Community*, Issues Paper No. 10 Community and Race Relations Unit, British Council of Churches

*CBI, (1995) *A Vision for Our Future: A Skills Passport*, Confederation of British Industry

*CBI, (1995) *Realising the Vision: A Skills Passport*, Confederation of British Industry

*The Council For Social Welfare (1996) *The Dole Truth: Voices of the Unemployed*, The Council for Social Welfare, Dublin

*Cox, G. (1994) *After the Safety Net - A Study of Pay Rates in Wages Council Sectors Post Abolition*, Low Pay Network

*Cox, G. (1995) *The Impact of Employment, Fiscal and Welfare Policies on the Structure and Extent of Poverty in the UK*, Briefing Paper No.32, Greater Manchester Low Pay Unit

*Cox, G. (1995) *Jobwatch '95: A Survey of Job Vacancies*, Greater Manchester Low Pay Unit

*Cox, G. (1995) *Strategies for National Renewal? A Critique of the Social Justice Commission Report in the light of employment trends*, Briefing Paper No.31, Greater Manchester Low Pay Unit

*Cox, G. (1995) *What Future? Jobs for Young People in Greater Manchester*, Briefing Paper No.29, Greater Manchester Low Pay Unit

*Church Support Group On Unemployment (Surrey and HE Hants) (1994) *Support Groups For the Unemployed: Handbook for Leaders and Helpers*

*Davies, M. (1992) Church Action With the Unemployed: *Unemployment - A Theological Perspective*

*Davies, S. (1996) *The Minimum Wage: No Case for Complacency*, Institute of Directors

*Department of Enterprise and Employment, Ireland (April 1996) *Growing and Sharing Our Employment: Strategy Paper on the Labour Market*

*Draper, R. *Community Projects in South Yorkshire related to unemployment*, revised November 1995, CHUG

*The Ecumenical Committee for Corporate Responsibility (April 1992), *'Buried Talents' 'Ethics and Corporate Responsibility - Why Should the Churches be Concerned?' Final Report of the Race Equality in Employment Project*, ECCR

*Finn, D. (1995) *Studying While Unemployed: The Jobseeker's Allowance and the 16 Hour Rule*, Part-time briefing 2, July 1995, Unemployment Unit

*Government of Ireland (1996) *Partnership 2000 for Inclusion, Employment and Competitiveness*

*Greater Manchester Churches Together (1995), *Action For Jobs: Towards Fuller Employment*, Greater Manchester Churches Together

*Griffiths, S. (1996) *Rotherham: A Poverty Profile*, Rotherham Corporate Research Group,

*Hall, B. *Impasse: A Possible Way Forward*, from Northern Economic Review

*Harber, B. Morris P. and McCormack I (1996) *Learning to Disagree: Peace and Economic Development in Ireland*, UNISON and IMPACT

*Harman, H. (1995) *Insecurity at Work - Interim Report to IRSF*

*Hartley, N. (1996) *Towards a New Definition of Work*, RSA

*Health and Safety Commission, (1996) *The Health and Safety Implications of Changing Patterns of Employment*, Health and Safety Executive

*Hewitt, P. (1995) *Social Justice in a Global Economy*, ICF Quarterly Papers Winter 1995/6

*Industrial Christian Fellowship (1990) *Wealth Creation and Christianity*, ICF 1990

*Institute of Management (1994) *Survey of Long Term Employment Strategies*

*Institute of Management (1995) *Directors' Remuneration*

*Institute of Management (1996) *Are Managers Under Stress?*

*Irish Business and Employers Confederation (1996) *Social Policy in a Competitive Economy*

*Irish Congress of Trade Unions, *Framework for a New Partnership: Statement from the Irish Congress of Trades Unions to the Economic and Social Summit*, 23 October 1996

*The Irish National Organisation of the Unemployed, (1996) *If you think the economy is working - ask someone who isn't: The Unemployed and a New National Agreement*

*The Institute of Employment Rights (1995) *Just the Job: A Consultation Document on the Future of Employment Law*

*Jenkins, R. (1991) *Changing Times - Unchanging Values?* William Temple Foundation

*Jones, I, Robinson, F, Dodd, P, Mchugh, M, Rafferty, G, Usher, F, (1996) *The Future of Work in the North East*

*Kessler I. and Undy R. (1996) *The New Employment Relationship: Examining the Psychological Contract*, Institute of Personnel and Development

*Lindsey, K. (1994) *A Stable Society Requires that Ordinary People Have Lives That are Stable and Fulfilling* (Talk to the European Ecumenical Commission on Church and Society in response to the White Paper 'Growth, Competitiveness, Employment')

*London Churches' Employment Development Unit, *Into the Lion's Den - Doing the Job: 21 projects for unemployed people run by churches*

*London Churches' Employment Development Unit, *Into the Lion's Den - What Do Churches Need to Tackle Unemployment?*

*McGregor, A. McArthur, A.A., (1990) *Community Enterprise in the Local Economy* Training and Employment Research Unit, University of Glasgow

*McOustra, C. (1994) *Job-Generative Models - A Proposal*

*Merseyside Economic Assessment, January 1996

*The Methodist Church SR (April 1995), *Economic Growth, Consumerism and Employment*

*Mills, J. (1996) *What is Wrong With Economics*, Labour Economic Policy Group

*Mounfield, P. and Clarke, M.L., (1989), *Voluntary Sector Provision for Long Term Unemployed People in Leicestershire*, Leicester Polytechnic Business School.

*Morrison, R. (January 1994) *Work and Unemployment: Theological Pointers for the Pastoral Task*, Derby Diocesan Council for Social Responsibility

*National Association of Citizens Advice Bureaux (1993) *Job Insecurity*, NACAB

*National Association of Citizens Advice Bureax (1994) *In Search of Work*, NACAB

*National Council for One Parent Families, (1996) *Returning to Work: A Guide for Lone Parents*, National Council for One Parent Families

*Newcastle Diocese BSR, *Hopeseeker* Unemployment Pack

*Northumbria Churches Training Consortium, (1996) *Churches Enquiry into Unemployment and the Future of Work*, 6th September 1996

*Ormiston, H. and Ross, D. (ed) (1990) *New Patterns of Work* St. Andrews Press for Scottish Churches' Industrial Mission

*Peart, P. and Holmden M. (1995) *The Pastoral Care of Unemployed People. The Challenge and Some Guidelines: A letter to the Churches of Newham*

*Parents at Work (1994) *UK Employer Initiatives: Working Examples of Family Friendly and Equal Opportunities Policies*, Working Mothers Association

*Parker H. and Raven S. (1996) *Basic Income for Intermediates*, Citizen's Income Bulletin No. 23

*Peacock, A. Work and the Economy Network in the European Churches (1995) *The Social Charter: A User's Guide Five Year Review*, The William Temple Foundation

*People and Work Programme (June 1995), *A Personal Ministry for Lay People*, Diocese of Peterborough

*People and Work Programme (June 1994), *Work in Worship*, Diocese of Peterborough

*Quigley, P. (1991) *A Future Out of Work? Finding Alternatives for Military Jobs in Coventry*, Coventry Alternative Employment Research (CARE)

*Race Equality in Employment Project, Wood-Sheppard Race Equality in Employment Pack

*RADAR (1995) *The Disability Discrimination Act 1995 - An Overview*, The Royal Association for Disability and Rehabilitation

*Respond! *Exploring a new vision in Teesside*

*Rose, R.A.L. (1994) *The Future of Work: A Discussion Document*, Occasional Paper Three, Chelmsford Diocesan Urban Theology Group

*Sentance, A. *Economic Prospects For Britain and Europe: The Employment Implications*; Presentation to Chelmsford Diocese 'Future of Work' Conference, 10th June 1994

*Smith, R. (1992) 'The Role of the Voluntary Sector in Tackling Poverty' *Community Development Journal* Vol.27 No. 3 July 1992

*South Hampshire Industrial Mission (1996) *The Minimum Wage*, SHIM

*South London Industrial Mission (1995), *Economic Developments and Multifaith Issues*, SLIM

*St. Antony's Centre for Church and Industry, (1995) *Job Security, Prosperity and the Arms Trade*, Centreview Issue 12, December 1995

*St. Antony's Centre for Church and Industry, (1996) *Stakeholding: A Christian Concept?*, Centreview Issue 13, March 1996

*St. William's Foundation, (1995) *Consultation - 'The Future of Work'* Occasional Paper No.19 27 October 1995

*St. William's Foundation, (1996) *The Future of Work - Dialogue With Students*, Occasional Paper No. 20 1996

*Tear Fund (1996) *Faces of Poverty: The State of Britain in the 90s*

*Trade Union Advisory Committee (1995) *Adaptability versus Flexibility*, OECD

*Trade Unions Congress (1995) *Black and Betrayed: A TUC report on black workers' experience of unemployment and low pay in 1994-5* TUC

*Training and Employment Agency, (June 1995) *The Corporate Plan for the period 1995-1998: developing a world class workforce in Northern Ireland*

*Usher, F. (1996) *Jobseeker's Allowance: A Briefing Paper for the Churches*, Churches Regional Commission in the North East

*Wales Rural Forum, (July 1995), *Rural Wales - The Way Forward : A Strategy Statement prepared by Wales Rural Forum.*

*Wales TUC Cymru (1995) *Unions Work for Full Employment*, Wales TUC Cymru

*Ward P.C. (1989) *Psychological Effects of Unemployment*, Gwent College of Higher Education

*Wardrop, K. (January 1996) *Glasgow Works*

*Williamson, R. (1994) *Work, Unemployment and Human Dignity*, Eureopean Churches' Committee on Justice, Peace and the Integrity of Creation

*The Working Mothers Association, (1991) *The Employer's Guide to Childcare*, The Working Mothers Association

*Young, M. and Halsey, A.H. (1995) *Family and Community Socialism*, IPPR

Literature from Organisations

We have also received additional information from the following projects and organisations;

Action Workwise, The Bexley Centre For the Unemployed, BIA Quaker Social Action, Black Country Industrial Mission, The Bridge Project, CHAR (Housing Campaign for Single People), Christian Aid, Christian Care Training (Exeter), Christian Unemployment Group (chug) (South Yorkshire), Highway (Part of West Doncaster CHUG), Church Action on Poverty, Church of Ireland ACE Ventures, Churches Initiative in Training Employment and Enterprise (CITTE Ltd) (Coventry), The Churches' Regional Commission in the North East, Churches' Trust Ltd (Northern Ireland), Clubhouse, Community Reaction Centre (Hampshire), Crisis Centre Ministries; Taking the Stress out of Distress (Bristol), Emmaus, Employment Policy Institute, First Move, Great Yarmouth Centre for the Unemployed and Unwaged, Frontier Youth Trust, Glasgow Works, Hackney Employment Link Project (HELP), Holme Christian Care Centre (Bradford), Industrial Mission Association, Industry Churches Forum, Instant Muscle Ltd, Institute of Business Ethics, ISR - The Churches' Council for Industry and Social Responsibility (Bristol), Jubilee Policy Group, Liverpool Industrial Mission, Local Exchange Trading Systems, London Churches' Employment Development Unit, London Docklands Development Corporation, Lower Don Valley Economic Development Project (IMSY), Luton Industrial College, National Federation of Credit Unions, Newham Community Renewal Programme, Norfolk and Waveney Industrial Mission, OK4 Young People's Centre (Cleveland), Opportunity Trust creating jobs for the poor, Parents at Work, PECAN (Peckham Evangelical Churches' Action Network), People and Work Programme, Diocese of Peterborough, People and Work Unit (Uned Pobl a Gwaith), The Pool Farm Church Listening Project, The Relationships Foundation, Respond! (Teesside), Scottish Churches' Industrial Mission, Scottish Low Pay Unit, Shoulder To Shoulder, South London Industrial Mission, Southampton and District Unemployed Centre, Springboard Resources Group

(Hampshire), Stepping Stone Project (Belfast), Teesside Employment Initiative, Teesside Industrial Mission, Tools With a Mission, Training Into Jobs: Building New Life (Chester), URC Industrial Mission, Von Hugel Institute, West Yorkshire Homeworking Unit, The Wise Group.

Annex A

CHRISTIAN TEACHING ON WORK AND THE ECONOMY

By Revd Dr Peter Sedgwick

The Biblical Teaching

There is a strongly realistic attitude to work and to economic life in the Old and New Testaments. Three aspects may be clearly distinguished. First, there is a recognition that work is a calling under God, linked to the need to respond to God as humanity engages with the world around them. Secondly, there is the description of work in the Wisdom literature, especially in Job. Thirdly, and much emphasized in recent years by some Church leaders, is the idea of Jubilee, and the ending of debts.

Work is a vocation. 1 and 2 Thessalonians, and Colossians 3:23 speak of

'work(ing) heartily, as serving the Lord and not men.'

In 1 Corinthians 7:20 Paul applies the term *Klesis* both to the calling of a person to follow Christ, and to the job being done by that person:

'Let every person stay in the same calling wherein he was called.'

This static view was undoubtedly due to the imminence of the end of the world in Paul's theology. It also, however, ensured that Paul emphasized his self-sufficiency.

'We did not eat any one's bread, without paying, but with toil and labour we worked night and day that we might not burden you... If any one will not work, let him not eat. For we hear that some of you are living in idleness, mere busybodies, not doing any work. Now such persons we command and exhort in the Lord Jesus Christ to do their work in quietness, and to earn their own living.' (2 Thessalonians 3:8 - 12).

Secondly, there is the description of work in the Bible. There is the myth of Genesis 3, speaking of the sweat of your brow as bread is produced and eaten, and the necessity of toil throughout life because the ground is cursed due to the Fall. Yet there is also the importance of creation, which persists even after the exile of Cain. Cain founds a city in his exile, and so perpetuates the command of God to Adam that he was to

'till it and keep it'

in the Garden of Eden. This creativity expands in the magnificent descriptions in Job 28 and the Wisdom literature.

'Iron is taken out of the earth and copper is smelted from the ore. Men put an end to darkness ... they open shafts in a valley away from where men live.'

Finally there is the concept of Jubilee. The family and its continuity was all important, as well as the safeguarding of family property. The go'el, variously translated as redeemer or kinsman, was meant to maintain the family. If anyone fell on hard times the go'el should come to his rescue, redeeming his property if he was forced to sell it and redeeming his person if he was sold into debt-slavery (Leviticus 25, Jeremiah 32, and Ruth 3 - 4). However at the same time there was the idea of Jubilee, when all debts would be remitted. Whether or not this was ever invoked, the concept remained powerful in Christian thought. Prophetic thought also judged the immorality of growing wealth at the expense of the poor. Amos describes vividly the idle rich living alongside enormous poverty. Both the idea of Jubilee every 50 years, and the prophetic demand for justice, make the important point that there comes a time when the family is unable to sustain itself, even with the aid of its go'el. Salvation, or redemption, must come from outside, otherwise debt will overwhelm it. There is a social dimension to all of life.

However Jubilee remained an ideal in the Jewish scriptures. It perhaps was never implemented, so one must look elsewhere for limitations on the work ethic. Two examples come to mind. One is the idea of the Sabbath, the other is the Deuteronomic legislation. In terms of Deuteronomy, the righteous person does not reap his field to its very edges, return to get the forgotten sheaf, or gather the windfalls. (Deuteronomy 24:19-21). There are also references in Leviticus (19:9-10, and 23:22) and there are limits to harsh contracts (Exodus 22:25-26). A discussion of poverty would take us too far afield, but it is important to mention that the poor (and slaves) had legal rights, which was highly unusual in ancient Near East society. Kings above all were protectors of the poor, and could not redistribute land (1 Kings 21). Job 29 describes how the ideal rich person functions in his community. Where the laws fail the prophets demand justice (Amos, Jeremiah, Isaiah). In relation to work it is significant that Jeremiah 22:13 criticizes the withholding of wages. The Sabbath also limited the amount of work that could be performed. Genesis places this prohibition in the context of God's own acting in creating the world.

It is worth pointing out two aspects of the Sabbath rest for a theology of work. (The term comes from the Hebrew verb to rest or Shabath.) First, Genesis 1 in its cosmology closely follows the Babylonian Creation Epic of the 23rd century BC (discovered in Nineveh in 1873) except that the Hebrew epic mentions the Sabbath, and the Babylonian one does not. It is a deliberate change. Secondly, the composition of Genesis 1 by the P narrator is dated from the exile in Babylon. Although rest days had been fixed before by the moon (2 Kings 4:23 and Amos 8:5), now it was fixed in accordance with the purposes of God. Severe penalties were prescribed for its infringement (Ezekiel 20 and Nehemiah 13). Here we have a community in exile seeking to reinforce its distinctiveness by the appeal to the higher purposes of God. Although work was important, it was subservient to the worship of Yahweh, which was the distinctive mark of the Jewish people in the ancient Near East.

The teaching of Jesus focused on the danger of wealth, especially in the parable of the unjust steward and the illustration of the camel going through the eye of the needle. The Gospel of Luke blesses the poor, while the rich man who turns away from Jesus' call in Mark 10 again shows the temptation of wealth. The rich and extortionate are condemned in Luke 16, while the open table fellowship that is a constant theme of the Gospels demands no economic conditions : it is simply open to all.

In the early Church there seems to have been a form of sharing, found in Acts 2. This is more the expression of a complete commitment to reconciliation and the breaking in of the new Kingdom than a model for social reform. Nevertheless the sharing of property found in Acts is of profound symbolic importance. It demonstrated vividly the need to overcome all attachment to wealth if one was to follow Christ, and it was a graphic illustration of the possibilities which life in Christ offered to his followers.

The Early Church Fathers

As the Church moved out of New Testament times, it spread across the Roman Empire. This was a vast, sprawling edifice, with self-governing cities which existed under the overall control of the Roman Emperor. The Church found itself involved in a society of manual labour, trade, commerce and luxury. Manual labour largely involved agriculture, with building, and fairly rudimentary metal work. Commerce and trade included long sea-voyages and the hazards of travel.

The Church at this time was hostile to military service, but it accepted the day to day economic world. Tertullian's well-known apologetic said that as Christians

> 'with you we sail the sea, ... work the land and trade in its fruits, just as we publicly sell for your use the products of our trades and labours.'

However few theologians actually wrote about why the economy mattered to Christians. There were two viewpoints. One is the traditional Greek one that the educated few engaged in philosophy. The rest should engage in economic life, for, as Origen said, the Creator did not give us a world which fulfilled all our needs without effort. That would have led to idleness.

A more substantial answer comes from the classic text of this period, which is Augustine's *On the Work of Monks*. Augustine wrote a treatise on behalf of the Bishop of Carthage, whose monks were refusing to engage in manual work. Augustine replied that labour is a means of self-expression, and the Garden of Eden was a place of work and delight. Work is not a consequence of the Fall. Selfishness is the sign of a fallen world, but culture springs out of the elemental experience of fashioning the world by manual labour and the use of reason. There is no weariness in work that is loved. Augustine contrasts the satisfaction which the North African farmers found in work, even if they were physically exhausted, with the idle monks. In this text Christian theology first engages with the reason why the economy matters to Christian faith.

At the same time the Church continued to accept slavery. In a striking phrase, Tertullian writes of the demons breaking out of hell just as slaves break out of '*prisons or mines or quarries*'. They are to be ruthlessly beaten back. Most Church leaders were kinder. Chrysostom said Christians should free their slaves whenever possible, although it was not a sin to keep them. Slavery was an Italian phenomenon : up to a quarter of the population of Italy may have been slaves in the Empire. What mattered was the quality of the slave-owner relationship in Church teaching. What were condemned were certain occupations. The Apostolic Tradition listed professions which Christians should avoid. Sculptors and painters could be involved in the manufacture of idols. Actors, dancers, gladiators and charioteers all fall under the ban on participating in luxury, just as the philosopher Cicero had condemned perfumerers. There is also a strong condemnation of excessive wealth.

The Early Church Fathers denied that there was a natural right to private property. Once, they held, all things were held in common. Then avarice created the rights of property. However these theologians said nothing about the common production of goods. It was often the case that a wealthy Bishop might share his private income with the poor, and in some cases give it away, but inequality as such was not questioned. Restraint was necessary in the face of luxury, and there was much alms-giving. However the Fathers are not to be seen as social reformers.

Usury was condemned because of pastoral reasons. Congregations were often poor, and high interest rates made matters worse. The practice of usury was forbidden at the Council of Nicea in 325, although there are condemnations of it much later, which shows that it was still prevalent, even among clergy. Usury was compared to gathering the harvest and recovering the seed, by digging under the roots. Chrysostom spoke of those who came looking for medicine in the form of financial aid and were offered poison, in the shape of usury. Early Christian thought tended to be more critical of usury than slavery.

By the collapse of the Roman Empire, and the Dark Ages, the Church had accepted wealth, while rebuking greed and luxury severely. There was an uncritical acceptance of trade, since it unified humanity (Basil of Caesarea) but not of usury. A favourite text was Ecclesiasticus 26:6

'*How hard it is for a merchant to keep clear of wrong or for a shopkeeper to be innocent of dishonesty.*'

It was not trade which was wrong, but the temptations which it offered. Augustine's justification of manual labour offered a significant advance on the Greek philosophical dichotomy between spirit and matter, or intellect and brawn. The main concern of the Church was the pursuit of a holy life, and the practice of Christian charity. There was frequent

221

compassion shown to the landless poor, who could be rendered destitute. It was this tradition which was to last through the Dark Ages, and to resurface in the medieval debates on usury.

The Medieval Period

By the thirteenth century the Italian city states, especially those on the coastline such as Venice or Amalfi, were thriving merchant cities as they traded with the East. They carried economic and social modernization into the feudal society of medieval Europe. At the same time the foundation of the universities at Bologna, Paris and Oxford led to a vigorous debate (often overlooked by social ethicists earlier this century) on the morality of property and economic life. The centre of the discussion lay in Paris, especially with the Franciscan theologians. As the thirteenth century elapsed, more positive attitudes to economics and wealth creation emerged. Private property was seen as not simply the result of the Fall, but as the most efficient means of administering society. The benefits of commerce and trade to a subsistence economy were not to be despised.

Compulsion was the central concept of scholastic economic ethics. If basic material needs failed then there was an obligation to respond : the *ius necessitatis*. This was in tension with the growing belief that the virtuous should enjoy the fruits of their labour. The increased emphasis on free social exchange as feudalism declined was difficult to combine with the social compassion of the relief of need.

Free and just exchange through the ideal of mutual advantage created the idea of the market, a revolutionary concept at the time. There were disagreements between Aquinas and Duns Scotus on whether private property was in any sense 'natural'. Although Scotus denied that it was, he accepted it on the basis of 'positive law' (made by societies) and developed the concept of the just price. A seller may guard against loss, but may not profit by another's need, however great. Peter Olivi, the greatest medieval economic commentator, discussed the question of local scarcity in the economy of medieval Europe. He allowed a limited amount of price-raising to overcome scarcity in order to obtain supplies from elsewhere, but feared the growth of monopolies.

Medieval economic ethics have had a bad press, partly due to the ignorance of these sophisticated debates from which seventeenth century ethicists derived concepts of justice on which Adam Smith built. At the same time discussion of medieval economics tends to focus on usury. Money was seen as non-vendible. It is a means of exchange, but no more. When money was borrowed, it was seen as a loan (mutuum) and not a lease. Loans transferred ownership to the borrower, and any profit on the loan should remain with them. The theory was elastic, however. It allowed for risk, and for credit transactions across currencies where the uncertainty of currency exchange meant that canon lawyers were unable to condemn transactions. It was not that the theory of usury simply collapsed, but that it became impossibly complex in a world of far-flung trading. At the same time Italian city states consolidated municipal debts and raised loans at fixed rates of exchange.

Usury was related to work and economic activity, since the economy of medieval Europe was primarily a trading economy in the Italian seaports and Hanseatic (Baltic) cities. However the one significant exception to the commerce-driven economy was the growth of wool, and the technological advances in treating it. It is very significant that this was developed by the great Benedictine monastic estates in England, especially in Yorkshire. The Benedictines united work and prayer, seeing prayer as the 'work of God' which should always be paramount, but also placing great emphasis on manual work as a disciplined way of serving God. Here again, as in Augustine, we see the growth of celebration of work for its own sake, even if this labour was placed within the context of a community dedicated to the service of God. The enormous wealth which this created, and the consequent problems of luxury and the corruption of the monastic ethic, should not blind us to the uniting of work, Christian faith and the care of the poor and needy. It is indeed here that the Christian work ethic first emerges, rather than the much vaunted Protestant work ethic (see below). It was an agricultural communal ethic that enabled England to join in trading with the continent, alongside the essentially mercantile ethos of Italy and the Hanseatic league.

For a while the collapse of the medieval economy, with the Black Death of 1340 (which ironically spread through the Italian seaports : rats and foreign currency came through Venice) and the renewed conflicts of the fourteenth and fifteenth centuries, halted the debate. Economic life declined. However by 1500 there were many signs of revival, only this time it was located in the Northern European cities of Germany and Flanders, as well as in Spain. It was here that economic historians earlier this century located the origins of capitalism, and related it to the Protestant work ethic. While this is now seen to be a mistake, since the sixteenth century economic boom was only the revival of the earlier thirteenth century growth of commerce, the views of the Church are of great importance. For the economic growth spreading across Europe in the early sixteenth century coincided with the Reformation.

The Reformation Debates

Luther gave substantial autonomy to the realm of daily work. Using the idea of 'orders', Luther believed that all social existence was preserved by God from chaos and injustice. Irrespective of religious belief, individuals found themselves in a series of different institutions, such as the family, the state, work and the church. Through these bodies God ruled the social order, and although each one was corrupted by sin, they were the means by which humanity worked out its vocation. These 'orders' are ordained by God to remain secular enjoying a relative autonomy under the will of the Creator. Reason and justice are normative for daily life, not faith and love. However, Christians who have responded to the word of God in salvation can illuminate the demands of daily life in seeing how love can transform the demands of justice to a compassionate identification with the poor and needy.

Luther developed the doctrine of the calling or vocation (German Beruft) which he found in I Corinthians. He saw the vocation of the Christian as found in daily work. If one is a blacksmith, then one's vocation is to act as well as one can. There is, however, an implicit compulsion in this theory. Left to oneself, one might be idle or selfish. Placed in the structures, social existence becomes possible. The consequences for economic life were profound. On the one hand, Luther felt that institutions could only be reformed by human law. Individuals could be transformed by the grace of salvation, in the Kingdom of God, but institutions were God's protection against sin and chaos. This led to a conservative view of social inequality. At the same time he gave economic freedom to the burgeoning middle classes and skilled workers to pursue their trades.

Calvin had a more dynamic view, reflected in the Catechism of the Church of England in the 1662 Book of Common Prayer:

'that state of life unto which it shall please God to call me.'

The Catechism, and the devotional prayers before public worship, spelt out the duties to God and neighbour. Calvin was the theologian who most developed this view. He himself set severe limits on usury, and believed that the wealth of an individual was a divine blessing which one could use to benefit one's neighbour. This is not a simple justification of early capitalism. However Calvin did believe that humanity could glorify God in daily work, and that the task of Church and state was to install discipline into the lives of Christians, as members of the church and as godly citizens. There was a strong emphasis on austerity, on thrift, hard work and responsibility. Thrift and saving led to capital accumulation, and investment, but this economic success also was a 'source of assurance'. It is too simple to say that wealth represented a sign that one would be saved, but it is true that a 'source of assurance' was the ability to perform good works. Self-discipline, self-examination, sobriety and obedience combined with social discipline. Contemporaries noted the growing prosperity of Protestant nations, such as England, and of Protestant cities, such as Geneva and Amsterdam. Calvin reluctantly agreed to usury, at a rate of interest of 5% (later 6½%), but it was his followers in the eighteenth century in Britain and in the United States who combined Calvinism with economic expansion.

The Industrial Revolution

From about 1760 in Great Britain, until 1830, there was a rapid process of industrialization. The rise in population and its concentration in cities led to profound changes in the pastoral needs of society. No longer could the parish priest visit his flock in a village, or market town. The few large cities before 1760 now became the norm, and the industrial use of new inventions also led to production being carried on in factories. These factories were often close to sources of power, and a new relationship was forged between human beings, machines and resources. In the nineteenth century this development spread both to Continental Europe and to the United States of America.

The initial reaction to industrialization is found in preachers like John Wesley. On the one hand he worked tirelessly to relieve poverty, founding schools and hospitals. He opposed slavery, and was highly critical of luxury. On the other hand he argued for great diligence in work, and in his Homily *Against Idleness* he wrote that

'*every one ought, in his lawful vocation and calling, to give himself to labour : and that idleness ... is a grievous sin.*'

He went on to stress the importance of

'*honest and godly exercise and labour, and every one follow his own business.*'

In his most well-known sermon on work, sermon 44 on *The Use of Money* he took as his theme: 'Get all you can, save all you can, and give all you can'. Wesley felt that people were only Stewards of their earthly possessions; and therefore they should be used as fruitfully as possible.

'*In what manner didst thou employ that comprehensive talent, money?*'

asks the sermon on *The Good Steward*.

At the same time theologians and Church leaders began to appreciate the importance of corporate structures and the economic ordering of society. Some nineteenth century theologians also wrote economic textbooks, and Archbishop John Sumner had been an economist in his early life. By the mid nineteenth century it was clear that a comprehensive reordering of society was needed as a response to the transformation of society by the Industrial Revolution. The first response was that of Christian Socialism, which first emerged in 1848 and became a dominant force by 1914 in Anglican social teaching in England. A second, and rather later, response was that of the Papacy in its social encyclicals from 1891 onwards. A third response, evolving out of Christian Socialism but tending towards a social reformism, has been characteristic of English Protestant denominations since 1945. Similar work can be found in (the former West) Germany from the Lutheran Churches, in the United States especially in the writings of Reinhold Niebuhr, and in the politically more radical pronouncements of the World Council of Churches. This brings us up to the present day. Finally, the very different arguments of conservatism and the Greens should be mentioned.

Christian Socialism

Its theologian was F D Maurice, who was greatly influenced by the poet-philosopher Samuel Coleridge. Maurice emphasized the partnership of society, and in his work *The Kingdom of Christ* he argued that the kingdom meant that human brotherhood was a present reality.

Christian social teaching should enable people to become what they already are.

'*The great practical existing reality which is to renew the earth*'

was his description of the universal community of Christ. Socialism meant

'*the assertion of God's order*',

which competition and possessive individualism contradicted. They became signs of hostility to the Gospel.

Maurice, Ludlow and Kingsley pleaded for social justice in the spirit of a crusade. Their practical attempts to found co-operative workshops did not flourish, but the long term effect was profound on the co-operative movement. By the late nineteenth century a series of clergy and radical social theorists were advocating the complete reconstruction of society. Stewart Headlam was prepared in the 1880's to collaborate with secular socialists. It was a socialism which wanted a minimum wage, wider land ownership and wealth redistribution, and universal education. Headlam thus becomes the first Christian thinker to advocate state intervention in society, and his high view of the state reflected his belief that the Industrial Revolution needed to be matched by a corresponding social revolution, not necessarily involving the use of force but certainly requiring legal compulsion from the state. Headlam also began to use social analysis, although his preferred use of Henry George and land taxation has not stood the test of time.

After Headlam's sermon on

'*the banner of Christ in the hands of the socialists*'

there came a great stream of politically radical social thinking. There were two main developments. One flourished in urban areas, often places of great poverty and bad social conditions, and this movement established the Church Socialist League of 1906. The rent strikes led by Fr John Groser in East London against absentee landlords, and his passionate support for the 1926 General Strike, are typical of this campaigning wing of the Christian left. The other was the Christian Social Union founded in 1889, and which lasted for thirty years. It involved William Temple and R H Tawney, and many Anglican clergy who belonged to it went on to become Bishops. Other theologians who belonged were Charles Gore and Henry Scott Holland. It sought to study and interpret Christian social principles, although it also campaigned against social abuses. Its importance lay in its social analysis, for it realized that state action can

'*hinder hindrances to the good life.*'

Industry was seen as a '*fellowship*', under the regulative control of the state, as the supreme authority. It influenced the 1909 Trade Boards Act, which produced statutes for setting minimum wages in industries where workers were disorganized. It eventually merged into the Industrial Christian Fellowship (ICF) in 1920, which still exists today.

Roman Catholic Teaching

In 1891 Pope Leo XIII published *Rerum Novarum*, dealing primarily with the rights of the worker. This was followed forty years later by *Quadragesimo Anno* (1931), and then a whole series of documents in the last twenty-five years from 1961. As well as the Papal encyclicals, there have also been national pronouncements, such as the United States Bishops' document *Economic Justice for All* in 1986.

Leo clearly condemns the excesses of the free market, reflecting both capitalism and socialism. He regretted the end of the medieval guilds for working-men which offered protection against employers, solidarity and a sense of community. Their demise has left the worker '*isolated and defenceless, to the callousness of employers and the greed of unrestrained competition.*' (RN 2).

Leo revived the medieval idea of the just wage, arguing that a wage must support the worker and his family in

'*reasonable and frugal comfort*' (RN 34).

He recommends strong government action when workers themselves cannot bring about change. Yet Leo defended private property, actually describing it as

'*sacred and inviolable*' (RN 35)

which the earlier medieval tradition had declined to do. He felt that the ownership of private property was part of human nature.

Rerum Novarum also sought better working conditions, and hoped that Catholic trade unions would be set up. There were limits to state intervention, and more action must not be taken than is required. By 1931 the well-known principle of subsidiarity spelt this out further. Where action could be taken by a smaller and more local body, it is

'*an injustice, a grave evil and a disturbance of great order*'

for the state (or any other larger body) to act instead (QA 79). Pius XI in *Quadragesimo Anno* also reminded the owners of property of the duties which ownership carried. Again, like Leo XIII, there is an attack on individualism in economic life.

In the last twenty years there has been an emphasis on human rights, including economic rights. The language of rights pervades the recent document of Catholic Bishops of England and Wales called *The Common Good* (1996), and it is there in the encyclicals of Pope John XXIII. In *Pacem in Terris* (1963) he spoke of the right to work, to safe working conditions, to own property and to a just wage. (PT 18 - 21). In *Gaudium et Spes* (1965) the list is expanded to economic rights which guarantee a '*truly human life*' including unions, employment, working conditions, shelter, food, and education (GS 26, 65, 68).

The documents of the late 1960's and early 1970's warn of poverty in the developing world, and now express the doctrine of '*common use*' of all goods. Private property and commerce can exist, but they should respect this principle. This reiterates some of the teachings of the Early Church Fathers and the medieval theologians described earlier. Finally Pope John Paul II in *Laborem Exercens* (1981), *Sollicitudo Rei Socialis* (1987) and *Centensimus Annus* (1991) bring the teaching of the Papacy up to the present day. The importance of work for human activity is stressed, but so too more recently is the place of wealth creation. There is a strong emphasis, found also in *The Common Good*, on the importance of society including all its citizens, which means those without work and in poverty as well as those who are employed.

Finally, the significant development of liberation theology should be mentioned. Primarily, but not entirely a Roman Catholic movement, this theological opposition to capitalism spread throughout South America in the late 1960's and early 1970's. It was nourished by the '*base community*' movement, which united people at the grass-roots to oppose the economic domination of South American society by an alliance of conservative land owners and powerful multinationals, usually from the United States. The Bishops of South America met for fifteen days in August-September 1968 at Medellin, Colombia and issued a declaration in favour of the poor. The Puebla episcopal document of 1979 is an attempt to steer a middle course between capitalism and socialism. Since then liberation theology has spread to parts of the world where there has been great poverty, such as South Asia, the Philippines, South Africa and the deprived cities of Europe and North America. It also was strongly advocated by the Jesuits in the 1970's under their charismatic head Pedro Arrupe. In the 1990's it reformulated its beliefs, becoming less dependent on Marxist analysis, but still remaining deeply critical of global capitalism. There would be extensive contact with the World Council of Churches (especially through the German Lutheran theologian Ulrich Duchrow) and the aid agencies, such as CAFOD and Christian Aid.

Protestant Church Teaching 1918 - 1996

The dominant figures in this period in England were William Temple and R H Tawney. Temple was Archbishop of York in the 1930's, and Archbishop of Canterbury during the Second World War, until his death in 1944 at the early age of 63. He was committed in 1908 to socialism as the economic realization of the Christian gospel, but moved in the 1930's to a more realistic position. He worked a great deal at the problem of unemployment, and spoke at all the major conferences called by the English Churches in the period from 1920 to 1944. He chaired many of them, and in his final major book on Christian social teaching *Christianity and Social Order* (1942) he developed a theology both of the central worth of each person and of the social structures within which full person-hood is realized. Persons do not flourish apart from communities and without the intervention of the state in creating the necessary social institutions and laws to enable human wellbeing. His basic principles in Christian Ethics were those of freedom, social fellowship and service, which he derived from Christian doctrine.

Out of these principles Temple developed what he called 'middle axioms'. These are middle level arguments, between detailed policy prescriptions and the principles mentioned above. They represent a provisional consensus on the work which needs to be done, such as on employment or the Welfare State. Temple also produced far-reaching conclusions on the future of capitalism in England, advocating nationalization where appropriate, but he emphasized that these were personal views, and he set them merely as an appendix to *Christianity and Social Order.*

R H Tawney represented a more egalitarian and radical Christian approach. As a lay Christian economist, he advocated economic democracy as far as possible. Working closely with Temple until 1944, his influence still pervades the Christian left. He died in 1962, and his writings on *Equality* remain influential. These two men did much to influence the future development of both Anglican and Protestant teaching in England until the present day. The tradition has also developed into a 'critical realism' with reference to political power, the working of the market, and globalisation through the writings of Neibuhr, Ronald Preston and John Atherton. The Board for Social Responsibility of the Church of England, and the Church and Society boards of the United Reformed Church, Methodist Church, the British Council of Churches and the Council of Churches for Britain and Ireland all stand in this tradition. The questions of economic justice, the conditions of the workplace and the future of work lead very naturally into the enquiry on unemployment and the future of work.

Conservative thought and the Green Movement

It is possible to unite these two movements by pointing to the external realities of social tradition and the environment which should limit unbridled economic activity. In this there would be a restraint placed on work, much as the Hebrew Shabath did with reference to Yahweh. The doctrine of Creation first came to influence Christian social ethics through the Jesuit palaeontologist and theologian Teilhard de Chardin in the 1950's. By the 1980's Protestant and Roman Catholic theology was deeply aware of the ecological limits to growth, with the Pope issuing the first document exclusively on this in 1990 entitled *Peace with God the Creator, Peace with all of Creation.*

There has been an intense re-examination of the notion of stewardship in Genesis, with a growing awareness that a non-anthropocentric ethic must portray the universe as loved by God in its own right. This harks back to St Francis of Assisi, although the intrinsic worth of the Creation is there in Augustine's writings. The World Council of Churches has especially monitored the impact of industrialization and technology on the environment since the 1979

American conference on science and religion. The former Archbishop of York, Lord Habgood, has been prominent here as theologian and scientist.

A conservative social ethic would reflect such ideals, seeing the organic nature of society as providing an analogy with creation. This gave a cautious welcome to the creation of wealth, so long as the social fabric is not disturbed. However in more recent years what is more properly called economic neo-liberalism has sought to justify free market operations by the religious justification of capitalism. A subtle attempt to reconcile Papal teaching with the working of the global, capitalist economy is found in the writings of the American Catholic theologian Michael Novak, who was closely associated with Ronald Reagan. *The Spirit of Democratic Capitalism* is Novak's best known work (1982) where he points to the positive role which wealth-creation has in society. An echo of his view is found in *Centensimus Annus*.

A different, but related, view is that of the English Evangelical lay theologian Lord Griffiths, who was an economic advisor to Mrs Thatcher for some years. He seeks to place capitalism within the framework of Christian social teaching, using a strongly Biblical ethic in his writings. He takes the Bible as giving a positive mandate to create wealth, but also recognizes the need to respect the created order. Part of the current debate within English Evangelicalism would be an attempt to balance the very different strands of Jubilee, wealth-creation and environmental stewardship, or nurture.

Conclusion

There are certain themes which run through Christian teaching on work and the economy. Most obviously, the treatment of the poor, the marginalized and the vulnerable is a constant concern throughout the whole tradition. Secondly, the doctrine of Creation recurs repeatedly in different forms. It may be the account of human activity in Job 28 juxtaposed with the activity of God, or it may be Luther's account of 'the orders'. In brief, there is a purpose to work and to the relations of human beings within employment. A full theology of work lies beyond this account, but the revelation of God through the creation is never to be ignored. Human beings find God through and in their daily life. Thirdly, there is a growing realization that the economic relations of human beings need careful scrutiny. The medieval input to this through the just price and law of necessity was one major contribution. So too are the explorations into 'socialism' by such people as Pope Leo XIII, Bishop Westcott of Durham and contemporary theologians such as R H Preston. Christian theology has tended to stress the compassion which one individual must show to another, but a fuller theology will include a full consideration of social structures in a discussion of employment and economic life. The sophistication of economic debate today must be related to the injustices of poverty and debt which remain nationally and internationally, but it also needs to be addressed as the context in which Christian understanding of the world of work is carried on.

Annex B

LOW PAY

By Gabrielle Cox

Definitions

In this paper *low pay* is taken to mean a low hourly rate of pay. There is no accepted definition of what constitutes low pay. Low Pay Units have in the past used a definition which was based on two-thirds of median male earnings. However, even such a definition has a range of outcomes, depending on what factors are included in the calculation, and there is no agreed figure amongst the Units for this reason. Nigel Lawson, when Chancellor, once spoke of 'half average earnings' as low pay, but translating such a concept into an hourly rate has the same problems as with 'two thirds median male earnings'.

Several trade unions are now campaigning for £4 an hour, with a view to trying to get all their pay settlements at or above this figure. At lower levels of pay, such as £1.50, £2.00 and £2.50 there would probably be universal agreement that such rates constitute low and unacceptable pay. At higher rates views begin to diverge. There are probably three elements which help to form views within the debate:

(a)   a comparative element - how the rate compares with what others get;
(b)   a subjective element - whether the rate is an acceptable return for someone's labour;
(c)   an element based on whether the hourly rate could produce a 'living wage' if paid for a full week's work (eg 40 hours).

This latter element brings us to the second issue related to low pay - namely low weekly earnings, which for simplicity's sake I shall call *low income* in this paper. Whilst low pay frequently results in low income, the two are clearly not synonymous. In particular, the government frequently claims that low pay does not matter because many of those who are *low paid* are in households with *high income*. (In fact this particular distributional outcome is one of the results of the growth of low pay.)

This paper can, inevitably, only be a brief overview of the evidence and the issues. There is obviously a great deal of detailed information on employment and on earnings which cannot be covered here.

The Context

It is important, I believe, to reiterate that the context within which low pay needs to be discussed is one of a vastly changed labour market. The latest employment figures (December 1995) show that since March 1979:
*   male full-time employment has fallen by 2.848 million (-22.9%)
*   male part-time employment has risen by 515,000 (+71.6%)
*   female full-time employment has risen by 132,000 (+2.4%)
*   female part-time employment has risen by 1.143 million (+30.3%)
*   all full-time employment has fallen by 2.716 million (-15.1%)
*   all part-time employment has risen by 1.658 million (+36.9%)

More recent figures are slightly more encouraging, with a rise of 14,000 full-time jobs and 152,000 part-time jobs over the year to December 1995, but even with these rises the number of full-time jobs lost since the last General Election is 485,000 (with a rise of 418,000 part-time jobs). (Labour Force Survey figures show that part-time jobs are on average equal to 40% of the hours of full-time jobs.) The shift from full-time to part-time and from male to female employment is largely to do with the loss of manufacturing jobs (over 40% since 1979) and the rise in service sector employment. The changes have had a significant effect upon pay and upon income, with pay falling as better-paid manufacturing jobs (eg in engineering) are replaced by poorer-paid jobs in the service sector (eg in hotel and catering), and income being affected not only by lower pay rates but also by the rise in part-time work.

We all know, too, that the labour market is becoming much more 'flexible', with more temporary employment, sub-contracting, zero hours contracts, etc. Of people placed into work by the Employment Service in 1994/95, 48% went into full-time permanent jobs, 23% into part-time permanent jobs, 20% into full-time temporary jobs, and 6% into part-time temporary jobs.

Mean duration of unemployment-related benefit claims has risen, and mean interval between latest and previous claim has fallen. In the three year period 1993-95, 23.5% of men of working age made a claim for unemployment-related benefits. 10% of men of working age made 2 or more claims for unemployment related benefit during that period.

The official position on earnings

Ministers have been asserting throughout the eighties and into the nineties that average earnings have risen substantially in real terms allowing for inflation and tax changes (roughly 40% since 1979). The statistics (such as they are) are technically correct but the conclusion drawn from them (that 'everybody is better off') is not. The average has gone up substantially for two reasons: high earners have had large increases in earnings; and high earners have also had significant tax breaks (the calculations are based on take-home pay). The real value of half average earnings rose by about 35%. Since 'half average earnings' is simply an arithmetic half of 'average earnings' the same process has applied although the effect of the tax changes is not so beneficial. Averages do not tell us what has happened across the range. (In fact the bottom 10% have seen no rise in earnings.)

However, there is another significant factor which makes the 'average earnings' figure increasingly unrealistic, and that is that it is based solely on full-time male earnings. With full-time male employment falling by nearly a quarter since 1979, this is an increasingly unrepresentative segment of the labour market. (Full-time male jobs made up 55.4% of employment in 1979, compared with 44.9% in 1995.) In fact, if you apply 1994 average weekly earnings for male and female full-time and part-time workers to the March 1979 and December 1994 employment profiles the average weekly wage for all workers would have been £285.20 in March 1979 and £261.29 in December 1994, a fall of £23.91 a week or 8.4%. This shows how the changes in the employment profile will have *reduced* average weekly earnings.

Moreover, such an exercise does not take into account the uneven coverage of the government's New Earnings Survey. The Survey covers only about 60% of part-time workers (the sample is traced through tax records and therefore does not cover those with low weekly income). The average pay for part-time workers used in the above exercise is therefore considerably higher than in reality; this will have reduced the impact on average earnings of the shift to part-time.

A further problem is that the New Earnings Survey is also uneven in its coverage of industry sectors. On average the NES samples 0.76% of all full-time male workers; however, it samples only 0.48% of full-time males in hotel and catering but samples 0.91% of full-time males in public administration. Since the average weekly pay for all full-time males is £240.90 in hotel and catering and £382.42 in public administration it is clear that this uneven sampling will also affect calculations of average male full-time pay.

Growth of low pay

The general shift in the nature of employment is not the only cause of low pay. There have been a number of significant policies which have encouraged low pay, for example:

* the revoking in the early eighties of the Fair Wage Resolution which ensured that contractors on government contracts paid union rates;
* the abolition of Wages Councils in 1993 (the very severe impact on wage rates of abolition has been well documented);
* privatisation of many/most local and health authority manual services, with contracts going to the lowest bidder (who usually makes the low bid on the basis of low pay and worsened employment conditions);
* changes in the financing of residential care for the elderly which effectively ensured the closing of local authority homes and the massive growth in private homes (with many paying well below local authority rates, eg £20 a night for 8.00 pm to 8.00 am is not unusual, although the local authority rate would be £4.17 per hour).

There are enormous pressures on people to accept low pay. The actively seeking work regulations allow for disqualification from benefit for refusing a job, even on the grounds that the pay is too low or the job unsuitable. The Jobseeker's Allowance regime will increase this pressure, with claimants being asked to state the lowest rate for which they are prepared to work, with no floor being contemplated by ministers. Employers routinely threaten employees with loss of their job if they do not accept adverse pay and conditions, including cuts in basic rate, loss of bonus, etc. With no legal right to overtime payments many workers get no overtime rate at all (very common, for example, in the security industry). Fewer workers are unionised; and even where workers are unionised many employers refuse to negotiate with the union. (It is not just small firms which refuse to negotiate with unions. Sainsbury's, for example, recognises unions for representation but not for wage negotiation.)

In contrast to official optimism about pay there are a number of indicators that low pay is widespread and growing. The Greater Manchester Low Pay Unit, for example, does Jobcentre surveys every year in Greater Manchester, and also produces similar surveys for various councils in Lancashire and Merseyside. The latest GM survey (for 1995) shows that average hourly pay for full-time jobs was £3.88 and for part-time it was £3.38. Average hourly pay for part-time jobs has remained fairly constant over the last four years, whilst average hourly pay for full-time jobs has fallen by 2.3% in real terms. More than 12% of jobs which gave a pay rate were paying less than £2.75 an hour, and more than 60% less than £3.50 an hour.

These specific findings for Greater Manchester are borne out by a wider Jobcentre survey undertaken by the government. This showed that in February 1994:
* 11% of vacancies were for £2.50 or below
* 47% were for £2.51-£3.50
* 27% were for £3.51-£4.50
* 8% were for £4.51-£5.50
* 7% were for over £5.50

Low hourly earnings are particularly prevalent amongst part-time, female and manual workers, as the following table of percentages of workers earning below £3.50 an hour shows:

	Non-Manual	Manual
Male		
Full-time	2.0	5.5
Part-time	18.2	38.3
Female		
Full-time	4.0	23.6
Part-time	15.4	39.5

Since these figures are based on the New Earnings Survey they are likely to under-estimate the proportions of workers earning below £3.50. The same is true for the following table which shows the proportions of female employees being paid below £1.75 an hour in 1994 and 1995, by region.

	1994	1995	
South East	0.3	1.2	+0.9
East Anglia	0.6	1.6	+1.0
South West	0.8	0.8	-
West Midlands	0.6	1.6	+1.0
East Midlands	0.6	1.0	+0.4
Yorkshire & Humberside	0.6	1.5	+0.9
North West	0.3	1.2	+0.9
North	0.5	1.2	+0.7
Wales	1.4	1.8	+0.4
Scotland	0.3	1.0	+0.7

Whilst the proportions paying below £1.75 are very low, the interesting point about this table is that for almost every region there has been a rise (in many cases more than a doubling) in the proportion paying below this figure, even though the effect of inflation ought to have been the reverse. Even official figures which under-estimate the extent of low pay, therefore, show increases in the proportions below very low thresholds (similar increases can be seen at other thresholds such as £2.00, £2.50 and £3.00).

A flavour of the kind of jobs which pay particularly low wages can be seen in the following table, drawn from the GMLPU Jobcentre Survey for 1995, which shows the proportions of different jobs which paid below £2.75 and £3.50.

	£2.75 or less	£3.50 or less
Security	49.1	89.6
Hairdressing	29.4	94.1
Clothing/machining	29.3	90.6
Factory	29.0	67.7
Warehouse	25.0	58.3
Cleaners	23.6	89.3
Care work	20.5	80.3
Managerial	18.2	36.4
Sales	16.8	52.1
Drivers	7.3	27.1
Building	7.1	14.2
Motor trade	6.0	18.0
Hotel and catering	5.2	81.4
Shops	4.5	78.0
Skilled	1.1	10.2
Engineering	0.0	3.5
Office	3.6	27.7

The table shows not only that some occupations had significant proportions of jobs below £2.75, but also that many low-paid occupations have rates falling between £2.75 and £3.50. (The residual effect of former Wages Councils can be seen in the figures for hotel and catering and for shops, both of which have low proportions below £2.75 but high proportions below £3.50.) All of these jobs are for adult workers, as young people's jobs have been excluded.

Low income

Low pay, plus the increase in part-time work, means that increasing numbers of jobs pay only a low weekly income. Thus, for example, GM Low Pay Unit Jobcentre survey shows a quarter of all vacancies paying less than the National Insurance threshold (then £58), and over 45% paying less than £100 a week. Over 90% paid less than £200 a week, with nearly 85% of the full-time jobs falling below this threshold.

Such figures indicate the kind of problems faced by people who are unemployed and looking for work: it is hard to get back into the labour market when jobs do not pay enough to support a family. According to tax benefit model tables produced by the government a family with one full-time earner and two children aged 4 and 6 on gross earnings of £200 a week would have a net income after housing costs of £135.09 per week, just £12.68 more than they would get after housing costs on Income Support. (The working family would have to find travel to work costs and would lose entitlement to free school meals.)

It is arguable that these are only vacancies in Jobcentres and therefore do not represent the whole of the labour market. However, government figures for all earners in the New Earnings Survey show that significant proportions earn below various Family Credit thresholds.

Proportion of all employees with earnings below Family Credit thresholds

Family type	Working 16-29 hours	Working 30 or more hours
One child under 5	79.4	27.7
Two children under 11	82.4	36.1
Two children 11-15	84.5	43.9
Three children under 11	85.0	46.2
Three children 11-15	87.6	57.5
Two children under 11, two 11-15	87.9	59.6

As the table shows, even in the New Earnings Survey (which over-estimates levels of earnings) more than a third of full-time jobs pay below the Family Credit threshold for a family with two children under 11. For a family with two older children or three children the proportion rises to well over four in ten.

The table does not include part-time jobs for less than 16 hours, since these are not eligible for Family Credit. However, the large majority of jobs for less than 16 hours will be below the Family Credit thresholds (pay rates in excess of £12 an hour would be required for a 15 hour week to meet even the lowest threshold). If we assume, therefore, that 95% of part-time jobs below 16 hours pay below FC thresholds for a family with two children under 11, and if we use the proportions in the above table, and apply these to the total labour market we find the following:

Type of job	Total number	Below FC level	
Below 16 hours a week	2.591m	95.0%	2.461m
16-29 hours a week	3.558m	82.4%	2.932m
30 or more hours a week	15.259m	36.1%	5.508m

This calculation suggests that around 10.9 million employees earn less than the Family Credit threshold for a family with two children under 11. This amounts to just over half (50.9%) of all employees. **Around half of all jobs in the economy, therefore, do not pay enough to support a family with two young children without recourse to top-up benefit.** (This is almost bound to be an under-estimate, given that significant numbers of part-time jobs between 16-29 hours will not appear in the NES because they pay too little.)

These figures explain why increasingly a family with children can only survive if more than one person in the household is in work. The one-earner household is becoming increasingly rare. In 1979 over 36% of the population lived in households with one full-time earner and one non-earning partner, whereas by 1991 this had fallen to 15%.

If we look simply at the workforce, rather than all households, we find that 26.2% of workers were in households with only one earner, 53.1% in households with two earners,

15.2% with three earners, and 5.5% with four or more earners.   Put another way, most workers (73.8%) were in multiple-earner households.   72.8% of full-time, 76.3% of part-time and 74.4% of self-employed workers were in multiple-earner households.

The increasing divide between 'work-rich' and 'work-poor' families must be of enormous concern.   Even where jobs are available, many unemployed households find that there is no point in taking the jobs because the weekly income is so low that they would be worse off than being unemployed.   The attached paper (appendix III) about new jobs in a supermarket in Stirling is a graphic example of the poor quality of many jobs available.   All but 4 of the 91 jobs paid below the National Insurance threshold, giving low weekly income and also excluding workers from the social insurance system.   (The paper also shows the fiscal problems arising from low income jobs - these fiscal problems then contribute to a vicious spiral downwards, where better-paid public sector employment suffers because of lack of revenue.)

The government consistently argues that low pay/income does not matter because there is a 'generous' system of Family Credit to top up wages.   Family Credit is available to households with dependent children where someone works 16 or more hours a week.   It is not available to single people and couples without children (though the government is now piloting a similar benefit for these groups, called Earnings Top-Up).

Family Credit claims have been rising continuously over the years.   Between 1990/91 and 1994/95 the number of cases roses by 83.5%, the number of children involved rose by 74.7%, and expenditure rose by 194.5%.

Latest figures show that in the year to July 1995 Family Credit claims rose by nearly 10% (with a rise of over 3% in the last quarter alone).   626,300 families are now claiming Family Credit, with average weekly earnings being under £108 and the average FC payment being £51.06 per week.   The cost of all in-work benefits was £2.333 billion in 1994-95 (this was a rise of 132.4% since 1990-91).   49.6% of all Family Credit claims are from the occupational category known as 'catering, cleaning, hairdressing and other personal service'.   However, all other occupations are represented, with over 11% coming from various managerial and professional occupations.

Whilst there is a degree of flexibility about Family Credit, in that awards are given for 26 weeks at a time and therefore someone can earn more in some weeks without benefit withdrawal (although the converse is also true), the fact remains that marginal tax rates for people claiming Family Credit, Housing Benefit and Council Tax Benefit are 97%.   The return for extra work is, therefore, very low.

A national minimum wage

There is a clear political divide on the question of minimum wages.   Britain is unique in Europe in having no minimum wage rates (except for the very small number of agricultural workers).   All other European countries have either national minimum wages or some other form of wage protection (such as legally binding sectoral agreements), and the same is true of the United States, Canada, Australia, and many other countries.

I do not intend to rehearse here all the complicated arguments about minimum wages. I believe that the principle that there should be a minimum wage is one that we ought to endorse, for a whole range of reasons, not least of which that it is right to offer some form of wage protection to workers.   We should not be in a position where unemployment and other pressures force people into working for exploitative wages.   The issue then becomes one of the level at which such a minimum wage is set.

Clearly a minimum wage set at £10 an hour would have significant effects on employment and inflation.   Similarly, a minimum wage set at £2 would be unnoticeable.   Thus it is the level which is crucial, not the principle.   I do not think we are able to make recommendations about level, since this is a complex issue, and anyway figures rapidly become out of date.   But it would be possible to look at some principles, such as:

(a) that once established a national minimum wage should be linked to earnings so that its relative value is not eroded (eg it could be expressed as a percentage of a specific definition of median male earnings and uprated accordingly each year);

(b) that it should cover all workers, including part-time, temporary, agency, homeworkers, etc.;

(c) that there should be one basic rate, not regional or sectoral or age-related rates (although it would make sense to have a training rate for young people if <u>real</u> training were offered);

(d) that overtime should be paid after a set number of hours (with Wages Councils overtime was paid at time and a half after 39 hours);

(e) that there should be adequate enforcement.

Lack of a minimum wage has meant that we are effectively providing a massive subsidy from the taxpayer to employers, in a way which is random, unfocussed, unproductive and may well be propping up inefficient and non-viable businesses at the expense of better ones. The growing in-work benefit bill is a serious problem. How is it to be financed if more people in employment are reliant on benefits? (The whole of the proceeds of the Railtrack privatisation will not fund the in-work benefit bill for one year.)

However, introducing a minimum wage (at any likely level) will not solve the problem of providing a living wage for families. For example, some unions have argued that the minimum wage should be £4.15 an hour. However, using 1995 benefit rates, a couple with two children aged 4 and 6 and one earner on £4.15 an hour for 40 hours a week would have net income after housing costs of £133.25 a week, whilst their net income on £2.50 an hour would be £131.25 (even at 16 hours on £2.50 net income would be £125.39).

So introducing a minimum wage even at £4.15 would not help families with children, because it would not take them above dependence on means-tested benefits. Whilst it is an important building block of any 'just' solution, it is not the sole answer, although it would have many beneficial effects for low-paid workers, particularly the feeling of getting a wage which more nearly reflected their worth to society.

A possible negative effect from introducing a minimum wage might be that employers would cut hours in order to keep weekly earnings below the National Insurance threshold. This would mean a proliferation of part-time jobs with low weekly earnings, whereas the ideal would be to increase earnings from part-time jobs and particularly to ensure that more employees become entitled to contributory benefits. (About 13% of employees earn below the NI threshold.) Extension of NI to all would help to solve this problem.

Benefits

Problems of low pay cannot be tackled by looking at pay rates alone. It is clear that the means-tested and contributory benefits systems ought to be looked at as part of the solution. I would argue that there should, in fact, be one means-tested benefit with more generous tapers, so that it was easier for people to move into work and so that they gained more from working more. (This could be financed from some of the savings on Family Credit produced by introducing a minimum wage.)

However, means-tested benefits should be the ultimate safety net, not an alternative way of providing income for a substantial sector of the population (eg over a third of families with children). This must mean safeguarding/improving universal benefits, giving all workers access to the social insurance system, and looking at partial individualisation of benefits. One of the major factors both in poverty and in inability to rejoin the labour market is the way in which the means-tested benefits system tends to lock all members of the family into unemployment.

Low pay causes immense problems. These are not just immediate ones. Many workers in today's labour market do not have occupational pensions and do not have sufficient income to afford private pensions. Indeed, many earn too little to pay NI contributions and therefore will not even qualify for a state pension. For some people, therefore, low pay means a lifetime of poverty and dependence on means-tested benefits, particularly as the labour market offers fewer and fewer chances of breaking out of the low pay sector.

Other issues

The problem of low pay, being trapped into poverty, lack of choice, etc. is compounded by the increased demands on income. Thus the lowest income quintile pays a higher proportion of income in tax than any other quintile (38.5% of gross income for lowest quintile, compared with 36.0% for highest). This is mainly to do with the shift to indirect taxation.

Housing policy has been significant. Escalating rents in local authority and housing association properties (as a direct result of government policies) has meant increasing reliance on Housing Benefit to subsidise housing. This has pushed up the benefit bill (to the extent that Housing Benefit is now being cut back for some groups). High rents mean that a family has to have a higher level of earnings to get beyond dependence on means-tested benefits - wages need to be higher to meet higher rents. This has occurred at a time when well-paid full-time employment has been less available.

Low pay, therefore, should not be seen as an isolated problem. It interacts with a number of issues, and has a significant effect on the possibility of labour market participation.

It also needs to be said that much low-paid employment is also very poor quality employment. Increasing numbers of workers have no right to paid holidays (though this should change with the implementation of the Working Time Directive in November, assuming the government loses its challenge to Europe on this issue). Employees are not generally protected from unfair dismissal until they have two years' service and our experience is that many employers exploit this fact unashamedly. It may be that we should be proposing improvements in employment rights and some kind of Employment Inspectorate to help people enforce these rights.

Beyond low pay

Hidden behind the official figures on rising earnings is the problem of the growth in low-paid and low-income employment due to the changing structure of the labour market. Whilst it is important to ensure that those who are unemployed are trained or retrained, I think it can be diversionary to look at the problem of getting people back to work as if it was an issue mainly to do with the lack of skills of the unemployed. The real problem is the lack of jobs (particularly full-time reasonably paid jobs). I recently spoke to a man who had worked for years as a skilled worker at British Aerospace, was made redundant, and could only find work as a security guard on extremely low hourly rates for very long hours. That experience is typical for many.

This is an area, I believe, where we need to challenge the inevitability thesis and question the outcomes produced by the market. Do we accept the decline in manufacturing industry, or do we argue for increased public investment in industry and in job creation, eg through support for research and development, training, etc.? Given that much manufacturing industry is no longer labour intensive, how is wealth-creation in some sectors to be translated into jobs in other sectors? (The market model is to let those with high incomes buy low-paid service from others; another model is to use fiscal and other policies to ensure wealth created in one sector funds reasonably-paid service to the community, eg teachers, home-helps, nurses, etc.)

The Churches have traditionally talked about work as giving a sense of worth and dignity. (Although it should not be the only source of worth and dignity.) There is little doubt that many jobs currently in the labour market make people feel of little worth - low pay, exploitative hours and conditions, etc. make people feel degraded and of no value.

'No house worth living in has for its cornerstone the hunger of those who built it...' ('Hunger', Ursula le Guin)

APPENDIX I

EXTRACTS FROM LETTERS TO GREATER MANCHESTER LOW PAY UNIT

'... The basic wage is £175 per week for a compulsory 72 hours Sunday to Friday inclusive, 6 - 6, with a £30 bonus which is paid if you have no time off.

'There are no breaks. You may get three ten minute breaks, if they have time. Thursday and Friday I personally had ten minutes at 10 am and 3pm. There are two girls on the night shift, one at 14 and the other 15 years old, doing the 6 pm to 6 am shift.

'The pay works out at £2.44 per hour. Something needs to be done about this company's pay policy and official breaks need to be introduced quickly. They say the breaks cannot be given because of staff shortages but there must be factory regulations regarding breaks for staff on 12 hour shifts. They have even put a camera in the staff canteen, which consists of a table with four stools and a single table with one chair and one tea machine. No clock! So you rush thinking your ten minutes are up.

'Please do not use my name and address or I will be dismissed...'

*****

'There should be enough to give me enough to provide a house mortgage for me and my family. After working 12.5 hours per day I find I cannot afford the cheapest housing.

'If they can give benefits why don't they put it in the weekly wage? When having worked all week I should not have to receive benefits. I do not think the MPs have to draw benefits, why should I after a full working week?

'Also we hear of MPs having not one job but two. I find after working 12.5 hours per day, having eight hours sleep, I would find it hard to cope with two jobs. If they have two jobs when already receiving good wages, in God's name how do they expect me to cope? I have the right I think, even if they don't, to live not exist.

'After working 62 hours per week, if I do extra work I still get the basic rate of pay for Saturday or Sunday.

'Words cannot describe the anger and frustration of being 26 and finding myself in the position of being not able to provide the cheapest housing for a wife and family after all the hours worked.

'If MPs have to have two jobs when one of their wages is twice or three times as much as mine, why should I be expected to be satisfied with my standard of living? Some MPs say we are jealous of their life style. Never mind being jealous, it should be classed as a criminal act to live such a life style when the lower paid find it hard to support a wife and family.

'Wouldn't Cedric Brown be jealous if he had to change places with me. We get sick and tired of low pay while seeing the top bosses riding in their thousands of pounds worth of cars. They have a hard time paying £3 an hour but have no problem finding the money for their cars.'

APPENDIX II

JOBS ON DISPLAY IN GREATER MANCHESTER JOBCENTRES : APRIL 1996

These are just a few jobs picked quickly out of data just collected on Jobcentre vacancies in Greater Manchester last month. They are all for adult workers. There are numerous jobs of this kind on display.

*Driver, 7.5 tonne vehicle, 'some experience in the trade not anything casual', current clean driving licence, aged 25+, £145 per week, 8.00 am to 6.00 pm Monday to Friday, 8.00 am to 12 noon Saturday (works out at £2.96 per hour).

*Part-time temporary cashier, aged 18+, betting shop, to cover summer racing - evenings, Saturdays and Sundays, £2.75 per hour to start, £3.57 when fully trained.

*Part-time sales person, aged 21+, experience essential, 9.00 am to 6.00 pm Saturday, 10.00 am to 5.00 pm Sunday, £2.50 per hour.

*Full-time dispensing assistant, chemist's shop, 9.00 am to 6.00 pm Monday to Friday, flexible - occasional weekends, £3.01 per hour.

*Static security officers, aged 21+, experience preferred, able to supply full work history and checkable references, 60 hours per week - 12 hour shifts nights and weekends, £2.75 per hour.

*Uniformed security guard, aged 21+, patrolling site as required, must have a ten-year checkable work history, references required, 8.00 pm - 8.00 am, 4 nights a week, £2.40 per hour.

*Full-time presser, must be experienced, using industrial press, references essential, 9.00 am - 5.30 pm Monday to Friday, £100 per week (£2.67 an hour assuming an hour's lunch break).

*Leaflet distributor, experience preferred, a lot of walking with heavy bag, 9.00 am - 4.30 pm, £75 per week (£2.31 per hour assuming an hour's lunch break).

*Part-time weekend laundry assistant, aged 20+, 8.00 am - 2.00 pm Saturday and Sunday, £2.55 per hour.

*Part-time general warehouse assistant, order picking, 2.00 pm - 6.00 pm Monday to Friday, £2.25 per hour.

*Temporary labourer (for 6 weeks), 7.45 am - 4.45 pm Monday to Thursday, 7.45 am - 12.45 pm Friday, £110 per week (£2.97 per hour).

*Flat or overlocking machinist, 40 hours per week, experience preferred but will train, £2.50 per hour.

*Part-time evening cleaner, aged 18+, experience preferred, 5.00 - 7.00 pm Monday to Friday, £2.40 per hour.

*Part-time catering and customer service assistant, 2-3 days Monday to Saturday, aged 18+, cafe bar, training given, £2.50 per hour.

*Part-time candle making assistant, 20 hours per week, will train, £2.25 per hour.

*Part-time nursery nurse, 27.5 hours per week, £2.75 per hour.

*Part-time radio operator, taxi firm, aged 30+, 20 hours per week to be arranged, £2.00 per hour.

*Spanner person, scrap metal merchants, own tools required, experience preferred, clean driving licence, 9.00 am - 5.30 pm Monday to Saturday, £15 per day (£2.00 per hour assuming an hour's lunch break).

*Temporary hairdressing salon manager, very well qualified, 9.00 am - 5.00 pm Tuesday to Thursday, 9.00 am - 5.30 pm Friday, 9.00 am - 2.00 pm Saturday, approximately £100 per week self-employed (£3.08 per hour assuming an hour's break each day, including Saturday).

*Part-time evening cook, experience preferred, 4.00 pm - 6.00 pm Monday to Friday, £2.90 per hour.

*Temporary process operative, aged 18+ (rigid), experience preferred, must be prepared to work in cold damp environment, £2.80-£3.05 per hour days, £3.96 per hour nights.

*Play assistant, aged 18+, experienced or qualified, 40 hour week, £2.50 per hour.

APPENDIX III

As part of a study of the impact of Wages Council abolition on pay rates, the Low Pay Network looked at pay rates of jobs on offer in Wages Council sectors in Stirling Jobcentre in January 1994. In the course of this survey it came across 91 jobs (on 15 cards) which were clearly all from the same employer, presumed to be a new supermarket. Analysis of these jobs gives a graphic picture of the nature of new jobs coming on to the labour market.

The jobs included grocery assistants, meat and dairy assistants, sales assistants, cashiers, grocery packers, canteen assistants and cleaners.

Hours

None of the jobs was full-time and hours of work varied between 8.25 and 25 per week. There was 1 job for 25 hours per week, 3 jobs for 20 hours a week, and 3 jobs for 16 hours a week. This means that only 7 (7.7%) of the jobs qualified for the same employment rights as full-time employees. All the other jobs were for less than 16 hours, in which case people taking up these jobs would have to wait five years before earning basic employment rights such as the right to notice, to redundancy pay, and to claim unfair dismissal.

· The average working week was only 11.36 hours.

· If the total hours covered by these 91 jobs were to be allocated to full-time jobs of 37 hours per week, then the total number of jobs would be 28.

Pay

there were three different pay rates on offer. 16 of the jobs had adult rates of £3.23 to £3.29, 64 had rates of £3.28 to £3.44, and 11 had a rate of £3.63 per hour.
Analysis of the jobs on offer shows the following:

· Only 4 jobs paid above the National Insurance threshold of £56 per week (3 paid £65.60-£66.80 per week and 1 £80.75-£82.25 per week).

· The average weekly income was £38.56 (if the lower hourly rate is used) and £39.05 (if the higher hourly rate is used)

Using the higher hourly rate to calculate weekly income, shows the following:

Weekly income	No of jobs	%age of jobs
Less than £30	30	33.0
Over £30, less than £35	15	16.5
Over £35, less than £40	7	7.7
Over £40, less than £45	12	13.2
Over £45, less than £50	14	15.4
Over £50	13	14.3

As the table shows, a third of the jobs paid less than £30 per week, and seven out of ten paid less than £45 per week.

If a worker earns less than the National Insurance threshold of £56 then neither the worker nor the employer pays National Insurance contributions (and the worker does not pay tax). The outcome for the worker is that s/he is not entitled to contributory benefits such as unemployment benefit, statutory sick pay, statutory maternity pay, and a state pension. The employer gains a worker without any social security oncosts.

Fiscal consequences

The fiscal outcome is that out of 91 new jobs created in Stirling, only 4 will make any contribution through tax and National Insurance to the Treasury. Many people taking up these jobs will, however, be entitled to means-tested benefits (either Income Support or Family Credit).

The **total** amount of tax and National Insurance payable on these 91 jobs by employees (assuming the higher hourly rate of pay and that taxpayers are entitled to the single person's tax allowance) is a mere **£15.02 per week or £781.04 per year.**

However, if the 91 jobs were translated into 28 full-time equivalents on £3.44 per hour (the higher rate of the most common rate), then the total amount paid by employees in tax and National Insurance would be **£570.92 per week or £29,687.84 per year.**

The **total** amount of National Insurance paid by the employer on these 91 jobs is **£13.26 per week or £689.52 per year.** This compares to a National Insurance bill of **£235.20 per week or £12,230.40 per year** if the jobs were full-time equivalents.

These figures can be summarised as follows:

- Total tax and National Insurance paid on these 91 part-time jobs is £1,470.56 per year.
- Total tax and National Insurance if they were 28 full-time jobs would be £41,918.24 per year.
- The loss to the Exchequer of having part-time jobs instead of full-time equivalents is **£40,447.68 per year.**

It is not being argued that all these 91 jobs could or should be translated into full-time equivalents. The cleaning jobs, for example, are likely always to be part-time. The case study does, however, show dramatically how severe can be the fiscal consequences of dividing full-time jobs into part-time jobs.

Annex C

THE IDEA OF AN EMPLOYMENT GUARANTEE

By David Price

Introduction

1.1 This paper was produced at the request of the Working Party. I was asked to develop ideas on an Employment Guarantee focused on the long term unemployed, involving 'real jobs' and 'the rate for the job'.

1.2 The paper was based in part on reading a good deal of the extensive literature on the subject, including evaluation reports, and in part on conversations with Andrew Britton, John Philpott (Employment Policy Institute), Pam Meadows (Policy Studies Institute), Mike Fogden (Chief Executive of the Employment Service) and various of his senior advisers, as well as academics at Sheffield Hallam University. They have all been very helpful, but of course I, not they, take responsibility for this report.

Summary

2.1. This paper considers the idea that 'The state should offer the opportunity of a paid job to anyone who is unemployed for more than a minimum period'. There is currently widespread interest in programmes to reduce long term unemployment. None the less, a proposal of this kind would be very controversial and the Working Party needs to consider the following *objections* that might be made:

> - *the extra cost to public funds would have to be met either by extra borrowing or extra taxes and might simply cause a corresponding loss of jobs elsewhere in the economy.* The assumptions here are highly debatable amongst economists. In the last resort this is a matter of priorities.It is right to target a small proportion of total public expenditure on labour intensive activity for a vulnerable group.

> *-a guarantee could be a hostage to fortune since it might prove impossible to maintain in a cyclical downturn in the economy or in other adverse circumstances.* This argument has some validity. The Working Party needs to consider whether it would be wiser to go for a *job offers programme* for half a million people, instead of a guarantee;

> - *such an intervention would have a distorting effect on the labour market.* This again is a matter of argument among economists; certainly, the design of any programme needs to take these factors into account;

> - *such an intervention may be unwise if there is a general decline in the number of jobs available.* On the contrary, if such a decline is occurring there is all the more need for large scale intervention and experimentation. However, it would be unwise to offer participants indefinite employment on schemes and it may be necessary to have a limit of,say, one year for initial participation.

2.2 The aim of the programme should be to provide work for the long term unemployed and , where possible, to achieve longer term resettlement into normal employment. To assist the latter aim, training and guidance in jobsearch should be provided.

2.3 The two main kinds of schemes are employment subsidy schemes and public or voluntary sector work schemes.The latter can embrace a variety of models, including the mainly local authority based scheme proposed by the Institute of Public Policy Research (IPPR) and the community-based scheme exemplified by the Wise Group. All these different kinds of scheme have their advantages and disadvantages and the disadvantages can increase as they grow bigger. It would be best to adopt an eclectic approach and recommend a funding framework which allows for a range of possibilities.

2.4 Pay should be based on the rate for the job, with a mix of full and part time opportunities and with a National Minimum Wage acting as a floor on wages under the programme. Special attention will need to be paid to the position of people with family responsibilities to ensure that they are not excluded by the 'benefit trap'.

2.5 The programme would be launched on a voluntary basis. Potential participants would be offered a choice between a range of opportunities and efforts would be made to help them overcome obstacles to their participation.

2.6 It should be possible operate such a programme for around half a million participants at a net cost to the public purse of very approximately £2 billion a year.

2.7 The programme would be administered by the Employment Service.

Background

3.1 In a paper on 'The Right to Work', Andrew Britton defined an employment guarantee as follows: 'The state should offer the opportunity of a paid job to anyone who is unemployed for more than a minimum period'.

3.2 The idea of such a guarantee seems to have originated with Professor Richard Layard in the early 1980s. Layard argued that the long term unemployed are to a large extent outside the labour market because of their own loss of confidence and the prejudice of employers and that it is in the national interest to draw them back in both on social and economic grounds, using the concept of a guarantee to ensure that this happened. Layard favours the concept of reciprocal obligations, so that benefit would be at risk if job offers were refused. He now favours a very simple model under which every employer taking on a 12 months plus unemployed person would receive a 6 month subsidy equal to their benefit.

3.3 Sir Ralph Howell MP (together with Frank Field MP) recently sponsored a Right to Work Bill which amounted to a radical programme for tackling unemployment. The main elements were:

- employer subsidies of over £2000 a year for employing people unemployed over 6 months;
- a Right to Work (RTW) scheme under which all those unemployed and fit to work would be entitled to a job (eg community service of some kind) at £3 an hour; £120 a week would be deemed to be their income for calculating means tested benefits;
- a Non-Workers Subsistence Allowance of £30 a week (and a Parents Grant of £60 a week) for those who opted not to join the RTW scheme.

Sir Ralph believed that this scheme would produce large net savings to the Exchequer.

3.4 In February 1996, the Commons Select Committee on Employment produced a Report 1996 called significantly 'The Right to Work/Workfare' which discussed at length and in favourable terms the idea of a guarantee and reciprocal obligations and urged the Government to experiment further.

3.5 Also in February 1996, IPPR produced a Report on 'Tackling Long Term Unemployment', recommending a voluntary scheme for up to half a million long term unemployed, offering work mainly in local authorities and paying the rate for the job, but capped so that most workers would be part time.

3.6 In November 1995, the Labour Party proposed a scheme for all under 25s out of work for 6 months or more. They would be offered opportunities with employers, the voluntary sector, education or an environmental task force and would forfeit 40% of their income support if they turned such opportunities down. The scheme might cost £900m and would be financed from a windfall tax on privatised utilities. Labour has been more cautious about a general scheme for the long term unemployed.

3.7. There is widespread international interest (eg in OECD) in schemes for the long term unemployed, particularly employment subsidy schemes, and rather patchy evidence about their effectiveness. Perhaps the most ambitious recent initiative was the 'Working Nation' programme introduced by the Australian Labour Government in 1994 which included an employment guarantee known as the 'Job Compact' for 232,000 people unemployed 18 months or more. The Programme was cut back by the new Liberal Government in 1996.

3.8 The UK Government has introduced a number of initiatives which are relevant to the idea of an employment guarantee, including the following:

- *Jobfinders' Grant* of £200 as an incentive to ease the movement into jobs of people unemployed two years or more; to be a national scheme from April 1997;
- *Workstart*- a pilot employers' subsidy scheme, in its original 1993-94 version offering £2340 a year to an employer who took on a long term unemployed person; further variants of this pilot are now in operation;
- *Project Work* - a pilot scheme for people over 2 years unemployed, offering 13 weeks intensive help with jobsearch; if not placed, they then have 13 weeks compulsory work experience; this pilot is to be extended to 100,000 people from Spring 1997;
- *Jobmatch* - following piloting, a national scheme from April 1997 designed to encourage young people aged 18 to 24 who have been unemployed for two years or more to take part time jobs by offering them a weekly allowance of £60 a week for 6 months;
- *Back to Work Bonus* - a national scheme introduced in October 1996 to enable some of the part time earnings of otherwise unemployed people to accumulate into a bonus payable if and when they get a full time job;
- *Northern Ireland*- an extensive and generous scheme for the long term unemployed has been introduced.

How strong is the overall rationale?

4.1 Despite the interest at home and abroad, there is no doubt that an employment guarantee would be highly controversial. Ministers of the present Government have made it clear that they are very strongly against the idea of the state acting as 'employer of last resort'. This section looks in some depth at arguments on both sides.

4.2. *The case for an employment guarantee* is as follows. Human beings were created in the image of God. We are all called to serve one another. It is wrong that large numbers of people should be placed for long periods in a position where they are in effect debarred from contributing to their own livelihood or (save through voluntary work) to the welfare of their fellows . We cannot avoid some short term unemployment, particularly as people move from job to job. But we need to make proposals that will address the evil of large scale long term unemployment. There is a case for various policy changes which might reduce unemployment in the long term, such as reducing the unemployment trap aspects of the benefit system, easing the movement of unemployed people into part time work, encouraging men to move into work traditionally regarded as 'women's work', removing income tax for low wage earners, encouraging reduced hours for those in work and improving education and training. But it seems unlikely that they would make a serious impact on long term unemployment in the 4 to 5 year lifetime of a Parliament. If we want to make a serious impact relatively quickly, then there is no alternative to a major state intervention to offer job opportunities to the long term unemployed.

4.3 We now look at some of the objections to such an intervention.

4.4 First, there is the *impact on public expenditure*. It is implausible to suppose, as Sir Ralph Howell does, that this can be a cost-free exercise. We discuss possible costs in Section 9 below, but they are likely to be substantial. Such costs have to be met either by increased Government borrowing (but borrowing is already reckoned by most economists to be too high) or by increased taxation. Increased taxation could simply have the effect of 'crowding out' other 'real' jobs, in favour of the 'artificial' jobs created under our scheme. This is highly debatable territory for economists, many of whom would not accept the 'crowding out' argument. The position of the Churches' Working Party might be to recognise that these proposals would lead to extra costs, at least in the short run, and that these would need to be met by taxation. But the net cost is unlikely to exceed 1% of total public expenditure and it is in the national interest to divert a small element of the national finances into ensuring labour intensive socially useful activities for the long term unemployed, even if this is at the expense of some other activity. In the long run, the approach should, by making the long term unemployed more competitive in the labour market, enable the economy to be run at a higher level of demand.

4.5 Secondly, it could be argued that an employment guarantee will be a *hostage to fortune*. It would be unwise for a Government to commit itself to an indefinite- or even a five year - 'elimination' of long term unemployment. Quite apart from the risk of shocks to the international economic system like the oil price hike, even a cyclical downturn in the economy might make such a guarantee prohibitively expensive. For example, the Finnish Government got into serious difficulties with a guarantee scheme when unemployment rose sharply. Quite apart from cost considerations, we could risk severe practical and administrative difficulties with an over ambitious programme. The Working Party needs to consider whether its overall aims could be met by a large *job offers programme*, without a formal guarantee.

4.6. Thirdly, it could be argued that a large scale intervention could have a *distorting effect on the labour market*. The view that high unemployment is essential as a constraint against wage inflation has been exploded by Layard's argument that the long term unemployed are not sufficiently competitive to influence wage levels. But the intervention could cause more subtle distortions, for instance in inhibiting normal hiring (see para 6.5 below). The Working Party might take the line that these are indeed risks to be addressed in the design of any scheme, but they are not a case for doing nothing..

4.7 Fourthly, we need to consider the implications for any intervention of the *long term future for jobs*. If Jeremy Rifkin is right to predict 'the end of work' owing to technological change, then is it wise to encourage people to believe that we can eliminate long term unemployment with a 'scheme'? There is evidence that the job market particularly for unskilled males is in long term decline (see IPPR 'Work and Welfare' by Ed Balls and Paul Gregg 1993). But even without taking a Doomsday approach, it is clear that in many localities a scheme for the long term unemployed is liable to include people who cannot find a future outside it. This was a problem with both Community Programme and Community Action and was addressed by setting a limit of a year or 6 months to people's stay on the scheme. There needs to be a strong emphasis on placement during the scheme period, but in practice many people will reach such a time limit still unplaced and, if they leave, will need to build up a new period of unemployment before they requalify. There will be a similar 'churning' effect in employment subsidy schemes, even if placement rates are higher. This is a major dilemma for the Working Party. It may be seen as uncaring to discharge participants after, say, a year. On the other hand, we live in an imperfect world and there is no way that we can quickly eliminate all the problems surrounding mass unemployment. It would be unwise to give people in effect a guarantee of *permanent* subsidised employment and, if we did, this might act as a disincentive to their return to the normal labour market. There may be no alternative to setting a time limit of, say, a year.

4.8 This leads us to the question of what is the *aim* of the intervention which we propose as between:

(a) getting the long term unemployed resettled in normal employment, and

(b) providing them with the opportunity, albeit not permanent, of a paid job.

The argument in the previous paragraph suggests that in the last analysis we are aiming at (b), but that our proposals should be so designed as to achieve (a) as well as far as possible, by enabling the long term unemployed people to compete more effectively in the labour market. In order to help achieve objective (a), some funding may be required for training and guidance in jobsearch skills. In addition, some participants in the programme may need pre-placement training if they are to make the most of their opportunity.

4.9 The argument about the long term future of jobs raises a fundamental issue. If the reality is that there is going to be a long term shortage of jobs, then the scheme we are proposing might provide experimentation in the provision of an 'intermediate labour market' (to use the Wise Group's terminology) or 'third sector' work (to use Jeremy Rifkin's terminology) on a virtually permanent basis.

Scope and scale

5.1 According to the Labour Force Survey, in Autumn 1996 there were 850,000 people who had been unemployed for 1 year or more.[1] We need to decide whether to target the whole of this group or to set a ceiling of, say, 500,000 as the IPPR does in their proposals. In view of the problems of both administration and effectiveness with very large schemes, the cost implications (see para 9.1 -9.3 below) and the Working Party's preference for a voluntary rather than a compulsory scheme (see para 8.1 below), it is suggested that we go for a *job offers programme for up to half a million people*. This is probably the maximum size of programme that would be administratively feasible in the first few years of operation. As it is, it would be the biggest work programme ever introduced in this country - roughly twice the size of the Community Programme at its maximum extent. The programme could be kept under review and it might be possible to increase the numbers later, particularly if the programme was proving successful in re-integrating people in the normal labour market.

Nature of scheme

6.1 There are broadly two kinds of scheme which we might consider:

(a) Employment subsidy schemes; and
(b) Public or voluntary sector work schemes.

6.2 *Employment subsidy schemes* are currently the subject of intense interest among labour market specialists, not only in this country but in many other OECD countries as well. Such subsidies can be paid either to the jobseeker or to the employer.

6.3 *Jobseekers' subsidies* are useful in addressing the financial problems and disincentives that unemployed people can face when they move into work after a long spell of unemployment. Some subsidies are designed to make part time jobs more acceptable either in themselves or as a stepping stone to full time jobs (para 3.8). Jobseekers' subsidies can be short term like the Jobfinders' Grant (para 3.8) or long term like Family Credit or the Earnings Top up which DSS is piloting for single people. But it seems unlikely that subsidies to jobseekers on their own could dramatically reduce long term unemployment, since the necessary jobs simply may not be there into which unemployed people can move and, even if the jobs exist, research suggests that employers are prejudiced against taking on long term unemployed people.

6.4 *Subsidies to employers* are therefore seen as necessary to encourage employers to offer the jobs. For instance, as we saw in para 3.8, the Government's Workstart pilot launched in 1994 offered a subsidy of £2340 to an employer who employed a 2 year unemployed person for a year. An alternative suggested by Professors Snower and Layard is simply to switch to the employer the money that would have been paid in benefit for a long term unemployed person. One of the major advantages of such schemes is that they offer opportunities for long term unemployed people to be re-integrated into a normal labour force and of continuing with the employer after the subsidy has expired. Employer subsidy schemes tend to be taken up mainly by the private sector (in the case of Workstart by small to medium firms); public sector bodies would not have the spare finance to cover the unsubsidised element in the pay packet. Subsidies to companies engaged in international trade could fall foul of rules of international competitiveness (eg. the Temporary Employment Subsidy of the late 1970s). By no means all of the subsidised jobs will be 'additional'. Indeed, an assessment of such schemes across OECD found in many cases researchers assumed that there would no effect on total unemployment[2]. In the original Workstart pilots, the proportion of additional jobs was in a range of 17-29% before displacement (which is very difficult to calculate)[3]. Whether the relatively low reduction in total unemployment matters depends on the aim of the scheme. It is clearly a major problem if the aim is simply to reduce unemployment. If on the other hand the aim is to bring down long term unemployment, even at the expense of generating more short term unemployment, then it does not matter so much. But it is important to face up to the financial implications of low levels of 'additionality'. In so far as what is happening is simply switching unemployment from one person to another, there will be no saving in benefit and the scheme will incur extra costs to public funds. Morover, one of the reasons for 'low additionality' may be high 'deadweight',which means that the state is simply paying employers for doing things they would have done anyway.

6.5 National Economic Research Associates (NERA) have carried out two major assessments of employer subsidies:

· Their review of employment subsidy schemes in OECD countries[4] expressed doubts about the likely effectiveness (and cost effectiveness) of a permanent full-scale wage subsidy programme eg for all people unemployed over 2 years. The review suggested that such a programme offered a potential for firms and unemployed people to learn how to 'play the system' strategically, so that employers converted their normal hirings into subsidised hirings, while individuals might suspend normal job hunting in order to wait to receive their scheme entitlement. Moreover, it was argued that such schemes can have the effect of stigmatising members of the target group and thus making it more difficult to achieve normal hirings. The review stressed that it was not hostile to such schemes, but hoped to encourage and focus debate on the conditions for making them effective.

· Their review[5] of Sir Ralph Howell's proposals (see para 3.3) which included a greatly enlarged Workstart or employer subsidy scheme. This scheme differed from many of the schemes reviewed in the OECD study in being open to all over 6 month unemployed and having stricter rules to discourage the displacement of existing workers. NERA estimated that 30% of the subsidised jobs might be additional and that 'it would be reasonable to expect a continuing benefit from Workstart in years 4 and beyond of very approximately 250,000 (reduction in unemployment), without causing inflation to accelerate.'

6.6 The main alternatives to employment subsidy schemes are _public sector and voluntary sector work schemes_, such as the Community Programme(CP) introduced in 1983 and its successor Community Action(CA) introduced in 1993 and recently abolished, making way, in part, for the pilot Project Work (see para 3.8) which however unlike CP and CA has compulsory work experience for people unemployed over two years who fail to leave unemployment after a period of intensive help with jobsearch. One advantage of these schemes as compared with employer subsidy schemes is that it is possible to make nearly all the jobs in them 'additional', by requiring that they should only undertake 'work which would not otherwise be done'. There are also social benefits in return for the investment in such schemes, in the form of environmental improvements, help to elderly people and so on. On the other hand, they have tended to operate with a segregated labour force which may have made it more difficult for participants to move from the scheme into normal employment. Placement rates from CP and

CA have not been high. In 1986/87, 28% left CP for a job or training and 35% were in a job or training when the evaluation survey was carried out.[6] The more recent CA had 25% 'positive outcomes' of which about half were into jobs[7]. In the Australian Job Compact scheme (para 3.7), only 22% of the people who had been on the New Work Opportunities (NWO) programmes (the element most like CP and CA) were in unsubsidised employment 3 months after the programme ended, compared with 41% of those who had benefitted from employer subsidies (though it is only fair to note that the NWO client group was a much more disadvantaged group).[8] There may also actually be an addictive element to such schemes; some people may prefer them to a normal job. The schemes score better against objective (b) in para 4.8 above (providing temporary work) than against objective (a) (resettlement).

6.7 Is it possible to recast these schemes to improve resettlement rates? For instance, instead of being segregated , could scheme workers be integrated with other public sector or voluntary sector workers? For instance, the scheme proposed by IPPR would operate predominantly in the local authority sector, enabling authorities to provide services currently not being offered for which there was demonstrable unsatisfied demand, eg extended opening hours for swimming pools or libraries or increased staffing for parks, retirement homes or meals-on-wheels. As the IPPR Report recognises, such a scheme could distort local authority behaviour (eg in switching 'normal expenditure' away from areas they could fund under the scheme), just as we have seen subsidies may distort the behaviour of private sector employers .There could also be problems around pay rates relative to the regular workforce. But none the less, these are interesting ideas and should not be rejected simply because there are complications and difficulties. In particular, they might offer work of greater social value than was possible in CP and CA.

6.8 Another model is the *community-based scheme*, of which the best example is provided by the *Wise Group*. They have a strong emphasis on partnership links with the local community and with urban regeneration. They have used funding from a variety of sources, so that they have some perceived independence of local and central government. As compared with other providers, they have been less at the mercy of the chopping and changing of Government schemes and have been able to build up a stronger basic organisation. Indeed, one of their most impressive features is their strongly philosophical approach built around the concept of the 'intermediate labour market'. Placement rates are better than CP and CA and have been around 47 % even in the difficult Glasgow labour market. The cost per job is relatively high at £14,000 a year, but the Wise Group reckon that two thirds are offset by savings in benefit payments and higher tax receipts. Similar to the Wise Group schemes is *Glasgow Works*, a pilot for 250 long term unemployed people offering paid employment in perhaps a wider range of socially useful work, together with assessment, guidance, training, help into regular jobs and aftercare. Over half of all leavers get jobs.

6.9 There is no shortage of socially useful work for such schemes. Possibilities include environmental improvement (eg canal clearance, reinforcement of paths, creation of cycle lanes, dry stone walling, home insulation, tree-planting), caring for elderly and handicapped people, work with children, leisure centre management, home security work and so on.

6.10 This review of alternative kinds of scheme suggests that, at the present state of knowledge, no one kind of scheme has so much edge over the alternatives that it would be sensible to put all our eggs into one basket. Each kind of scheme brings its own advantages and disadvantages and unfortunately the disadvantages (eg game playing behaviour by employers) are likely to grow as a scheme gets bigger or lasts longer. It will be best therefore to go for an eclectic approach and provide an overall Government funding framework which caters for:

- subsidies to employers
- subsidies to jobseekers
- grants to public sector bodies, including local authorities

- grants to other scheme providers, including voluntary bodies and community based providers.

In view of the concerns set out in para 6.5 about the risks involved in very large employer subsidy schemes, it might be best for the larger proportion of the programme (perhaps 60%) to be public and voluntary sector work schemes, including community schemes. Criteria would need to be set that ensured that the money was spent on employment opportunities for long term unemployed people, with perhaps differing emphases on additionality as against subsequent placement according to the nature of the scheme. While there would be an emphasis on experimentation and evaluation, it would also be important to make the framework stable for, say, 3 years, to enable providers to build up their expert staff.

Pay

7.1 The Community Programme paid the 'rate for the job' - in practice about £60 a week for mostly part time jobs; the funding of CP was not sufficient for full time jobs. Since then, Government schemes have been run on the basis of 'benefit plus £10'. The Working Party was clear at its March meeting that it wanted to pay 'the rate for the job', because it was important to people's self respect to emphasise that these were 'real jobs' which were properly paid. ' The labourer is worthy of his hire'. This view is strongly endorsed by the Wise Group and Glasgow Works. Presumably, if the Government were to introduce a National Minimum Wage at about the same time as it introduced this programme, the new National Minimum would also set a minimum for the programme.

7.2 There are some problems associated with the 'rate for the job'. First, various experts, including analysts in Sweden and in OECD and in IPPR, argue that full time work at the rate for the job, particularly if on an indefinite basis, could create artificial disincentives against returning to the normal labour market. It is this line of argument that leads OECD to favour 'benefit plus' and leads IPPR to advocate capping the number of hours worked.

7.3 Secondly, the benefit trap may mean that people with heavy family responsibilities lack an incentive to join the scheme at 'the rate for the job'. This is particularly likely if hours are capped as in CP and in the IPPR's scheme. Indeed, IPPR recommend some further social security assistance to make up the difference in such cases.

7.5 The Working Party might recommend:

·   the rate for the job, with the National Minimum Wage acting as a floor;
·   a mix of full and part time jobs; while full time should probably be in the majority, it would be a mistake to rule out part time jobs, as some people prefer them; they are an increasing feature in the normal labour market and they also allow more time for jobsearch;
·   guidance on existing in-work benefits to potential participants;
·   action to reform the benefit system so as to reduce the 'benefit trap';
·   in the last resort, consideration of 'family subsidies' to ensure that people with family responsibilities are not excluded.

Compulsion

8.1 In this context, compulsion means that there is some loss of benefit as a penalty for non- participation. There is a growing orthodoxy in favour of compulsion, reflecting the concept of reciprocal obligations. Benefit itself has always been conditional on active participation in the labour market and conditions were tightened with the Jobseekers Allowance in October 1996. The Government is testing the use of compulsion in temporary work schemes in its Project Work pilot (see para 3.8). Gordon Brown's scheme for young unemployed under 25 entails 40% loss of benefit for those who refuse to participate. Sir Ralph Howell's Right to Work Bill had a similar provision (para 3.3). However, voluntary sector bodies like the Princes's Trust and the Wise Group and most church groups active in this field are strongly against compulsion.

8.2 There are arguments both ways. Sometimes, we need to be cruel to be kind. Long term unemployed people may hold back from joining schemes because of a deep seated lack of confidence which is difficult to address without an element of compulsion. Public opinion would probably question why people should receive public funds if they turn down a place on a scheme. Compulsion may also deter fraud. Indeed, 25% are said to have 'disappeared' when confronted with the Project Work pilots (though there could be other reasons than fraud for this; moreover, the scheme applied only to those unemployed 2 years or more, so the effect might be different with other groups)[9]. But there are powerful arguments against compulsion. Compulsion will make scheme management much more difficult. It seems most unlikely to work in the case of employer subsidy schemes; employers will not want conscripts. In other kinds of schemes, voluntarism puts a salutary pressure on the state and on providers to make sure that schemes are attractive. From a Christian point of view, as was argued in a paper for the Working Party, 'no-one should be beyond the reach of our concern and compassion'.

8.3 The Working Party might take the line that the programme should be *launched* on a voluntary basis. This would help to ensure that its offerings were attractive. Specialist help would be available to help overcome people's genuine difficulties in joining the scheme (eg financial or child care problems or alcohol or drugs). Potential participants would be given several alternative offers to increase the chances of them joining the programme.

Cost

9.1 There are great difficulties in achieving a consensus about the net cost to public funds of the kind of programme we are considering. One of the key questions is the extent to which expenditure on the programme would be offset by savings in benefit expenditure and gains in tax and national insurance contributions. The Government generally takes a rigorous view about the extent to which employment schemes produce additional jobs and would only allow benefit expenditure as an offset where jobs were additional. The following are some examples of estimates of the net costs of schemes designed to address long term unemployment:

- John Philpott writes:'A very crude estimate- based on conventional analysis- would suggest that a wholesale attempt to tackle long-term unemployment by creating temporary jobs in the public/voluntary sectors or subsidising private sector jobs might require extra (i.e. net) public spending of around £4 billion per annum'. [10]
- The IPPR Report suggests a net cost of £1.7 billion a year for a programme for half a million long term unemployed mainly employed part time in local government.
- The net unit cost of CP in 1986 was less than £2000, equivalent to £3100 at 1996 prices, and suggesting a net cost of £1.5 billion for a similar programme today of 500,000 places.
- NERA's thorough costing of Sir Ralph Howell's extremely radical and far-reaching scheme suggests an Exchequer cost of rather over £3 billion in year 4.[11]

9.2 Some labour market analysts like Professors Snower and Layard would argue that these estimates are much too high and indeed that there should not ultimately be a net cost at all. According to them, the reintegration of long term unemployed in the labour market will have beneficial effects on labour supply; because, even if it leads initially to larger numbers of short term unemployed, their presence will influence wages downwards. This in turn will create conditions for more jobs, less benefit expenditure and a higher tax take. Other arguments can be brought in about state expenditure on health and crime which might be reduced if unemployment were brought down .

9.3 Based on comparisons with the costings of other schemes and reasonable assumptions about the rules which might be applied, we might assume that the programme proposed here for half a million long term unemployed people might have a net cost of very approximately £2 billion per annum.

Administration

10.1 The running of individual schemes would rest with public and private sector providers and voluntary bodies. But a Government agency would need to market and administer the overall programme, allocate grants and subsidies and see that the necessary conditions were met. Possibilities are :

- the Employment Service
- the TECs
- a new agency or agencies

10.2 The advantage probably rests with the Employment Service. Setting up a new agency would cause delays whereas the ES already has a well established presence in about 1,000 locations across the country. ES has more experience than the TECs of running employment, as against training, schemes. It ran CP and CA and is currently running Workstart, the Jobfinders' Grant and Project Work. It is used to working with outside agencies. ES is moreover already closely involved in assisting the long term unemployed and would need to submit people to the programme.

---

[1] The claimant count gave the much lower figure of 700,000 (GB Oct 1996) but for the purposes of an employment guarantee it seems more appropriate to take into account those not qualifying for Jobseeker's Allowance (eg because their family income or wealth exceeds the means test levels) who are actively seeking work.

[2] NERA: 'OECD Wage Subsidy Evaluations: Lessons for Workstart' Vol 1 para 3.3. Nov 1995.

[3] NERA: 'Right to Work Assessment'. An Independent Inquiry requested by the Prime Minister. Dec 1996. Appendix 6. para 6.7.4.

[4] NERA Nov 1995 report (see footnote 2). Vol 1. Section 6.1.

[5] NERA. December 1996 Report (see footnote 3).Para 3.3 and 5.3.4, 5.4.3 and 5.5.

[6] Manpower Services Commission. Annual Report on the Community Programme 1986/87.

[7] Information form Employment Service.

[8] NERA Right to Work Assessment. Appendix 17.

[9] NERA Right to Work Assessment. Vol 1. para 7.1.1.

[10] 'Work Out or Work In' Ed Pamela Meadows. Joseph Rowntree Foundation . 1996. Page 136.

[11] Ibid. Page vii.

Annex D

THE FUTURE OF WORK
Evidence to the Churches' Enquiry into Unemployment
and The Future of Work

Submitted by Church Action on Poverty

Church Action on Poverty is grateful to all those who freely gave up their time to participate in the discussion processes that enabled this document to be produced. The views expressed are those of the group and do not represent CAP's views. CAP is committed to developing processes that enable people affected by particular social and economic issues to speak out on their own behalf. This document is a product of such a process.

Church Action on Poverty is grateful to the following people who generously gave their time to enable this document to be produced:

Phil Burke   Colin Lidster
Terry Burton   Jamie Michelle Phillips
Linda Granville   Lewis Rose
Wayne Green   Marion Seddon
Sean Jones

David Cross, CAP's Community Linkworker facilitated the process.

1.   INTRODUCTION

1.1   In Britain today there are over two million people registered as unemployed, with almost the same number who want to work and are looking for work but do not appear in the unemployment statistics because for one reason or another they are ineligible to 'sign on'. When seen in this light the problem of unemployment poses a far greater question for us than many politicians and economic commentators are prepared to admit. Much of the debate surrounding unemployment focuses on reintegrating the unemployed into the workforce and taking them off state benefits. Whilst being a laudable aim, dealing with unemployment in such a way only serves to blame the victim as the cause of the problem rather than the complex interactions of our economic, political and social systems. It assumes that there are plenty of jobs if only the unemployed would look for them and they are more likely to do so if Welfare Benefits are less generous and more difficult to obtain. Such an approach neglects to take into account the almost constant changes taking place within the work processes at every level.

1.2   This document is a contribution to the debate from the perspective of people experiencing unemployment and the poverty it inevitably brings. Those involved came from different parts of the UK and were either unemployed, had been unemployed, on state benefits or involved at a grassroots level in their own locality in practical initiatives aimed at dealing with unemployment. There were no professional economists, politicians or business people. CAP aimed to facilitate a process by which the group could meet to share their experiences and insights into how we as a society can develop a fairer and more just pattern of work and distribution of opportunities and financial resources. The group met on two occasions. After identifying a number of priority issues, members agreed to take responsibility to write up their own concerns and ideas. These were brought back to the second meeting and discussed at length. This document is the outcome of that process.

1.3   The areas which were given priority were: The Changing Nature of Work; Training and Education; Jobseeker's Allowance; Short-term Contracts; Job Sharing; Tax and Benefits; Voluntary Work; Prospects of Young People; The Role of Europe and How Work Could Be. Needless to say, the document calls for radical changes to the way we structure work, the economy, benefits and tax systems. It is an earnest attempt to offer positive recommendations which challenge society to redefine work and reassess its priorities.

2.   THE CHANGING NATURE OF WORK

2.1   'Industry is constantly adapting to changing world markets. Some years ago a large company would do everything for itself. It would employ drivers for its transport fleet, its own cleaning staff and teams of people who were capable of repairing anything that could go wrong. Today such firms employ directly many fewer people who are paid more highly, regularly re-trained and long hours are expected of them. All except the core tasks are tendered out to contractors. Where industry has led the way local authorities have followed. Previously they built and repaired roads, managed local authority housing, provided services for the elderly and so on. Today the same services are bought in from small businesses with contracts being awarded to the lowest bidder. In addition education, health and social services are undergoing massive changes in terms of ethos, structures and staffing. Professional workers are required to meet an increasing array of performance indicators imposed from above'. (Keith Lindsay, Growth, Competitiveness and Employment).

2.2   The above quote was used by one of the group as she felt it summed up most adequately the problem being faced. She went on to say, 'People need different skills from before. The ability to be adaptable, to train for new things, to have confidence to move freely between employment, self employment and unemployment. Sadly a lot of people do not have this ability and feel thrown on the scrapheap. People are in constant competition and our basic need to support and help each other as a community is being eroded. The 'Every man for himself' syndrome is taking over'.

2.3   The group felt that this had the effect of creating the selfishness that has governed our society for so long. It recognised that changes need to take place in all aspects of society but none more than in the field of employment. The changes mentioned above have brought with them unemployment, low pay and job insecurity along with the abandonment of the aim of full employment. Another group member said, 'Full employment, be it in a modified form from that of the 1960s and 70s, must not be abandoned. To do so would be immoral as we would be knowingly consigning people to the scrapheap. There is endless work to be done in areas that have suffered years of neglect. I cannot believe that full employment is beyond the ingenuity of our nation provided we have the will to secure it'.

2.4   The present situation has led us to the point where we have very high levels of unemployment and at the same time many people in work are expected to work long hours, often unpaid, and are put under extreme pressure. The group felt that given proper thought and attention the scenario we are now experiencing is quite unnecessary. Work must be looked at from more than just the point of making money and creating wealth. 'The needs of people are not just physical but social, emotional, intellectual, spiritual and physical. Work and the economy should serve the needs of all people and not vice versa. We need a long term perspective. We do not so much inherit the earth from our ancestors as borrow *it from our children. We should make sure the unemployed are involved in the decision making process on unemployment and the future of work'*. (Group member from Teesside).

3. JOBSEEKERS ALLOWANCE

3.1 The Jobseeker's Allowance (JSA) was a main point of concern for the group and was seen to be a punitive rather than a helpful measure to enabling the unemployed re-enter the workforce. *'The JSA is plainly an attempt to reform the labour market and a flagrant attempt to reduce the numbers of unemployed by any means possible. It is designed to save money by forcing claimants to fight for either full time or part time, low paid jobs or risk losing benefit. It suggests that there is plenty of work out there if the jobseekers would only look for it. All they need is the motivation and jobsearch skills. This is a punishment not an aid for the unemployed'*. (Group member from Teesside).

3.2 Under JSA, claimants will be expected to sign a Jobseeker's Agreement confirming their availability to work and be expected to take any job they are deemed capable of doing irrespective of hours, travel distance or level of wages. It is feared that *'Since 16 hours work per week is considered full time, refusing to work such hours for low pay, probably lower than current benefit levels, will not be tolerated by Benefits Agency staff and will be likely to result in loss of benefits'*. (Group member from Teesside).

3.3 JSA gives the claimant advisers too much power to direct or compel people into actions they may not feel comfortable with. Some requirements, for example, regarding appearance could result in serious confrontation between Benefits Agency staff and claimants. Demanding that a person conform to a dress code decided by a claimant adviser is surely a breach of civil liberties. Satisfying many of the rules of JSA could be largely a matter of the opinion of the claimant adviser. The result could be the loss of up to 40% of benefit until an appeal is heard. A claimant who falls victim of this could end up with debts that take years to clear, even after benefits are restored. S/he may have had their gas, electricity and water disconnected because they were unable to pay the bills during the period of benefit reduction and may have had to take out expensive loans to see them over the period.

3.4 Reasonable steps to find work will depend solely on whose definition of reasonable is used - the claimant's or the adviser's. The Jobseeker's direction will almost certainly have to be followed and the claimant's own initiative will eventually count for nothing. There are some incentives within JSA but these were viewed as short term bribery that would most likely put the Jobseeker in a situation where the loss of a job for whatever reason will mean losing part if not all of one's benefit until the facts are known and a decision is made. The Employment on Trial Scheme was seen as only being able to work in areas where there were relatively high numbers of jobs available and would be unlikely to make much impact where major base industries have been lost and not replaced by any extensive alternatives.

3.5 The group agreed that JSA is not a welcome incentive for the unemployed but a further attempt to punish them and move towards reducing and finally ending Welfare Benefits altogether. One member argued, *'Rather then moving forward towards a better future this scheme is purely a throwback to the Poor Laws of the 16th and mid 19th centuries which treated the unemployed as criminals'*.

4. SHORT TERM CONTRACTS

4.1 Over the last twenty years we have witnessed a growth in the number of companies employing people on temporary or short-term contracts. This has resulted in many people feeling vulnerable and insecure. Current changes to benefits and the introduction of JSA has fuelled the concern not only of those on short term contracts but also those on benefits who are now afraid of taking short-term work because of the risks of losing benefits should they be forced back into unemployment. One group member from the south of England said, *'People are in fear of unemployment, whilst the unwaged wish to seek long term, stable employment. Surely this is not too much to ask? I believe such contracts in no way help the employee or the employer to feel any responsibility towards each other. This creates discontent and feelings of mistrust. If a contract is not renewed one not only has the fear of unemployment but the whole task of claiming benefit all over again which, under JSA, is likely to force people to seek any type of employment'.*

4.2   It was suggested that workers ought to be protected by a state contract which is built into all short-term and individual contracts. This would enable workers to enter into discussions with employers on a more equal footing. Such a contract could include a right to state benefit on expiry of the contract between employee and employer. In turn this would protect people from unscrupulous employers who are merely out to exploit the current job market and take advantage of the tightening of benefit rules.

4.3   It was noted that one in nine of British workers do not have paid holidays and that such an incidence would be very high among those who start on short-term contracts. The group felt that people ought to be protected from this with more holidays being made statutory. The amount of overtime being worked by those on short-term contracts is likely to be very high and the group felt that people in this position were not working so much for themselves or their family's subsistence but were merely a resource to enable employers to make profits. People are not getting anywhere because they are not earning enough to live on and those on short-term or temporary contracts are more affected than others.

5.   JOB SHARING

5.1   A group member from Reading talked about his vision of redistributing work. *'Job Share is based upon the premise that if there is an unemployment rate of, say, 8% then the redistribution of work by a similar percentage could produce full employment, albeit in a reduced form. The guiding principle being that to secure a free, moral and just society the well off must agree to accept a little less'.* The following is a list of measures that he sees as being able to achieve that objective:

1.   The introduction of maximum working hours complete with a minimum hourly wage. Overtime is an insult to every unemployed person and its strict curtailment would make a considerable impact in providing additional real jobs.

2.   Regular breaks for employees to develop skills with 'life time' education and training coupled to extensive further education to ensure all school leavers are equipped to meet the challenge of work on an equal footing with other European countries.

3.   Control on multi-income families where this is not necessary for a secure and reasonable lifestyle.

4.   In two parent families with young children, one parent should be at home to look after the children's welfare up to a certain age.

5.   Encourage early retirement on an adequate pension whilst giving special assistance to support the long term unemployed back into work.

6.   The need to foster a spirit of co-operation, as opposed to competition, between individuals and social groups. This would include giving proper support to one

parent families who are either in or out of work.

7.   We must seriously consider the restoration of benefits to 16 and 17 year olds.

5.2   *'The immediate question is can we afford these changes? My answer is can we afford not to? Such changes would not only enhance the lives of those in difficulty and would improve the nation's performance at the same time benefiting those in power, as their wealth, which they guard so savagely, will be only slightly affected. In return they will get a society of freedom and security that they will not have if current policy continues. Some may consider this to be only a dream but some dreams turn into reality and it is essential that this one does. On reflection it only goes to show how far we have fallen when we contemplate fellowship and a fair chance for everyone as a dream'.*

6.   TRAINING AND EDUCATION

6.1   A group member from Dundee gave his insights on training and education in relation to employment.

As a society we should be investing in our people from an early age through education and training. This has not been the case in recent times. Training companies have been set up with this in mind but at the back of their thinking training has been seen as a good way to make money. In talking to some people who have been on recent training schemes it appears to them that they get little out of it. Some are used as cheap labour, not paid the going rate for doing the job while others are not given the necessary skills or training. One company which recruits from training agencies was asked by its workforce why those from training agencies did not get the going rate for the job, as opposed to benefits plus £10 per week. As a result of this pressure the company now pays those recruited from training agencies the rate for the job on completion of a trial period. This did not go down too well with the agency.

6.2   If we wish to be a progressive society then we must look further ahead than just tomorrow. We need to put in place a system whereby education, training and life skills are taught from an early age and are in the curricula of schools and continued through college, university and workplace. One way that this is already being done is by firms linking with those responsible for investment along with colleges to discuss the skills and qualifications required. This has happened in Inverclyde, an area once at the heart of shipbuilding until the late sixties and now part of the sunrise industrial sector. A firm was looking to set up its operation in the area and once it secured factory premises it consulted with the local college and asked it to put together a training programme for a potential workforce. The company guaranteed everyone who completed the course a job interview. This seems a sensible way to structure training and for firms to recruit. From this experience it can be seen that access to good training, education and a skilled workforce are prerequisites to enticing firms to an area.

6.3   Training and education goes against the thinking of many people who are unemployed because it has been used purely as a way of providing cheap labour giving people little sense of self worth. The WISE group in Dundee has pointed out that the long-term unemployed have usually had a bad experience of training and education. Therefore when taken back into such situations they often rebel. The group also argues that vast numbers of people are not stupid. They realise that training is put forward as a substitute for work rather than as a means of finding a job. Many involved in education feel that our system fails in some ways. One of the reasons for this is that it sets targets at the top end of the spectrum, leaving those who find it difficult to struggle along with little or no encouragement. It is perceived that all pupils must have academic qualifications but there are those who are not interested and ought to be encouraged to work towards good vocational qualifications using the skills they no doubt have.

6.4 Another area of concern is the way we restrict people. A leaflet published by the Scottish Enterprise Trust states that recruits should be aged eighteen or over and be unemployed for a minimum of six months. This is discriminatory. A person keen to get on is barred from participating because they do not meet the criteria. This can be very discouraging with the person involved losing the interest s/he may have had. The Government recently introduced 'Skillseekers' which will provide a workforce with the competence to do the job but with little wider knowledge or theoretical background. We should be aiming at developing an integrated approach whereby there is a combination of theory and skills, which the old apprenticeship scheme required, giving a qualification that could be built upon. On Tayside alone the Government, through the Scottish Enterprise Trust, is allocating £7 million to 'Skillseekers'/Youth Training. This amounts to over one quarter of its current budget. When the question '*Is there value for money?*' is posed the answer is rather bland - if you get a job then there is value for money. One the other hand, if you don't then there isn't. If we are to be a society in which all have a chance it is going to cost money and take effort. Maybe our schools are where education and training should be carried out instead of channelling money to training agencies that are profit motivated. In the UK we ought to be trying to develop a system of education and training that fits our needs instead of looking to import methods from places like the USA. We must also convince the unemployed that training is not an easy option compared to work and that it can be relevant to them in helping them find work. Whether such work is part time, full time or job share is another question.

7. BENEFITS AND TAXATION

7.1 The Jobseeker's Allowance has already been mentioned as one of the most crucial benefit changes yet to occur. However, a number of benefit changes in other areas have been introduced. The effects of these are now being felt. A group member who is a student living in the North West talked of the changes to housing benefit and the effects these were likely to have on vulnerable people.

7.2 '*Housing Benefit will no longer cover the full rent where this is seen to exceed a reasonable level. The result of this is that those on Housing Benefit will have to make up the shortfall out of their Income Support or Jobseeker's Allowance. Yet people are being told that the amounts of benefit allowed for different elements of living costs do not cover any additional amount which they may have to pay in rent. Those who will be particularly hard hit are young, single adults under twenty five whose benefit is less and who are unlikely to receive any additional discretionary Housing Benefit. Many people will be placed in a desperate situation with the increasing risk of homelessness. This could result in families being pushed into poorer accommodation. These problems may be exacerbated by the increasing number of people on benefits being forced to take short term tenancy agreements as their only alternative to being homeless*'.

7.3 One group member from the South Coast told of his experience:

'*If one rents a private dwelling the standard contract is a six month shorthold tenancy. This contract favours the landlord and puts an unfair worry on the tenant. By the time one has moved into a dwelling and settled in it is not long before the end of the contract. If the landlord wishes the contract can be terminated within two weeks should s/he require the property back. Such a situation does not help the unemployed or those on benefits react more flexibly to labour market changes. Tenancy agreements ought to cover a much longer period - for example 1 - 3 years. This would give the tenant the type of security and time to find employment and re-enter the workforce should they have been unemployed*'.

7.4 Even with existing arrangements for Housing Benefit the length of time that people have to wait for a Rent Officer's assessment is resulting in the tenant accruing a debt with the landlord. Under the new rules this debt may not be totally covered by the amount of Housing Benefit allowed. The Government argues that the changes give tenants the incentive to find reasonable rented accommodation or to negotiate lower rents but the reality is that landlords will be less likely to rent to people who require Housing Benefit in order to afford the rent. The plight of the homeless, jobless and the low paid is worsened by the shortage of affordable, good quality social housing. These problems could be dealt with by initiating house building programmes for this sector of society. Some areas have set up self-build schemes which enable the unemployed to build their own dwellings whilst at the same time developing their skills in construction. It is a positive use of people's time and talents.

7.5 Another member from the South made the case for tax and benefit reform:

'Unemployment could be decreased by creating more part-time jobs. The problem with this is that part-time jobs rarely, if ever, pay enough wages for someone to live on. If transfer payments between benefits and wages were fairer top-up benefits for the low paid would mean that part time work could be a more viable option. The problem with the present system is that the wages of the top fifth wage band have moved much further away from the bottom fifth. This can be rectified by restructuring the tax system. VAT should be reduced on all goods other than true luxuries such as expensive electronic equipment. Income Tax ought to be increased but should be carried out carefully. The base rate of tax should not be increased as this would be a disincentive for those on lower wages to work. The system should have many different tax bands. The lowest should be set at a level that will avoid those on low incomes being worse off working than on benefit. This would reduce the burden on lower income groups with a more progressive system being aimed to get more from those that can afford it. Restructuring in this way would result in a more equitable distribution of income and would also make part-time work more viable.

The ceiling on National Insurance contributions should be increased so that those earning more pay more. At present the ceiling means that high earners are not really paying in an amount that is representative of their income'.

7.6 A further suggestion came from a member in Teesside who talked about the development of a Citizens Income. This would result in abolishing conventional benefits and replacing them with an equal, guaranteed income for every man, woman and child which is set at a higher level than present benefits. Work is then taxed according to the amount that is done but at least everybody starts from an equal footing. 'The only reason why this cannot take off is because those with lots of money will have to give some back to society to pay for it'.

7.7 It was also argued that we ought to steer clear from linking benefit payments to compulsory work schemes. This has been tried in the USA under Workfare and has been shown to fail. The benefit system is a prerequisite for an industrial/post industrial society. If structured fairly it can be a positive aid in helping people take advantage of the requirements to be flexible in the economy. More attention needs to be paid to how benefits can be used to ease the unemployed back into the workplace rather than pulling the rug from under them. The underlying philosophy of the Welfare State should be to alleviate and eventually eradicate poverty whilst at the same time allowing people to preserve their dignity and self respect.

8. THE PROSPECTS FOR YOUNG PEOPLE

8.1   A number of group members were aged between 17 and 21 years of age. This gave the group an extra dimension in that it brought the needs of young people into the debate. The main points of concern were job opportunities, lack of benefits for 16 & 17 year olds and the current student grants/loans situation.

8.2   One member, a full-time student at Liverpool said, '*Grants barely cover accommodation costs. This means that other living costs such as food, clothing, fuel and books have to be paid for out of student loans, overdrafts and parental support. Many students leave education with debts of between £5,000 and £7,000. Almost every student now has to seek work throughout the Summer, other holiday periods and during term time. There are fewer jobs available leaving many students who cannot find work unable to afford to live or even complete their studies. Some have been forced into 'slave labour' work and even into 'Escort' jobs, prostitution and drug dealing. Students are a cheap resource for employers who under-employ staff and build up backloads of work. This has an effect on the job market for everyone and helps to depress pay rates and reduces job security. Most students now face the prospect of unemployment after university. My personal experience seems to be that of the student population in general. With less ability of parents to help out, fewer people from poorer backgrounds go to or can stay at university. The effect of poverty on students threatens and harms their education, participation in university life, health and well-being and the effects of debt last for years longer*'.

8.3   Another group member is 17 years old and is living in council care. She said:

'*You think young people have problems but not serious ones. Well, young people do have serious problems, especially those who do not have families or anyone to help and support them. When young people enter care they are automatically labelled. This label carries many things on it and results in us not being given a chance by society. People expect us to be thieves, drug users, brainless, always in trouble and scum. The public have a negative opinion of young people who are or have been in care. It is harder for us to get jobs because once an employer finds out that you are or have been in care you get told that you are not wanted. I have an example of how employers can be unfair. One girl who lived in the same place as me got a job in a cafe. She thought she was getting on the right track and was able to have a better life. She went to work one morning and was told that the employer did not need her. When she asked the manager why he said it was down to her background of being in care. This should not be allowed to happen. Some kind of rule should be introduced to stop employers treating us this way. They should give us a chance and make a judgement on our work and not on our backgrounds. I passed ten GCSE's with four at A-C grades. Many others don't pass any at all -I was lucky.*

I want to see my brother, who has learning difficulties, get the career he wants which is joinery but I bet something to do with being in care will stop him. I would like to have better things offered to us instead of second best youth training schemes and slave labour jobs. We would like apprenticeships brought back, more jobs introduced and more Government help'.

8.4   This was supported by the other group members who had pointed out the impact that the removal of benefits for 16 and 17 year olds had had on the young. When young people leave school they have three options open to them: 1) to find their own job; 2) to take up a YT scheme; 3) to go to college. The first option is not viable since jobs are few and far between for this age group. Youth Training does not pay a wage. Young people should not be expected to work all week for £29.50. Thirdly, a lot of young people cannot get financial support from their parents because many of them are unemployed and college grants do not provide an adequate level of income on their own.

8.5   A member from Manchester added:

'In the community where I live 16 and 17 year olds have fallen through the net. They have turned to crime. In some cases they have been turned out of their homes by parents who cannot afford to keep their own children and so they are turned out onto the streets. We have seen some of the effects this has had on young people and their parents. I am amazed that people in the community with no experience in Government can see what the effects of benefit withdrawal from the 16 and 17 year olds is having on them. The present Government, along with the main political parties need to address this situation. A starting point would be to restore benefits to 16 and 17 year olds. This would also make them eligible to 'sign on' for work which would at least give them the same opportunities as adults in finding a job. At the moment they are in limbo and have nowhere to turn except to crime. We must help these young people, do all we can for them because I cannot bear to think of what the future holds for the next generation'.

9.   VOLUNTARY ACTIVITY AS PAID WORK

9.1   The annual value of voluntary work in the UK is put at £41 billion (report in The Times, 4 June 1995). This report by the Home Office was aimed at increasing the numbers of volunteers by encouraging community action by people of all ages. A group member from Teesside developed the following argument for linking benefits to voluntary work as a wage and not as a punishment: 'With Government plans aimed at making the unemployed earn their benefits it should be pointed out that many unemployed people already earn their benefits and contribute a great deal to society by the voluntary work that they do at present.

9.2   'For many people voluntary work presents an opportunity for training as well as providing work experience. It also provides value for that training as they are engaged in actual work. The cost of training can be absorbed by the voluntary agency, saving the taxpayer's money. The training given is that which is actually needed and not just to give someone something to do as most Government schemes appear to be. Voluntary work provides training, work experience and current references which are vital for things like Jobsearch. Training can be added to as need arises depending on resources. Personal development is an important factor particularly if the voluntary work is linked to further education. This would mean allowing those in voluntary work to add to their qualifications through educational courses designed to complement their field of activity. We may even begin to view voluntary work as a job in its own right. If voluntary work was to be considered in such a way then the current benefit changes would need to be reversed. Furthermore we should not confuse what is being suggested here with 'Workfare' which the UK Government seems bent on introducing.

9.3   'Our suggestion is to make benefits into a wage for people involved in voluntary work with a relaxing of the rules concerning the number of hours those on benefits can do voluntary work for. Although a subsidy greater than the current benefit plus £10 per week on present training schemes would be needed, the annual value of these extra volunteers would add to the £41 billion already established by current volunteers. Extra funding could be obtained through existing voluntary agencies fund raising strategies, from local businesses and local and central Government. Volunteers would be liable for Income Tax and NI contributions. Benefits would have to be flexible - Housing and Council Tax benefits would still be required to protect volunteers from falling back into the poverty trap. Some existing schemes are already incorporating the idea of benefits and work into what may prove to be a viable proposition. The Community Work Programme (Northern Ireland) offers training in contracts of up to three years. Participants receive a weekly training allowance equivalent to their benefits and also an additional training premium depending on the position held. For example, standard £20, skilled £25, supervisory £35 and managerial £55. This is for social, cultural and environmental projects. Such an idea could be adapted to voluntary work on a larger scale than for just the above mentioned projects.

9.4 'The idea of voluntary work as paid work through the benefit system could still fit in with JSA criteria. Participants would be engaging in jobsearch activities through their voluntary agencies thus improving their chances of finding a job. It would be hoped that the aggressive and punitive elements of JSA could be scrapped for those engaged in this scheme. Government schemes such as Restart and Job Plan would lose their significance for volunteers as they would already be involved in the type of activity these schemes were designed to produce. Volunteers could be considered as trainees for social security purposes. Although this initiative would ideally be run on a regional basis with each area planning for its own needs, it would be vital to introduce a national policy to ensure that the rules were universal. This scheme would be particularly beneficial to areas where unemployment is high due to the closure of previously stable industries. Voluntary work may be referred to as social working and if linked to benefits as wages it may eventually be accepted as work in its own right. This would change the way we consider employment and finally accept the value of voluntary work and its importance to the UK economy'.

9.5 Some group members felt that voluntary work in its present form was seen as a sector sustaining an immoral government as it fills the gaps in provision that the state ought to be looking after and that it was quickly replacing the notion of paid jobs. There are many strands to voluntary work which go beyond assisting the service delivery of organisations. One member talked of the development of Local Exchange and Trading Systems (LETS) in which people barter with their talents and skills, working for each other as another dimension. However, those on benefits were excluded from this due to benefit rules and restrictions. On the other hand all members felt that voluntary work gives us a glimpse of how work can be in the future.

10. WORK: A VISION FOR THE FUTURE

10.1 As a final part of the process the group was asked to consider the shape of work in the future. We asked people to develop their own vision. The following is what they came up with.

Work should be people centred and not just concerned with making profits. There should be a maximum 4 day (32 hour) working week, with no overtime, that can incorporate flexible working hours. Every job should carry a reasonable living wage and have an element of Citizens Income within it. Work inside the home, rearing of children, housework should be given greater value and recognised as work in itself. Wage regulation should occur both at the top and bottom end of the pay scale. There should be a minimum and maximum wage.

10.2 We should stress the interdependency of people as opposed to individualism. Many unemployed people are doing vital work in the community. This ought to be more highly valued and the benefits system should not bar them from doing such work. People should be trained for jobs that exist or will exist rather than being shunted onto totally irrelevant training schemes. Work itself must be linked to lifetime learning. People could be given sabbatical leave to re-educate or re-train for three years or so. This would create a job opportunity for someone to fill in the meantime.

10.3 It was felt that Britain should adopt the Social Chapter and the Government should stop publicising it as something wicked and brutal. We must also be prepared to offer a central and more constructive role within the European Community. By reducing the hours of work and linking work to lifetime learning, many benefits will be brought to wider society. The group identified things like increased literacy, reduced levels of stress, greater efficiency and productivity, a healthier society which will reduce the costs of the

Welfare State through reducing absenteeism at work and increasing employment opportunities. Developing our nation's greatest resource, its people, will create a broad skill base that will enable us to compete economically with any country. We will also have a nation in which its citizens feel valued and appreciated. All can and must have a place in society if we are to flourish as a nation. Our participation in society and freedom should not be limited to whether we own property, shares or have secure well paid jobs.

10.4   The main political parties' commitment to cutting taxes and public spending are also a major contributing factor to unemployment and poverty. One member said that he '*found it refreshing that the EU had recently warned the Chancellor not to cut taxes again*'.

10.5   The group realise that these may appear to be dreams but it believes it is much more concrete than that. '*There is plenty of money around, it is just that we have the wrong sets of priorities about what we are prepared to pay for as a society. We keep looking to the trickle down theory: this is wrong. We may also be asking the wrong question because we are always talking about how much 'the poor' cost society. Maybe we should change the emphasis and begin to ask how much does it cost to keep the rich rich? We should not talk about the system as though it were something with a nature of its own. Any system is made up of people and this involves relationships. We ought to examine more closely the relationships between banks, business, communities and individuals and begin to understand how these fit together*'.

11.   CONCLUSION

11.1   This document throws down a challenge for the whole of society. It asks for courage from those in positions of wealth, power and authority to dare to change the direction towards restoring fairness and justice within the fields of economic, social and political activity. It urges us to make the aim of full employment a serious and integral pursuit in the development of our nation.

11.2   Those involved in the discussions that produced this document are fully aware of the size of the problem facing us as we head towards the twenty first century. Nevertheless, they have an optimism and vision that few of those who are wealthy or gainfully employed have. The members of the group stated their position on certain issues and give no apology for that stance. Throughout the meetings that were held and in all the pieces written by the members runs a continuous commitment to the poor and marginalised in the UK. A final point was made by the group which sums up everything it has attempted to achieve through this process: '*There is still a lack of awareness about what it is like to be unemployed even though many people live in constant fear of it. We must keep bringing the unemployed and employed together in dialogue. The unemployed are not lazy and they can have a positive input to the debate about the future of work, benefit reform, political and economic direction. It is important that we get this message circulated more widely and the process used more often*'.

SOCIAL SECURITY AND UNEMPLOYMENT

By David Price

1. INTRODUCTION

1.1 This paper discusses the link between social security and unemployment

· how far the social security system alleviates the impact of unemployment,
· whether, as some would argue, it exacerbates the problem of unemployment and
· whether there are changes in social security provision which could improve the present situation.

In preparing this paper I have benefitted from the advice of Professor Alan Deacon, Gabrielle Cox, academics at Sheffield Hallam University and elsewhere and officials, and I have studied some of the relevant literature. It is a huge subject and my coverage has inevitably been partial. In particular, I have not attempted to cover:

· the question of benefit sanctions to ensure that unemployed people participate in the labour market; and
· the question of fraud and abuse.

Both of these are large subjects in their own right which I have not had time to research properly.

2. EXECUTIVE SUMMARY

2.1 The main social security provision for the unemployed is the Jobseeker's Allowance, though there are significant numbers of unemployed people who are not JSA claimants. The main reasons for providing benefits to the unemployed are to reduce financial pressures during jobsearch, to facilitate change in the labour market, to avoid social exclusion and to alleviate poverty. Benefit levels in the UK have fallen significantly relative to the income levels of those in work. There is public recognition that benefit levels may be too low and may cause hardship.

2.2 Government policy in recent years has been driven on the one hand by an understandable wish to contain expenditure on benefits for unemployed people and on the other hand by a concern to improve incentives to work. In practice, expenditure has remained high - currently over £8 billion a year - while some of the economies introduced have had a perverse effect on incentives.

2.3 Research suggests that the level of unemployment benefit is not the major determinant of unemployment duration, particularly for men, though important disincentives to work exist for two groups among whom women predominate - the partners of unemployed people and lone parents. Research also suggests that the labour market behaviour of unemployed people (particularly long term unemployed) is determined by a complex of factors, including household needs, support networks, institutional arrangements for paying benefits and finding jobs, the morale of the individual and what is on offer in the local labour market. A major problem is the prevalence of insecure, short term and part-time jobs in the labour market. Long term unemployed people are cautious about putting their fragile household finances at risk for an insecure job, particularly given their concerns about the problems of re-instating their JSA when the job ends and adjusting their Housing Benefit and Council Tax Benefit. .

2.4 The Government has taken a number of measures, notably in the 1994 Budget, to help unemployed people to bridge the gap between welfare and work. In particular, they have sought to address the problem of incentives by the provision of *in-work benefits*, of which Family

Credit and Housing Benefit are the most important. In-work benefits have their value but it would be unwise to make them the central foundation of a back to work strategy. Family Credit is restricted to families with children, though DSS is piloting an extension to single people and childless couples. The biggest problem is that in-work benefits are means-tested which means that they create disincentives as well as incentives - disincentives for partners of recipients and for recipients wishing to better themselves. Unemployed people regard them as a more risky source of income than normal wages. They do not feel that they can trust the authorities to adjust benefits (particularly Housing Benefit) quickly as their circumstances change. Further consideration should be given to administrative changes and *bridging mechanisms* which help to provide unemployed people with assurance that their financial position will not be at risk as they move into jobs:

- Guaranteeing that in-work benefits will be paid promptly enough to replace the JSA girocheque;
- Paying the Jobfinder's Grant of £200 to all people at least one year unemployed who move into jobs
- in the longer term, seeking to bring in-work benefits under a unified system of administration, so as to simplify the handling of changes in circumstances.

2.5 JSA has, among other things, involved some simplification and streamlining in the benefit system, but further efforts in this direction are needed when there has been time to evaluate the effect of JSA. The system needs to become more transparent and more reliable in its operation. This would not only help the long term unemployed to move into jobs, but also greatly assist people moving in and out of a succession of low paid jobs with spells of unemployment in between.

2.6 *Part-time jobs* are now very prevalent, but reliance on benefits makes many unemployed people reluctant to take them, given the tight 'disregard' provisions under which they cannot retain much money without a corresponding loss of benefit. It is suggested that people should be allowed to retain at least £20 without loss of benefit. The Government has introduced a number of measures to help unemployed people to move off JSA into part-time jobs, but these arrangements are limited in scope and/or excessively complicated. A major reappraisal is needed to see whether a system of *part-time unemployment benefit* could be devised as part of a wider insurance-based reform.

2.7 There is a need to re-instate a national scheme to provide support to unemployed people who move into *self-employment.*

2.8 Government policy has encourage a major shift towards *means-tested benefits* for the unemployed. While bringing short term economies, this trend reduces incentives, discourages savings and arguably fosters dishonesty and fraud. It is not conducive to building up personal responsibility and its long term effect on public expenditure may be deleterious. There is a strong case for a programme designed to *rebuild social insurance* including

- reducing the present level of exemptions from National Insurance contributions, and
- relaxing substantially the contribution conditions for receipt of contributory JSA.

In addition, some of the incentive problems with the present benefit system would be alleviated by

- removing the joint income test for means-tested JSA, at least for childless couples;
- introducing a National Minimum Wage; and
- lowering taxation on low paid entry level jobs.

3. SOCIAL SECURITY AND THE DEFINITION OF UNEMPLOYMENT

3.1 As from October 1996, the main social security provision for the unemployed has been the Jobseeker's Allowance (JSA) which replaced both Unemployment Benefit and Income Support for the unemployed. JSA takes two forms - contributory JSA which lasts for up to 6 months and 'means-tested' JSA which lasts indefinitely, provided that the necessary conditions are fulfilled. These conditions, which apply to both kinds of JSA, include being 'available for work', 'actively seeking work' and agreeing to, and carrying out, a 'jobseeker's agreement' on jobsearch.

3.2 One Government measure of the number of unemployed is the 'claimant count', i.e. the number claiming JSA. However,this measure does not give a complete picture of potential labour supply. There are others who may be 'unemployed' in the sense of wishing to participate in the labour market, although they do not claim JSA. There will be some of these in each of the following categories:

·   Those under 18, who do not normally qualify for benefit;
·   Lone parents who can receive income support without actively seeking work;
·   Unemployed non-claimants, mainly married women;
·   Students and trainees;
·   Older workers, below pensionable age, who can receive benefits or credits without actively seeking work, but may still seek work;
·   Pensioners.

There are in addition people who are on Incapacity Benefit, who by definition are not labour market participants when they are sick but may subsequently return to the labour market.

4 WHY PAY BENEFITS TO THE UNEMPLOYED?

4.1 Three kinds of argument can be put forward for paying benefits to the unemployed - labour market arguments, social arguments and ethical arguments.

4.2 From the point of view of the labour market, unemployment benefits have the function of providing people with financial support during a period of job search. It may be beneficial to the national economy that unemployed people are not under such extreme financial pressure that they take the first job that comes along, when a longer period of job search might have led them to a job which made far better use of their skills. A reduction in financial pressure will also help to maintain people's confidence and keep them in touch with others in society at a difficult time; research shows that informal networking is the best route back into employment for the long term unemployed . A further labour market argument is that the availability of financial support during unemployment may reduce resistance to change among the workforce, since the adverse consequences of change will be reduced.

4.3 The social argument for financial support is that it is undesirable that there should be groups in society who are so impoverished as to suffer from social exclusion. A divided society will be an unhappy society. More practically, such a society may suffer from high crime levels, as indeed tends to occur in the USA, where unemployment insurance is cut off after 29 or 36 weeks, without much in the way of subsequent welfare provision.

4.4 Thirdly, from the point of view of Christian ethics, there is a strong case for giving assistance to the unemployed as victims of misfortune - 'Inasmuch as ye do it to the least of these my brethren, ye do it unto me'.Questions could arise as to whether it is right for this assistance to come from the state, rather than the charity of individuals or groups, but it has long been seen as a state responsibility in this country, presumably because the potential cost can be so great.

4.5 An OECD Report distinguishes between unemployment insurance and unemployment assistance and says that:

> 'The positive labour market role of unemployment insurance is to minimise unnecessary disruption caused by unemployment, allowing people who become unexpectedly unemployed to concentrate their time and energies on job search rather than costly adjustments to their life style.... ..Assistance benefits have as one of their main aims to prevent poverty among persons who do not get insurance benefits.'

It is doubtful however whether this particular conceptual difference between insurance and assistance benefits can be sustained, since both insurance and assistance payments can be seen as fulfilling all the various arguments for financial support. In practice, in Britain the distinction between these two kinds of benefits has in any case been reduced. There is no difference in the basic rates of contributory and means-tested JSA, whereas in many other countries people face a decline in income when they move from insurance benefits to assistance benefits. The insurance-based system seems almost in terminal decline: in 1994, only 17% of unemployed claimants receive insurance benefits only, while only 4% received both contributory and means-tested benefits. These proportions will fall yet further as a result of JSA. Later on in Section 12 we discuss important and controversial issues about the growth of means-testing and the case for rebuilding insurance-based support.

5 THE LEVEL OF BENEFIT

5.1 There are major tensions around determining the right level of benefit - as between, on the one hand, pitching it high enough to fulfil the purposes set out in the previous section and on the other hand avoiding excessive pressure on public finances and avoiding disincentive effects.

5.2 There are reasons to think that the level of benefit paid to unemployed people has fallen to a level which is insufficient to meet the criteria implied above of preserving people's confidence and their social networks and avoiding social exclusion. Research into the long term unemployed found that 84% said that they could not afford to go out much. This would prevent them from networking. 80% said that they could not afford to buy new clothes, whereas we know that presentation is important for successful job interviews. It is argued that the level of benefit has kept pace with the cost of living but even this is debatable when all the detailed changes to social security are taken into account, such as the introduction of the Social Fund as a replacement for one-off grants for essential expenditure. What is indisputable is that the level of benefit has fallen sharply as compared to average earnings. It fell by 20% between 1979 and 1988. One of the best sources of information is the Households Below Average Income Statistics produced by DSS. These statistics show an increase in the proportion of families with no working or self-employed member in the population as a whole - from 23% in 1979 to 35% in 1993/94. In the same period, they also show a striking difference in income growth between these families and those in work - the unemployed showed a small rise in average household income of around 8% after housing costs, compared with large real increases of the order of 40-50% for all of the in-work groups in the sample. This means that those who are unemployed and their families will feel an increasing sense of social exclusion, as they compare themselves with increasingly affluent people who are in work. This is an important part of the poverty problem identified in reports sponsored by the Rowntree Trust.

5.3 It should not be assumed that public opinion condones or supports this worsening of the relative financial position of those who are unemployed. The British Social Attitudes Survey found that in 1994 53% of the public regarded benefits as too low and causing hardship, whereas only 24% thought they were too high and liable to stop people from getting jobs. 38% favoured spending more on unemployment benefits, 44% favoured maintaining spending at current levels and 18% favoured spending less. It is only fair to add that far more people favoured spending more on health (88%), education (76%) and pensions (78%) than on unemployment benefits.[1] But this survey casts doubt on the idea that the majority of the British public would oppose an improvement in benefit levels.

6 RECENT GOVERNMENT POLICY

6.1 The priorities of the present Secretary of State for Social Services for the social security system as a whole were stated in 1996 to be:

1.   to focus benefits on those who need them most;
2.   to encourage personal responsibility;
3.   to improve incentives to work and save;
4.   to bear down on fraud and abuse; and
5.   to ensure that the system does not outstrip the nation's ability to pay.[7]

6.2 In the same 1996 report, the Department of Social Security declared its '*Back to Work Strategy*' to be as follows:

6.   ensuring a positive return from working;
7.   smoothing the transition from unemployment to work, by reducing the gaps in income;
8.   encouraging employers to take on long term unemployed or those with lower skills;
9.   providing incentives for those on Income Support or JSA to find and keep part time work.

6.3 We now look more closely at these priorities.

6.4. The first theme coming out strongly in the last priority in para 6.1 -ensuring that the system does not outstrip the nation's ability to pay - is that of *saving public expenditure*. This has been particularly influential in determining policy towards unemployment since 1979. This is understandable. After all, in the inter-war years, the cost of unemployment was such a controversial issue as to precipitate the fall of at least one government. Moreover, as the Green Paper on 'The Reform of Social Security' stated in 1985:

'the cost of social security must not be allowed to become a millstone preventing the general economic improvement on which the real alleviation of poverty depends'.

One might dispute the assumption that the only way ultimately of alleviating poverty is to increase general prosperity so that it can then 'trickle down' to the poor and needy. But equally Government has a responsibility to ensure that welfare costs do not weigh so heavily on the economy as to inhibit economic progress. Even so, after many years of trying to contain or reduce expenditure on unemployment, in 1995 the Treasury was still forecasting total expenditure on benefits for the unemployed of over £8.6 billion per annum both in 1996/97 and 1997/98; even with recent reductions in unemployment, expenditure is likely to be around £7 -£8 Billion.

6.5 A second theme coming strongly through these objectives is that of *creating incentives to work*. For much of the time, this has seemed compatible with, and indeed supportive of, the first theme of saving public expenditure. The policy of the early 1980s of abolishing earnings related benefit and detaching movements in unemployment benefits from movements in earnings was seen as simultaneously containing public expenditure and increasing the incentive to work.

6.6 In reality, however, there can be considerable tension between saving money and providing incentives and Government has had to choose where its priorities lie. For instance, the Jobseeker's Allowance has been driven largely by saving public expenditure and was expected to save £240 million in 1997/98, its first full year of operation. But, by extending means testing, it must reduce work incentives for partners of unemployed people, since a partner's full-time job or earnings above the JSA level can eliminate entitlement to means-tested JSA[3]. Similar contradictions arise from the introduction in October 1995 of a 6 to 9 months delay in the eligibility of newly unemployed people for mortgage support (unless they had been in work for less than 12 weeks); this is a money saving measure which could discourage people from returning to work.

6.7 We now look in more detail at key elements in Government social security policy as they affect unemployment:

- the question of incentives;
- in-work benefits, including housing benefit;
- short term and temporary work;
- part-time work and the question of disregards;
- self-employment;
- means-testing versus social insurance.

7. THE QUESTION OF INCENTIVES

7.1 We saw in para 6.1 and 6.2 that the issue of incentives is central to the present Government's policy on benefits for the unemployed. This concern is nothing new but has been around for centuries. Beveridge said that:

'The State in organising security should not stifle incentive, opportunity, responsibility; in establishing a national minimum, it should leave room and encouragement for voluntary action by each individual to provide more than that minimum for himself and his family.'[9]

Throughout the period since 1979, the British Government has been openly concerned by what has been called the 'Why work? dilemma' or the risk that state benefits may create a 'dependency culture'. Norman Fowler's Green Paper on Social Security of 1985 stated:

' While it is one of the functions of the social security system to help those who are unemployed, it is self-defeating if it creates barriers to the creation of jobs, to job mobility or to people re-joining the labour force. Clearly, such barriers exist if people feel themselves better off out of work than in work; or if employers regard the burden of national insurance as a substantial discouragement to providing new jobs.'[10]

7.2 It would be difficult to take exception to these principles as they stand. However, the argument can be carried further than this to the point where the level of benefits is thought to be the major determinant of the level of unemployment, because higher benefits are thought to erode work incentives. The available evidence refutes this simple thesis. Andrew Dilnot examined the evidence in 1992 and concluded:

'the level of unemployment benefit does have some impact on the duration of individuals' unemployment spells, but the effect is rather a small one. To have a dramatic effect on the level of unemployment, massive cuts in unemployment benefit levels would appear to be required. And such cuts would create a regime so different from the regime under which the estimates of elasticities were derived that their predictive usefulness must at best be doubtful.'[11]

Dilnot goes on to acknowledge that women's behaviour is more influenced by benefit levels than that of men and to point to severe potential disincentives to work for two groups:

partners of unemployed people; this tends mainly to affect women, who can earn very little without it affecting their partner's benefit, thus helping to create the phenomenon of *work-rich and work- poor families*; we have seen that the extension of means testing under the Jobseeker's Allowance is liable to increase this problem (para 6.6 above);

lone parents, who may find it difficult to get work which makes them better off than under benefit after child care costs have been covered (though this problem has been alleviated by the introduction in October 1994 of help with certain childcare charges in Family Credit).

Even in the case of men, it would be wrong to dismiss the work incentives argument entirely. A man with family commitments may be reluctant to take on a job as a security guard at £3 an hour, because of a variety of relativities -with his benefit rate, with his previous earnings, with his sense of what he is worth and his family needs. But research, both in the UK and internationally[7], does not support the view that benefit levels are an overwhelming influence.

7.3 Recent research suggests that there remains a strong commitment to work among the unemployed[8] and that their labour market behaviour is influenced by a whole variety of factors including:

- household financial needs, which appear to be the main factor determining the wage that long term unemployed people seek; and there is evidence of 'flexibility' in the wages they seek [9];
- their social and household networks, which may provide both financial and social support and job contacts;
- the institutional framework and regime within which they obtain benefit;
- opportunities for finding out about jobs, training and work experience;
- costs likely to be incurred as a result of work, together with any likely delays in receiving wages from the new job; 'you have to eat meanwhile';
- the psychological state of the individual, whether confident and enterprising or demoralised and fatalistic or somewhere between these extremes;
- the characteristics of jobs in the local labour market : temporary or permanent, wage rates, hours of work, whether part-time or full time, the extent to which employers are prepared to consider unemployed (particularly long term unemployed) candidates; and
- the degree of security offered by particular jobs as against the degree of security offered by the regular arrival of the girocheque.

7.4 This last factor is particularly important. Unemployed people can be severely constrained by the labour market. The range of jobs available to them in many labour markets may be very limited and poorly paid. Some recent research found that 'the typical entry job pays only 44% of gross weekly wages observed in all other jobs'.[15] Moreover, employers are highly risk averse when it comes to recruiting long term unemployed people.[16] At the same time, unemployed people may be constrained by their own circumstances. Professor Eithne McLaughlin writes of 'the fragile and precarious nature of unemployed people's budgeting'[17]. It is entirely rational for them to be cautious about putting the household finances at risk by taking an insecure, temporary or part-time low-paid job. Experience has taught them that getting back onto benefit can be a wearisome and time-consuming process. Indeed, they may fear possible penalties for making themselves 'voluntarily unemployed' (though there is a helpful Employment on Trial provision - see para 9.3). They may hesitate even more to disturb the flow of Housing Benefit payments, given the administrative delays that can occur in many local authorities. The Government have tried to address this by allowing Housing Benefit to run on at its existing level for 4 weeks for people 6 months unemployed who move into a new job; this is helpful, but may not be long enough for some local authorities and would not cater for a succession of short term jobs.

7.5 To sum up, while direct financial incentives are of some importance if unemployed people are to get back to work, a range of other factors can be just as important and these need to be addressed as well, as indeed increasingly has been the case in recent years.

8 IN-WORK BENEFITS

8.1 Building on its concern about incentives, the Government has since the mid 1980s given a great deal of emphasis to providing in-work benefits in order to ensure that unemployed people are 'better off in work'. The main in-work benefits in social security are:
- Family Credit;
- Disability Working Allowance;
- Housing Benefit;

- Child Benefit;
- Council Tax Benefit.

Both the Benefits Agency and the Employment Service provide advice to unemployed people on how they could take advantage of in-work benefits to ensure that they are 'better-off' even in relatively low-paid jobs.

8.2 *Family Credit* was seen as the centrepiece of Norman Fowler's reform of the social security system. In 1996, over 700,000 people were receiving Family Credit and DSS believed that 81% of those eligible were taking advantage of the benefit[18]. Payments were around £50 a week. Research suggests that Family Credit 'improves families' incentives to get paid jobs at the expense of reducing the incentives of those with jobs to do more or better work. And it operates rather differently for one- and two-parent families'.[19] Lone parents gain relatively more because, in the case of the two parent family, Family Credit creates a disincentive for the partner of a Family Credit claimant to get a job. In 1995, 44% of recipients were lone parents.[20]

8.3 One major limitation of Family Credit at present is that it is confined to working families with children. But clearly problems of incentives to work could also affect single people and couples without children. The Government has therefore launched a pilot known as the *earnings top up* to test out the worthwhileness of a special in-work benefit for this group. DSS plan to run the pilot for 3 years before reaching a decision on whether to implement the scheme nationally.

8.4 *Housing Benefit* is the other in-work benefit which operates on a massive scale. It is only available to rent-payers. Mortgage payers who are unemployed have been able to receive Income Support Mortgage Interest (ISMI) but have no financial support on moving into jobs. The latest research[21] suggests that

- Only about half of those interviewed reached decisions on the basis of a 'better off' calculation; others overrode such a calculation or did not even carry it out, being driven by a stong work orientation;
- Many rent-payers were unaware that they could continue to receive Housing Benefit if they got a job; others were aware, but declined to take advantage;
- There is now an increased disincentive for mortgagors to take a low paid or insecure job, as repeat claims for ISMI made after 12 weeks are now subject to the full qualifying period of 9 months for a new mortgagor and up to 6 months for an existing borrower;
- The researchers' conclusion is worth quoting :

   'Current policies are resulting in considerable tensions between the housing sector and the labour market. The former is characterised by high housing costs (particularly rents), while the latter has a growing proportion of low wage, often flexible jobs. The costs of in-work benefits (particularly Housing Benefit) have increased as a result of this tension...at the wages available to most returning claimants (given current housing costs), the costs of in-work benefits will continue to grow. Reductions in in-work benefits will either encourage withdrawal from the labour market or result in growing hardship or debts among those remaining in work'.

8.5 In-work benefits have their value, but it would seem unwise to make them the central foundation of a 'back to work strategy'. The biggest problem is that they are means tested (see Section 12 below). This inevitably create disincentives as well as incentives - disincentives for partners and a 'poverty plateau' problem for beneficiaries who are deterred from increasing their earnings when in a job. Here it is worth noting that a National Minimum Wage is at least a partial alternative to in-work benefits and would have the advantage that it would not create problems of disincentives. It would also avoid some of the features which make unemployed people cautious about putting their faith in in-work benefits. Research[22] suggests that unemployed people see a combination of a wage and an in-work benefit as inherently less reliable and more risky than a higher wage. This is partly because of the problems of form-filling and bureaucracy inherent in such benefits and affecting the risky transition from unemployment to work. Many long term unemployed people are in debt[23] and getting a job may cause creditors to renew their demands. The new job, particularly if monthly paid, may cause a temporary hiatus in household income. Long term unemployed people need *bridging mechanisms* to help them cope with the financial transition.

8.6 The Government has taken a number of steps to address these problems. But other measures are worth considering:

- To find ways of guaranteeing to unemployed people moving into a job that they will get some in-work benefits by the day that they would otherwise have received their next JSA girocheque and for a period of some months thereafter. Some steps in this direction have already been made with the the 4 week extension of Housing Benefit at its existing level and the commitment to deal with Family Credit claims within 5 days;

- To build on the Employment Service's *Jobfinder's Grant*; this is a grant typically of £200 to an unemployed person who gets a job; it is intended to help with the problems of transition into work; evaluation found that it showed 'strong positive effects on the quality of people's lives.....self-respect and confidence had grown and their view of future possibilities had changed...'[24] This provision has the attraction that it is not restricted to people with families and does not involve means-testing; it is simple and easy to administer; however, it is at present confined to the relatively small group who are 2 years unemployed and should be extended to the one year unemployed; and

- To bring in-work benefits under a single system of administration, so as to minimise the form-filling, disturbance and delay when circumstances change; this clearly would be a very radical long term measure but there might be cost savings here as well as greater convenience and simplicity for claimants, who would only need to notify a change once.

9 SHORT TERM AND TEMPORARY WORK

9.1 We have already seen that one of the fundamental problems for longer term unemployed people returning to work is the insecure and temporary nature of many of the jobs on offer. In 1994, nearly 20% of the jobs obtained by people unemployed a year earlier were temporary.[25] Such jobs are perhaps more likely to be taken by non-claimants, by the newly unemployed or by students than by long term unemployed people, although in principle they could be valuable in getting long term unemployed back into the rhythm of working life.

9.2 As we saw in para 7.4, long term unemployed people are influenced by quite rational concerns about the process of getting back onto benefit after a short spell in work. One study found that:

'for a third of the sample the perceived or experienced difficulties of the signing on process could act as a disincentive to taking on a short term or 'risky' job and contribute to a general perception of unreliability or opacity concerning the benefit system'[26]

9.3.It is useful to list some of the worries that a long term unemployed person may have about the problems of getting back on benefit after a temporary job comes to an end:

- In order to get back onto JSA, people have three 'waiting days' without any benefit at all;

- Fears that, even after the three days, there might be a hitch in JSA payments;

- Fears (perhaps misplaced) about the process of agreeing a Jobseeker's Agreeement with an ES official;

- Fears that, despite DSS's and local authorities' best efforts, the delays and confusion in in-work benefits, particularly Housing Benefit, will last longer than the temporary job;

271

Fears that the job will prove unsuitable but that leaving it will lead to a 6 months benefit sanction for *voluntary unemployment*. (The extension of the penalty period introduced in 1988 may have had the perverse effect of making unemployed people more cautious about taking risky jobs). In this connection, the Employment on Trial provision under JSA (carried through from a previous provision) is helpful in offering people who have been unemployed for 13 weeks or more the chance to try out a job for at least 4 weeks without penalty if they leave; however, this does not address the problems of a person who takes a succession of temporary jobs.

9.4 A further deterrent to taking temporary jobs arises from the preferential treatment given to the 'long term unemployed' under a wide range of government schemes; a short term job could debar you from jobclubs, training, job subsidies etc. To remove this problem, it would be highly desirable to reintroduce eligibility criteria of the kind used for the Community Programme in the mid 1980s which were at least 12 months unemployed in the last 15 months (for those over 25) and 6 months in the last 9 months (for those aged 18-24).

9.5 Ultimately, any solution to the problem of the reluctance of long term unemployed people to take temporary jobs will *not* depend on building a further array of special provisions on the already Byzantine structure of the benefit system. Both staff and public already find the system cumbersome and hard to understand and unreliable in its operation. Now that we have a flexible labour market, what is required is a high degree of administrative streamlining and simplification, so that the system is more transparent and more predictable in its operation and can be highly responsive to the financial problems of people moving in and out of a succession of insecure and low paid jobs, with spells of unemployment in between. It is recognised that the introduction of JSA has involved some useful administrative streamlining and also far closer integration of the contributions of the Benefit Agency and the Employment Service, with the Jobcentre identified as the principal point of contact with the public. It would obviously make sense to evaluate the administration of JSA before contemplating further major administrative changes.

10 PART-TIME WORK AND DISREGARDS

10.1 Another feature of a flexible labour market is the proliferation of part-time jobs. In 1994, around one third of the jobs taken by people who had been unemployed a year earlier were part-time[27]. We saw in para 6.2 that providing incentives to take part-time work was one of the four planks of DSS's current Back to Work Strategy. Under JSA, part-time earnings which exceed £5 (or £10 or £15 in certain cases)[28] cause equivalent deductions in benefit. The implications merit some attention. We saw in para 7.1 Beveridge's plea that benefit provision should not stifle incentive, opportunity, responsibility, but should leave room for voluntary action by each individual to provide more than a minimum for himself and his family. No doubt, Beveridge had in mind the values currently espoused in DSS of encouraging personal responsibility (para 6.1). Yet the effect of the policy on 'disregards' (i.e. the small sums that are disregarded in the sense of not causing a deduction in benefit) is to offer the following choices to unemployed people:

- to engage in little or no paid activity;
- to do some part-time work above the disregard limits and declare it, thereby losing most of the reward for the work and causing a reduction in benefit, which might in turn disrupt the regular flow of benefit payments;
- to do some part-time work and not declare it, putting themselves at risk of accusations of fraud from the growing army of fraud staff and from neighbourly informers.

As one researcher has argued:

'Insisting on complete inactivity as the price to pay for receiving unemployment benefits is far more likely to create a culture of welfare dependency than allowing unemployed people to take up whatever small scale opportunities come their way.'[29].

In 1994, following the Report of the Commission on Employment Opportunities, the Australian Government substantially extended the disregard under their income support system (which was already much more generous than those in Great Britain). It is suggested that it would be desirable to increase the disregard levels in this country considerably, say to a standard level of £20. This would encourage self reliance and reduce fraud, since it would legitimise current minor infringements. It is difficult to see that it would be costly in public expenditure terms since there is little incentive at present to declare earnings.

10.2 Much of the debate about 'disregards' relates to jobs amounting to only a few hours a week. But there is a more fundamental issue here about the relationship between the benefit system and the growing proportion of part-time jobs of all kinds in the economy. The proportion rose from around 15% in the early 1980s to 24% in 1995.[30] In 1994, Professor Eithne McLaughlin commented:

' Many employment problems arise from the failure of any British government to depart from the premise that the bulk of working age man's and family income should come from regular full time employment....the issue of how and whether it may be efficient to permit, even to encourage, combinations of part-time or temporary employment with a range of other economically and socially necessary and productive actions (such as education, caring for children, supporting frail, elderly or disabled people, voluntary work) has been completely absent in policy discussions of the labour market...'[31]

While there has not been the kind of fundamental re-appraisal that Professor McLaughlin is looking for, the Government has introduced a range of policies to help people move into more substantial part-time jobs:

·   People working 16 hours or more qualify for Family Credit and nearly one third of recipients (mainly lone parents) work in that band of hours;[32]
·   following piloting, the Employment Service are introducing Jobmatch nationally in April 1997 under which people aged 18 - 24 who have been more than two years unemployed and take a part-time job receive a weekly allowance of £50 for 6 months and a training voucher while they build up their working hours or seek a portfolio of jobs to make the equivalent of full-time work;
·   In Oct 1996, DSS introduced the Back to Work Bonus, under which people who have claimed JSA for 91 days or more and who take a part-time job retain benefit plus £5 a week from their earnings, with half the remainder of their earnings accumulating into a bonus payable when they move into a full-time job.

10.3 Given the prevalence of part-time work and its potential value as a route out of unemployment, more attention needs to be given to the best ways of handling the benefit problems. The Family Credit provision is helpful, but only applies to people with children. Of the two subsidy schemes described above, Jobmatch seems far more helpful and straightforward in building towards a portfolio of part-time jobs (1.13 million people held second jobs in 1994[33]), as compared with the unnecessarily complicated Back to Work Bonus, where any gain for the individual is dependent on ultimately getting a full-time job, which may not be possible or desired. But Jobmatch will be narrowly confined to young people over two years unemployed. The Commission on Social Justice, of which Professor McLaughlin was a member, recommended part-time unemployment benefit and offered three models for the design of such provision. The problem is that there are some 4.5 million part-time employees and it would be difficult to introduce cover for those moving from unemployment into part-time work without taking on massive deadweight from the existing part-time workforce. It should not however be assumed that the problems are insoluble as some other EU countries have begun to create part-time unemployment benefit systems[34].

10.4 To sum up, there is an inconsistency between on the one hand a labour market in which part-time work is becoming increasingly prevalent and in which permanent jobs may be unavailable and on the other hand a social security system which is still very largely built on the concept of full time work. A major reappraisal is needed to see if a practical insurance-based system of part-time benefits could be devised.

11 SELF EMPLOYMENT

11.1 In accordance with its principles of encouraging personal responsibility (para 6.1), the present Government has greatly encouraged the increase in self-employment. The number of people working as self employed has increased to over 3 million in 1995. Self employment is among other things a route out of unemployment. However, the Government has curtailed the financial support that it earlier gave to people moving from unemployment into self-employment. Under the Enterprise Allowance Scheme (EAS) which operated from 1983 to 1991, unemployed people could receive £40 a week during the first year of running a new business. This scheme was introduced partly because of dissatisfaction with a situation in which unemployed people trying to better themselves by starting a new business immediately lost their benefit at a time when they most needed it. Research found that 63% of those supported under EAS were still self-employed 2 years later.[35] The replacement in 1991 of the EAS by the Business Start Up Allowance, along with accompanying changes in eligibility criteria and transfer of responsibility from the Employment Service to the Training and Enterprise Councils, has meant that there is no longer effective national provision to help unemployed people starting a new business. [36] Such provision needs to be restored and the simple and effective EAS could be used as a model.

12 MEANS TESTING VERSUS SOCIAL INSURANCE

12.1 Means testing was one of the most detested features of the unemployment benefit system of the 1930s. In his 1942 Report, Beveridge said that :
'To reduce the income of an unemployed or disabled person, either directly or by the application of a means test, because the unemployment or disablity has lasted a certain period, is wrong in principle.'[37]
In view of this he recommended 'making of unemployment benefit at full rate indefinite in duration, subject to requirement of attendance at a work or training centre after a limited period of unemployment.'[38] This recommendation was not accepted and instead the duration of contributory unemployment benefit was limited to one year until the introduction of JSA in October 1996 when the period was cut to 6 months. Even before 1979, exclusive reliance on contributory benefit was in decline as can be seen in the following table:

Year	Total Unemployment	UB only %	UB plus NA /IS %	NA/IS only %
1951	303,000	67	11	11
1961	389,000	45	7	26
1971	736,000	41	13	24
1981	2,195,000	43	10	33
1991	2,048,000	22	5	59
1994	2,551,000	17	4	68

Notes: 1. Table taken from Frank Field 'Making Welfare Work' 1995, quoted in Prof. Alan Deacon's paper 'The Social Policy Response'. See also Hansard 2 February 1995. Col 823-824.
2. UB = contributory Unemployment Benefit. NA = National Assistance. IS = Income Support.
3. Figures do not add up to 100% in any year, because there was an additional category receiving 'no benefit' eg 11% in 1994.

But what is most striking about this table is the extraordinary increase in reliance on means testing between 1981 and 1991. In part, this increase will be due to a more insecure and flexible labour market in which it is more difficult to achieve the contribution conditions. But in addition there has been a deliberate tightening of the contribution conditions[39]. The further impetus towards means testing arising from JSA seems likely to push the proportion relying exclusively on the contributory benefit down to 10% or less.

12.2 The emphasis on means testing also arises, as we have seen, in the in-work benefits that are available, including Housing Benefit which is available both to unemployed and employed people.

12.3 Frank Field MP has for some time been waging a one-man crusade against the emphasis on means testing in Government policy. In his latest book, he argues as follows:

'Means test do not operate in a vacuum. It is the way in which the eligibility rules for such benefits interact with human character which creates today's welfare disaster. If eligibility for a benefit is determined primarily on the grounds that income or capital is below a statutory level, then a penalty is imposed on honesty, effort and savings. In short, means tests:
· cripple incentives - as income rises, means tests bite and benefit value falls;
· penalise savings - people who save are likely to make themselves ineligible for benefits;
· tax honesty - those who are honest about their earnings and savings make themselves ineligible for benefit.'[40]

12.4 This debate brings out the internal inconsistency in the Government's priorities for social security policy (para 6.1). The Government has been driven by a combination of the first priority (focusing benefit on those who need them most) and the last (ensuring the system does not outstrip our ability to pay), at the expense of the other three priorities. In no way can means-tests be said to 'encourage personal responsibility'; indeed, as Field argues, they discourage saving. Nor can they be said unequivocally to 'improve incentives to work', since we saw in connection with in-work benefits that, while they may create incentives at one level, they also create unemployment traps for partners and poverty plateaus for recipients. As to the Government's ever growing emphasis on 'bearing down on fraud and abuse', means-tested benefits can, as Field argues, create an environment in which fraud and abuse are more likely to occur. Field contests whether the Government is right in its belief that means-testing helps to control the social security budget:

'Far from limiting claims, each £1 of means-tested benefit helps to generate the next £1 claim of benefit.'[41]

This is because of the indirect impact on personal responsibility, on incentives and on honesty, the erosion of which, he argues, will give rise to an ever increasing social security bill. This is a critical argument. If it could be *proved* that the shift to means-tested benefits was increasing benefit dependency over the long term, then, quite apart from all the other arguments (which might appear more important to a church committee), the *public expenditure* arguments for rebuilding social insurance would be overwhelming. The JSA policy of reducing the duration of contributory benefit by 6 months would be seen as demonstrably unsound and as something that the Treasury should never have supported. Frank Field's thesis is probably inherently difficult to prove because it relates to subtle and hidden aspects of human behaviour. But Field's view has some influential support. For instance,the European Commission commented as follows in 'Employment in Europe 1996':

' recent research has drawn attention...to the potentially positive effects of unemployment insurance schemes (as opposed to means-tested assistance), which may encourage labour force participation and favour regular rather than marginal employment...... reducing the duration of insurance benefits and extending means-tested assistance can potentially discourage people from taking up work, particularly those at the lower end of the earnings scale who might find it difficult to earn more in employment than when unemployed (or in the case of working wives, difficult to compensate through their earnings for the loss of means-tested assistance that these earnings entail). Nevertheless in most Member States, the emphasis has been on tightening eligibility criteria and/or on reducing the duration and level of benefits....'[42]

Another supporter of the rebuilding of social insurance was the Commission on Social Justice who argue that:

'social insurance should act as a 'time bank' which enables people to invest resources they earn during some parts of their lives, and draw on them to finance time off work for family responsibilities and education at others'.[43]

12.5. It would not be sensible to go exclusively for an insurance based system. A thorough international study[44] argues that a purely contribution-based financing system would not encourage active labour market policies, because 'contributory systems always imply an identifiable link between contributions and benefits.' Moreover, a purely contributory system is unlikely to be able to meet the strains of a major recession or to meet the needs of those who cannot meet contribution conditions. Mixed financing from contributions and taxes is needed but with a marked shift towards **more** contributions-based insurance and **less** tax-based means-testing.

12.6 One factor in the decline of the insurance-based system is the substantial group of labour market participants who are now outside it. The Commission of Social Justice in 1994 identified these gaps in coverage as follows:

- more than 3 million employees, two thirds of them women, earn less than the lower limit on contributions (currently £61 per week),
- 850,000 self-employed people paid no contributions,
- another 2.3 million self-employed people paid limited contributions but earned no protection for unemployment or family responsibilities and
- more than 1 million temporary or seasonal workers pay only irregular contributions, so that they are unlikely to qualify for benefit when they need it.[45]

The Commission suggested that social insurance membership should be extended to all those employed for an average of 8 hours or more a week. This would no doubt be controversial and fears would be expressed that Britain's 'flexible labour market' and international competitiveness would be put at risk. But it seems difficult to justify an otherwise 'compulsory' National Insurance system which allows such enormous exceptions (a quarter of the labour force), which encourages reliance on means-testing and creates an artificial bias in favour of part-time and other 'atypical work'. It is true that many in these groups are not well paid, so that contributions would have to be kept very low (even with exemptions at the lower levels) to avoid a disincentive effect .

12.7 Rebuilding social insurance would also require reforming the contribution conditions for receiving contributory benefit. The Commission on Social Justice commented that the UK now 'has some of the most demanding qualifications in the EU which merely serve to exclude many contributors from receiving benefit'.[46] Frank Field criticises 'what is in effect now a two year period in work for the restoration of insurance entitlement' and suggests instead 'a 13-week period back in work and paying contributions before entitlement for a 3 month duration of insurance benefit is restored. Those with fuller insurance records, or those who have been unemployed but who have been back at work for 6 months, will gain a 6 month eligibility for insurance cover.'[47]

This illustrates how an insurance-based system could be devised which was adapted to a 'flexible labour market', in which many people were repeatedly moving between spells of work and spells of unemployment.

12.8 The British unemployment insurance system is by now in such a debilitated state that it would no doubt take some time to revive it. Meanwhile, it would be useful to look at the rules of the means-tested benefits to see if they could be made to reduce their adverse impact on partners' employment (see para 7.2), which is one of the worst features of the present regime. The Australian reforms (see para 10.1) included a useful proposal to abolish the joint income test for unemployed couples without children, ie to treat each person individually for benefit purposes (as is now the case in the UK for tax). It would clearly be much more complicated to introduce similar principles for families with children. It is suggested that a provision of the lines of the Australian proposal should be introduced under JSA and that the scope for extending this approach to other means-tested benefits and to families with children should be examined.

12.9 There are two other measures which, as argued in a recent paper by Paul Gregg and Jonathan Wadsworth[48], would help to correct the problems created by the combination of an increasingly flexible labour market and increased reliance on means-tested benefits:

- A National Minimum Wage, which would have the advantage of improving work incentives and reducing reliance on in-work benefits;
- Raising the tax threshold for low paid jobs; even after the November 1996 Budget, people are taxed at 20% on any earnings above £4045 a year; this is an exceptionally low wage at which to start paying tax at 20% and must have a disincentive effect.

12.10 It is recognised that significant extra short term costs could arise from a programme of this kind. But Field and others present cogent arguments that the long term effect of a shift towards insurance-based provision would be beneficial to the public finances in the long run. After all, it is not clear that the means-testing approach has led to savings: in real terms, benefit expenditure on working age claimants and their dependents rose from £19 billion in 1978/79 to £45 billion in 1994/95.[49] The success of any such policy of building up social insurance would depend on a favourable public climate. But people are more likely to support an increase in National Insurance contributions than an increase in taxes; insecurity arising from the 'flexible labour market' arouses deep public concern and many people would welcome any new scheme which addressed this disturbing environment in a positive and forward looking way.

---

[1] Les Dawes: Long-Term Unemployment and Labour Market Flexibility. Centre for Labour Market Studies, University of Leicester. 1993. Page 9.

[2] Oecd Economic Outlook 1991. Chapter 7.

[3] Dawes. Op cit. Page 33.

[4] A Dilnot and I Walker; 'The Economics of Social Security'. Oxford 1989. Article by Tony Atkinson and John Micklewright, page 23.

5 DSS announcement 96/250 dated 14 November 1996.

[6] British Social Attitudes . The 12th Report. SCPR. 1995. Chapter 11 by Professor Peter Taylor.

[7] Social Security Departmental Report. The Government's Expenditure plans. 1996/97 - 1998/99. March 1996. Para 2.

[8] Government booklet: 'Jobseeker's Allowance:Helping you back to work' JSAL5. page 23. 'Partners of jobseekers who get income-based Jobseeker's Allowance can work up to 24 hours a week on average. Where partners' earnings exceed the amount of Jobseeker's Allowance after the disregard, your entitlement to Jobseeker's Allowance will cease'.

[9] Sir William Beveridge: 'Social Insurance and Allied Services' 1942 Para 9.

[10] Green Paper on 'The Reform of Social Security.' Cmnd 9517. 1985. Vol 1 page 3.

[11] Ed E Mc Laughlin. Understanding Unemployment. Routledge 1992. Paper by Andrew Dilnot. page 130.

[12] See for instance G. Schmid, B. Reissert and G Bruche: 'Unemployment Insurance and Active Labour Market Policy'. Wayne University Press. 1992. Page 160.

[13] Ed.M.White. 'Unemployment and Public Policy in a Changing Labour Market'. PSI 1994. Article by D Gallie, Y Cheng, M. Tomlinson and M White. Page188.

[14] Dawes Op cit pages 9 - 10.

[15] P Gregg and J Wadsworth ; 'The Importance of Making Work Pay'. Employment Policy Institute Vol 10 No 3 March 1996.

[16] Dawes Op cit page 12.

[17] E Mc Laughlin. 'Flexibility in Work and Benefits'. Commission on Social Justice Issue Paper No 11. 1994.

[18] DSS Announcement 96/254. 18 November 1996.

[19] A Marsh and S McKay:'Families, Work and Benefits'. PSI. 1993. Page 186.

[20] Social Security Departmental Report 1996.

[21] J Ford, E Kempson and J England: 'Into work? The Impact of Housing Costs and the Benefit System on People's Decision to Work.'. Rowntree 1995.

[22] A Bryson and S McKay:' Is it worth working' PSI 1994. Paper by Jane Millar. pages 84 - 85 Also E McLaughlin, J Millar and K Cooke: Work and Welfare Benefits 1989.

[23] Dawes. Op cit. Page 118. 40% of males and 28% of females said they were in debt.

[24] Employment Service evaluation.

[25] Gregg and Wadsworth. Op Cit.

[26] Dawes Op cit page 43.

[27] Gregg and Wadsworth Op cit.

[28] Under JSA, you can earn the following weekly amounts before your benefit is affected:
- £5 if you are single, or you have a partner and you get contribution-based JSA;
- £10 if you have a partner and you get income-based JSA;
- £15 in special circumstances (if you receive income based JSA) eg lone parents, people with disabilities, carers, men over 60 part time fire fighters , territorials,etc.

£15 in special circumstances (if you receive contribution-based JSA), eg part time fire fighters, territorials etc

[29] Ed E Mc Laughlin 'Understanding Unemployment'. Routledge 1992. Paper by C Hakim on 'Unemployment, Marginal Work and the Black Economy.'

[30] Julian Morgan: 'Labour Market Recoveries in the UK and other OECD Countries'. Labour Market Trends Dec 1996. Page 534. Also EU 'Employment in Europe. 1996'. Page 162.

[31] Employment Policy Institiute. Economic Report Vol 10 No 3 'The Importance of Making Work Pay' March 1996   E. McLaughlin. Paper at footnote 17.

[32] Social Security Departmental Report. 1996.

[33] Butcher S and Hart D 'An analysis of working time 1979 - 1994'. Employment Gazette. May 1995.

[34] Commission on Social Justice. 1994. Page 236.

[35] N A Maung and R Erens 'EAS: A Survey of Participants two years after leaving.' SCPR. 1991.

[36] Commission on Social Justice. 1994. Page 178.

[37] Beveridge. Op cit page 57.

[38] Beveridge. Op cit page 16.

[39] eg the lengthening of disqualification periods for voluntary unemployment and the provision in the Social Security Bill 1988 making UB dependent on contribution records for two years rather than one. Ed Dilnot: The Economics of Social Security. pages 44-45.

[40] F Field MP 'How to pay for the future: Building a Stakeholder's Welfare' . Institute of Community Studies. 1996. Page 9.

[41] Field. Op cit page 10.

[42] EU. Employment in Europe. 1996. Page 132-133.

[43] CSJ. Op cit. page 229.

[44] Schmid etc Op Cit. page 267.

[45] CSJ page 227-229.

[46] CSJ. page 234 -235.

[47] F.Field: Op cit. page 96.

[48] Employment Policy Institute. Op cit.

[49] Ibid.

Annex F

THE CONCEPT OF THE WORK ETHIC

By Rt Revd Michael Bourke

People work for a wide variety of reasons - many because they have to in order to survive, others to supplement their income, to seek satisfaction, to express their creativity or to serve the community. The concept of a 'work ethic' attempts to analyse and deepen individual motivations and link them to broader philosophical and religious views about the purpose of life.

Three aspects of the 'work ethic' demand our attention:

1. *The Content of Work*

   Work, paid or unpaid, is about making the things or providing the services needed to sustain and enhance life. Very few individuals or families are able to be self-sufficient: since the days of palaeolithic hunters human beings have co-operated to provide life's necessities. Martin Luther saw this fact of co-operation through the division of labour as an expression of the Second Commandment: our primary vocation as Christians is to love our neighbours by working to provide the necessities of life for them, and not just for ourselves. The supreme value which Christianity ascribes to love thus translates into a work-ethic based on service. The goods and services provided by work may address basic survival needs, such as food, shelter and clothing; or they may address the more diverse cultural needs of a civilised community. A biblically-based 'option for the poor', and an incarnational theology, would suggest that survival needs must take priority over, say, luxury goods. A fundamental question therefore is whether the economic system to which people are contributing is meeting, or ignoring, the basic needs of the world's population.

   If human needs are to be addressed (at whatever point in the 'hierarchy of needs') there is an over-riding need to **work well**. This is not necessarily the same as the traditional work-ethic of 'working hard'. It may involve working either physically or intellectually and it will usually depend on 'working together'. But the key ingredient in 'working well' must be an attention to quality, reliability and detail. Both the Protestant work ethic and the Confucian work ethic of the Japanese and Chinese manifest a certain obsessive perfectionism which is one of the engines of progress. Sometimes this may be the fruit of fear, or of the search by exiled or immigrant people for acceptance, security and success in a strange land. Perfectionism can have destructive aspects if it leads to a neglect of rest, family life and friendships. Nevertheless, if the quality of goods and services is neglected, the result is not only a loss of competitiveness, but also a lowering of the quality of life, sometimes with serious results.

   This element of striving to maintain and improve what is produced has strengths and weaknesses from a Christian perspective. It can result in an anxious attitude of 'justification by works', in which personal identity is found through achievement and destroyed through failure. On the other hand, it can be a valid expression of the human need for self-transcendence - the need for us always to be on our toes, and a pointer towards the new creation which is God's purpose for us. The purpose of work is not just to maintain the existing order of things, but to transform the world. Made in God's image, we are transformative beings. Miroslav Volf's book 'Work in the Spirit' speaks of the 'human project' to transform the world, in which the contributions of individuals are like links in a great historical chain. It is true that, in Christian understanding, the

281

new creation is not a human achievement, but the gift of God; nevertheless the 'human project' waits for God's transformation of the existing order not passively, but actively. The relationship between the present order and the new creation is full of tension and paradox. God may 'outwit' us and stand against us in judgment. Yet even when we are found wanting, God is working with the raw material of human history.His purpose is, not to destroy the world we have made, but to redeem it. God's promised transformation is what makes our fallible efforts worthwhile, and gives us the courage to risk making mistakes. That is why St Paul in 1 Cor. 15 v.58 concludes his great vision of the resurrection life with a practical call to work, 'knowing that, in the Lord, your labour cannot be lost'.

Miroslav Volf argues that the human stewardship of the natural world should be considered from this perspective of the new creation. Human beings are placed in the world not just to preserve it as it is, but to bring it to perfection. Adam and Eve are not jungle conservationists but gardeners. This perspective is in opposition both to environmental destruction and irresponsibility, and also to the kind of ecological extremism which is opposed to human activity. I wonder what Miroslav Volf's theological critique of landscape gardening might be?

2.   *The Psychological and Spiritual Value of Work*

Much thought about the work ethic has focused on traditional masculine values such as working hard physically, and fighting and winning wars, whether military or industrial. The feminist movement has challenged this by reminding us that at least half of the work done by human beings is performed by women, and that traditional women's work has been unpaid and non-competitive. The entry of women into the organised commercial world of work on an increasing scale inevitably entails a re-assessment of the work ethic.

Work offers people a number of psychological and spiritual benefits. It offers them a sphere of service, an opportunity to fulfil one's basic Christian vocation to serve one's neighbour. It heightens a person's confidence by assuring them that they are needed: to some small degree the world depends upon their intellect or their muscle, and there is a proper sense of pride which individuals and groups can develop in feeling that they are needed. Conversely, to be out of work is to be told that one is not needed, and the sense of confidence and self-esteem is damaged.

Another benefit to the individual is the opportunity to develop his or her potential. It is through our work that we become in some measure the co-creators of our own destinies. The lack of work spells not only a lack of usefulness, but also a stunting of one's development as a person.

One of the chief benefits of work is the opportunity to share with other people in a common task. Many close relationships and friendships are born in the working environment. Work provides a ready-made framework in which we have to relate to other people, and work at our relationships. 80% of the population are alleged to be extrovert rather than introvert - they form their ideas and their sense of creativity through inter-acting with other human beings. To be out of work is often to be condemned to spend hours sitting at home, perhaps in front of a television, living in effect in a world of one's own.

The importance of work in the socialisation process is particularly significant for young people. Going to work has traditionally been for most people the initiation process into the adult world. It is the point at which young people begin to take life seriously, and to face up to its demands and opportunities. Positive role-models are particularly important for young men. A society where the burden of unemployment falls disproportionately on the young will inevitably see disruptive effects on the maturing process: if work is not available for young people, acute questions are raised about ways in which this vacuum in the initiation process can be filled.

3. *Rights and Responsibilities*

In a Christian philosophy, rights and responsibilities go together. There is a duty to work to support oneself and one's dependents, and to achieve self-respect in doing so. In an increasingly flexible labour market the duty to work will include the duty to look for work, to seek training, to be enterprising, and to be prepared for mobility (like Abraham). At the same time, the duty to work becomes problematic when for many, and especially for the low skilled or the unskilled, the opportunities for work are limited.

There is a tendency for society to 'blame the victims' by putting more emphasis on the duty to work at the very time when employment opportunities are contracting through the combination of recessions and technology. It is part of the individualism of modern culture that the blame for unemployment is attributed more to individuals than to the corporate failure of society to provide enough jobs. It is particularly invidious when the affluent tell the unemployed to solve the problem for themselves by accepting very low wages.

This raises in a new form the old question about the right to work. Should individuals, or at least households (not necessarily the man) have a right to a job? If so, what does this mean in an economy where the labour market is increasingly deregulated and the prospects of life-long employment are diminishing? Ought society to create incentives for work to be shared, so that more people have an opportunity to exercise this right? If so, what are the implications for people's standard of living, where the income of many depends on working long hours? How can we redress the imbalance between those who are working too much and those without a chance to work at all - both extremes damaging a healthy work-ethic?

Another aspect of the rights-and-responsibilities debate concerns rewards for work. Should there be a right to a social wage, regardless of whether one is 'in work' or not - and if so, where should the money come from? Such a social wage would presumably cover those outside the traditional labour market, including for instance voluntary workers and houseworkers etc. At the other end of the scale, there is a 'work ethic' argument which is sometimes deployed to justify the right of individuals to keep as much as possible of what they 'earn' through their work. This is used to defend high salaries against redistributive taxation. There are economic arguments about incentives here which have to be taken into account; but from an ethical point of view it is unsatisfactory to isolate the right to a reward from the responsibility to contribute according to one's means towards an equitable social framework aimed at maximising participation.

In thinking about social issues, we are often challenged to make a distinctively Christian contribution.One such contribution will be to point beyond specific policies to deeper questions of belief. In an age of economic turbulence, the contest between rival systems of belief is heightened, and there are new opportunities both for mutual learning and progress, and also for conflict and exploitation. Christians will want to expose the inadequacy of policies based on a view of people as cogs in an impersonal economic machine, or on the idea of the world as a game with winners and losers. Instead, Christians will seek a work-ethic which witnesses to the dignity of human beings, the importance of service, the priority of trust, and the transformation of existing power structures into signs of the Kingdom of God.

Annex G

SIMONE WEIL
ON "THE SPIRITUALITY OF WORK"

By Revd Dr Andrew Shanks

What specific difference might - or should - religious faith, as such, make to the considera-tion of 'unemployment and the future of work'?

Simone Weil suggests one possible answer:

'Workers need poetry more than bread. They need that their life should be a poem. They need some light from eternity.

Religion alone can be the source of such poetry'.

But when she looks for the 'poetry' that is needed in mainstream church-religion she does not find it.

These words come from one of Weil's fragmentary notes, put together after her death by Gustave Thibon into the collection translated into English as *Gravity and Grace*. The full passage runs as follows:

'To strive from necessity and not for some good - driven not drawn - in order to maintain our existence just as it is - that is always slavery.

In this sense the slavery of manual workers is irreducible.

Effort without finality.

It is terrible - or the most beautiful thing of all - if it is finality without an end. The beautiful alone enables us to be satisfied by that which is.

Workers need poetry more than bread. They need that their life should be a poem. They need some light from eternity.

Religion alone can be the source of such poetry.

It is not religion but revolution which is the opium of the people.

Deprivation of this poetry explains all forms of demoralization'[1].

The 'poetry' in question will, on the one hand, be a registering of sheer horror at the 'slavery' of so much of industrial working class life - that is, insofar as it remains unredeemed by the transforming power of 'poetry' itself. And yet, on the other hand, it will also be a recognition of the 'beauty' paradoxically co-existing with that horror - Weil means a certain beauty of spirit, only to be found among those whose whole identity has been shaped by a life of affliction - which is indeed for her potentially 'the most beautiful thing of all'.

Religious faith is often supposed to be consolatory, reconciling people to their fate by easing the grief of it. ('How I envy you your faith', people say). But there can be no question in this context of any merely consolatory reconciliation. The spectacle of the 'beauty' she speaks of 'satisfies'; it does not console. On the contrary: 'it is not religion but revolution which is the opium of the people'. The intoxicating dream of revolution may help soften the immediate anguish of oppression. True 'religion', as Weil envisages it, does the exact opposite. It involves the most radical possible exposure to the actual reality of injustice - completely undistorted by any sort of propaganda-interest.

Weil herself had been a dedicated trade union activist; heavily involved during the early

1930s, above all, in the struggle to maintain the French trade union movement's independence from the growing power of the Communist Party, with its special expertise in propaganda. And it would seem that her subsequent turn to religious faith essentially represents a further radicalization of the same basic anti-propagandistic impulse that had inspired her then. The 'poetry' she has in mind would thus, in the first instance, be a bearing of effective public testimony to just those moral realities which it suits the more conventional propaganda-interests of both right and left either to ignore or else to over-simplify. It would take shape, very much, as a systematic strategy of resistance to the entire propaganda element in politics. Or, for that matter, in 'political theology'.

But this is, at the same time, surely also the sense in which it would be a celebration of the latent 'beauty' of lives which tend to be all 'effort without finality' (without any clear future goal towards which they are 'drawn'); or whose only finality (if 'finality' just means 'drivenness') is the 'finality without an end' of lives lived, as it were, for the bare love of life alone - more or less drained of any other kind of 'end', or ambition.

For those who live like that are beyond the propagandist's reach.

'No terrestrial finality', as she also puts it in another note, 'separates the workers from God'. - When she speaks of 'the workers' in this way the category is evidently quite a narrow one: she means those whose energies are virtually exhausted by the immediate struggle for survival. -

'No terrestrial finality separates the workers from God. They alone are so situated. All other conditions imply special aims which form a screen between man and pure good. But for them no such screen exists. They have nothing superfluous of which they have to strip themselves'[2].

No 'superfluous' yearnings or frustrations, in short, for the propagandist's art to play upon to manipulate them.

Every social class has both its particular problems and its characteristic virtues. Insofar as they lack the redemptive 'poetry' that is needed, those who are the most oppressed naturally tend also to be the most demoralized. Of course - one only has to look at the crime statistics. And yet Weil is nevertheless far more concerned with trying to discern and to give expression to the inarticulate gospel of the oppressed than she ever is with constructing a gospel for the oppressed. The gospel of the oppressed is inarticulate, to begin with, almost by definition: oppression, after all, deprives people of both the space and the resources needed for sophisticated reflection. But society in general tends only to respect the articulate. In direct contradiction to that tendency, Weil's thinking is conceived in a spirit of the most radical respect for the very people most often unjustly deprived of it.

No doubt she is thinking, primarily, of the various people she had got to know during her year as a shop floor worker in the Alsthom, Carnaud and Renault factories, or during her time as an agricultural labourer. She is looking for a 'poetry' to make some sense of their lives - the deepest possible sense. It is, she suggests, the special vocation of the present epoch to construct, for the first time ever, a civilization founded upon 'the spirituality of work'. This is the one aspect of life with which the philosophic wisdom of ancient Greece never even began to get to grips. There are scattered hints of what is required in the writings of Rousseau, George Sand, Tolstoy, Proudhon and Marx; also in the encyclicals of Pope Leo XIII. But only hints. Herein though, she further argues, lies the one true remedy against the new disease of totalitarianism.

Another note expresses the core insight of this 'spirituality', as she conceives it, in terms of an analogy between manual labour and death. The fundamental thought in this passage clearly relates to the Pauline notion of 'dying to sin' so as to be raised to new life in Christ:

'Through work man turns himself into matter, as Christ does through the Eucharist.

Work is like a death.

We have to pass through death. We have to be killed - to endure the weight of the world. When the universe is weighing upon the back of a human creature, what is there to be surprised at if it hurts him?

Work is like a death if it is without an incentive. We have to act, renouncing the fruits of action.

To work - if we are worn out it means that we are becoming submissive to time as matter is. Thought is forced to pass from one instant to the next without laying hold of the past or the future. That is what it means to obey'[3].

'To obey' - that is, for the fussy ego to drop away. It is that ego which both seeks to manipulate others and is itself manipulated. But the countervailing 'obedience' in question here is a suffering of coercion which paradoxically liberates the soul from the more seductive dynamics of manipulation. Again, what Weil is thinking of is the labour of those who labour simply in order to survive. This 'obedience' therefore stands in absolute antithesis to the titillations of consumerism, the governing spirit of contemporary mass democracy.

And the evil in long-term unemployment, one might add, is not only that it negates the dignity of individuals and dissolves community. In this sense, it is also the destruction precisely of a spirituality. It removes a passageway to salvation.

'Workers need poetry more than bread': the need Weil sees is for a 'poetry' both of protest and of celebration.

But it is **'poetry'** that is needed. Not propaganda. Some 'light from eternity'; nothing merely manipulative, in the service of more limited interests.

And that is surely the essential point she is making when she says that

'religion alone can be the source of such poetry'.

NOTES

[1] Simone Weil, *Gravity and Grace*, translated into English by Emma Craufurd (London: Routledge & Kegan Paul, 1952), p. 159.

[2] Ibid.

[3] Ibid. , p. 160.

Annex H

INTRODUCTION TO PAPERS SUBMITTED BY THE BAPTIST UNION

By Revd Simon Jones

'Like most Microsoft employees, I consider myself too well adjusted to be working here, even though I am 26 and my universe consists of home, Microsoft, and Costco.' So observes the narrator near the beginning of Douglas Coupland's sharp and funny novel *Microserfs*. A little later he further notes: 'Most staffers peek at Winquote a few times a day. I mean, if you have 10,000 shares (and tons of staff members have way more) and the stock goes up a buck, you've just made a grand! But then, if it goes down two dollars, you've just lost twenty grand. It's a real psychic yo-yo. Last April Fool's day, someone fluctuated the price up and down by fifty dollars and half the staff had coronaries.'

This is the world of work for Generation X, the twenty and thirty-somethings comfortably embracing the new world of cyberspace, so ably chronicled by Coupland. Optimistic and techno-friendly, most of them are bugged by fears that the corporation is withering their souls and will use them up and spit them out, but they're too deeply bedded in by stock options, high salaries and company shopping malls.

At the other end of the spectrum are those who feel excluded from this brave new world. Those who didn't achieve a lot at school by way of formal qualifications, those with skills acquired at the heavy end of industry which are now surplus to requirement, those who have a twenty year clean track record behind the wheel of a van or lorry but can't get a driving job because they lack the computer skills necessary.

And in the middle are most of us, carrying on, making the best of it we can, but somewhat breathless at the pace of change that means we learn from our kids how to programme the video or work the cordless phone.

When we left school, we got a job, chose a career and assumed that we'd be on a gradual ascent to retirement. We assumed that we'd do a fair day's work - around eight hours - for a fair day's wage - enough to feed the family, pay the rent, buy a few luxuries and put a little by for a rainy day.

Now we find ourselves in offices doing 50 hour weeks, on factory floors doing at least one full shift's worth of overtime - though possibly not getting one full shift's worth of overtime pay. Now we find ourselves in our mid-30s, mid-40s changing careers, going back into training, having to add to our portfolio of skills just to keep our heads above water.

Companies talk of 'downsizing' when what they mean is shrinking the workforce by voluntary and compulsory redundancies as technology and the ever-present need to pare costs to the bone, make more and more workers surplus to requirement. As Anthony Sampson shows in his book *Company Man*, this does not just apply to manual workers. Increasingly these changes are hitting the one-time secure tiers of corporate life - middle managers, administrators, even professionals like accountants and lawyers.

Perhaps in a bid to get their own back, the young, articulate, multi-skilled middle class are 'downshifting'. Bailing out of companies, simplifying their lifestyles, trading wealth for happiness. One commentator describes it as 'dropping out without any hint of being a hippie.'

The world of work is changing rapidly and few of us see clearly where it is going. All we know is that the old values that sustained us, the old values that everyone - bosses and workers, teachers and politicians - shared have all gone and have not yet been replaced by anything we hold in common.

And in churches we commit ourselves to the creeds and confessions that generations of Christians have recited through the ages, we worship our creating, working God, we pray for strength to serve him in the world of human affairs and commerce. And yet we sense that

289

there is a widening gulf between what we sing and say on Sundays and what we are experiencing during the week at work.

And then there is a growing pool of people, Christian and non-Christian, coming to terms with unemployment, living in near-poverty, feeling trapped in a workless lifestyle by an economy in a state of flux and a benefits system that offers no incentives and no clear direction back to employment. The frenetic pace of change in society carries the world of work further from their grasp, causing increasing dislocation not only in their families and communities but also in their spirits as their confidence, self esteem and sense of dignity is shredded by the experience of worklessness.

And the young feel the effects of these changes no less than the old. Many young people leaving school with GCSEs or A-levels join the queues of unemployed signing on only to find that those ahead of them are last year's pool of jobless graduates. Disaffection sets in early and sensing that they'll not get any qualifications and so not get a job, many in their teens drop out of school and fall out of the networks of adult society, inhabiting a parallel but largely unseen world of transient relationships, drugs, petty crime, rootlessness and the risk of permanent exclusion from mainstream community life.

Charting a way ahead

So, it is not enough for politicians and trade unionists to spout about full employment. It is not enough for governments to tinker with the figures and introduce schemes and reforms that seek to restore the status quo - or at least get the jobless total down to around a million.

The changes in the world economy, in the processes of manufacturing, in the ways of creating wealth mean that we need a fundamental rethink of policy in relation to the world of work and how we as a community ensure that all our people enjoy a right to useful toil and reap the rewards of wealth creation.

But something even more basic needs to happen. We must reassess our values in relation to work. Using the tools of Christian revelation - especially the Scriptures and the Spirit - we must rethink our theology of community, work and wealth, our pastoring of people who live in the world of work and those who gaze on from the sidelines and most fundamentally the way we think about people.

This set of papers from the Baptist Union's working group on unemployment and the future of work does not do all that. But it does set down a few markers and point to a few of the issues that need to be tackled if this fundamental reassessment of values is to happen.

So, in his major paper Albert Richards outlines the issues that need to be taken into consideration when formulating a theology of work in the 1990s. Robert Paul in two linked papers considers the effects of changes in the workplace on people and reflects on what Christian teaching says about this. Paul Allen looks at pastoral approaches to people at work through the lens of Niebuhr's *Christ and Culture*. Doreen Landriau examines young people's expectations about work with reference to two recent major studies.

The question of lifestyles

One issue that isn't tackled in the papers is the whole thorny area of lifestyle. This is an issue that Christians are theoretically in a good position to talk about - given the weight of biblical teaching and Christian tradition dealing with the topic of our attitude to material possessions. Unfortunately, it is all too often the case that there is a massive disjunction between what Christians say and what they do.

But it seems right to raise it here and urge the Enquiry team to examine the issue for two reasons. The first is that there is much in Christian revelation to suggest that this is a crucial issue for the church and the world, something that is definitely on God's heart and so should be on ours. Secondly, nearly all discussion about work, unemployment and the future of both assumes constantly rising standards of living. This second reason needs to be explored further.

No political party goes to the poll saying 'vote for us and cut your standard of living'. All of them urge voters to put a cross against the candidate that they believe is not only going to protect their standard of living but raise it, give them more prosperity and boosted spending power. Indeed modern consumer economies rely on people having increasing levels of disposable income for if the shops are full and the tills are ringing, the factories are busy, the transport sector, construction industry, finance houses, security business, advertising agencies and packaging manufacturers are wringing their hands with glee.

When people suggest reducing - or even pegging - standards of living, there is usually a sharp intake of breath followed by an explosion of amazed indignation. The topic is dropped. Conversations return to how we can boost sales without stoking up inflation and how by making the rich richer we'll raise the living standards of everyone because wealth somehow has a way of trickling down the social order. If only..!

Christians need to try to keep the conversation on the living standards issue. It's not about the salaries paid to top executives - though the question of huge salaries paid to give a few executives the incentive to perform better is intriguing when put next to the suggestion that the unemployed need to have their benefits cut to give them the incentive to get back to work! It is about how much we all need to live on. So, it affects everyone in society from the company boss to the car park attendant, from the newspaper vendor to the TV executive to the policeman to the parish priest to the short order chef at McDonald's. And it's not about demands, desire or wants, but needs. What do we each need to live on?

This is an issue that needs thorough investigation and a thorough airing. It has implications for how households are organised. One of the reasons frequently touted for the rise in the level of male unemployment is the entry of larger numbers of women into the labour market. The question 'Has the one caused the other?' leads to a sterile debate about women's rights/ women's place (depending on which side you come down!).

As Albert Richards points out in his paper, this is a trend with massive implications for the future of work. The kind of jobs being created, he argues, are jobs that women tend to do and that men don't. This is forcing some couples - regardless of their social attitudes - to change traditional roles with men staying at home as full-time parents and women going out to work.

Albert further suggests that some men go after what are traditionally seen to be women's work in order to maintain the traditional male role of being the family bread winner. But this has led to problems in the way men feel about themselves and their role in society. The chattering classes are, of course, much exercised by the crisis in masculinity caused by the rise of feminism and changes in the economy. Albert's paper shows that this crisis has profound implications for the workplace and is rooted in economic realities.

What we should be doing is asking do both partners need to work outside the home, indeed should both partners work - especially when there are young children to be cared for? Is there mileage in exploring the possibility of using the tax and benefits system to encourage the creation of single income households where one partner or the other works outside the home for a salary and the other doesn't? This doesn't preclude the 'non-employed' partner being involved in community/voluntary/'gift' work outside the home. But it seeks a way of obviating the necessity of both partners working for money solely to balance out the family's finances.

It seems to us that there is something worth exploring here. It would, of course, sit comfortably within a discussion of basic income and changing the tax and benefits system to ensure a 'social wage' of one sort or another is paid to everyone. Tony Walter and the Basic Income research group has done a lot of good work in this field. Walter has also written imaginatively on the whole issue of work and worklessness in *Hope on the Dole* (SPCK 1985)

These are fundamental questions to do with the nature of persons and the society we live in. As such they are theological questions. And Christians need to answer them within a theological framework that takes seriously the fact of our creation by a personal, loving God and which takes seriously the biblical emphasis on the involvement of God in his/her creation.

But such answers are not abstruse or other-worldly. They have a direct bearing on how our economy is organised. At the end of November a single mother won her case against London Transport in an industrial tribunal on the grounds that new rostas did not take account of her family circumstances. The tribunal argued strongly that companies must recognise the family needs and responsibilities of its employees. It could well be a landmark judgment unless overturned on appeal!

These theological questions feed into what we believe about the roles of men and women in society and the workplace, about the legitimacy of types of family organisation and whether the state should support and encourage one type at the expense of others, about the kinds of contracts we all have with our employers.

The moral maze

Undoubtedly the debate over the future of work is at root a moral debate. We cannot leave it to market forces to dictate how society is to be organised. We cannot allow notions of efficiency, return on investment and maximisation of profit and shareholder dividends to dominate discussion of what companies are and what role they have in our society.

The Churches' Enquiry is in an ideal position to raise broader, more fundamental and decidedly moral questions relating to the future of work, because the issue is at the end of the day not just about economics, it is about what kind of society we are creating for ourselves and our children.

Annex I

SOME THOUGHTS ON THEOLOGICAL METHOD

By Revd Malcolm Brown

Eleven years ago, *Faith in the City*[1] was published to great acclaim, continuing controversy, and a persistent charge that it was theologically 'weak'. Whilst the impact of the report was considerable and lasting, the lack of theological rigour - the sense that it adopted an 'implicit' theology in an age where such a stance could not go unquestioned - diminished its impact both in the churches and beyond in ways which subsequent attempts *Theology in the City*[2], *God in the City*[3] to redress the balance have never fully overcome.

If the theological context of 1985 was more complex and controversial than the authors of *Faith in the City* realised, how much more is this true in 1996? *Faith in the City* neglected a widespread sense that the connections between theology and social action (and even more, between theology and specific social choices) were not straightforward or able to be made without, as it were, 'showing one's working'. That generalised sense of unease - that the theological methodology which had served the churches well enough through the years of the post-war consensus could not seamlessly accommodate the ideological upheavals and uncertainties of the Thatcher years - marked the beginning of a debate about theological method which is still continuing and shows no signs of early resolution. Unless a church enquiry on social issues has a clear position vis-a-vis this debate, it will not only fail to convince the church-based constituency upon which it depends for its legitimacy, but its findings risk being judged to be remote from the contemporary debate.

What was the theological weakness of *Faith in the City*? The report stood more or less within a tradition that had become second nature to church people - especially Anglicans - addressing social issues, but could be said to be a debased example of that tradition. Often called 'Middle Axioms'; developed in England by William Temple and championed today by Ronald Preston, the methodology was founded upon a serious and mutually respectful dialogue between theology and other disciplines. The primacy of' 'the facts' was recognised and simplistic leaps from Biblical texts or doctrinal themes to policy choices were eschewed. The role of theology was to set out certain fundamental principles and the role of the dialogue with others was to establish 'intermediate' positions which lay somewhere between bland generalities and specific policies.

Properly - and openly - handled, this approach can be more sophisticated than it sounds. It is able to handle the pragmatism of 'balance' rather than the certainties of ideology and it recognises the practical necessities of compromise and negotiation. It accepts the autonomy of other sorts of knowledge than the theological but does not reduce theology to baptising every 'expert' thesis. It could be said that the 'Middle Axiom' approach balances idealism with pragmatism because it is based on a theology that recognises the ambiguity of many aspects of Christian understanding, but that it encourages a *principled* pragmatism.

Faith in the City, in terms of the methodology of its working party, conformed to the dialoguic, middle-axiom, approach. Nevertheless, it was deeply influenced also by the impact of Liberation Theology and the 'bias to the poor' which self-evidently connected with the issues they confronted in the UPAs. What they neglected was that Liberation Theology is, of its essence, theology done by the marginalised not by the comfortable on their behalf. The result was that *Faith in the City* was open to attack on two fronts. To the proponents of Middle Axioms it strayed dangerously in the direction of precise policy recommendations which could not be supported out of an understanding of the proper role of theology and the church. To the liberationists, the voice of the report lacked genuine authenticity and resembled too much the angst of concerned, but unaffected, liberals.

Much more would need to be said to make a just critique of the theology behind Faith in the City. But, from a distance, it is possible to see that its problems stemmed from its positioning 'on the cusp' of a new philosophical understanding of social relationships. The Middle Axiom model essentially depended on the 'experts' in many fields (including theology) sharing a fundamentally common discourse and rationality. As a method, it had little to say to the particularity of perspective brought to the table by women, black people or those outside a fundamentally liberal social model. The development of feminist theologies, black people's theologies and liberation theologies from various 'perspectives from beneath' has gone too far to ignore and has been mirrored in secular disciplines. Perspective is all. The middle axiom model, which saw the danger as too much specificity, is ironically more in danger of being unable to move beyond banal platitudes in a plural world where the notions of consensual politics and academic impartially have been (perhaps fatally) damaged.

A church-based social enquiry into an issue like the Future of Work, taking place in the mid 1990s, finds itself in the context of a tradition lost but not yet a tradition rediscovered. For there is no clear methodology or understanding of context that will be acceptable to a very wide church consensus. The recent BSR report on 'the family' *Something to Celebrate*[4] fell foul of this controversy by failing to recognise that the methodology of theological enquiry and reflection must be overt and argued for. In *The Church Times*[5], Michael Banner - an exponent of what might be called the neo-Orthodox tendency - slated the report for its susceptibility to affirming secular trends without a clear enough grasp of moral relativity and without a sharp enough sense of Christian distinctiveness. The response by Peter Sedgwick[6], basically reaffirming Temple's middle axiom approach, failed to address the difficulties of a church struggling to find its identity in relation to those outside the Christian community in a deeply plural world where the right of the church to comment on social trends is not self-evident. 'Christendom' thinking in the 1990s has had a big boost from John Milbank's book *Theology and Social Theory*[7], in which he argues that, with the post-modern breakdown of the meta-narrative, the task of Christian theology is to 'out-narrate' other, rival, inferior narratives. The strength of the 'Christendom' theologies is a clarity about the distinctiveness of the Christian community. Its weakness, briefly stated, seems to be principally that its relation of Christian ethics to wider society is essentially aggressive - because Christianity is the best way to understand reality. This does not sound promising in a multi-cultural and non-consensual world.

On another flank, the middle axiom approach is under attack from the liberationist model and its developments in the context of Western theology. This strand is particularly evident in papers from the World Council of Churches and can be characterised by the 'confessional' approach of theologians like Ulrich Duchrow in Germany and Michael Northcott in the UK. With a strong focus on 'good news for the poor', the approach here is to argue from Biblical principles to social and economic choices as tenets of faith. Thus (to over-simplify greatly) it becomes impossible to hold Christianity and capitalism together and the churches' task must be to overturn the structures of injustice whilst those caught up in the structures are called to penitence and re-orientation.

Again, the confessional distinctiveness of the Christian community is emphasised - and to those who make the accusation that this is 'salvation by (political) works' the response is that belief, action and spirituality are integral elements.

This brief thumbnail sketch of the three main theological approaches to social Christianity highlights the problem facing the Enquiry on the Future of Work. In none of the three cases is implicit theology allowable. The Enquiry could, possibly, choose to place its report within one or other school of thought, thus endorsing a particular methodology. Or it could openly acknowledge the problems and seek tentatively to affirm a theological approach that addresses the concerns and conundrums around which the theological debate revolves.

In many ways, the economic issues which the Enquiry is addressing lend themselves not only to a theological concern and commentary but to a methodology. And this is particularly true in the context of the central issue of plurality. The handling of plurality is a crucial issue in economic theory and there is a good case to be made that economic ideology of left and of right has failed to make sense of it. The command economies of the former Soviet bloc were incapable of making any realistic accommodation of difference. For the neo-liberal right, plurality is an essential tenet. Since, in a plural society, there are no agreed values whereby goods can be distributed, it is argued that state action in the name of social justice is no more than the imposition of one set of values on everyone. Thus only the 'amoral' market - the unintended and unforeseeable outcomes of millions of autonomous individual choices - can distribute goods 'fairly'.

These ideological approaches to distributional questions are now very widely discredited - that of the left self-evidently so and that of the new-Right shown to be deficient in both its internal logic and its empirical outcomes, not to mention its palpable neglect of 'the social fabric' which is an essential pre-requisite of the market's flourishing (see Raymond Plant in *Theology in the City*, Fred Hirsch's *Social Limits to Growth*[8] etc.)

It is particularly when we look at the structural unemployment that has followed from neo-liberal economic policies (at least those policies were a very major cause) that the social consequences of an ideological approach to economic policy become clearly unacceptable. Nor is an ideological economics of the left an answer if the competing 'goods' of democracy, choice and 'freedom to' as well as 'freedom from' are to be kept in creative tension.

Yet it may be in the juggling act of competing values that a way forward may be found which combines notions of Christian distinctiveness with an ability to work creatively in a plural context. For all the issues facing an economist or a politician attempting to create conditions for sustainable, participative, democratic and fair employment, are issues of tension and balance - dilemmas between objectives and values that cannot all be achieved in full at once. The distribution of work and reward achieved by the market is unequal and - some would say - unjust, but so is too much central command which can also be deeply inefficient. Economic efficiency is a good, but how is a practical, comprehensive, measurement of efficiency to be attained? Maximising economic activity and growth may be a way forward, but it has to be balanced against fair trading conditions for much poorer economies around the world. Investment needs to be deeper and more long-term (*pace* Will Hutton[9]) but it also needs to be able to react quickly to changing circumstances.

In short, the economist faces dilemmas on all fronts. So, profoundly, does the theologian. The divine drama of the Christian faith is played out in paradox and dilemma. Christ's strength and triumph is exhibited most clearly in the self-giving weakness of the cross. Our salvation is present with us now, yet sin is persistent and structural. We live as if the Kingdom of God were a present possibility, yet are faced always with the contradictions of a fallen world. Choices are rarely between good and evil, right and wrong whatever the moralists would tell us, since such categories do not precisely correspond with the Christian understanding of the nature of things. Yet that is not to embrace relativism or 'situation ethics'. There remains a balancing principle which informs dilemmatic choice. A theology of 'the virtues' derived from Alastair MacIntyre[10], and others is helpful here. 'Tragic' dilemmas, in which there is no 'right' choice are everyday matters in the political economy. But the choices are informed by values and how those values are arrived at is central to the morality of the outcome.

Something of this approach is to be seen in a paper currently being drafted by a small international group of the Work and Economy Network in the European Churches. Entitled 'The Future of Work Beyond Employment'[11], the paper seeks to assess the political choices facing a Europe of high and rising unemployment against an attempt at a Biblically-sourced 'theology of work'. This theological excursion leads into the presentation of nine 'dilemmas' in the pursuit of a more just employment market and concludes with some policy options for the governments of Europe.

Now this approach is not far in principle from a Middle Axiom methodology and it could be criticised on similar grounds except that the theological reflection is explicit and precedes the formulation of the dilemmas from which policy options emerge. Theology is not treated as a 'tacked-on' chapter, but is integral to the process. None the less, the paper as it stands (it is only a draft) is deficient in failing to demonstrate how it moves from theology to dilemmas and from dilemmas to policies.

The move from theology to dilemmas could be explicated by an expanded version of the argument I have just set out about the essentially dilemmatic nature of theology itself. Indeed, the theological principles espoused by the WEN paper are themselves often only one side of an ambiguity. For instance, the concept of 'the human being as an active, responsible individual' which lies behind the German Roman Catholic and Protestant churches' paper "On the Economic and Social Situation in German" has sound theological roots, but must be held in tension with the equally theological understanding of the Christian life as one marked by 'being chosen' rather than exercising choice. Similarly, the concept of work as a co-creative activity in which humanity works with and in the image of God needs to be balanced with the sense of work as, if not exactly a curse, frequently necessitated by the sinful, fallen, nature of the world. The paper does usefully contrast the importance of work with the necessity of rest - and the need to balance both. What still needs to be dealt with is the theology which connects work and rewards - and the relation of work to the tensions between individual and community.

The point I am making is that there is a strong case for holding that a dilemmatic approach to social questions reflects in its essence the nature of the Christian understanding of life in the world and that a process for theological enquiry must reflect this. However this does not in itself resolve the challenge posed to theology by the plural nature of society. All we have established is that no single solutions, no one set of priorities and no ideology of distributive justice will be sufficient for all time since all structural solutions tend towards their own distinctive sins.

The fact of plurality challenges us to find a participative method for arriving at the preferences, or virtues, that inform our approach to dilemmas. One solution for Christians is to set out their stall of 'Christian' values and offer them to the world as the best solution possible. Thus a church report on the future of work might say "our Christian principles lead us to say *this* about the nature of work and therefore to say *that* about how work should be ordered in our society". But this 'Christendom' approach does not take much notice of competing values or virtues nor of the idea that 'the Christian faith' is not one thing but many depending upon one's perspective - for there are many Christian communities. Alternatively, the report could prioritise the experience of those marginalised in the current labour-market - not least those marginalised in the global economy. The call to the wealthy and to the developed nations of the G7 and others would be to penitence and renunciation in the name of justice. There is a spirituality in this position which is attractive, but as a strategy for change rather than a prophetic call to what might be, it has little to say that can inform a dilemmatic choice.

I believe that the challenge is to find a methodology of encounter which encapsulates 'Christian distinctiveness' not in credal propositions but in *process*. Ian Markham comes close to this in his book Plurality and Christian Ethics[12].

The first step is to know who we mean by 'we'. The fond belief that 'we' can speak for all people of good will must be finally exploded. 'We' are always an interested party and a partial observer of incomplete 'facts'.

But a belief in a God can be a safeguard against irrevocable relativism. The believer in an 'ultimate reality' cannot treat every value as relative, for the 'ultimate reality' is knowable, though never (in this world) fully known.   So a respect for other perspectives is in order (provided it is reciprocal) but in the context of mutual exploration rather than the chaotic Babel of 'postmodernism' at its bleakest.

A colleague who is very active in community relations in Handsworth once said to me: "I am totally fed up with people who say they want to unite the black community. Can they not see that we are not one - we are diverse and hold very different values. But on some things, many of us can come together - and when the objective has been achieved we regroup in a new formation to tackle the next one. But we are not 'one thing'. That to me represents the clearest statement of a renewed 'liberal' approach to theological enquiry which takes plurality seriously. It is not a return to 'middle axioms' but reflects the strengths of that position in accepting the integrity and potential for alliance between theology, other disciplines and those beyond the church.

So the process would look something like this: first, know yourself. Who constitutes 'we'? Which is the community we represent and where do we place ourselves within the diverse array that is the Christian community. Models of theological reflection drawn from Liberation Theology help here, not least because the concept of 'ideological suspicion' draws out the way in which our beliefs and knowledge are shaped by a social construct and mind-set which is not given but is contingent and subject to interrogation from other perspectives. Then find who in the wider society can work with us for now, on one theme - not for ever on every issue. The 'ecumenical confusion' is a parallel here - ecumenism has tended to take unity as its goal rather than collaboration which respects diversity. Paralysis has tended to result. It can be argued that the ecumenical Enquiry on the Future of Work has been hamstrung by this very factor: because difference is seen as dangerous in ecumenical politics, theological method (which is highly controversial) was not on the agenda at the early moment when it could have influenced the methodology of the Enquiry.

Having found partners and allies and having explored the limits of agreement and discovered what unity there is to be had in diversity, the values whereby dilemmatic choices can be addressed may be striven for. The presentation of the dilemmas may be the province of those well schooled in relevant disciplines - economists and labour-market experts in this case - though, conscious of plural perspectives, never one alone. The theological task is to discern the values which must interrogate the dilemmas (the 'virtues' which faith lives by) and to show how these values may be better realised in practice by taking particular policy options. Unlike the middle axiom approach, this method is not afraid of detailed policy options, although - taking dilemma and ambiguity seriously - it understands them to be contextual in time and place. Nor can it, as a method, bring everybody with it - even all Christians - because values, virtues and Christian principles are always controversial. But by being clear who is promulgating these values, how they are arrived at and how they connect with policy, the process is overt, subject to challenge and debate but capable of reasoned defence. It echoes to a degree the 'Christendom' approach, in that it is prepared to defend itself in terms of the attractiveness of the Christian narrative, but refuses either to profess a single 'Christian' position or to confront uncompromisingly those who differ.

Can it be done? I don't know. The process does not lend itself to the compressed timescales necessitated by public debate. But can we afford any alternative? The debate on methodology in social theology is too vigorous to allow the theological issue to be fudged. The CCBI Enquiry on Unemployment and the Future of Work is of crucial importance, not just for its subject matter which is of urgent concern, but as a step in the history of the churches' social engagement. The various reports since *Faith in the City* have shown that theological confidence has not been restored in the churches - it may even be that the problems are still not understood. The Enquiry is the first time such an exploration has been undertaken in the name of the churches rather than a denomination. Early hopes that this would bring the question of diverse approaches to social theology to the fore have not, as yet, been realised. But if the Enquiry fails to move the process on from *Faith in the City* who will take social theology seriously again, let alone the findings of this or subsequent reports?

The world may set the agenda. 'Society' may be the intended constituency for the report's findings. But whose report is it? Where does it come from and with what credentials? The answer must be 'the churches' and so there must be an answer to the question of why 'work' is any of the churches' business. If there was controversy over the report on 'the family' (which the church is expected to have a view on) how much more will the fur fly over work and the economy which is not supposed to lie within the churches' sphere of authority?

Employment and the Future of Work are desperately pressing questions for everybody - that's why they raise such passions. Theology generates passion too because it matters desperately to those who have a stake in it. If we are to put the two together credibly, we not only need to be clear who 'we' are, - and who we are able to work with - we have to 'show our working', and preferably not in the margin.

1 Archbishop's Commission on Urban Priority Areas, Faith in the City, Church House Publishing. 1985.

2 (ed) A Harvey, Theology in the City SPCK, 1989.

3 (ed) P Sedgwick, God in the City, Mowbray, 1995.

4 Board for Social Responsibility, Something to Celebrate, Valuing Families in Church and Society. Church House publishing. 1995.

5 M Banner, "Nothing to Declare" in The Church Times 16 June 1995.

6 P Sedgwick, "Refusing to Despair over Families" in The Church Times 30 June 1995.

7 J Milbank, Theology and Social Theory, Blackwell, 1990.

8 F Hirsch, Social Limits to Growth. 1977.

9 W Hutton, The State We're In, Jonathan Cape. 1995.

10 (eg) A MacIntyre, After Virtue, Duckworth, 1981.

11 Work and Economy Network in the European Churches, The Future of Work Beyond Employment. The William Temple Foundation (forthcoming)

12 I Markham, Plurality and Christian Ethics. C.U.P. 1994